MAPS AND MAP-MAKERS OF THE AEGEAN

MAPS AND MAP-MAKERS OF THE AEGEAN

VASILIS SPHYROERAS
University of Athens

ANNA AVRAMEA
University of Crete

SPYROS ASDRAHAS
Professeur associé à Sorbonne

Translation from the Greek
G. COX and J. SOLMAN

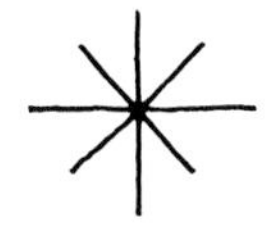

OLKOS LTD

ATHENS 1985

The subject of this book is the mapping of the Aegean Sea, or the Greek Archipelago, as it was perhaps better-known to foreign cartographers and travellers. The maps the book contains – which have necessarily been the result of a process of selection – span the period from the early 15th century, when the first attempts were made in the West to depict a specific area in the form of a map, to recent times. With the exception of the manuscript maps of Buondelmonti and some manuscript portolans, all the maps are printed: many are copper engravings, with woodcuts and lithographs being encountered less frequently.

Throughout this period, lasting more than five hundred years (the most recent map is that of the North Aegean published by the Greek Hydrographical Service in 1967), and through copying, repetition, alteration and additions large and small, the maps record and bear witness to the development of cartographic tools and techniques, to the gradual formulation of the modern concept of geographical space, and, primarily, to the particular interest which the Aegean has always had for the countries surrounding it. Our book's ambition is to provide a reading of this three-fold yet unified phenomenon.

It frequently happens that a map is at the same time a work of art, a scientific record and a political document, and the co-existence of these three features constituted the basic criterion on which the maps were selected. The persistent mapping of a specific area, by cartographers of various countries often acting on the orders of their governments, is never a matter of chance. It would not be an exaggeration to say that before a country sends its gunboats and troops into a particular area it sends its travellers and its map-makers.

The Aegean Sea, an indispensible link in the chain of highly significant relations between East and West and a point of meeting and so of friction between two different civilisations, became, at a very early date, the object of observations, descriptions and representations of various kinds, involving not only maps. It has never been a neutral geographical area. The geographical co-ordinates which criss-cross it combine in the thickest of networks with the co-ordinates of its history and its ancient civilisation.

This network is most evident in the imperfect maps of the first centuries recorded here. All the particulars which gave the place identity are recorded clumsily but characteristically on the surface bounded by the equally clumsy geographical outline: ancient ruins, Byzantine churches, Frankish castles and the ancient Greek place-names taken straight from Strabo and Ptolemy. The more recent maps gradually subject the part to the whole and while sacrificing descriptive detail to an overall concept reveal something considerably more substantive: that the islands of the Greek Archipelago form a geographical, historical and cultural unit, that they constitute "a far-flung Greek city, scattered over the face of the waters".

We would like to acknowledge our debt of gratitude to the historian Voula Konti, to Commodore Varfis, Deputy Governor of the War Museum, to Dimitris Tsitouras and above all to Stathis Finopoulos, whose contribution to making this book possible was a most considerable one.

The Publishers

THE AEGEAN SINCE THE 15TH CENTURY
A HISTORICAL OUTLINE

The effects of the fall of Constantinople were not felt immediately in the islands of the Aegean. With the exception of the occupation of the islands in the Sea of Thrace in 1456, the islands fell under the rule of the Ottoman state gradually, and it took two centuries for Turkish domination to become fully established. Mytilene was captured in 1462, Euboea in 1470 and the taking of the petty state of the Knights of St John of Rhodes occurred in 1522. Some 40 years later, in 1566, Chios and what remained of the Venetian Duchy of the Aegean were incorporated into the Ottoman administrative system. In the place of the last Venetian Duke, Giacomo IV Crispi, Sultan Selim II installed his protégé Joseph Natsi, a Jewish merchant from Spain, whose influence at the court of the Sultan was considerable[1]. In 1571 Cyprus fell to the Turks and a century later, in 1669, the Venetians abandoned Crete after a lengthy war with Turkey.

Ottoman domination in the Aegean, taking hold gradually (the survival of the Venetian possession of Tinos down to 1715 is a complete exception), determined the shaping of the political, social and economic life of the islands. Small islands which had been abandoned by their inhabitants in the face of pirate raids were repopulated and on the larger islands, from the beginning of the 17th century, limited shipping and commercial activity began to develop. This continued to grow and reached its highest point in the 50 years immediately before the revolution of 1821.

Although the economic progress of the Aegean islands was achieved by the general conditions created in the area by the international situation, the decisive factor in the development of most of them were the special privileges granted to them by the Sultan. These were the pre-condition for the organising of an initially rudimentary form of self-government, which developed, by the end of Turkish rule, into semi-autonomy.

In 1580 a delegation of islanders from Paros, Naxos, Santorini, Melos and Syros arrived in Constantinople – one year after the death of Natsi – and sought an 'order as to privileges' to govern relations between the island population and the Ottoman rulers. Sultan Murat III then granted them privileges similar to those granted to Chios in 1567 and 1578. These privileges meant that the enforced levy of Christian children and the installation of janissaries on the islands were forbidden, taxes levied in other areas were reduced or abolished, freedom in the performance of religious duties was accorded, the system of administration of justice in force before Turkish rule was recognized and the Turkish presence was limited to two officials on each island, the bey and the kadi.

This arrangement, although originally covering only the Cyclades and Chios, applied, from the 17th century on, to a large number of the islands – 34 in all – subject to the jurisdiction of the capudan pasha (admiral). Belonging to this administrative unit, apart from the Cyclades, were the islands of the Argolic and Saronic Gulfs, the Sporades, Psara, Kasos, Patmos and Astypalaea of the Dodecanese and Trikkeri at the mouth of the Gulf of Pagasae[2]. In the case of the larger islands of the Aegean – Lesbos, Samos, Rhodes and Crete, whose importance for the Ottoman Empire was such that other administrative arrangements were required, the policy of the Sultans was different and oppressive measures retarded their development for a considerable period. At the same time, compulsory conversion to Islam and the importation of populations from Asia Minor – chiefly to Crete and Rhodes – posed a temporary threat to the ethnological composition of their population. There is clear evidence that certain tax and administrative privileges were granted to islands in the Dodecanese in an attempt to put a stop to a tendency among the population to flee elsewhere. The records which have so far come to light do not allow description of the regime implemented in Crete after the fall of the Venetian feudal system.

The information provided by travellers during the first two centuries of Ottoman rule is equally scanty and unreliable in regard to living conditions on the Aegean islands and the number of their inhabitants. We have very little knowledge of the occupations of the population[3], but it seems certain that chief among these must have been farming – limited in extent by the nature of the soil – and stock-breeding to meet local or even exclusively family requirements. Among the very few islands which are exceptions to this rule are Crete, Chios and Rhodes, whose vital position on the sea-lanes favoured the development of shipping and trade and the setting up at the end of the seventeenth and the beginning of the eighteenth centuries of small handicraft firms processing local raw materials. The ships of Crete had been voyaging to Venice, Dalmatia and Constantinople before the Turkish conquest of the island, and after a brief decline soon reappeared on the waters of the Eastern Mediterranean. Towards the end of the seventeenth century mention is first made of the manufacture of soap in Crete, and in 1723 the number of firms engaged in soap-making was in excess of twenty[4]. Only a few years after the fall of Chios to the Turks, merchants from the island had established themselves in Constantinople, and after about 1600 conducted their activities in Smyrna as well. The port of Rhodes, a way-station for pilgrims en route both to the Holy Land and to Mecca, did good business and the shipyard there employed local craftsmen in the repair and also the building of ships. The start of the shipping trade of Kastellorizo and Mykonos and of the manufacture of barrels on Kos can also be placed in the early years of Ottoman rule[5].

The degree to which an island was fertile and the level of its production was not always reflected in the commercial achievements of its inhabitants. Trade tended to be in the hands of foreigners (the Dutch, the English and the French) or more rarely in the hands of locals who were usually descended from the former class of Venetian feudal lords.

The consuls of the European countries in the islands usually belonged, too, to the old noble families. England,

France, Holland, Venice and Spain, Denmark later and Russia after 1774 had all opened consulates or sub-consulates to protect the interests of their subjects, even on small and at the time unimportant islands such as Antiparos, Ios, and Kimolos. It was not uncommon for the same individual to perform the duties of consul for more than one country[6]. These consuls were responsible for providing hospitality for travellers calling at their island's port en route for Smyrna, Constantinople, Alexandria or the Holy Land, and this is why most travellers' descriptions of the social life of the islanders go no further than that of the 'nobles' who as a rule lived in the old Venetian castles.

These castles, built between the thirteenth and fifteenth centuries to combat the Turks or the pirates who roamed the Aegean, had lost much of their former glory. Their bastions and cannon-ports were in many cases out of commission, their sturdy gates rarely closed at night except in emergencies, and, with the passage of time, Orthodox churches to Our Lady or to the soldier saints – St Demetrios, St. George, and the Archangels Michael and Gabriel – were erected within their walls. It is worth noting that as time passed many of the castles built in the hinterland of the islands came to be abandoned, while the same is not true of those which stood above the harbours. Around these castles the few poor dwellings which in former times had housed the families which tilled the land for the nobles multiplied, growing, on the passing away of the power of Venice, into new settlements, called 'burgi' or 'burga'. These later became the homes of the merchants and handicraft workers. The strongholds of the feudal lords, where their ownership did not come into the hands of the inhabitants of nearby villages, were used by their owners only as a residence during harvest-time. Under the new conditions, the population of the villages remained stable, but that of the settlements on the coast rose, especially after the early eighteenth century, when the final retreat of Venice from its last possessions in the Aegean – Tinos and the Peloponnese – meant the end of the wars between Venetians and Turks.

We can unhesitatingly trace the beginnings of the social and economic restructuring of the Aegean to the early eighteenth century. Increased commercial transactions during this period in the areas which surround the Aegean, in conjunction with the growth of a large number of 'urban' centres along the coasts of Asia Minor and mainland Greece, the appearance in the Greek seas of more commercial vessels of the European maritime states than ever before, the curbing of piracy and the more active participation of the Greek element in foreign trade all led to a broader mobilisation of the island populations.

However, what was of decisive importance for the islands of the North and Central Aegean was the creation of the institution of 'dragoman of the fleet', which probably dates from 1701. The occupants of this post, islanders at first and later Phanariots from Constantinople, were direct assistants to and stand-ins for the capudan pasha in the administration of the Aegean. The involvement of these officials in the affairs of the island communities gave the area under the jurisdiction of the capudan pasha an administrative form of its own and had a wider influence on its economic and social activities and on the progress of its culture[7]. Questions of taxation, the appointment of headmen or the ratification of their election, the codification of customary law, the administration of justice, matters relating to the church and education and a whole host of other issues were dealt with by the dragoman of the fleet, who could unreservedly be claimed to be co-governor of the region. His enormous influence on the circle around the Sultan allowed him to intervene in more general matters of the Porte's policy towards the islanders. It seems highly likely that it was dragoman of the fleet Nikolaos Mavroyenis, a Parian whose term of office coincided with the Orloff revolt (1770-74), who arranged the amnesty granted to the islanders and also saved the inhabitants of Psara from the certain extermination decided upon by the capudan pasha as a punishment for their share in the revolt. More or less the same happened after the withdrawal of Lambros Katsonis from the Greek seas in 1792, when the inhabitants of Psara were saved by Constantine Hadzeris from the mass deportation to Asia with which they were being threatened by the capudan pasha.

The temporary occupation by the Russians of the Cyclades and Samos during the Russo-Turkish War in 1768-74 was the first sign that Ottoman dominance in the Aegean was crumbling. But this period is most notable for the tremendous boost given to development of the island economies by the Treaty of Kuchuk Kainarji (1774), the convention of Ainali-Kavak (1779) and the commercial convention of Constantinople (1783). These treaties enabled Greek merchants, with their ships flying the Russian flag, to sail not only to the Eastern and Western Mediterranean but also into the Black Sea, which until then had been closed to them. In the Aegean islands themselves, where, as we have said, the English, French and Dutch had controlled trade, the presence of the Russians created a bridge to another Orthodox country, and one in which the Greek nation had invested its hopes of liberation.

These new conditions, together with a number of extraneous factors, brought about a shift in Greek shipping activity from the western parts of Greece – Galaxeidi and Messolonghi – to the Aegean. Hydra, Spetses and Psara, which with very few exceptions had in mid-century confined their shipping to the Greek coast, now set their sights on more distant seas. The heavy supply of labour by the Greek inhabitants of the islands stabilised or even reduced the wages of Greek crews, thus bringing freighting costs down to levels at which the foreigners could not compete, and this was especially true of the French, who even earlier had been concerned about the development of local commercial fleets within Greece and had seen it as ruinous for their own mercantile marine[8].

An insufficiency of sources prevents us from seeing from an overall point of view the rapid growth of shipping among the inhabitants of the Aegean islands. We know very little about the fleets of Mykonos, Skopelos, Santorini, Kasos, or Crete, and there are large gaps in our knowledge even of the three naval islands which we shall now be going on to discuss.

Psara had been a pirates' nest until the late seventeenth century, and lay far from the cluster of islands in which the other maritime centres lay. Merchant shipping in Psara began to develop around the middle of the eighteenth century. The first ships, known as 'sakoleves' (vessels with sprit sails) with which the islanders had voyaged to Chios, Mytilene, the coast of Ionia and westwards to Euboea and Thessaloniki, were replaced by larger vessels, of which there were 36 by the time the Orloff revolt broke out. At least 45 galliots were built in Psara during the period 1770-74, as well as the first three-master, which belonged to Ioannis Varvanis. In 1790, 57 ships from Psara, with a total displacement of 36,280 kantaria (approximately 18,000 tons) and a total crew of 850 men were under sail in the Mediterranean. Spetses began to grow as a mercantile power after the Treaty of Kutchuk Kainarji, and built a first 250-tonner as early as 1792, but the island's shipyards were engaged mainly in the construction of smaller vessels, lateen-rigged vessels and other small sailing ships (sachtouria); in 1813, the total fleet amounted to about 60 ships. The ships of Hydra had made their appearance on the Greek seas in the first decades of the 18th century, and by 1764 the island had one hundred and twenty vessels afloat, all with the last word in equipment. Two years later the French consul in Korone estimated that the number had risen to two hundred and considered the ships a threat to French shipping, as they voyaged throughout the Mediterranean and particularly to the Italian peninsula. Towards the end of the century, the Hydra fleet received significant reinforcement in the form of large-capacity ships and the island became the leading naval power in the Aegean: the islanders set up the first naval school in the Greek world and invited Italian and Portuguese experts to come and teach young men the art of the sea in a more systematic manner. In 1803, the islanders drew up a merchant shipping law "that good order and good command may be preserved" in relations between ship-owners and crews and in transactions. The islanders were in the special favour of the Turkish Grand Admiral, who received part of the crews of the Ottoman fleet from Hydra, with compulsory enlistment. The sailors of Hydra who had served in the Turkish navy during the first two decades of the nineteenth century were to form, along with the 'pressed' men from other islands (and especially from Spetses and Psara) the crews of the 'three-island fleet' which dealt so successfully with the Turkish armada during the years of the Greek War of Independence[9].

Apart from these islands, shipping developed at other points throughout the islands of the Aegean, as we have already seen. Mykonos had 25 ships in 1770, Kasos, Kastellorizo and Syme had about 120 at the end of the eighteenth century, the seamen of Santorini no longer confined themselves to trips to nearby islands but went as far afield as Smyrna and Constantinople, and the islanders of Skopelos sold their wine "in the cities of Turkey and of Europe, to which they themselves conveyed it in their ships". Chios turned itself over mainly to trade. As the island was the last stop for ships on their way to Smyrna or Constantinople, after the mid-18th century some 150 European ships, on average, passed through the harbour each year. The inhabitants of the island devoted themselves almost exclusively to trade, and merchants from Chios settled in Central and Western European countries – Holland, France, and others.

Rhodes was the major merchant shipping centre of the South-East Aegean, as a reception centre for foreigners trading in the Eastern Mediterranean and also for the building and repair of ships. The Rhodians themselves, with approximately fifty ships by the end of the eighteenth century, voyaged mainly to Alexandria, but also went to the other ports of Southern Europe.

In the Southern Aegean, Crete became the target of French trade after the departure of the Venetians in 1669. A French consulate was set up at Chania in 1679, with a subconsulate at Herakleio and agencies from time to time in Rethymno. Reports submitted by these consulates always laid particular stress on the importance of Crete for French trade. In the years leading up to the French Revolution the level of purchases and freighting of Cretan products reached those the French were already conducting with the Peloponnese, and one third of the business they did with Constantinople. During the period 1766-1785 an average of 75-115 ships per year docked at or sailed from Chania, and most of these were French. Cretan ships, too, played their part in this trade, and it is indicative that in his 'Thourio' of 1797 Rigas Pherraios calls upon the "sea-birds of Hydra and Crete" to aid the struggle for the liberation of Greece. The heroic spirit of the island, which had repeatedly shown itself in risings against the Venetians, reached a climax with the Daskaloyannis revolt of 1770. After this had been put down, Turkish oppression became intolerable.

The improvement during the eighteenth century of living conditions had an effect on cultural development in the islands, and especially on education. After 1750 schools were founded on almost all the islands, by the community and at its expense, while this had previously been true of only a very few islands. The most important of these schools were on Chios, Patmos, Andros, and Naxos, and apart from able teachers the schools had well-organised libraries containing the works of classical writers and the fathers of the church as well as translations from the European languages of works in the sciences.

The outbreak of the War of Independence in 1821 found the Aegean populations prepared for the great struggle which was to follow. The wholehearted support given to the Orloff brothers in 1770, the participation of many islanders in the operations of Lambros Katsonis and, later, in 1807, the assistance extended to the Russian admiral Seniavin, who planned operations to remove the Turks from the Aegean, were the preliminaries to armed combat with the Turkish fleet. The commercial vessels of Hydra, Psara and Spetses were converted into warships in record time and managed not only to confine the Turkish armada to its bases in Constantinople and the ports along the Asia Minor coast but also to carry out victorious sorties against any Turkish units which did dare to venture out into the Aegean. The use of fireships counterbalanced the difference in fire-power between the two fleets, inspiring the island populations and giving fresh heart to the freedom fighters. From the very first use of fireships, off Eresos in 1821, to the final stages of the War of Independence, the island fleet was able, despite internal disputes which led from time to time to dangerous moments of crisis, to act as a breakwater on which every Turkish attempt to regain control on the naval front broke in vain. The destruction of Chios in 1822 and of Kasos and Psara in 1824 revealed the importance of those islands for the Struggle, as an advanced line of listening posts in the North and East Aegean. By eliminating them, the Porte hoped to be able to reverse the advantage held by the Greeks.

The fixing by the Great Powers of the borders of the new Greek state, in 1832, left all the islands of the North and East Aegean, and Crete, beyond the frontiers. In Samos alone the situation was defined by a 'Charter of Privileges' of December 10, 1832, by which the autonomous 'Hegemony of Samos' was set up. The island was to be ruled by a Christian Governor-General appointed by the Sultan. The refusal of the islanders to accept the new arrangement was finally overcome in 1834, when a Turkish fleet arrived off the island and imposed the Powers' decision by force. Lykourgos Logothetis, leader of the island during the War of Independence, and other leading figures in the struggle for liberation were forced to leave the island, along with some 6,000 inhabitants opposed to the settlement forced on them, without their consent, by the Great Powers. The "General Assembly of the Samiots", without the most vital and liberal section of the population, proved to be the prime organ of the new regime, but the period of autonomy was not without its upheavals. The rising of the population in 1849 – which was not unrelated to the movement for social liberation throughout Europe the previous year – compelled the Porte to issue a new Charter introducing liberal ideas into the administration of the island.

Despite the contribution it had made to the success of the War of Independence, Crete remained outside the borders of the Greek state: in 1831 it had been ceded by the Sultan to Mohammed Ali of Egypt, in return for services rendered to the Porte during the War of Independence. The Egyptians remained on the island until 1840, when they were forced to withdraw under pressure from Britain, Austria, Prussia and Russia. This change of regime provided the signal for an uprising, which came to an end without success some months later. This first revolutionary move by the Cretans since 1821 was followed by the great Cretan revolt of 1866-69, the rebellion of 1877-78, and the rising of 1896, which was the final one before at last liberation came.

The inhabitants of the other islands which had not been included in the Greek state turned their attention mainly to the economic and cultural sectors. On Chios, the old and famous school acted as a nucleus for efforts to promote education which grew in strength and extended to nearly all the villages. At the same time, increased attention to shipping brought the island into the front rank of mercantile centres throughout the Greek world. Towards the end of the first half of the nineteenth century, Mytilene had a high school of outstanding quality, with excellent teachers; in 1859, instruction was conducted with aids imported from Europe. At the end of the century two periodicals, the *Pittacus* and the *Sappho* were publishing studies of local writers and scholars, the fame of some of whom had spread beyond the island itself. There can be no doubt that a Lesbos intellectual school had come into existence, and some of its representatives gained fame in letters and sciences throughout Greece.

As we have seen, some of the Dodecanese islands had special privileges. During the nineteenth century the islands were active mainly in the fields of ship-building, shipping and trade. The shipyards of Syme and Kasos built vessels of various types of up to 1000 tons and used them for the transportation of the products of the islands (and other goods) to ports in Asia Minor, Syria and Egypt. The Dodecanese islands were famed for their achievements in sponge-fishing –an activity which continues today, particularly in Kalymnos– and in ceramics and pottery.

Turning to the Aegean islands which were included within the Greek state set up in 1832, special attention must be devoted to Syros. This little island, most of whose inhabitants were Catholic during the period of Turkish occupation, was a shelter for refugees from Chios, Psara and elsewhere during the War of Independence. These fugitives settled around the hitherto uninhabited harbour below the old town[10]. They gave their new home the appropriate name of Ermoupolis and returned to their traditional activities in merchant shipping, which had been violently interrupted when their islands were laid waste during the course of the struggle for freedom. A new, urban society grew up in Ermoupolis, and the port became for some years the chief shipping, industrial and commercial centre of the new Greek state. As Ermoupolis flourished economically, it was also the scene of noteworthy cultural occurrences, such as that of the foundation of its high school, in 1834, where some of the most famous scholars of literature of the 19th century were to teach. Ermoupolis also had literary and arts clubs, printers of fine editions, and theatrical performances at the 'Apollon' Theatre (a version in miniature of the Scala of Milan), all of which gave the town the air of a small city in Western Europe. However, the rise of Piraeus in the second half of the century and later the construction of the Corinth Canal caused its importance for shipping to shrink, although the town kept its character as one of the more unusual places in the Aegean islands.

Despite the individual differences between the islands of the Aegean, despite the trials and tribulations they suffered over the centuries at the hands of pirates, as a result of military conflict and through their domination by foreign powers, and despite the lack of soil capable of cultivation, their populations retained their vitality and also characteristics whose origins are lost in the years of the Byzantine Empire. The vital position of the islands as a link between Europe and Asia and Africa was decisive in defining their course through history. This integral geopolitical region, which had become the scene of competition since the thirteenth century, which was divided up between the Genoese, the Venetians, the Turks and the Knights of St. John, and which from time to time other states had designs upon, was finally reunited in 1913, when the Greek fleet liberated the islands of the North and East Aegean during the Balkan Wars, and when Crete was once more joined to Greece.

At the end of the Turkish-Italian War of 1911 and under the Lausanne Treaty of October 18, 1912, the Dodecanese were ceded to Italy. They were to remain outside the frontiers of Greece until after the Second World War, being unified with Greece by treaty on February 10, 1947. It took ten years from their liberation during the course of the First Balkan War for the legal status of the other eastern Aegean Islands to be settled once and for all. Under the Treaty of Bucharest, 1913, only Thasos was returned to Greece. Final arrangements for the other islands (Lemnos, Samothrace, Lesbos, Chios, Ikaria and Samos) were made by the Treaty of Lausanne of July 24, 1923, by which Turkey recognised Greek sovereignty over the islands. Imbros and Tenedos, which had been granted to Greece under the Treaty of Sèvres in 1920, were returned once more to Turkey.

Vasilis Sphyroeras

1. For the status of the Aegean after the dissolution of the Duchy of Naxos, see P. Grunebaum - Ballin, *Joseph Naci, Duc de Naxos*, Paris, Le Haye, 1968, and B.J. Slot, *Archipelagus Turbatus, Les Cyclades entre colonisation latine et occupation ottomane c. 1500-1718*, Leiden - Istanbul 1982, pp. 88-97.
2. Vasilis Sphyroeras, *The Dragoman of the Fleet, the institution and holders of the office* (in Greek), Athens 1965, pp. 21-29.
3. Vide Slot, *op. cit.*, pp. 13-65.
4. Vasilis Kremmydas, *The soap manufacturers of Crete in the 18th century* (in Greek), Athens 1974, p. 16ff.
5. M. Efthymiou - Chatzilacou, *Rhodes et sa région élargie au XVIIIe siècle: les activités portuaires*, (doctoral thesis), Paris 1984, p. 262.
6. Pantelis Kontoyannis, "Under protection", (in Greek), periodical *Athena*, vol. 29 (1917), pp. 62-80.
7. Sphyroeras, *op. cit.*, pp. 13-20, 61-84.
8. Georgios Leontaritis, *Greek merchant shipping (1453-1850)*, reprinted from the work under the same title published in 1972 by the National Bank of Greece, Athens 1981, pp. 52-62.
9. Vasilis Sphyroeras, *Greek crews in the Turkish fleet* (in Greek), Athens 1968, pp. 85-86, 128.
10. Andreas Drakakis, *The history of the town of Ermoupolis, Syros* (in Greek), vol. I, Athens 1979, pp. 110-121.

MAPS OF THE AEGEAN

The islands of the Aegean Sea, territorial units isolated by the barrier of the waters, but with close ties with the nearby mainland shores, constitute a unity as a geographical concept. Scattered over the surface of the sea in a unique pattern, they describe the arc of a circle formed by Euboea, the islands of the northern Aegean and those along the Asia Minor coast, with the Cyclades forming a link, and with Rhodes, Crete and Cyprus on the southern boundary. This group makes up so formal a pattern that the term 'archipelago' has become a descriptive one, by synecdoche, of seas with scattered islands. A terse geographical description in a Byzantine text of the 10th century likens the mainland part of the Empire, Europe and Asia Minor to the head and the tail, while the islands of the Aegean form the middle of a complete full-length figure.

The great sea routes pass through the world of the Aegean. Landing places and supply points for shipping in times both of the burgeoning of trade and of the outbreak of war, the ports and anchorages of the islands of the Aegean have been visited in the course of their long history by vessels carrying warriors, merchandise, pilgrims, crusaders and the learned. War and trade, trade and crusades, rediscovery and antiquarianism have succeeded one another and have gone on side by side.

The vessel which crosses the Black Sea and emerges from the Straits into the Mediterranean encounters the island way stations of the Aegean. Tenedos, a maritime fortress controlling the entrance to the Propontis, opens the way to Lemnos and Thessaloniki, but also to Chios, Samos, Kos, Rhodes and Cyprus. Rhodes lies on the sea route which links the Near

East with the Western Mediterranean, on which Crete is also situated. Another route takes in the Cyclades, Euboea, Kea and skirting the eastern and southern shores of the Peloponnese makes its way to the Sea of Sicily.

Maps showing sea routes, identifying harbours and sheltered coves and sketching not only the coastline but also the interior of these links in the great chain of islands of the Aegean were a necessity. Equally necessary was a text describing in detail mariners' experiences of sailing conditions, winds, the depths of the waters, settlements on shore and sources of supplies for vessels.

In studying the maps depicting the islands of the Aegean, we can trace the stages through which map-making passed: from antiquity to the Arab representation of the Middle Ages, so different from the theological concept of the picture of the World held by Christian geographers; from the empirical progress of Western marine map-making to the discoveries of the Renaissance combined with the knowledge of antiquity, to the gradual understanding of how the various regions of the Earth can be most correctly and accurately represented.

Although the geographical works of the ancients have not survived, we know from historical sources the wealth of their geographical and nautical knowledge, accumulated over a period of centuries, and the attempts, particularly of the Ionian school, to depict the then known world. The oldest cartographical work on the Aegean to come down to us is that of Ptolemy (Claudius Ptolemaeus) (2nd century AD) and is included in the 'Map of Greece' in his *Geographia*. Manuscript variants and copyists' errors make it difficult to reconstruct the picture of the islands as given by Ptolemy. When, at the end of the 15th century, the manuscript works of the Alexandrian geographer were printed, they had a profound and lasting influence on Western cartographers.

The ancient seamen's guides ('periploi') giving sea routes and distances are works which presuppose the existence of marine charts. This tradition continued into the Byzantine period, as can be seen from a 10th century manuscript in the Madrid Library (Codex 4701), entitled 'Survey or Periplus of the Great Sea' and based on an older original. Marine charts must also have accompanied Byzantine texts on navigation. One such is preserved in the works of Constantine Porphyrogenitus and is placed by him at the end of the catalogue of ships which were fitted out to take part in the unsuccessful campaign of 949 to recover Crete from the Arabs. The 'Stadiodromikon', as it is called, gives way stations and the distance between them on the course to be followed by the imperial fleet. The route starts from Constantinople and via the Hellespont and the islands of Tenedos, Mytilene, Chios, Samos, Naxos and Thira reaches Crete. The oral tradition of the portolans, descriptive navigation texts, also survives in another Byzantine document: "...those with accurate experience of the sea... which winds cause it to swell and which blow off the land; so that they should know also the hidden rocks in the sea and those places which are without depth and the land on shore and how far distant these havens are the one from the other...".

The inadequate knowledge of the Middle Ages produced pictures of the world, but not maps. The 12th century Arab geographer Al Idrisi, who lived at the court of King Roger II of Sicily, attempted the charting of the Aegean. Al Idrisi produced a representation of the known world on a silver disk, divided into eight sections and, in order to provide a guide to understanding it, wrote a book entitled *The diversion of him who would traverse the world.* As he himself states, he made used of older Arab sources, checked against the accounts of contemporary travellers. The disk of Al Idrisi has been lost, but many manuscripts of his book are accompanied by a map of the world and by particular maps with a schematic outline. Also schematic is the representation of the islands of the Aegean, including Crete, Mykonos, Delos, Naxos, Amorgos and others. In the text accompanying the map the distances between the islands are given in miles.

The first marine charts (portolans) which have come down to us were produced by the map-makers of the West. The awakening of cartography is to be traced to the new era which dawned, from the end of the 11th century, when the Byzantine emperors granted privileges to the maritime cities of Venice, Genoa and Pisa, which allowed them to trade freely in the ports of the East. The marine charts were necessary for navigation to the ports where this colonial trade was carried on. At the same time, a species of descriptive text, the Italian portolan, also evolved. These texts, pioneering in form and modelled on the Byzantine portolans, have been preserved in Greek. Greek manuscript and printed portolans are written in a kind of 'Mediterranean koine', which took form during sea voyages and meetings of mariners in the ports of the Mediterranean.

The oldest marine charts or portolans which have come down to us from medieval times date from the 13th century. Drawn on parchment, these valuable tools of cartography were intended for the libraries of the nobles, the merchants and the shipowners of the period and so were spared the perils and wear and tear of voyages at sea. Today they are preserved in such major libraries as the British Museum, the Paris National Library, the Correr Museum in Venice, the Lorenziana in Florence and elsewhere. These maps have been drawn in accordance with the direct observations of seamen using the compass and give the plan of the shores with the place-names along the coastline. In spite of the fact that this form of cartography was carried out in an empirical manner, these marine charts are more faithful than those drawn according to the Ptolemaic system. The distances are estimated and the maps which include the whole of the Mediterranean must have been put together from individual maps of the different sections, which have not survived. A common feature of all the portolans is the use of the same colours: black for the outline of the shores and the place-names, red for the harbours and red, blue or gold for the islands. In the hinterland the mountains are shown schematically, while plans of fortified cities are reproduced and the map is decorated with flags, fabulous beasts and trees. The charts are covered with thumb or plane sailing lines whose intersections form the 'compass rose'. The oldest example of these charts is the so-called 'Pisa Map' of the 13th century, in the National Library of Paris, with a schematic representation of the islands of the Aegean. In the last years of the same century this species of map flourished and progress was achieved by the maps of

Petro Vesconte of Genoa at the beginning of the 14th century.

Since the scale of the portolans is very small, it is not possible to expect an accurate plan of the islands. From the 15th century these charts multiplied, though the plan remained unimproved, while repeated copies contributed to its distortion. In 1520 Ioannis Xenodochos of Corfu mapped, with Venetian nomenclature, the eastern Mediterranean, with the Aegean strewn with its islands. Special leaves devoted to the Aegean were drawn by Gaspar Viegas in 1534, while the map of Salvator Oliva (16th century) includes the Greek Archipelago. The leaf designed by Georgios Sideris or Kalapodas in 1560 is in the Correr Museum. The nomenclature of the map of the Archipelago by Mohamet Raous (1590), which was based on an Italian original, is Turkish.

The marine charts or portolans, often works of art of rare beauty, show that their designers were at the same time navigators and artists who described the world they discovered, mixing myth and reality. As we look at them today, we can share in the dreams and the chimaeras which they pursued.

It is to a 15th century humanist, the Florentine cleric Christoforo Buondelmonti, that we owe the first specialised maps of the Aegean. Based on Rhodes, where he had settled to study Greek literature, he visited the islands of the Aegean, collecting manuscripts. In 1420 he dedicated to Cardinal Giordano Orsini the *Liber Insularum Archipelagi.* Prior to this he had produced a description of Crete. In studying ancient writers, Buondelmonti noted their historical oddities and the myths connected with the Aegean. This aspect of his work stirred the interest of the contemporary learned world and the *Liber Insularum* had a wide circulation. Until the end of the 18th century this work remained the basis of the geographical knowledge of men of letters, who were interested by its description of the islands and its cataloguing of monuments, as well as by the large number of maps by which it was accompanied. In 1824 L. de Sinner published the Latin text and in 1897 Emile Legrand the manuscript of Buondelmonti, which was translated into Greek anonymously. At the end of his edition Legrand printed 16 maps from the

Latin manuscript of Buondelmonti, No. 4825 in the Paris National Library, while he included in the text 36 printed maps, reproduced by the zinc-plate method from originals belonging to the 'atlas' of C. Schefer, about which more will be said below.

The maps which are reproduced with considerable care in the various manuscripts of Buondelmonti are all of the same type. The outline of the islands is traced carefully and we conclude that Buondelmonti was not copying from the portolans, but was attempting, without intending to be purely scientific, to give their shape. In one of the manuscripts – Res. Ge FF 9351 in the Paris National Library – which contains 79 water-colour maps of the Aegean, the topographical details which they provide are of interest. On the map which shows the coast of Asia Minor opposite Tenedos, with a wealth of classical remains, Buondelmonti names the area as the site of ancient Troy, a view which was later to be vindicated.

The great influence which the work of Buondelmonti had is obvious from a series of geographical works containing descriptions of islands and accompanied by maps, the species being known as an 'isolario'. The imitation of the Florentine humanist in these works is obvious. In the verse work of Francesco Berlinghieri, printed in Florence around 1480 and entitled *Geografia in Terza Rima...*, Ptolemaic maps are included, but it is clear that there are borrowings from Buondelmonti. Chronologically this was followed by the isolario of Bartholomeo dalli Sonetti, the 'good Venetian', as he called himself on the title page, which was printed around 1485. The dominating factor in these verse works is the practical purpose for which they were written, though historical details are not lacking. The influence of Buondelmonti is apparent here too, but, as can be seen from the maps, particularly of the bigger islands, the writer had a profound knowledge of the Aegean. The influence of Buondelmonti can also be seen in the work *Insularum Illustratum* by the German cartographer Henricus Martellus Germanus, finished about 1490, but not printed. Written in Latin, it is accompanied by maps of all the islands of the Mediterranean, drawn in colour. In 1528 Benedetto Bordone published in Venice an isolario in prose, without original features. The text for the most part is borrowed from Buondelmonti, while the maps are a more schematic reproduction of those of Bartholomeo dalli Sonetti.

The 'Book of the Sea' (Kitab-i Bahriyyé) of the Turk Pîri-Re'is, presented to the Sultan Selim I in 1526, was influenced by the Italian portolans and contains geographical observations and historical and archaeological data, as well as accounts of mythology. Intended as a marine guide for the Ottoman fleet, which at that time was fighting for the mastery of the Mediterranean, it was widely circulated, if we are to judge from the large number of manuscripts which have survived. Its maps follow the pattern of those of dalli Sonetti.

Works describing and mapping the *most renowned islands of the world* by Camocius (Venice 1562) and Porcacchi (Venice 1572) also had a wide circulation.

The work composed by the French historian and 'Cosmographer to the King' André Thevet in 1584 with the title "Le Grand Insulaire et Pilotage.." dans lequel sont contenus plusieurs plants d' isles habitées et deshabitées et description d' icelles... has remained in manuscript (Paris National Library Ms. 15452-15453). It contains, as its title suggests, printed maps attached to the pages corresponding to the description. These maps had been ordered by Thevet for the printing of his work, which, however, he either did not live to see or had not the means to carry through. A section of these maps was found in the forged 'atlas' bought in Turin by C. Schefer and passed on by him to Emile Legrand. As mentioned above, Legrand reprinted 36 maps from this 'atlas' in his edition of the Greek manuscript of Buondelmonti. Thevet himself states, in another work – *Vrais Portraits et Vie des Hommes Illustres* – published in 1584, that this 'atlas' contained some 300 maps. Today a part of these maps is included in the d' Anville collection in the Paris National Library.

The manuscript isolario completed in 1590 by Antonio Millo imitates the maps of Bartholomeo dalli Sonetti, but the outline of the islands is distorted. The same type of map was reproduced by Marco Boschini in *Archipelago con tutte le isole, scogli, secche e bassi fondi,* printed in Venice in 1657. He collected plans from earlier cartographers, and engraved them himself. The text which he supplies also includes elements from earlier works. We also find the pattern of dalli Sonetti in the maps of Widman, of the mid-18th century, whilst the text which accompanies them is more or less copied from Boschini.

Two general maps of Greece of the 16th century, of large dimensions, include the Aegean and served as originals for more than a century. The Corfiot man of letters Nikolaos Sofianos for his map '‘Ἑλλάς' borrowed the outline and the plan of the Aegean from Ptolemy. He records the names as they appear in ancient authors — Herodotus, Thucydides, Strabo and Pausanias, but he also drew up a table in which he attempted to identify these with the contemporary ones.

The Aegean is shown with greater accuracy in its representation in the map of Eastern Europe (1560) of Jacopo Gastaldi, which was inspired by the portolans. The work of Gastaldi was used by Ortelius for his map of 'modern Greece' and was followed by Mercator.

From the end of the 16th century and into the 17th a type of cartographical representation which derived from on-the-spot research and travellers' accounts and was used to adorn travel books had a considerable vogue.

The attention of the learned world was directed towards the actual sites of military conflicts and commercial dealings. Cartographers, as many of them claimed, gave information about 'existing conditions', while, apart from geophysical features, they note the archaelogical remains in the places which they visited. Fortresses, monasteries and remains of temples adorn the maps and they are careful to give the ancient place-names alongside the contemporary ones.

In 1688 Francesco Piacenza, who travelled in the Aegean, published *Egeo Redivivo,* a survey of the Sea. The text is a hotchpotch of earlier works and the plan of the maps follows that of Boschini. At the same period the prolific writer O. Dapper published at Amsterdam his *Exact Description of the Islands of the Archipelago,* the fruit of the knowledge of an intellectual well acquainted with contemporary bibliography. The most outstanding example of the genre of travellers' descriptions is the work of the Cosmographer of the Venetian Republic Vincenzo Coronelli, which includes many place-names, ancient and contemporary, historical elaborations and plans which are without any particular geographical interest. At the beginning of the 18th century the French botanist Pitton de Tournefort, who possessed all the qualifications of the observant traveller, visited the Aegean and produced detailed maps on a scientific basis. In the work of the French Ambassador at Constantinople, Choiseul Gouffier, the well-known *Voyage*, we find a combination of archaeological research and contemporary fact. The maps which accompany his work note details of the hinterland and the coastline.

Although men's desire to acquire a picture of the world as a whole shows scientific curiosity and although navigators always needed to be able to recognize the shores of a particular region, the need for accurate knowlege of a particular region was most keenly and chiefly felt by soldiers on campaign and, subsequently, by a public interested in conflicts as contemporary events. This is the reason why the majority of cartographical works with the representation of localities were related to military operations.

The wars between Venice and Turkey gave the impetus for the publication of local maps dealing with the islands, 'the theatre of war'. Public response to such productions can be gauged by the fact that the publishers of Venice and Rome, pioneers in this area, such as Bertelli, Lafreri and Duchetus, and later the Dutch and the French, had no hestitation in bringing out large numbers of local maps, which found their place in their atlases.

Although the maps which accompanied an isolario or travellers' account were repeated without any progress being made, a new concept was introduced into cartographical representation by hydrographic maps. From the mid-18th century, the Dutch, the French and the British, who had acquired privileges from the Ottoman Empire and carried on competitive trade in the ports of the Eastern Mediterranean, were in need of more accurate maps. The Dutch were the first to produce hydrographic maps, which were to replace the Italian portolans. In 1621, W.J. Blaeu, a competent and cultivated cartographer, drew and published maps of the Mediterranean, accompanied by a text containing useful advice and depictions of the coastline. Blaeu established a firm which was to become famous and his maps had many imitators, as in the case of the atlas of Pieter Goos, in which the general map of the Archipelago is included (1669). Also of importance is the work of the Dutchman J. Van Keulen with its map of the Archipelago (1680).

However, the Dutch maps remained at the empirical stage and were not based on detailed representation or accurate astronomical definition. It was the French who attempted to make their maps accurate, with latitude and longitude and the projection introduced by Mercator for marine charts. On the inspiration of Colbert, the composition of the memorable work *Neptune de la Méditerranée* was embarked upon, with hydrographic expeditions being organised for the purpose. In June of 1685 the French hydrographers were ordered to map the islands of the Aegean. It can be seen from the documents relating to these expeditions how closely they were bound up with French policy towards the Ottoman Empire. In the 'Instructions of the King' to the leader of the 1685 expedition, La Motte d' Ayran, we read: "He should be aware that all the maps made up to the present have been found incorrect and, in consequence, His Majesty has determined that a new one shall be made, on which shall be shown all the principal features of the coastline, shoals, inlets, bays, harbours and anchorages... When all the maps and the necessary instruments have been collected together, every measure is to be taken for the expedition to be seen as a commercial one... the orders are to be kept secret...".

The map of the Archipelago was drawn in 1695 and again in 1715 and 1730. In the 18th century the work of Bellin (1738), d' Anville (1756), Chabert (1794) and later of Gauttier and Benoist (1818-1819) was to predominate.

The contribution of the British to the cartography of the Aegean is indicative of their interest in the region, particularly after the establishing of the Levant Company at the end of the 16th century. Their work was collected together in the *English Pilot*, issued for the first time in 1677 and subsequently republished many times. However, it was the accurate hydrographic maps of the British which, in the 19th century, superseded every other work. The map of the Archipelago published by the Hydrographic Service of the British Navy in 1847 was a landmark in the mapping of the Aegean.

Anna Avramea

SELECT BIBLIOGRAPHY

Avramea, Anna: "Coastal Map-making," *Greek Merchant Shipping (1453-1850)*, (in Greek), National Bank of Greece, Athens 1972.

Armao, Ermanno: *In Giro per il Mar Egeo con Vincenzo Coronelli*, Firenze 1951.

Bagrow, Leo: *History of Cartography*, revised and enlarged by Skelton, R.A., London 1964.

Delatte, Armand: *Les Portolans Grecs*, Bibliothèque de la Faculté de Philosophie et Lettres de l'Université de Liège, CVII, Liège - Paris 1947. *Les Portolans Grecs, II, Compléments*, Bruxelles 1958.

Hasluck, F.W.: *Notes on MSS in the British Museum*, Annual of the British School at Athens, 1905-1906.

Kretschmer, Konrad: *Die italienischer Portolane des Mittelalters. Ein Beitrag zur Geschichte der Kartographie und Nautik*, Berlin 1909.

Nordenskiöld, A.E.: *Facsimile – atlas to the Early History of Cartography*, Stockholm 1889.

Stylianou, A. and J.: *The History of the Cartography of Cyprus*, Nicosia 1980.

Tooley, R.V.: *Maps and Map-makers*, London 1949.

Tooley, R.V.: *Tooley's Dictionary of Mapmakers*, Tring, England 1979.

Zacharakis, Chr.: *A Catalogue of printed Maps of Greece, 1477-1800*, Nicosia 1982.

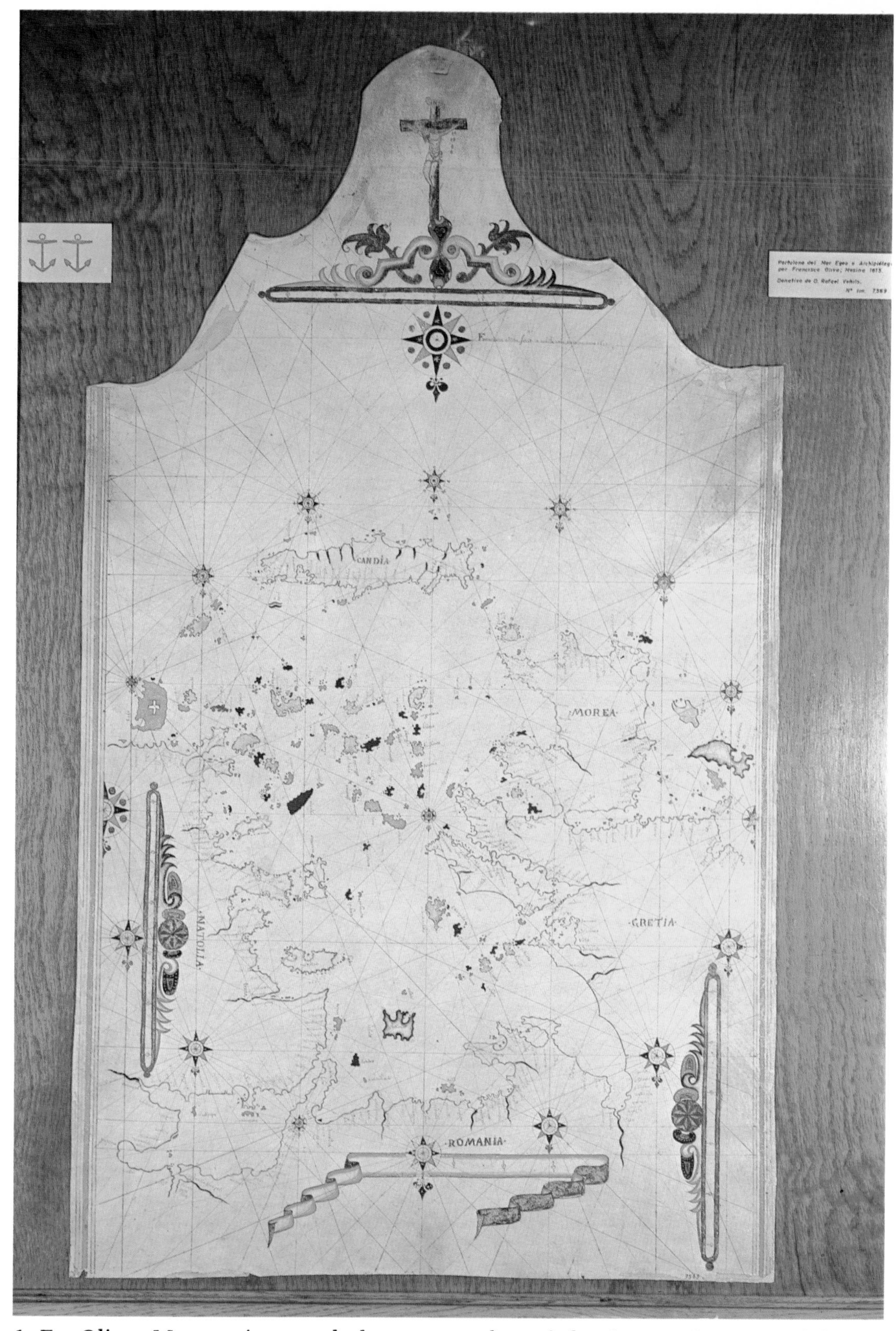

1. Fr. Oliva: Manuscript naval chart - portolan of the Aegean Sea, Messini 1615

1 a. Manuscript naval chart - portolan of the eastern Mediterranean and the Black Sea, on parchment, the work of Ioannis Xenodochos of Corfu, 1520

MAR MAZOR
ANTOLIA
CARAMANIA
ARMENIA
MARE MEDITERANEVM
ARABIA FELICE
MARE RUBRO
damasco

2. *Portolan of the Mediterranean, Europe and Africa, 1561*

3. Manuscript portolan of the Aegean, 1664

AFRICA
Barcha
Alesandria
Eggito
Candia
Cipri
Soria

Romania
Natolia
ASIA
Caramania
Salonice
Lembalo
Nicalidi
Longisto
Grisopoli
Tristopolo
Cavalla
Gaurelli
Asprosa
Fanal
Magri
Mariza
Eneo
Cezari
Ziani
Chisa
Gallipoli
Sindra
Androbo
Schiro
Tino
Scio
Pelegia
Saline
Marmara
Costantinopoli
Galata

I. CHIOS
melaneto
Scta elena
Vichio
Cardamile
portus cardamile
Strimili
Sctus Stephanus
portus delphini
pitio
S. elyas
S. Angeli
S. Iohes
mons altissimi
Litimmena
hic erat civitas chy olim
CHIOS
Coron ata
portus late
portus chy
S. Gregorii
Campus fertilis
Castellu recouera
pigri
Sa Anastasia
Calamoti

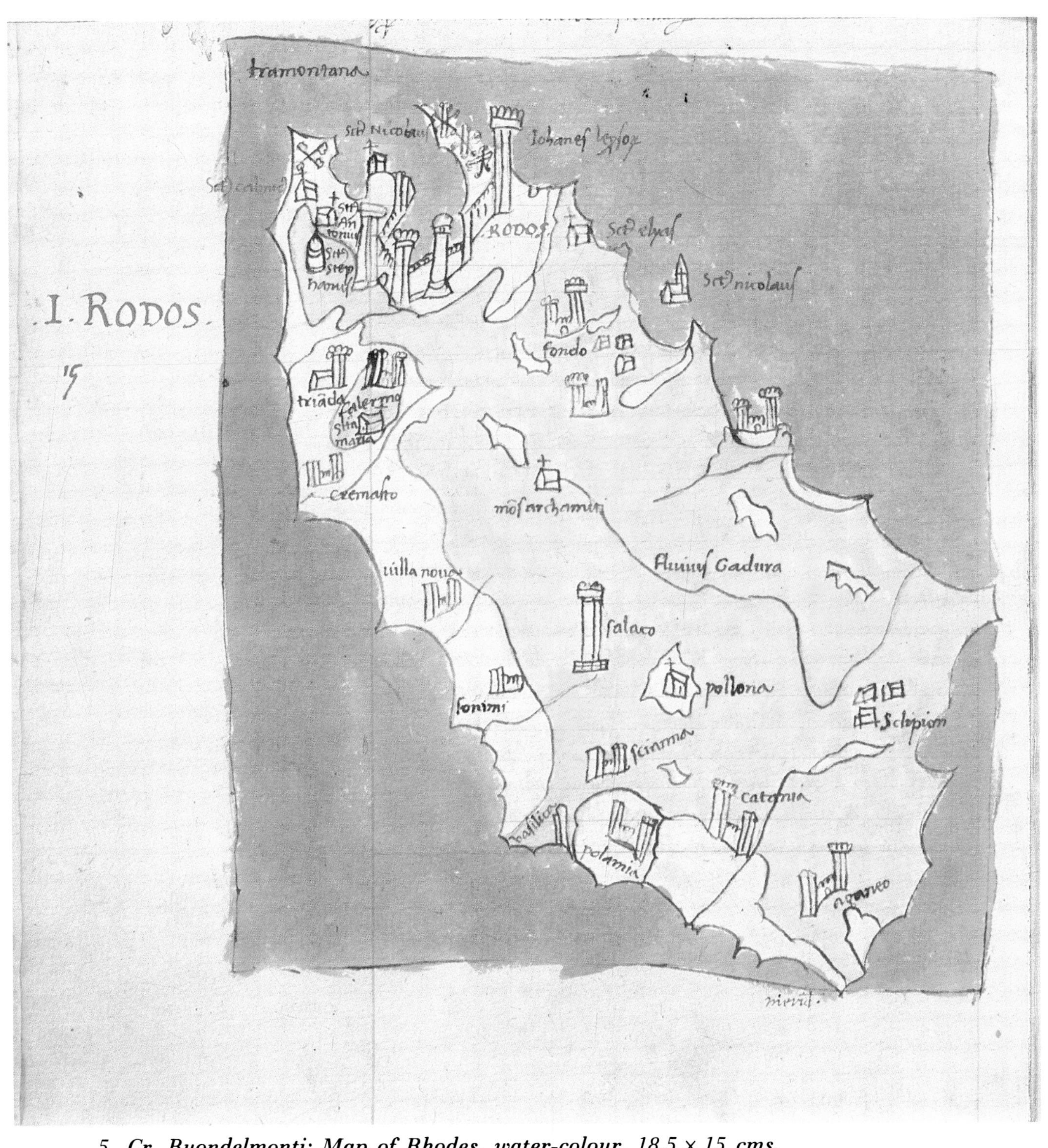

5. Cr. Buondelmonti: Map of Rhodes, water-colour, 18.5 × 15 cms, from a 15th century manuscript

4. Cr. Buondelmonti: Map of Chios, water-colour, 23 × 17 cms, from a 15th century manuscript

31
.I. ANDROS.
31
Andros
Oriens

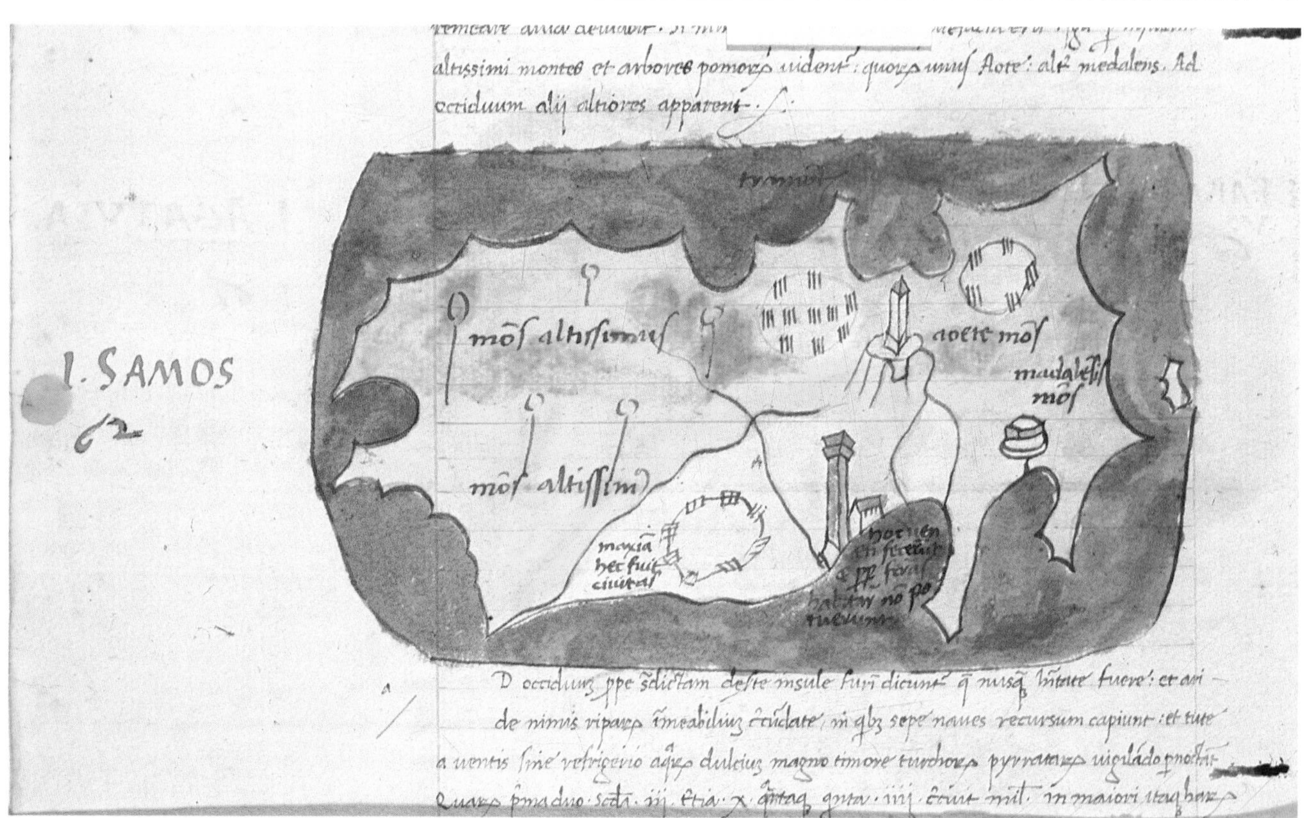

I. SAMOS
62
mōs altissimus
mōs altissimi

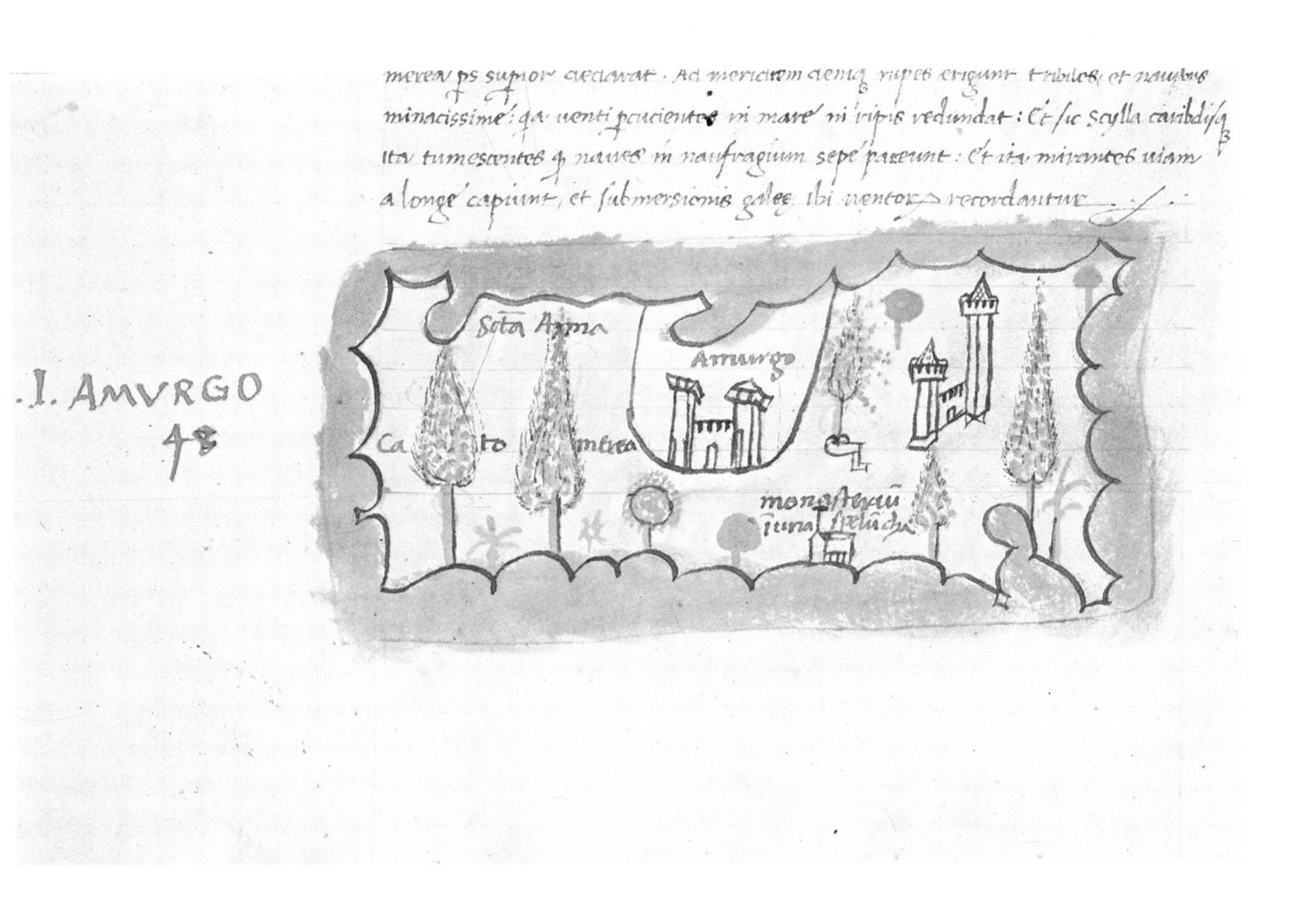

6. Cr. Buondelmonti: Map of Andros, water-colour, 11 × 14 cms, from a 15th century manuscript
7. Cr. Buondelmonti: Map of Samos, water-colour, 8.5 × 15 cms, from a 15th century manuscript
8. Cr. Buondelmonti: Map of Amorgos, water-colour, 6 × 12 cms, from a 15th century manuscript

Bartolomeo dalli Sonetti: pseudonym of the writer of a portolan giving a description of the Aegean islands in verse and mapping them. The entire text is in sonnet form, from which the author, an experienced and widely-travelled Venetian sailor, gained his soubriquet.

Bartolomeo's Isolario was printed first at Venice, in 1485, and re-issued in 1532. It is the first printed atlas of the Greek islands based on real measurements. There is one sonnet for each island, with the exception of the larger and more famous ones, such as Crete, Rhodes and Euboea, to which Bartolomeo devoted more of his compositions. The work contains a total of 49 maps of the islands.

All are woodcuts, and occupy one page of the atlas, again with the exception of Crete and Euboea, which are accorded two pages. The information provided by the Isolario is historical and nautical, and its general accuracy meant that it must have been of considerable use to sailors of the time. The writer must have had earlier manuscript portolans in mind, and particularly the *Liber Insularum Archipelagi* of Buondelmonti.

9. The cover and the beginning of the Isolario *of Bartolomeo dalli Sonetti, 1485*

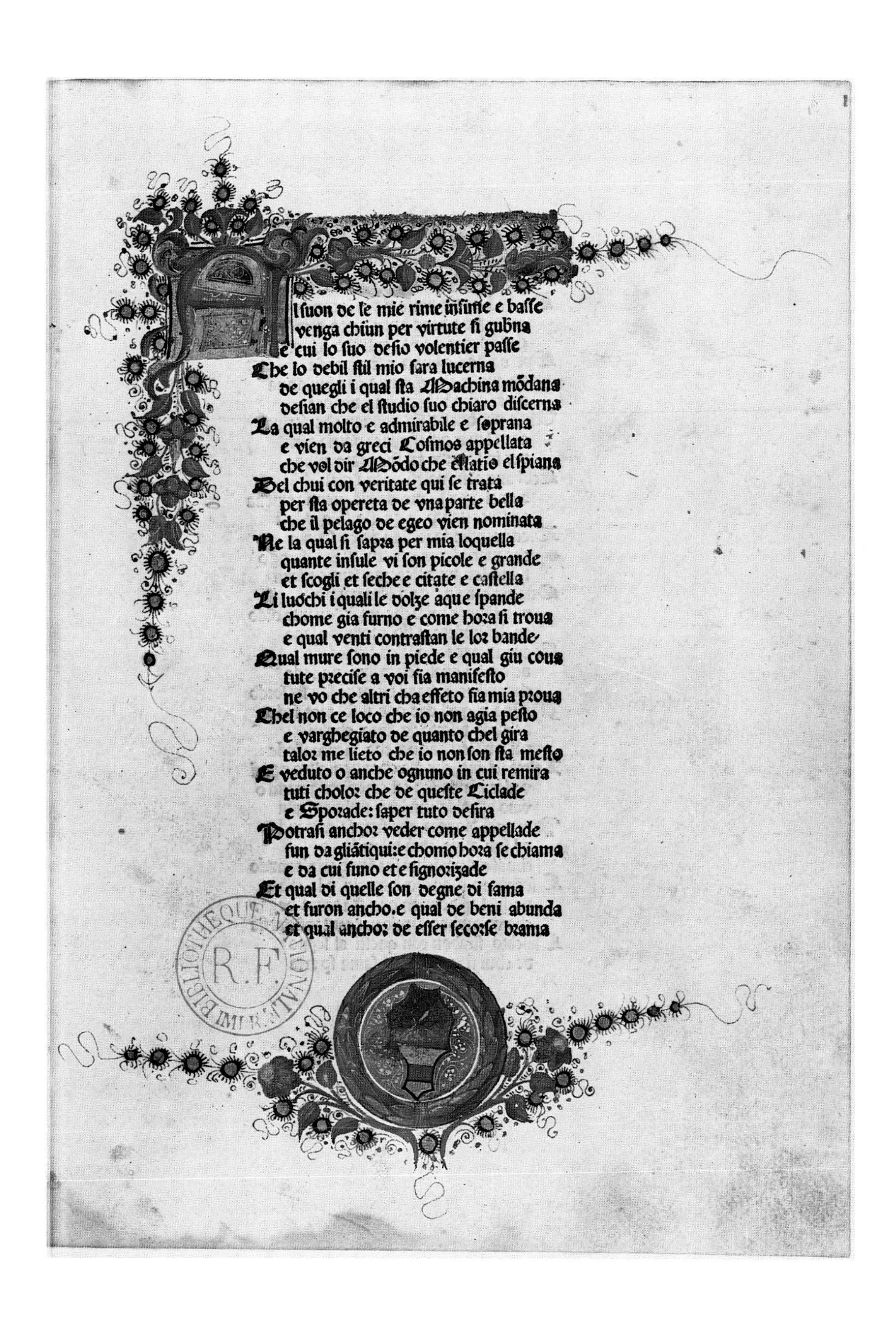

Al suon de le mie rime insume e basse
venga chiun per virtute si gubna
e cui lo suo desio volentier passe
Che lo debil stil mio sara lucerna
de quegli i qual sta Machina mõdana
desian che el studio suo chiaro discerna
La qual molto e admirabile e soprana
e vien da greci Cosmos appellata
che vol dir Mõdo che ellatio el spiana
Del chui con veritate qui se trata
per sta opereta de vna parte bella
che il pelago de egeo vien nominata
Ne la qual si sapra per mia loquella
quante insule vi son picole e grande
et scogli et seche e citate e castella
Li luochi i quali le dolze aque spande
chome gia furno e come hora si troua
e qual venti contrastan le lor bande
Qual mure sono in piede e qual giu cous
tute precise a voi fia manifesto
ne vo che altri cha effeto fia mia proua
Chel non ce loco che io non agia pesto
e varghegiato de quanto chel gira
talor me lieto che io non son sta mesto
E veduto o anche ognuno in cui remira
tuti cholor che de queste Ciclade
e Sporade: saper tuto desira
Potrasi anchor veder come appellade
fun da gliãtiqui: e chomo hora se chiama
e da cui funo et e signorizade
Et qual di quelle son degne di fama
et furon ancho. e qual de beni abunda
et qual anchor de esser secorse brama

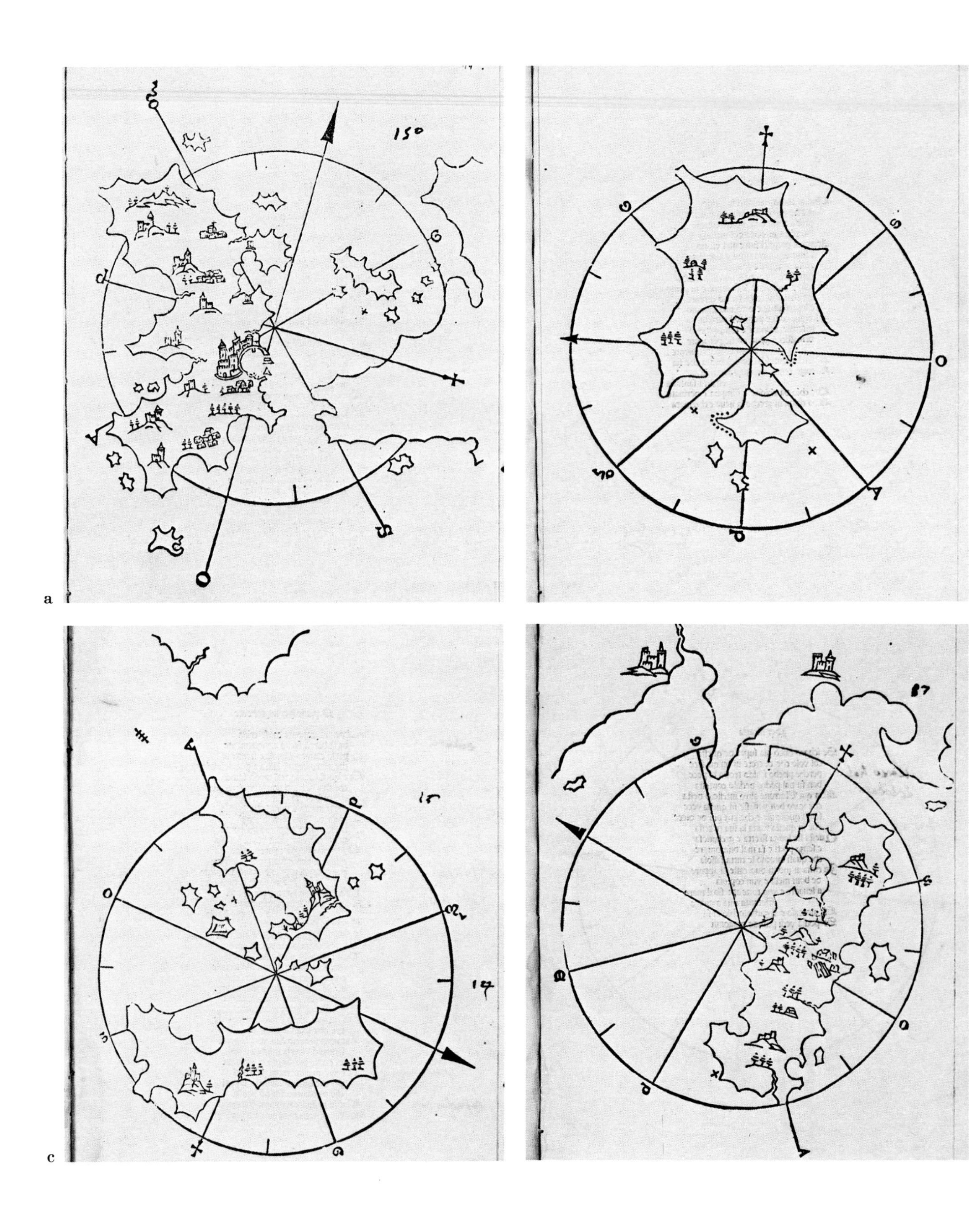
a
c

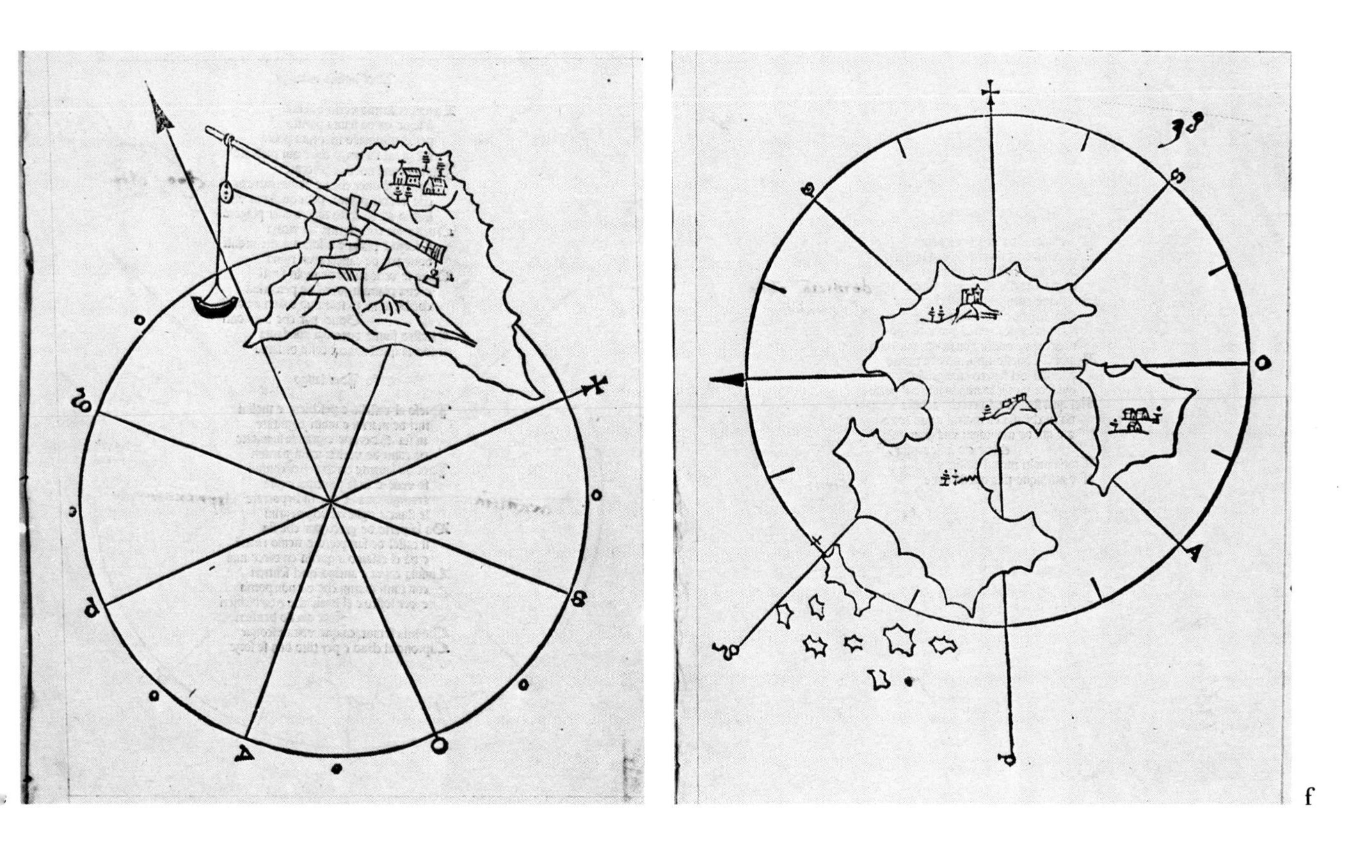

10(a). B. dalli Sonetti: Map of Chios, woodcut, 19 × 15.5 cms, 1485
11(b). B. dalli Sonetti: Map of Psara, woodcut, 19 × 15.5 cms, 1485
12(c). B. dalli Sonetti: Map of Skopelos and Skiathos, woodcut, 19.5 × 15.5 cms, 1485
13(d). B. dalli Sonetti: Map of Samos, woodcut, 17 × 15 cms, 1485
14(e). B. dalli Sonetti: Map of Kalogeros, woodcut, 20 × 15.5 cms, 1485
15(f). B. dalli Sonetti: Map of Leros, woodcut, 15 × 15.5 cms, 1485

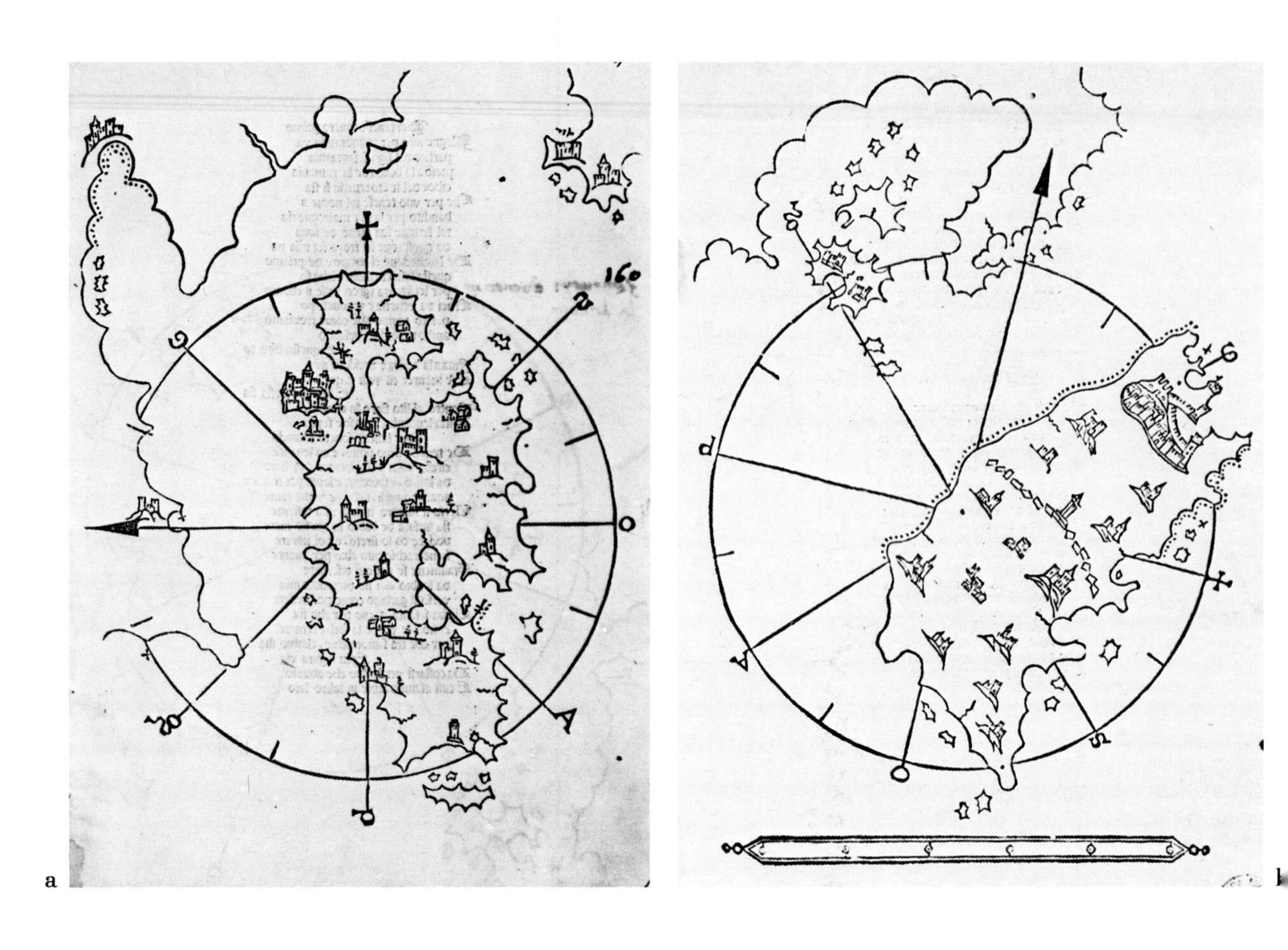

16(a). B. dalli Sonetti: Map of Mytilene, woodcut, 21.5 × 15.5 cms, 1485
17(b). B. dalli Sonetti: Map of Rhodes, woodcut, 21 × 15.5 cms, 1485
18(c). B. dalli Sonetti: Map of Cyprus, woodcut, 28 × 19 cms, 1485

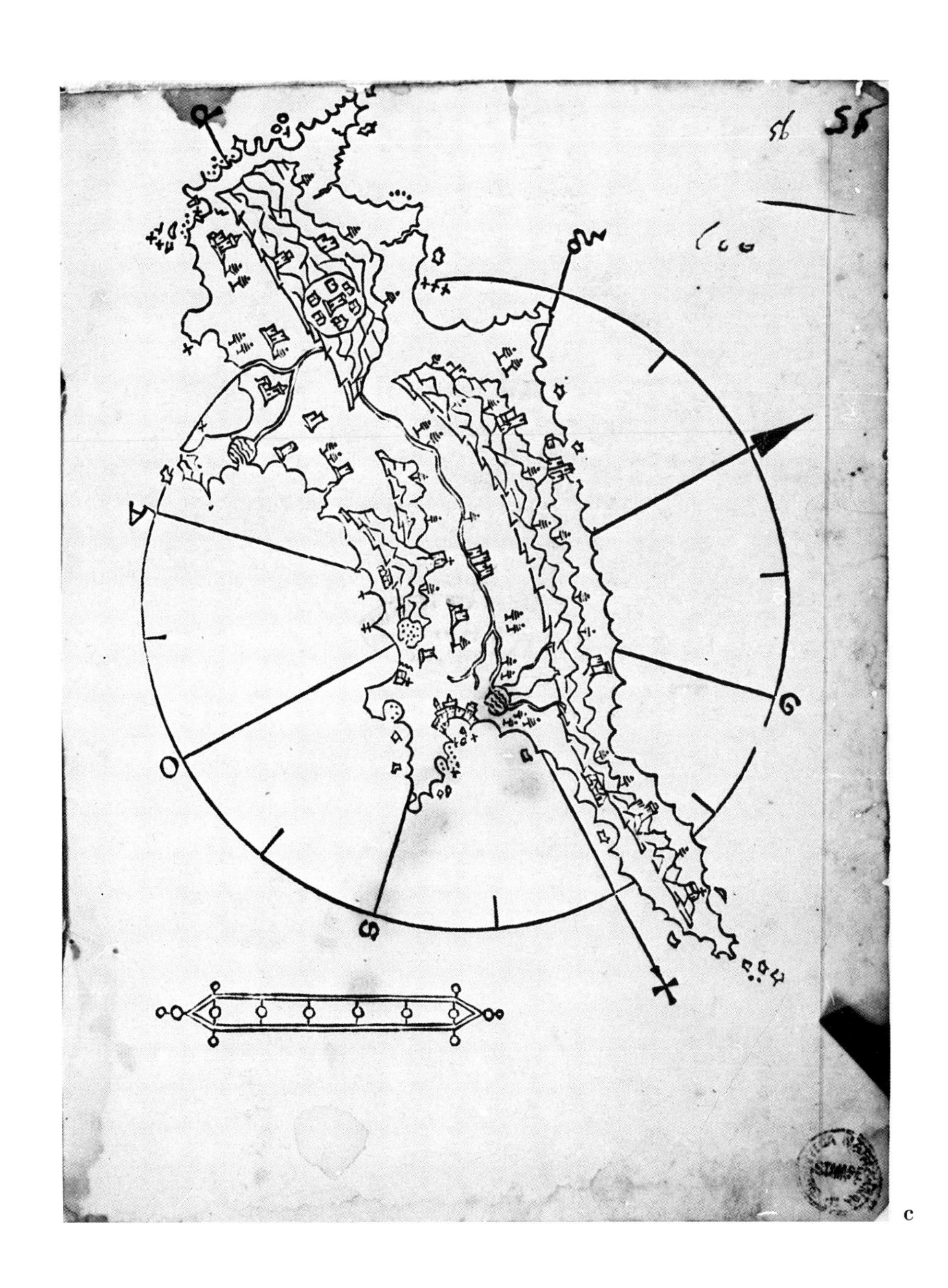

c

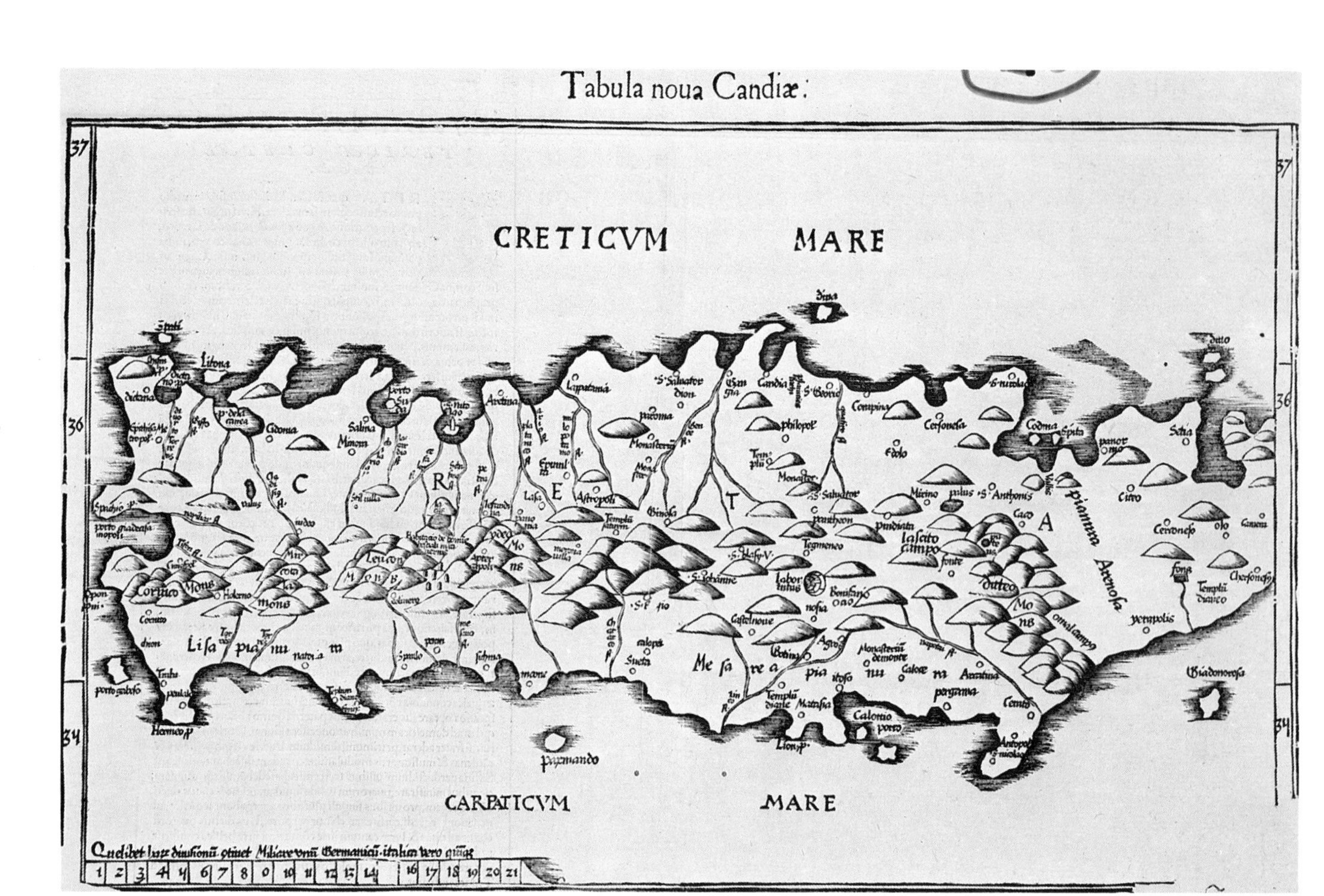

19. Map of Crete, woodcut, 1522

The work of the Alexandrian astronomer and geographer Claudius Ptolemaeus (Ptolemy) (87-150), known to the West through Byzantine and Arabic manuscripts, had a profound influence and for 1500 years dominated the development of geography and map-making. From the 15th century his *Geography* went through repeated editions, of which the following are the most important. The first edition, without maps, came out in Venice in 1475, whilst the first, rarer, edition with maps was that of Bologna (1477). In Germany the *Geography* was printed for the first time in 1482 at Ulm, with 32 woodcut maps. The most important edition of Ptolemy is that of Martin Waldseemüller, Strasbourg 1513, with 20 'contemporary' maps, including the first map of the New World. The Venice edition of 1548 has a text in Italian. The maps were drawn by Jacopo Gastaldi. The maps in the Cologne edition (1578) were drawn by Mercator and those in the Venice edition of 1596 by Girolamo Porro. The map of Crete (no.19) is from Joannes Gruninger's Strasbourg edition of 1522. This included 50 woodcut maps, of smaller dimensions, however, than those in the 1513 edition, as well as three new maps drawn for this edition.

Benedetto Bordone (1460-1531): cartographer, miniaturist and engraver, was born at Padua and worked in Venice. Among his works is the Isolario from which the maps of the Aegean islands we show are taken. The book was first published in 1528, and further editions followed in 1532, 1534, 1537 and 1547.

The 1537 Isolario, the edition used here, was printed in Venice, and illustrates its text with 78 woodcut maps of the islands described. There are also four double-page maps which do not accompany the text: the Eastern Mediterranean, the Western Mediterranean, the World and the City of Venice. Bordone numbered himself among "the high-minded and lion-hearted knights who, at great cost to their vital spirits and even with loss of their lives, have explored the oceans in the mighty fleet of the lords of Venice". With the aim of providing a background for young seafarers, he gives a general summary of the cosmographic theories of his day, explains the criss-crossing of parallels and meridians on the globe and describes the positions of the points of the horizon and the directions of the wind. In his introduction, Bordone explains that the study of the ancients formed one of his sources, while the initial incentive for his writings was his desire

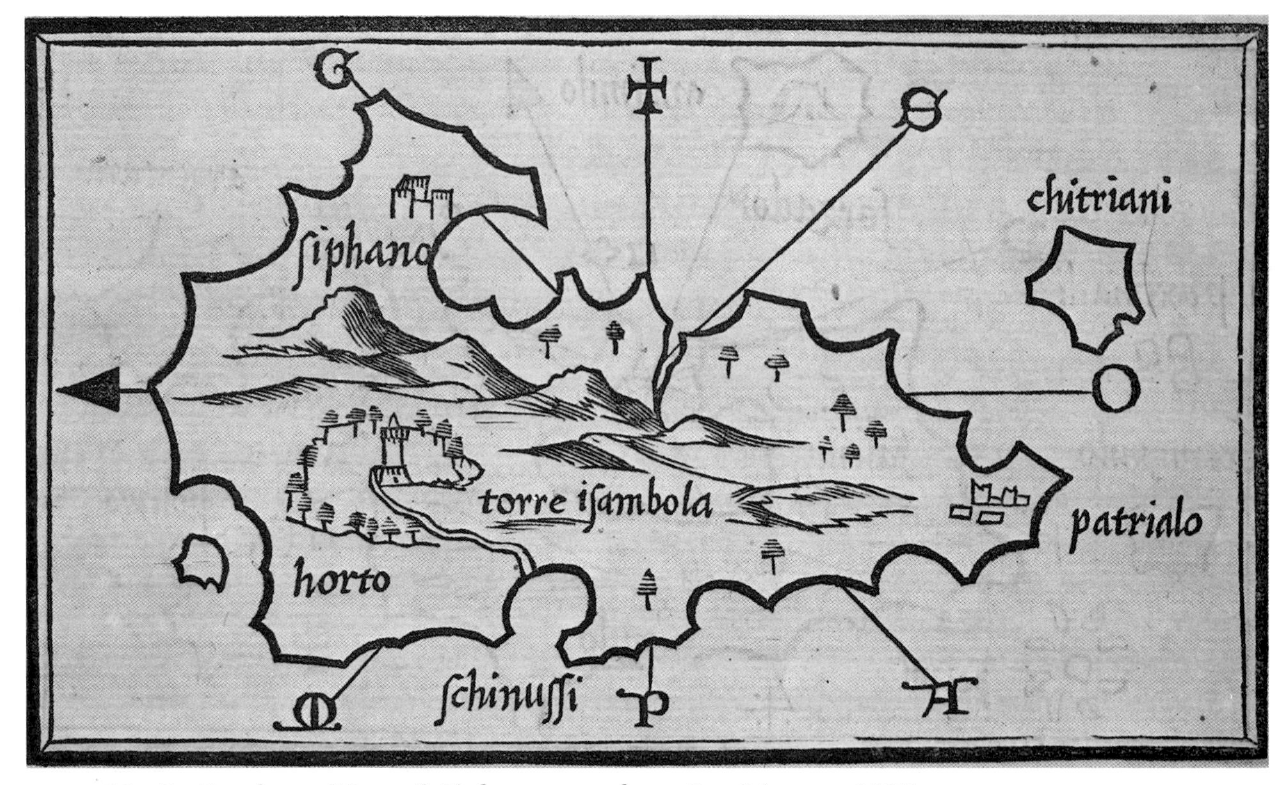

20. B. Bordone: Map of Siphnos, woodcut, 8 × 14 cms, 1537

to communicate his knowledge to benefit and entertain those who read him. Thus in his exciting narrative more attention is paid to the myths about the various islands rather than to the scientific recording of their characteristics.

In the particular case of Bordone's maps of the Aegean islands, coastlines are shown according to their shape and

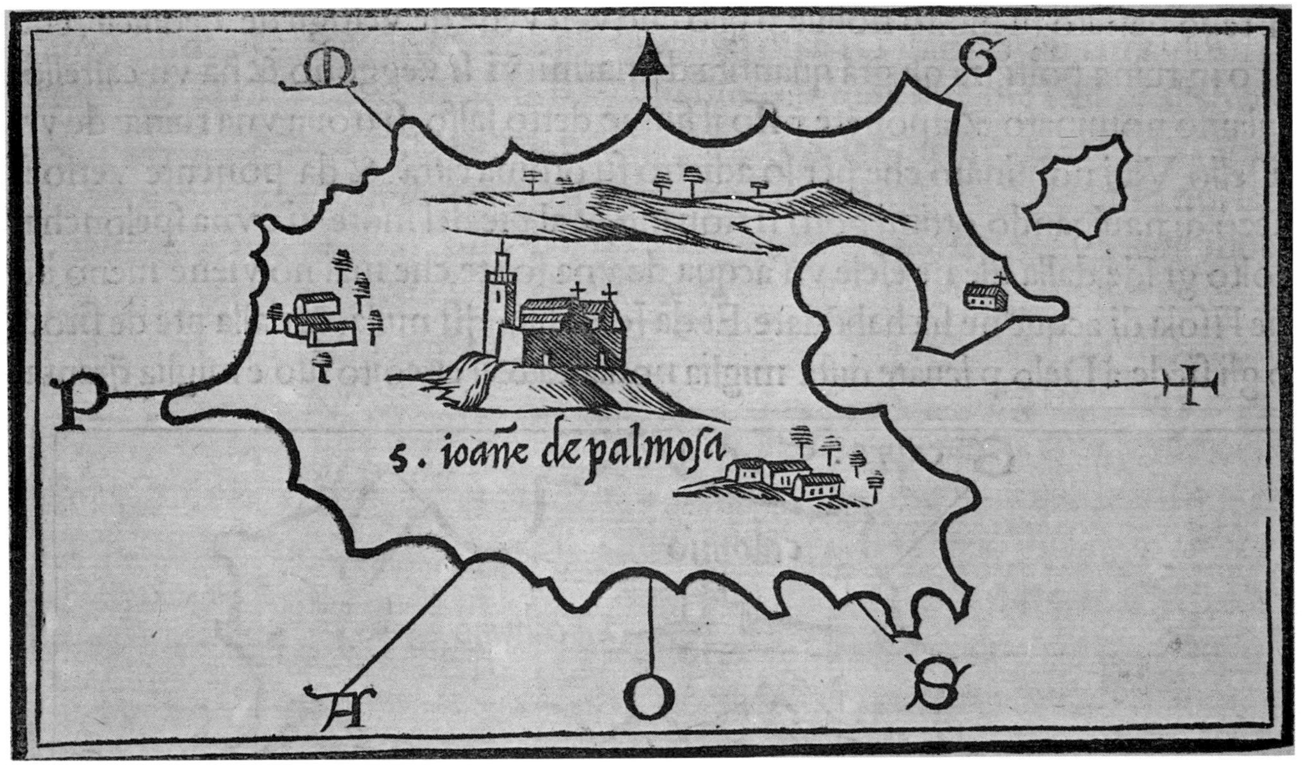

21. B. Bordone: Map of Patmos, woodcut, 8 × 14 cms, 1537

place-names are not given. The map of the Aegean does, however, give the Greek names for the seas — in more or less corrupt forms — such as Mare Egeo Arcipelago, Pelago Cretense, Mar Carpathio, Sinus Termaïcus and Propontide, and the names he uses for the lands surrounding the Aegean are also Greek: Morea, Macedonia, Thracia, and Asia Minor.

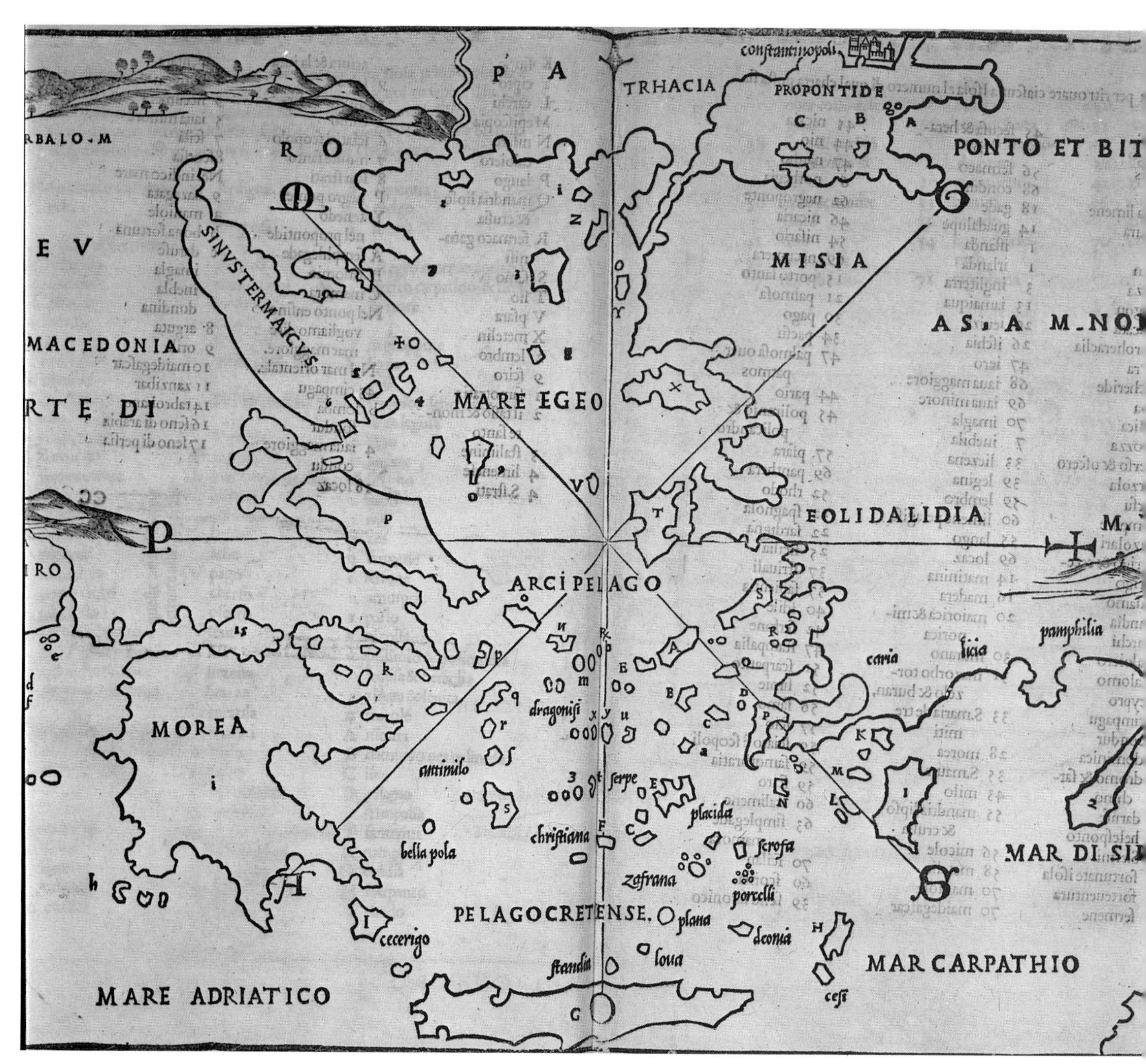

22. B. Bordone: Map of Greece, woodcut, 28 × 38 cms, 1537

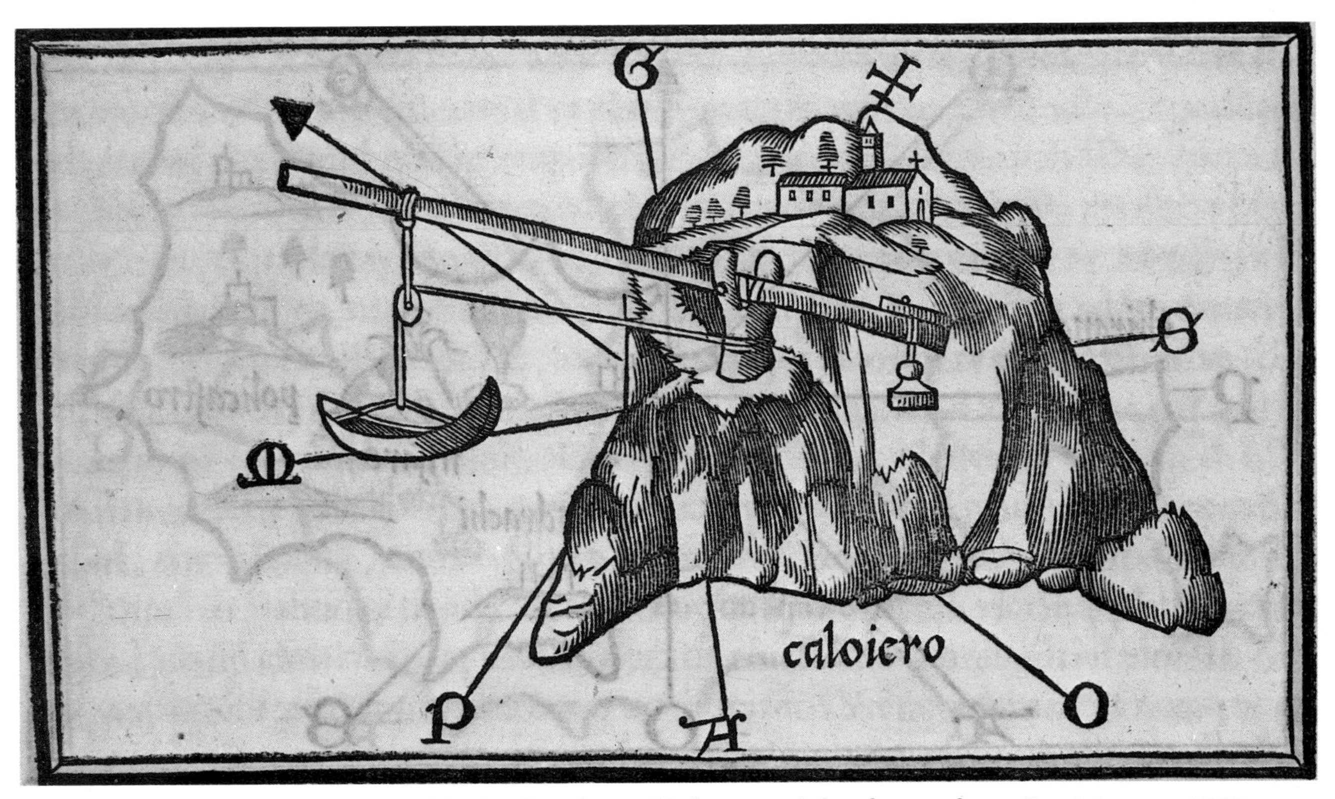

23. B. Bordone: Kalogeros island, woodcut, 8 × 14 cms, 1537

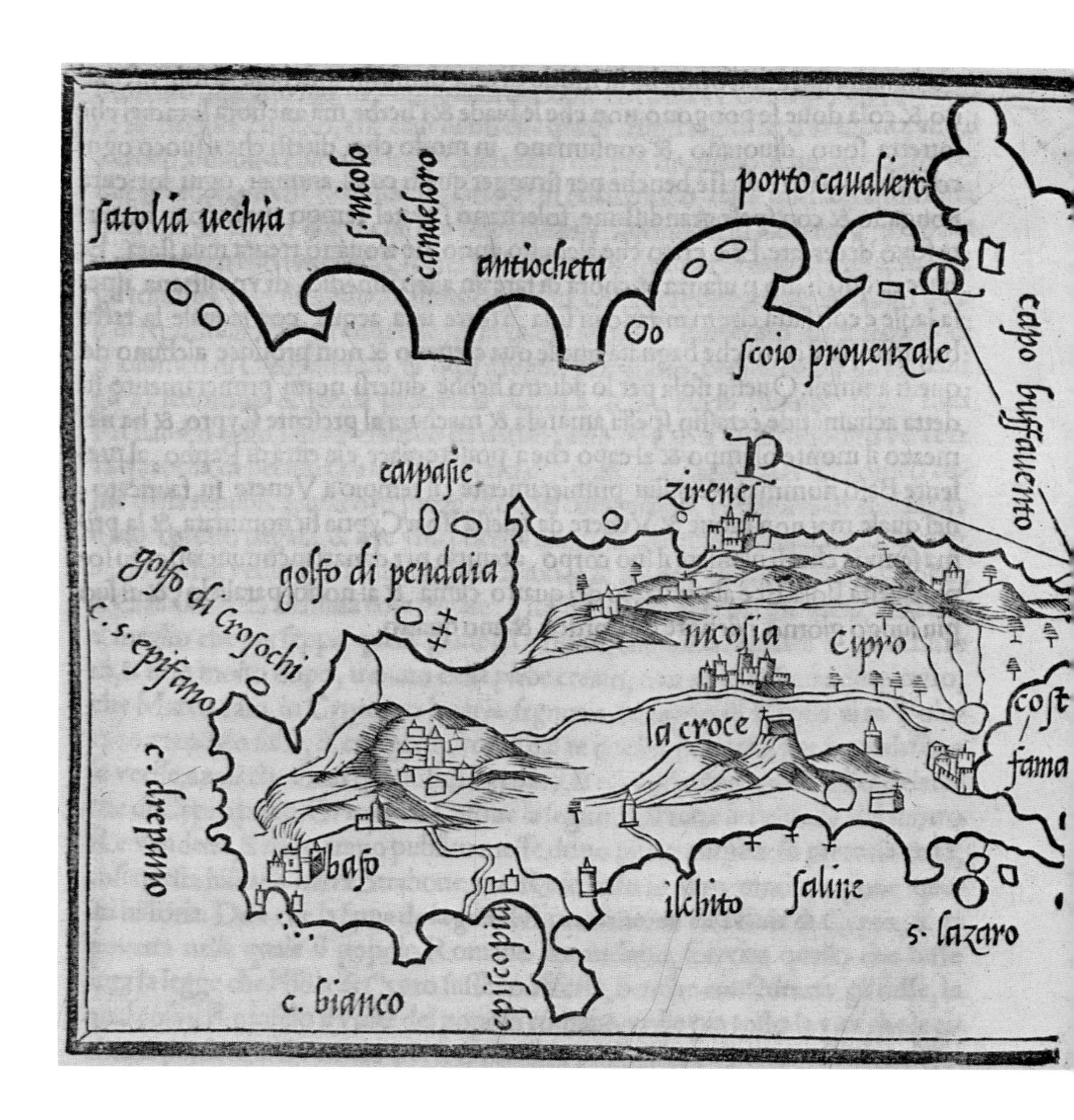
satolia uechia
s. nicolo
candeloro
antiocheta
porto caualiero
scoio prouenzale
capo buffauento
carpasie
zirenes
golfo di pendaia
golfo di Crosochi
c. s. epifanio
c. drepano
nicosia
Cipro
cost
fama
la croce
baso
episcopia
ilchito
saline
s. lazaro
c. bianco

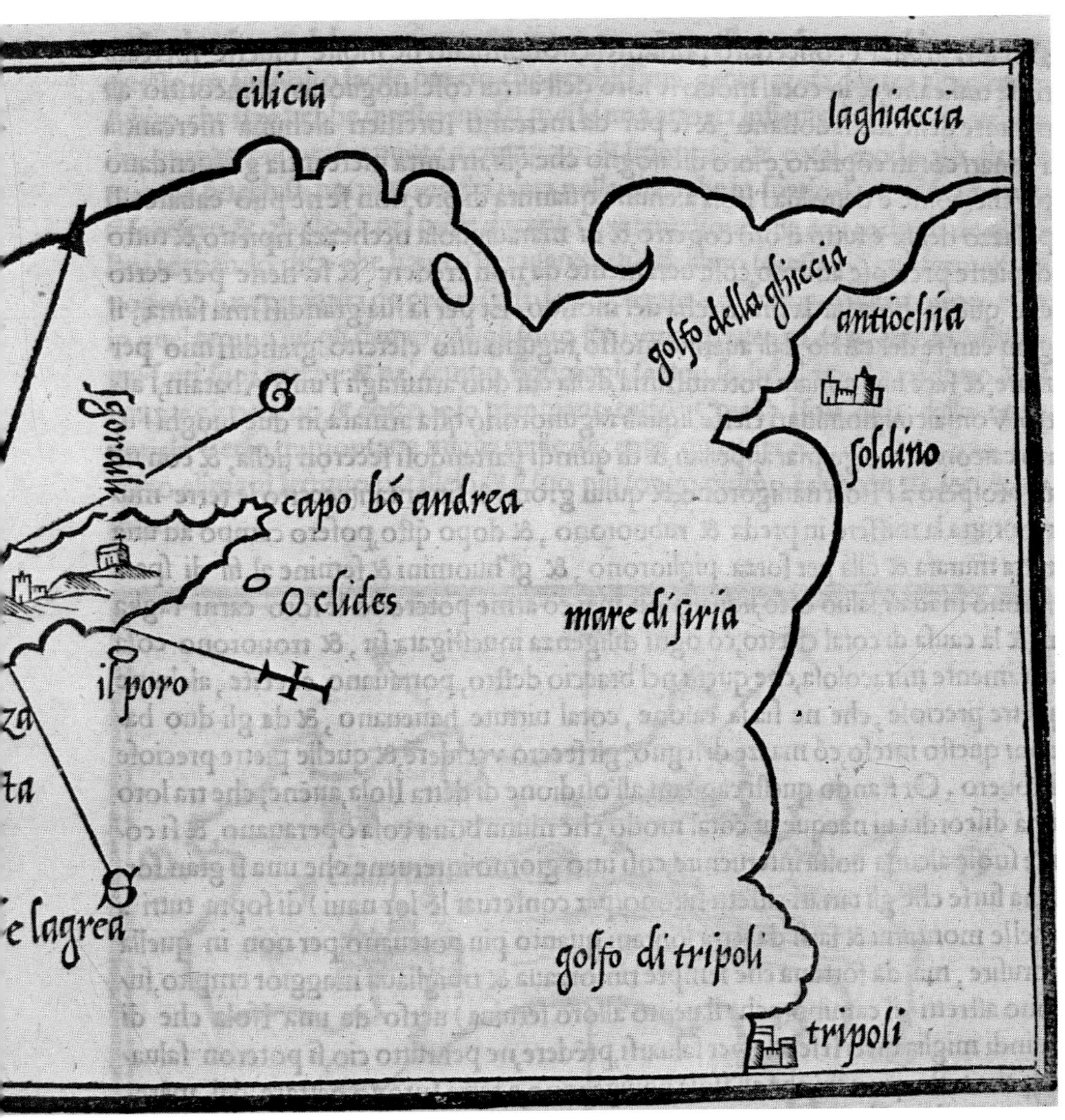

24. B. Bordone: Map of Cyprus, woodcut, 15 × 33 cms, 1537

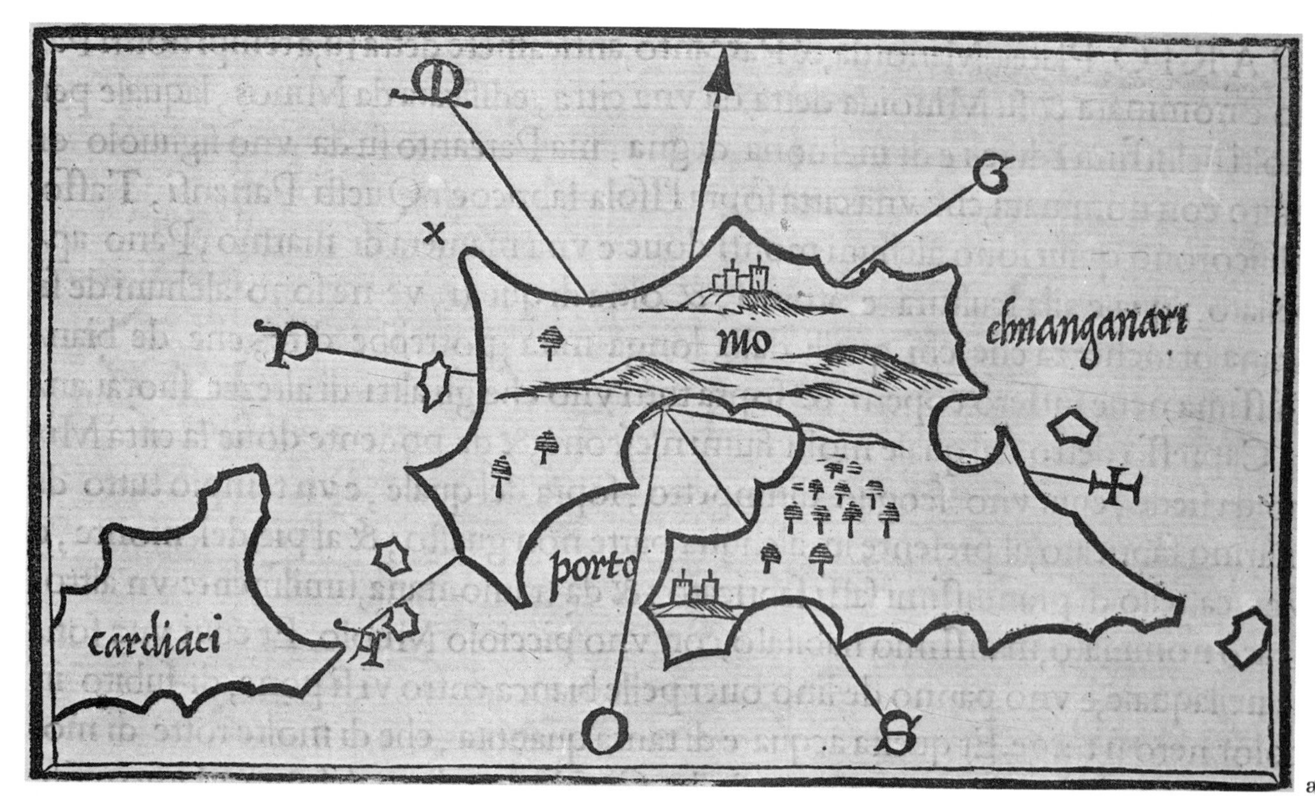
ehmanganari
porto
cardiaci

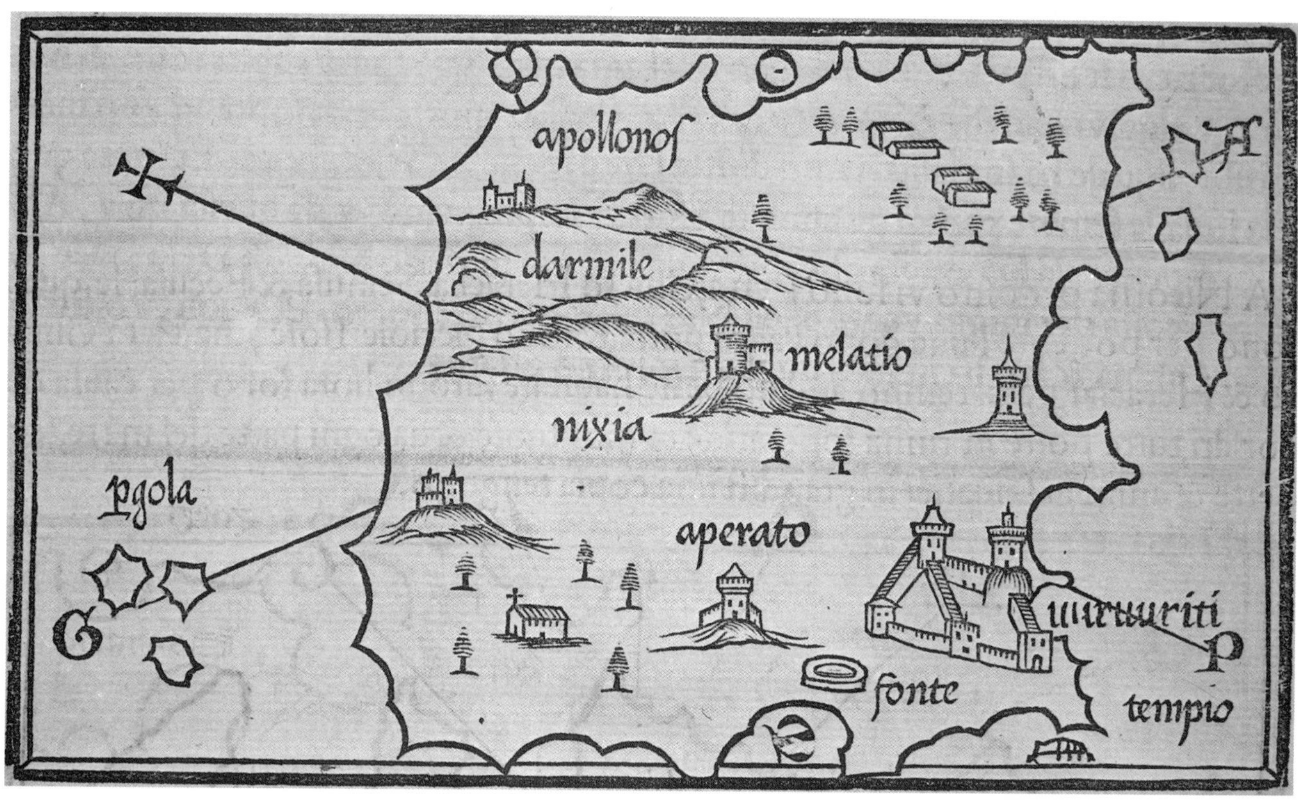
apollonos
darmile
melatio
nixia
pgola
aperato
fonte
tempio

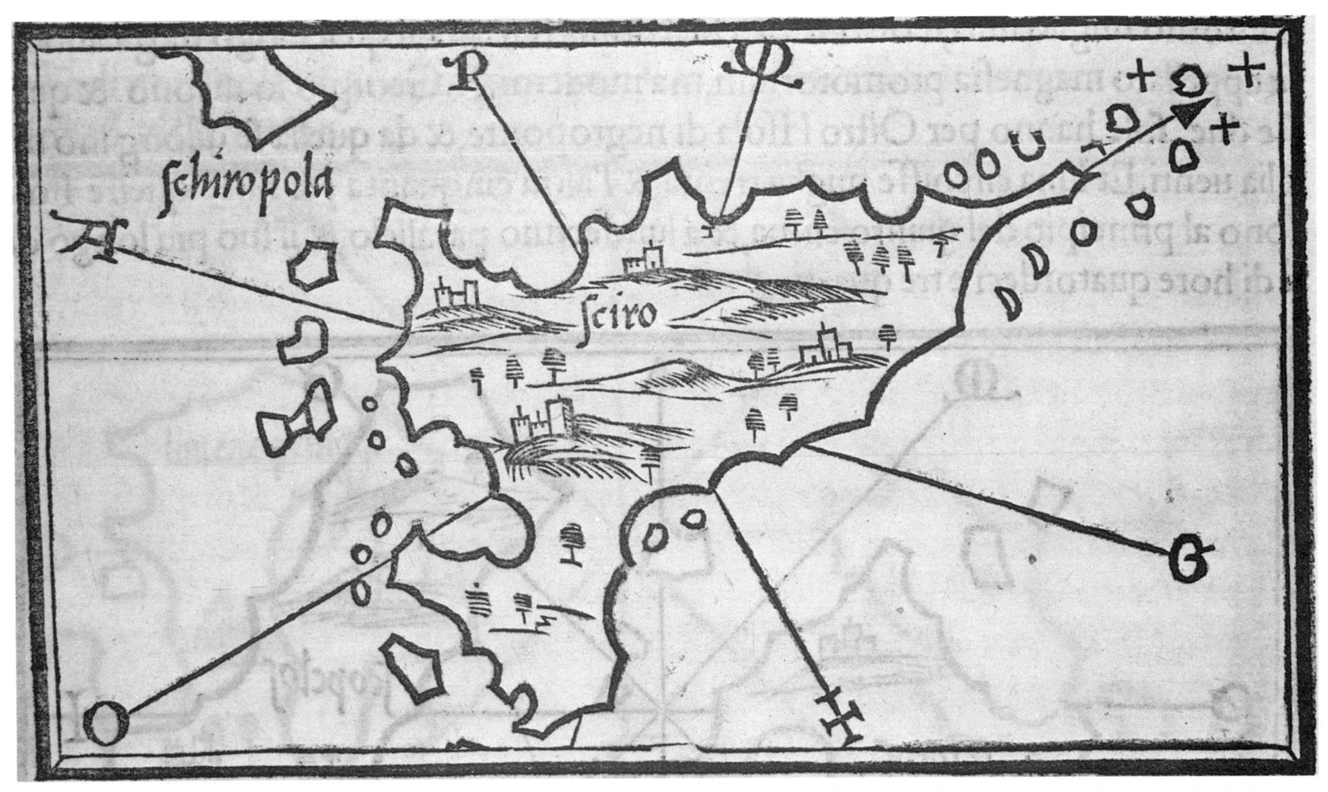

27. B. Bordone: Map of Skyros and Skyropoula, woodcut, 7.5 × 14 cms, 1537

25(a). B. Bordone: Map of Ios, woodcut, 8 × 14 cms, 1537
26(b). B. Bordone: Map of Naxos, woodcut, 8 × 14 cms, 1537

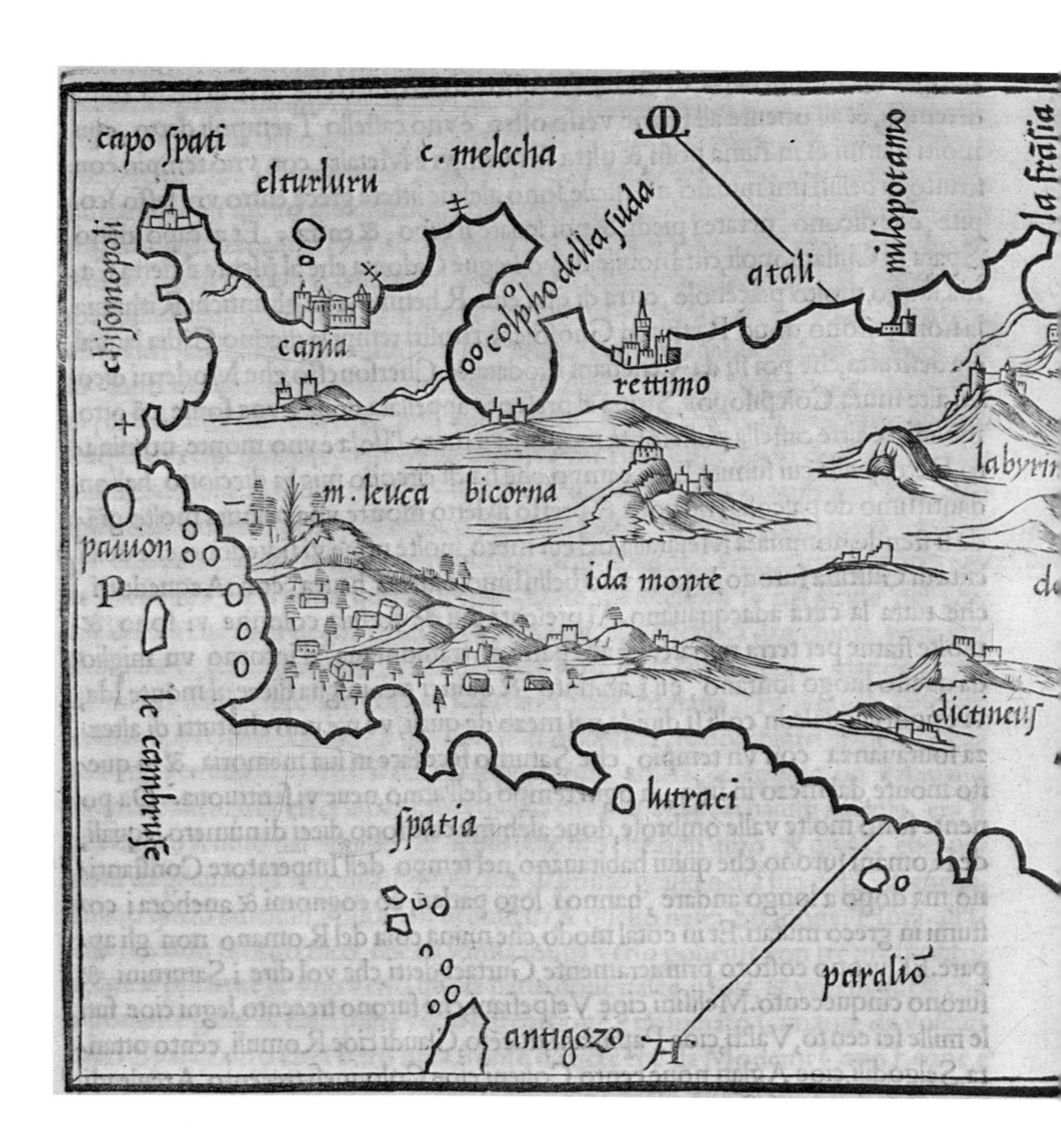
capo spati
elturluru
c. melecha
colpho della suda
atali
milopotamo
la frasia
chisomopoli
cania
rettimo
m. leuca
bicorna
pauion
P
ida monte
le cambruse
dictineus
lutraci
spatia
paralio
antigozo

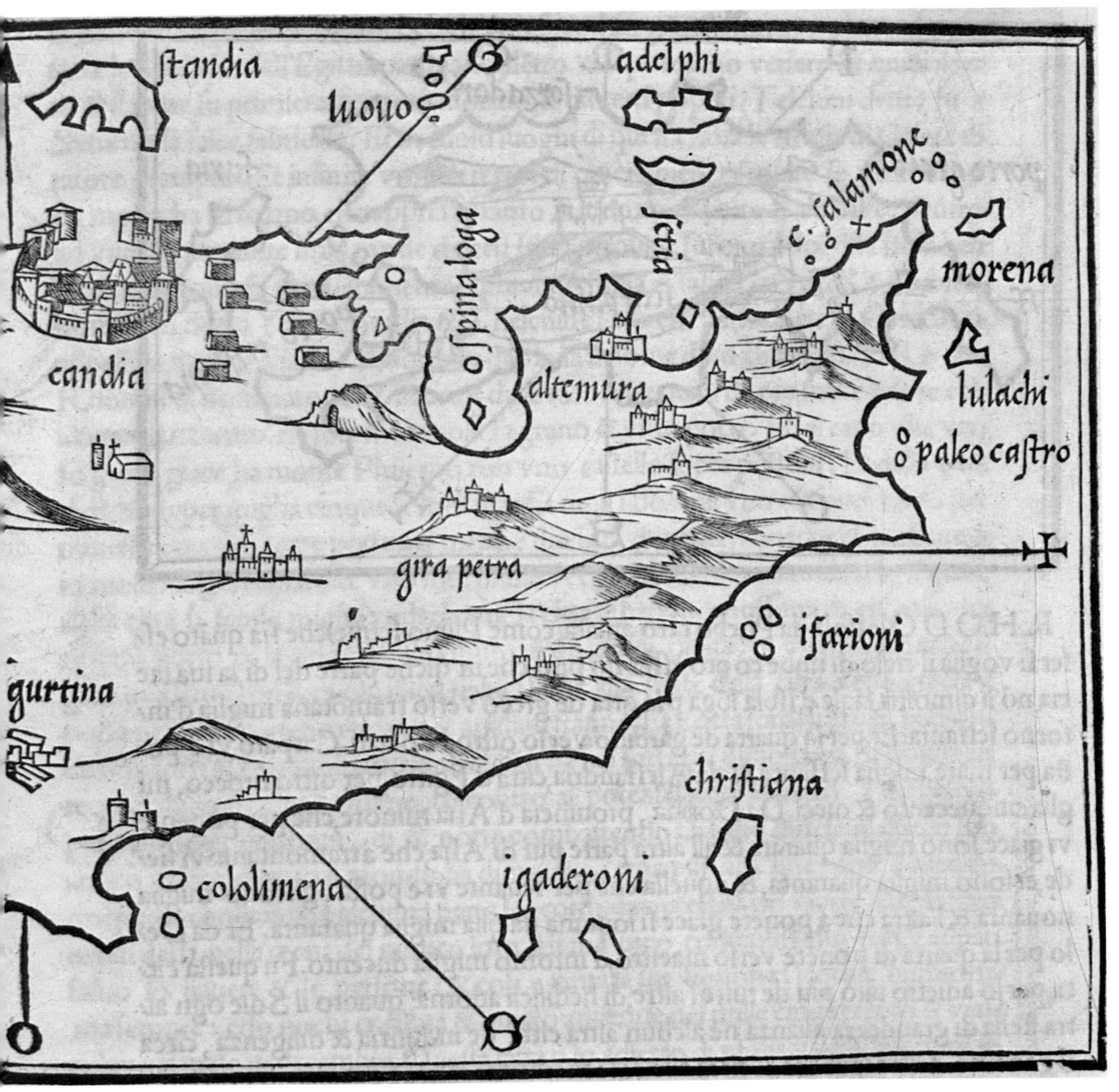

28. B. Bordone: Map of Crete, woodcut, 15 × 33 cms, 1537

29. S. Münster: Map of Greec

odcut, 32 × 36 cms, 1545

Sebastian Münster (1489-1552): German cosmographer, author of a famous *Cosmography* which was to be found in circulation for more than a century after its first edition in 1544. The Cosmography was the first extensive description of the world, with 471 woodcuts and 26 maps in six volumes. Münster also published the commentary of C.J. Solinus along with up-to-date (1538) maps added to Ptolemy's *Geography* – 12 maps were added to the first edition of 1540 and 24 to the second of 1542. The same maps were included in the first edition of the Cosmography, which was itself revised by Münster in 1550 with the addition of 52 new maps.

The maps of Chios, Patmos, Euboea and Tinos printed here are from the *Isolario* of the Venetian cartographer and engraver Giovanni Francesco Camocio. His work was published in 1571-72 and includes maps of the islands and representations of the Venetian - Turkish War (1570-73). Camocio published, inter alia, a map of Europe (1579), of Asia (1575) and of America (1576).

30. G. F. Camocio: Map of Chios, hand-coloured copper engraving, 16 × 22 cms, 1571-1575

PARTE DI SOPRA
Cardamilla
Fonte
nao
Vlißo
Monaleßo
Molini
Vichio
Pino
Cardane la
Porto del fino
Panaize insule
S. Angelo
Heluesono
Torre p guardia d'porto
Reccouero
Catonati
S. Antomista
PARTE
Monte corona
Leßeme
SCIO
Porto della citta
Polignoti
DI
Pigri
Mastico
SOTTO
Parte di Natolia
C. Biãco
Passagio
Paßaggio
Capo mastico
Venetico insula
SCIO. Chio antiquam.te detto Insula posta nello Ar-
cipelago distante da Capo bianco della Nattolia mill: 10.
gia tempo signoreggiata da Genauesi et hora dalla caxa
Ottomana, Qual Insula antiquam. hebe di molti scienciati
et ha tenuto imperio cõ armata nel mare, et è divisa
luna d'lle quali è tutta mõtuosa, laltra amena, et frutife-
ra tenẽdo una bella Cittade et porti bonissimi, il circui-
to d'lla quale si estende mill: 124.
57

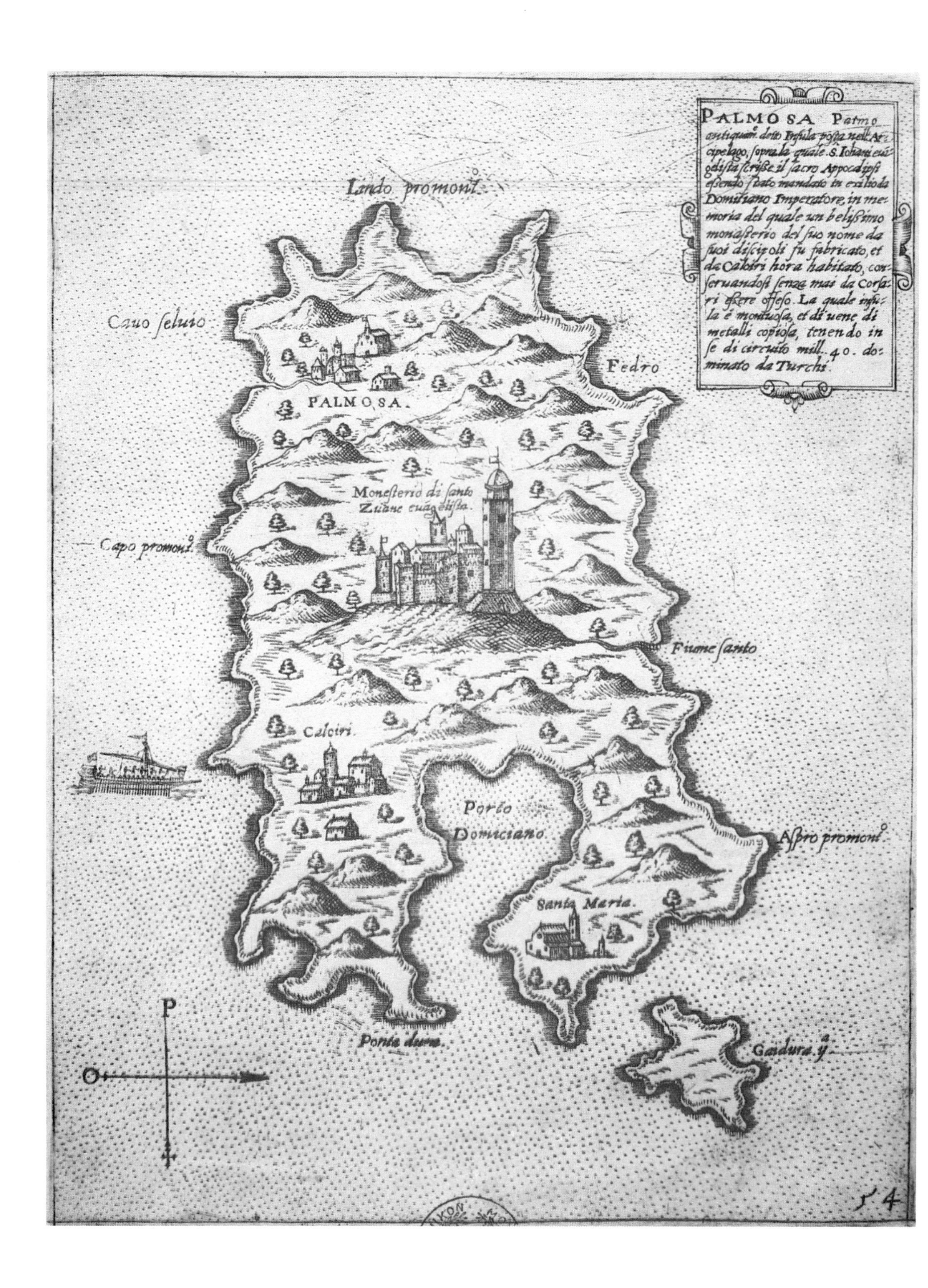
PALMOSA Patmo antiquam. detto Insula posta nell'Arcipelago, sopra la quale S. Iohani euãgelista scrisse il sacro Appocalipsi essendo stato mandato in exilio da Domitiano Imperatore, in memoria del quale un belissimo monasterio del suo nome da suoi discipoli fu fabricato, et da Caloiri hora habitato, conseruandosi senza mai da Corsari essere offeso. La quale insula è montuosa, et di uene di metalli copiosa, tenendo in se di circuito mill. 40. dominato da Turchi.
Lindo promont.
Cauo seluio
Fedro
PALMOSA.
Monesterio di santo Zuane euãgelista
Capo promont.
Fiume santo
Calciri
Porto Domiciano
Aspro promont.
Santa Maria
Ponte duro
Gaidura
P
O
54

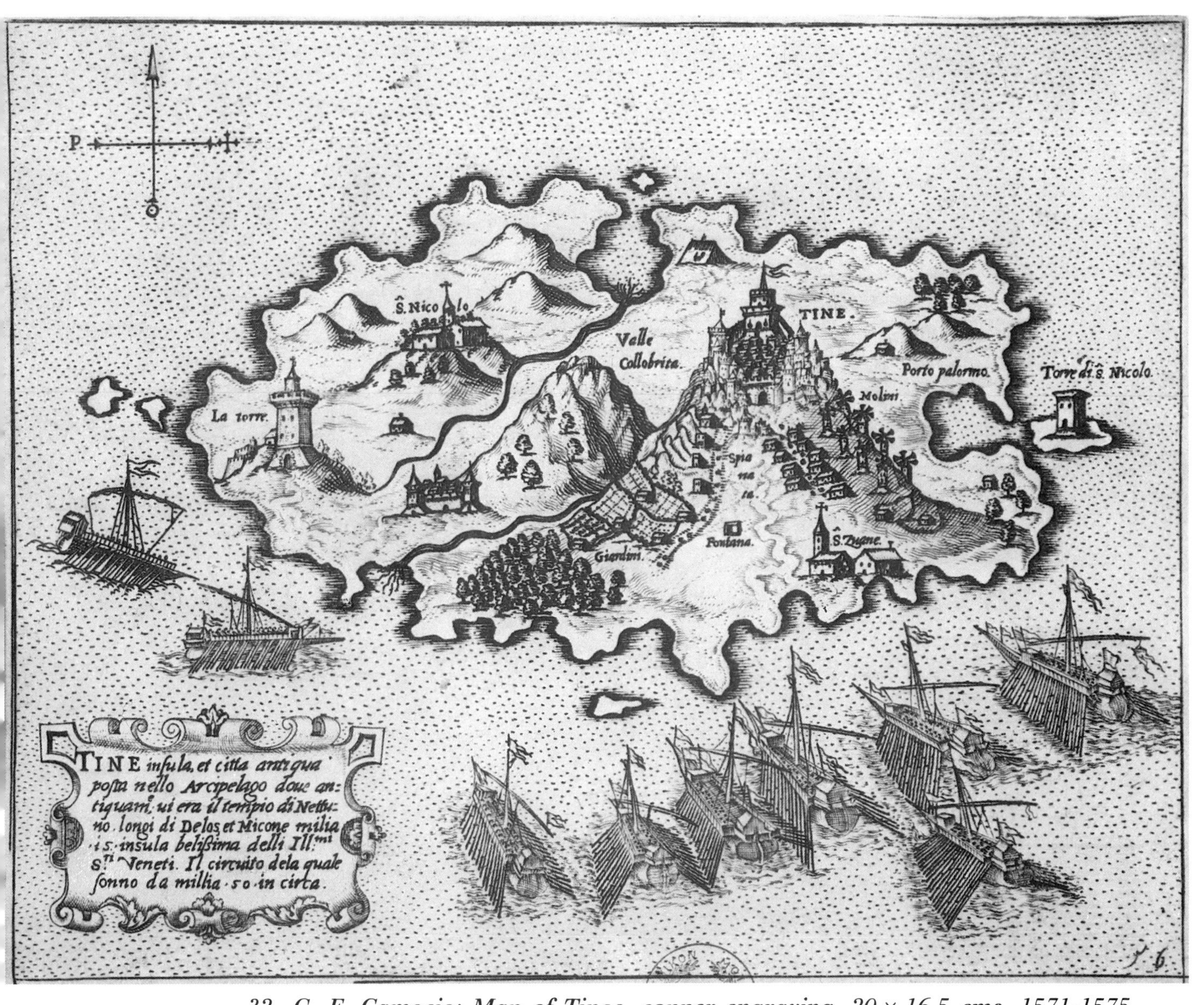

32. G. F. Camocio: Map of Tinos, copper engraving, 20 × 16.5 cms, 1571-1575

31. G.F. Camocio: Map of Patmos, copper engraving, 20 × 15.5 cms, 1571-1575

NEGROPONTE
Insula
ΠΟΛΕΜΙΚΟΝ ΜΟΥΣΕΙΟΝ
230
C. delle colone.
C. matello
Castri
Spiulo.
Athica.
Athene.
CauaLeni
Marafona
Diro.
Selina.
Caloiero.
Cupa.
Protimo
Cardi
Longan.
Megra.
Vatia.
Valoni.
Lanto.
Badia.
Trocco
Politica
Limne.
Lipso.
Oreo.
Ponico.
Beotia.
Talindi.
Pondico.
Cancua.
Ialita.
NE
GRO
PONTE.
ISO
LA
A C
CHAIE.
PARS.
NEGRO
PONTE.

Tomaso Porcacchi da Castiglione (1530-1585): author of *L' isole più famose del mondo* (1572), from which the maps illustrated are taken. The book was published in quarto, and contained 117 pages, while the text was illustrated with 29 maps by the engraver Girolamo Porro, of Padua (1520-1604). Porro, also a publisher, worked in Venice. Among his works are maps of Europe and North Africa (1567), an edition of Ptolemy (1596) and Mercator's *Atlas Minor* (1596).

The maps he drew of the islands are adorned with imaginary creatures of the sea, dolphins, sea-horses, Tritons, mermaids and brigs and galleys skimming over the foaming waves. Porcacchi's Isolario contains a general map of the Aegean, entitled "Arcipelago", showing Greece and a section of the Asia Minor coast. The map records the names of certain islands and of the cities with their castles.

In his text, Porcacchi uses previous writers as his sources — "those whose works have come down to us, and not those whose names have survived while their work remains hidden in the darkness of ignorance". He describes a total of 28 islands and island groups, including Venice, Greenland, North America, Cuba and the islands of the Aegean. Of his information, only a part is correct, showing the level of geographical knowledge in his day. Porcacchi's book went through repeated editions until 1686.

33. G. F. Camocio: Map of Euboea, copper engraving, 21 × 16 cms, 1571-1575

34. T. Porcacchi: Map of the Aegean, copp

graving of Girolamo Porro, 10 × 14 cms, 1572

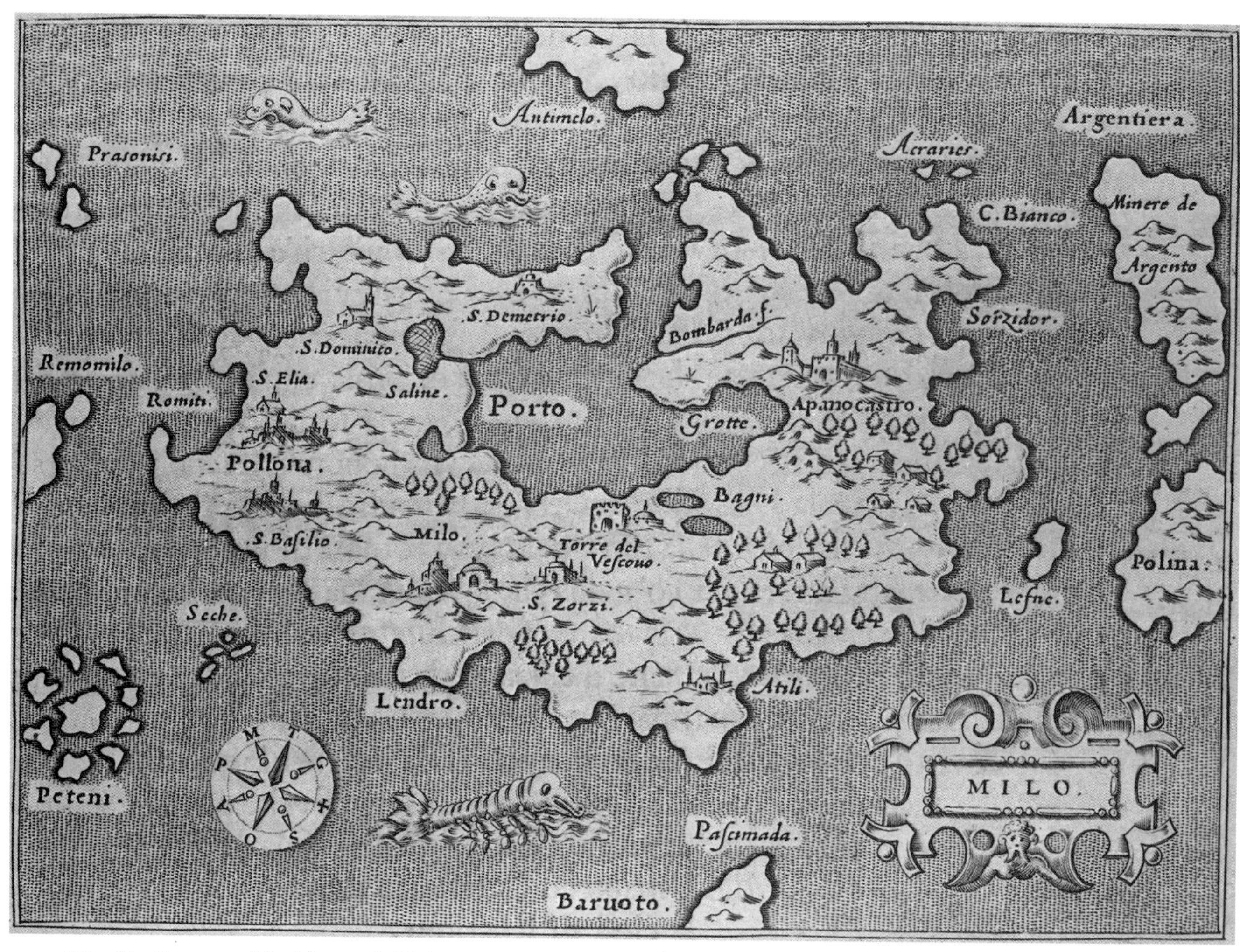

35. *T. Porcacchi: Map of Melos, copper engraving of Girolamo Porro, 10 × 14 cms, 1572*

36. T. Porcacchi: Map of Kythera, copper engraving of Girolamo Porro, 10 × 14 cms, 1572

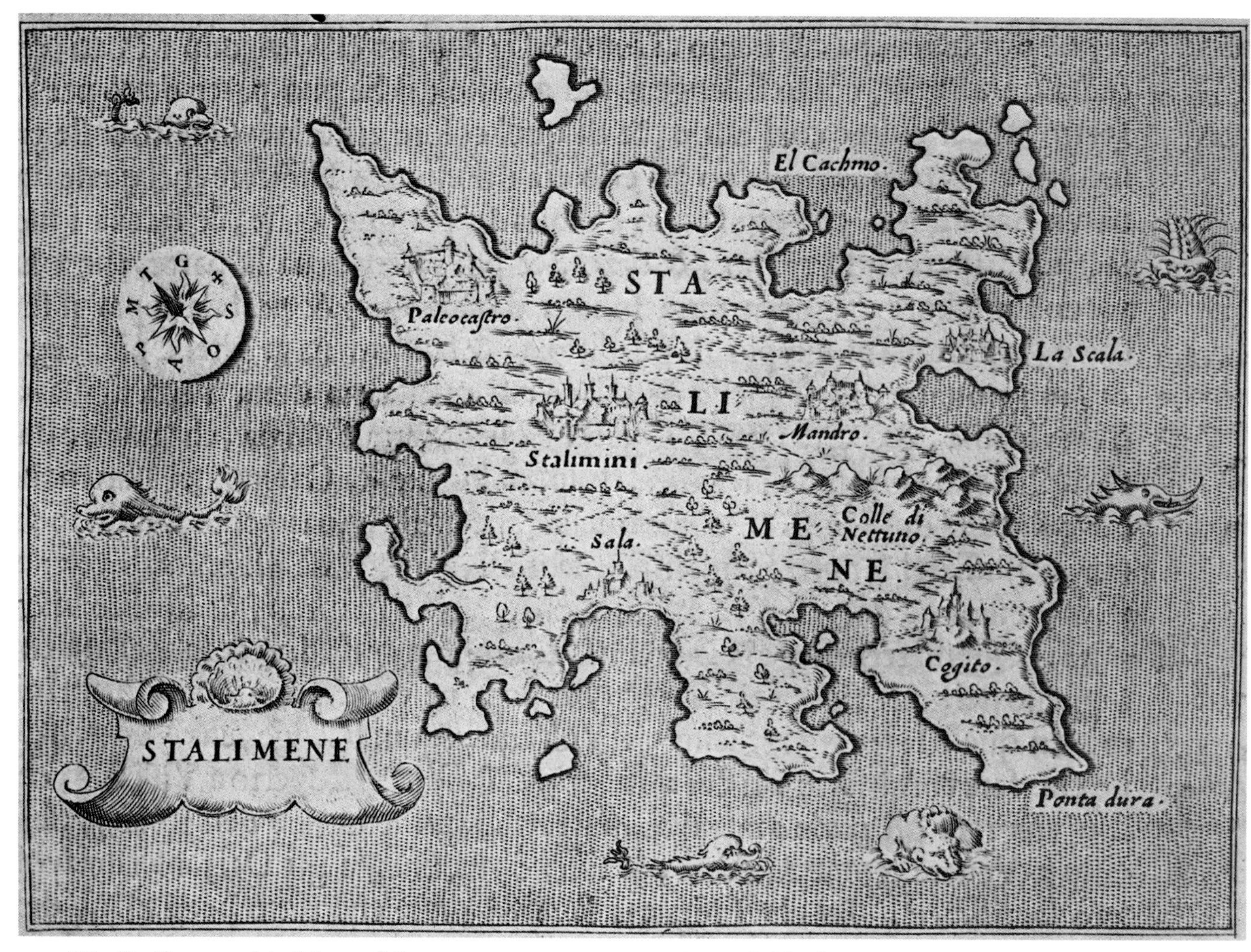

37. T. Porcacchi: Map of Lemnos, copper engraving of Girolamo Porro, 10 × 14 cms, 1572

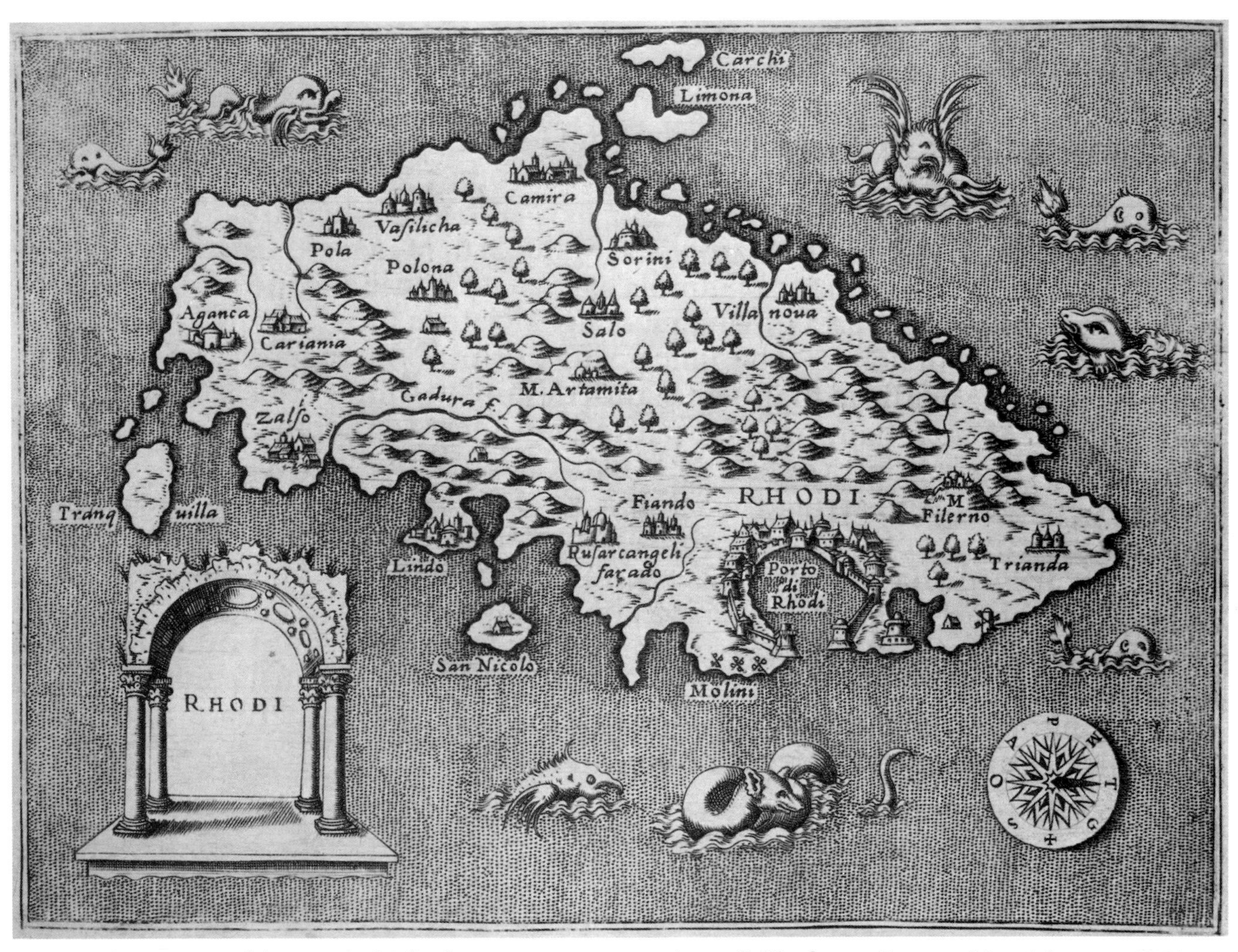

38. T. Porcacchi: Map of Rhodes, copper engraving of Girolamo Porro, 10 × 14 cms, 1572

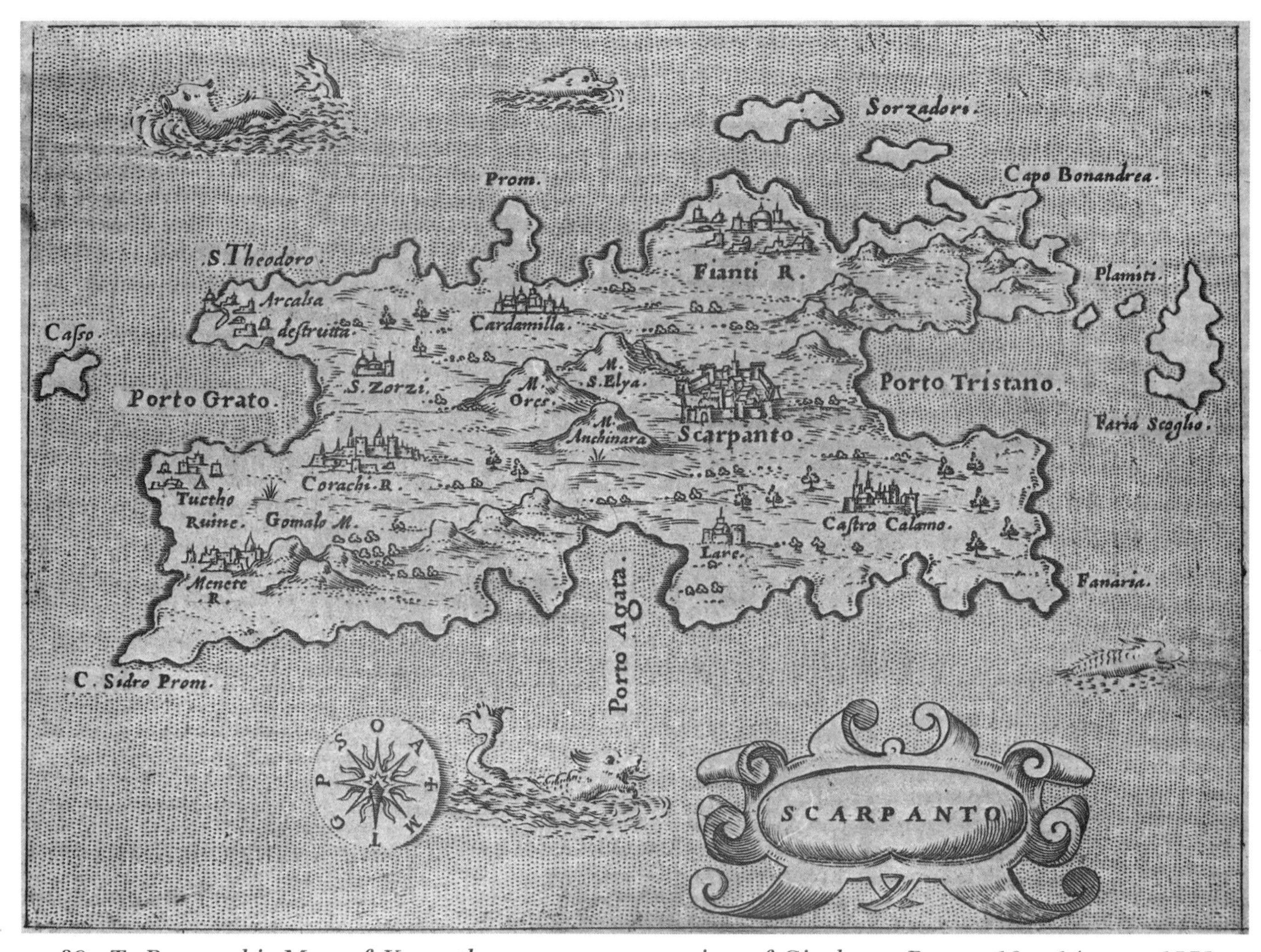

39. T. Porcacchi: Map of Karpathos, copper engraving of Girolamo Porro, 10 × 14 cms, 1572

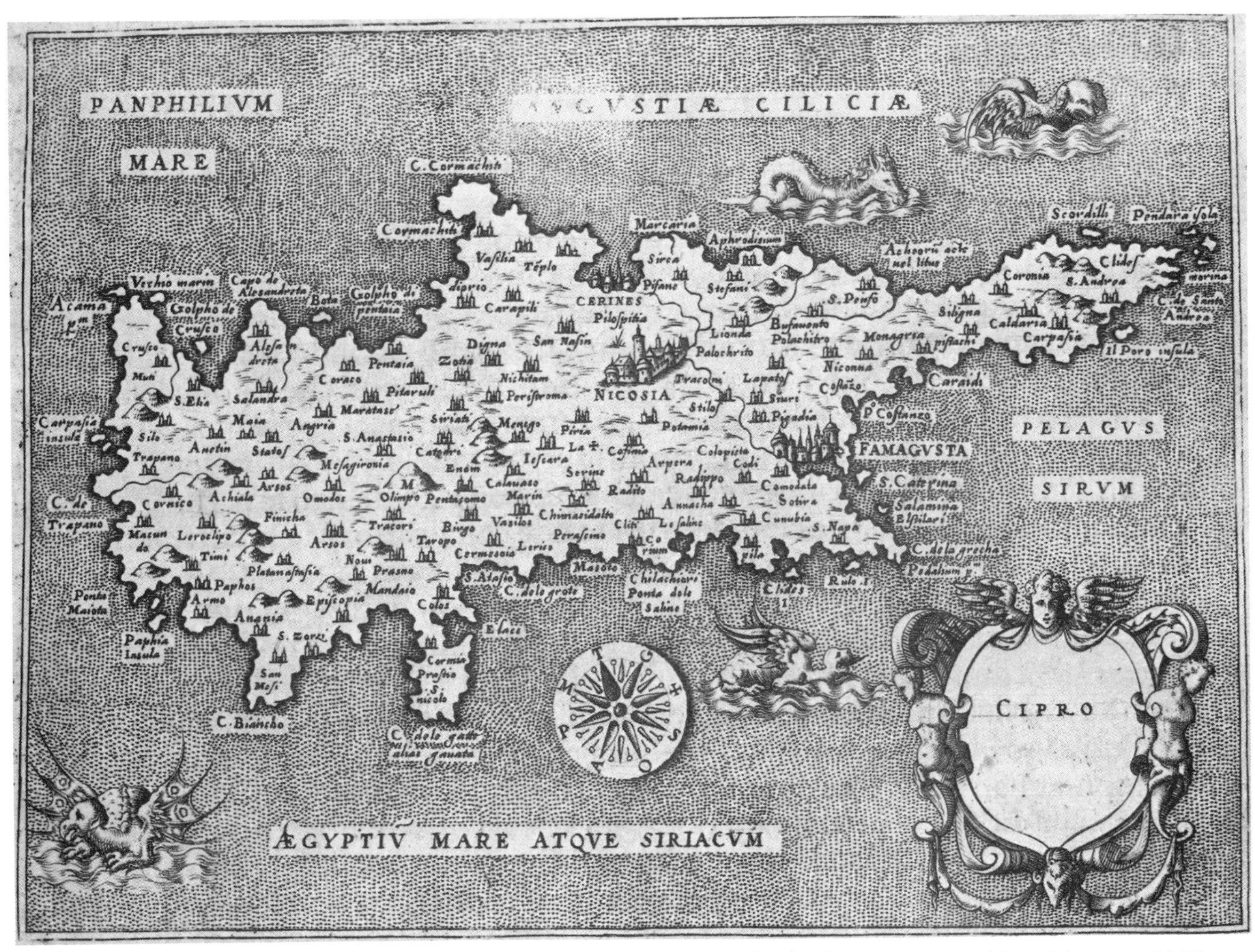

40. T. Porcacchi: Map of Cyprus, copper engraving of Girolamo Porro, 10 × 14 cms, 1572

56
41
41
Alexandria
Assum
Methymna
Antissa
S. Theodorus
Sinus
ÆOLIS
Sigrium p.
Adramytius
LES
BOS
Argenum p.
METELIN
Turris
40
40
Pyrra
Mytilene
Imera
Eressus
Mania ert
MARE
ÆGÆVM
Segr
56

41. Map of Lesbos from H. Petri's edition of Strabo, woodcut, 12 × 8 cms [1571]

The map of Lesbos (no. 41) is part of Gulielmo Xylandro's 'Strabonis Rerum Geographicarum libri septemdecim', 1571.

This edition is among the works of cartography based on the geography of antiquity – on the work, that is, of Strabo and Ptolemy. The map of Lesbos uses Ptolemy's co-ordinates and is the work of cartographer Sebastian Henric Petri. In obedience to the spirit of fondness for things archaic which was characteristic of map-making of this kind, the placenames are in the ancient form, and in Latin.

The map of Lesbos thus bears the ancient placenames Eressus, Methymna, Pyrra, Sigrium, Antissa and so on, and the descriptive text is based on Ptolemy and Strabo.

Franco Ferretti: sea-captain from Ancona, author of the *Dipporti notturni. Dialloghi familiari...*, published in 1580. The book contained 28 maps drawn by the engraver Michel' Angelo Marrelli Anconitano.

The circular perimeter of the maps is reminiscent of the medieval T within an O, very much in the same way as the sea monsters around the islands constitute the relics of the medieval mythology of travellers' tales. Depiction of castles, mountains and wooded areas is typical of 16th century cartography of the islands.

RAGIONEVOL' FORMA
ET VERA POSTVRA
DEL' ISOLA DI SAMO
T
S
M
O
P
A

a

RAGIONEVOL' FORMA
ET VERA POSTVRA
DEL' ISOLA DI CERIGO
S
G
O
T
A
M
P

b

RAGIONEVOL' FORMA
ET VERA POSTVRA
DEL' ISOLA DI STALIMINI
T
M
G
P
A
S
O

d

RAGIONEVOL' FORMA
ET VERA POSTVRA
DEL' ISOLA DI SCIO
T
M
G
P
A
S
O

c

f

42(a). F. Ferretti: Map of Samos, hand-coloured copper engraving, 13 × 8.5 cms, 1580
43(b). F. Ferretti: Map of Kythera, hand-coloured copper engraving, 13 × 8.5 cms, 1580
44(c). F. Ferretti: Map of Chios, hand-coloured copper engraving, 13 × 8.5 cms, 1580
45(d). F. Ferretti: Map of Lemnos, hand-coloured copper engraving, 13 × 8.5 cms, 1580
46(e). F. Ferretti: Map of Naxos, hand-coloured copper engraving, 13 × 8.5 cms, 1580
47(f). F. Ferretti: Map of Andros, hand-coloured copper engraving, 13 × 8.5 cms, 1580

48(a). F. Ferretti: Map of Mytilene, hand-coloured copper engraving, 13 x 8.5 cms, 1580
49(b). F. Ferretti: Map of Tinos, hand-coloured copper engraving, 13 x 8.5 cms, 1580

André Thevet (1502-1590): Franciscan monk and cosmographer to the King, born in Angoulême. In 1549 he set off from Venice on a voyage to the Holy Land, stopping on the Dalmatian coast and at Corfu, Crete (where he stayed for four months collecting information), Milos, Chios, Mytilene, Lemnos and Constantinople. He toured the Black Sea coast, visited Rhodes and then went on to Egypt, Mt. Sinai, Jerusalem, Damascus, Antioch and Cyprus. The fruit of this

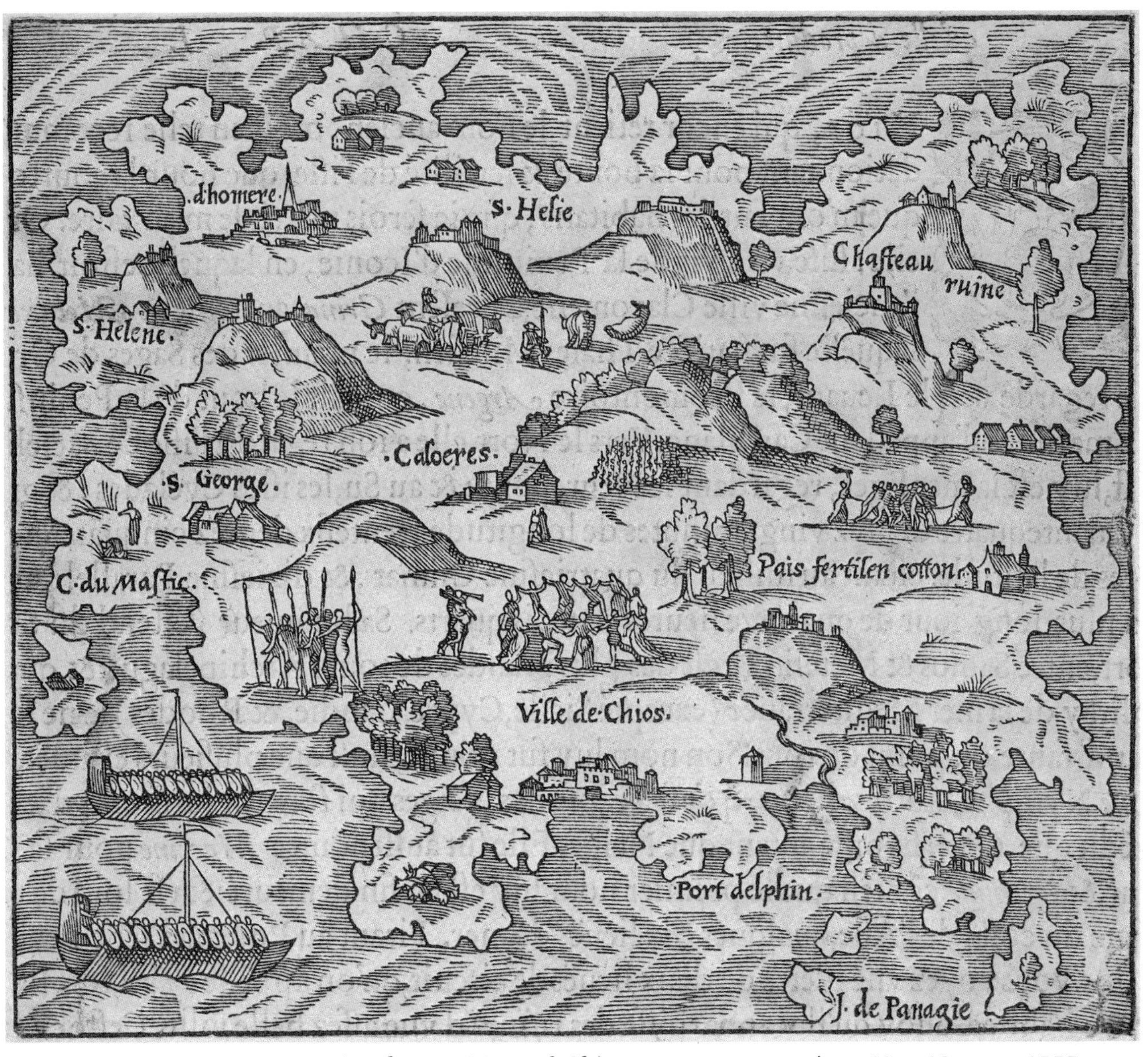

50. A. Thevet: Map of Chios, copper engraving, 15 × 18 cms, 1575

voyage was his *Cosmographie du Levant,* published in 1554. Thevet also accompanied a French mission to Brazil in 1555. Thevet wrote a *Cosmographie Universelle* (1775), which, among other maps, included the Greek islands of Euboea, Chios, Lemnos, Kos, Rhodes, and Mytilene and a map of Mount Athos.

Other works: *Grand Insulaire et Pilotage* (1584), unpublished, with maps of the Greek islands , *France Antartique* (1585), *Nouveau Monde* (1584).

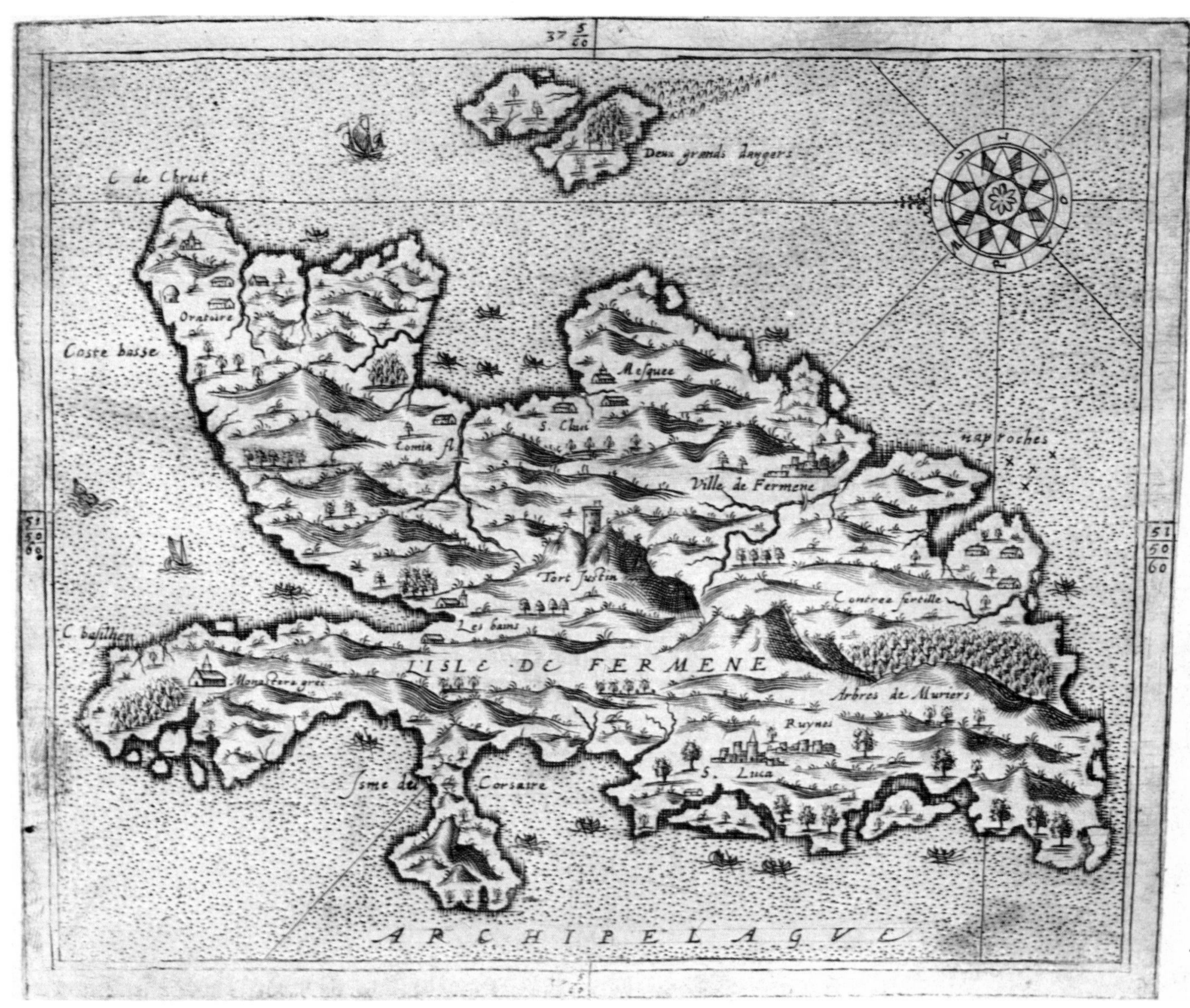

51. Anonymous: Map of Kythnos, copper engraving, 15 × 18.5 cms, 1584

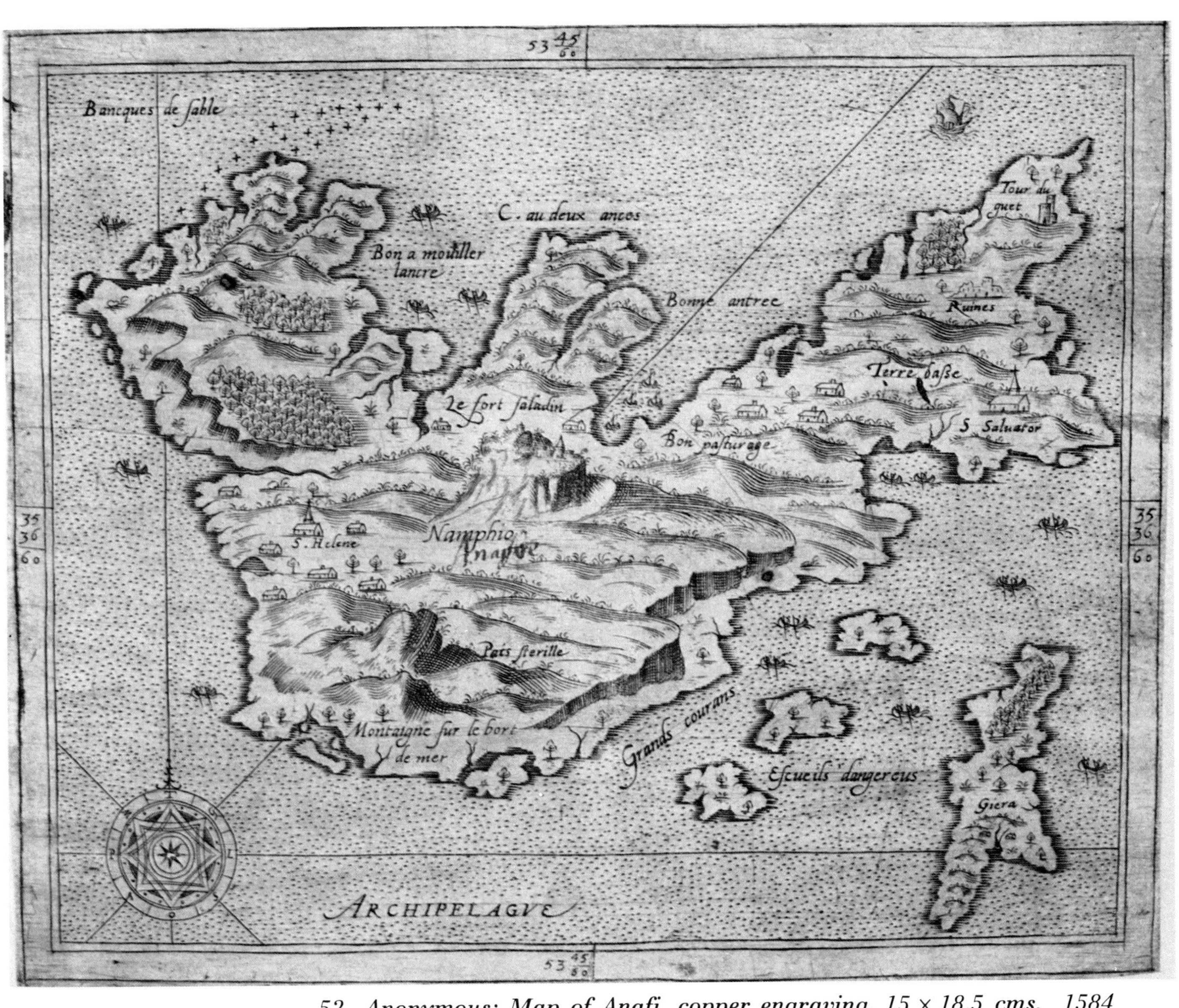

52. Anonymous: Map of Anafi, copper engraving, 15 × 18.5 cms, 1584

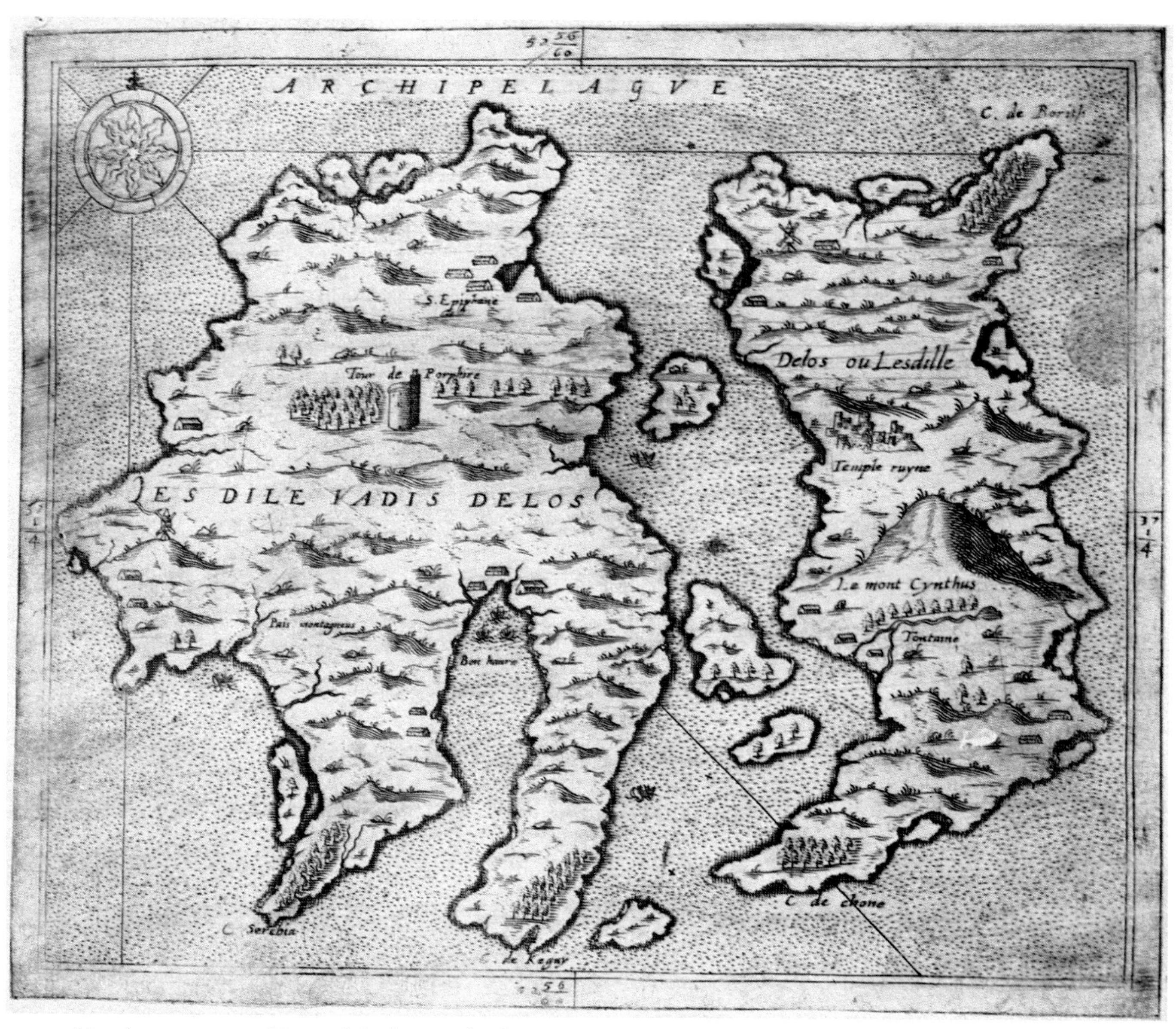

53. Anonymous: Map of Delos and Rheneia, copper engraving, 15 × 18.5 cms, 1584

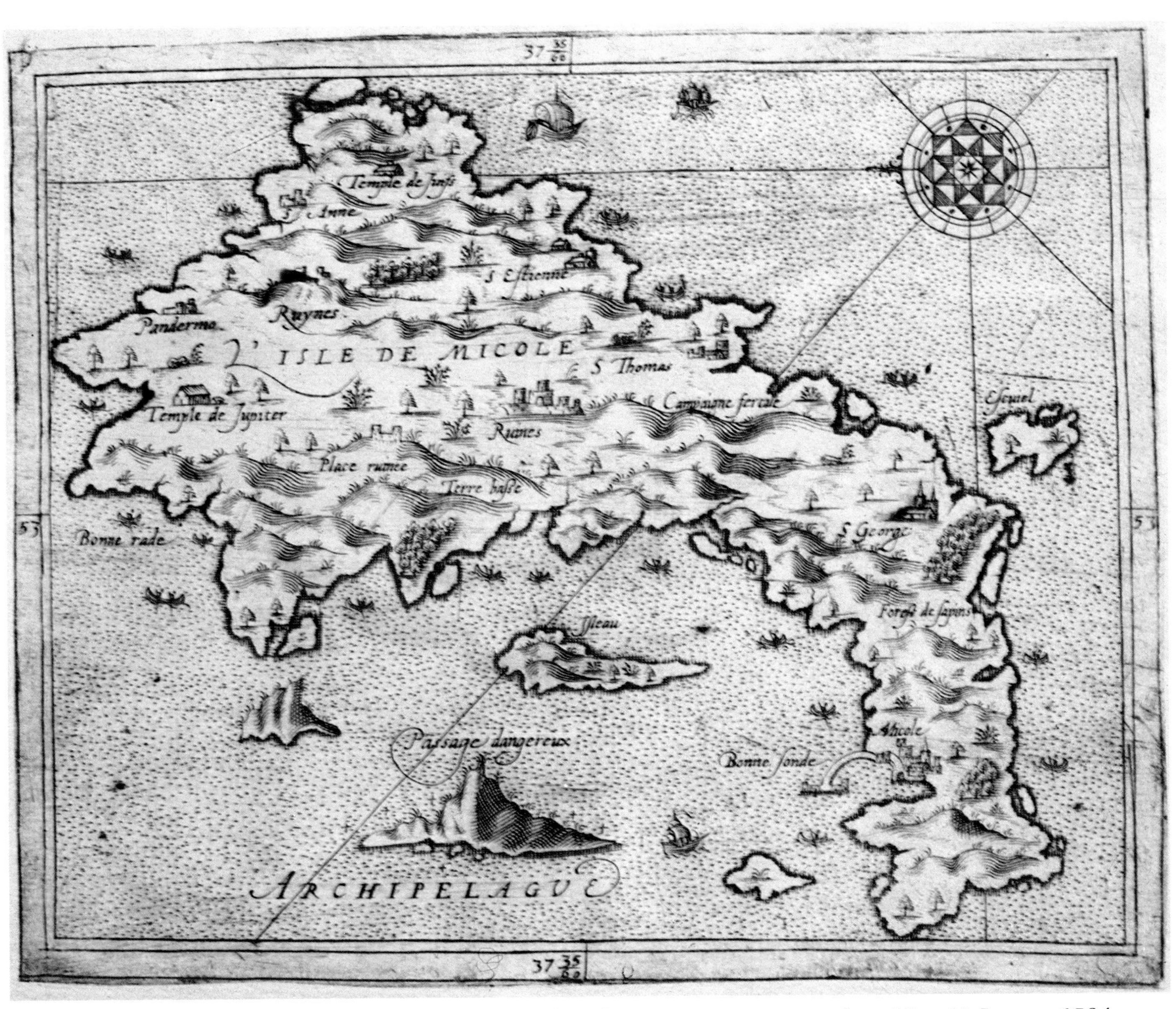

54. Anonymous: Map of Mykonos, copper engraving, 15 × 18.5 cms, 1584

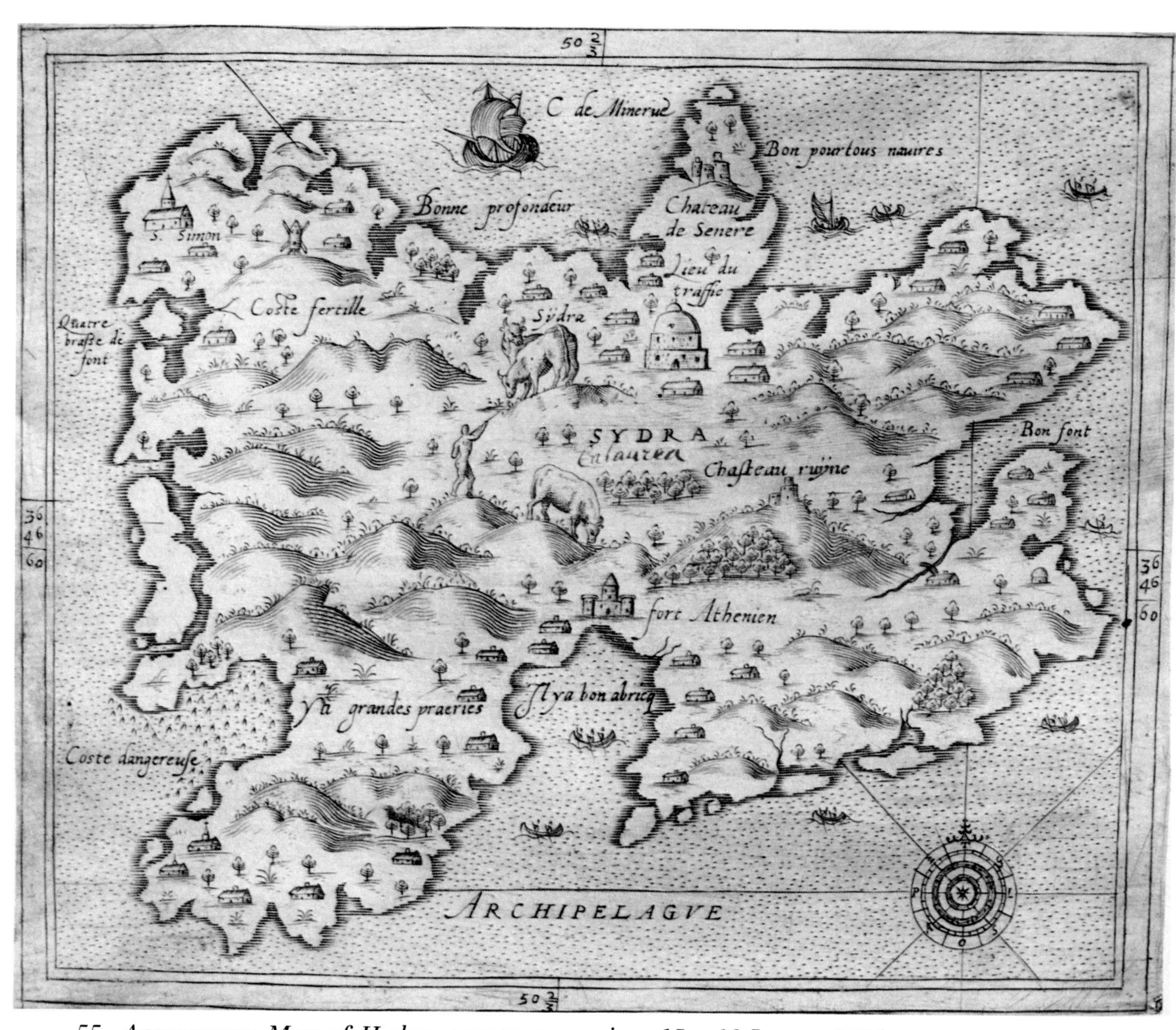

55. *Anonymous: Map of Hydra, copper engraving, 15 × 18.5 cms, 1584*

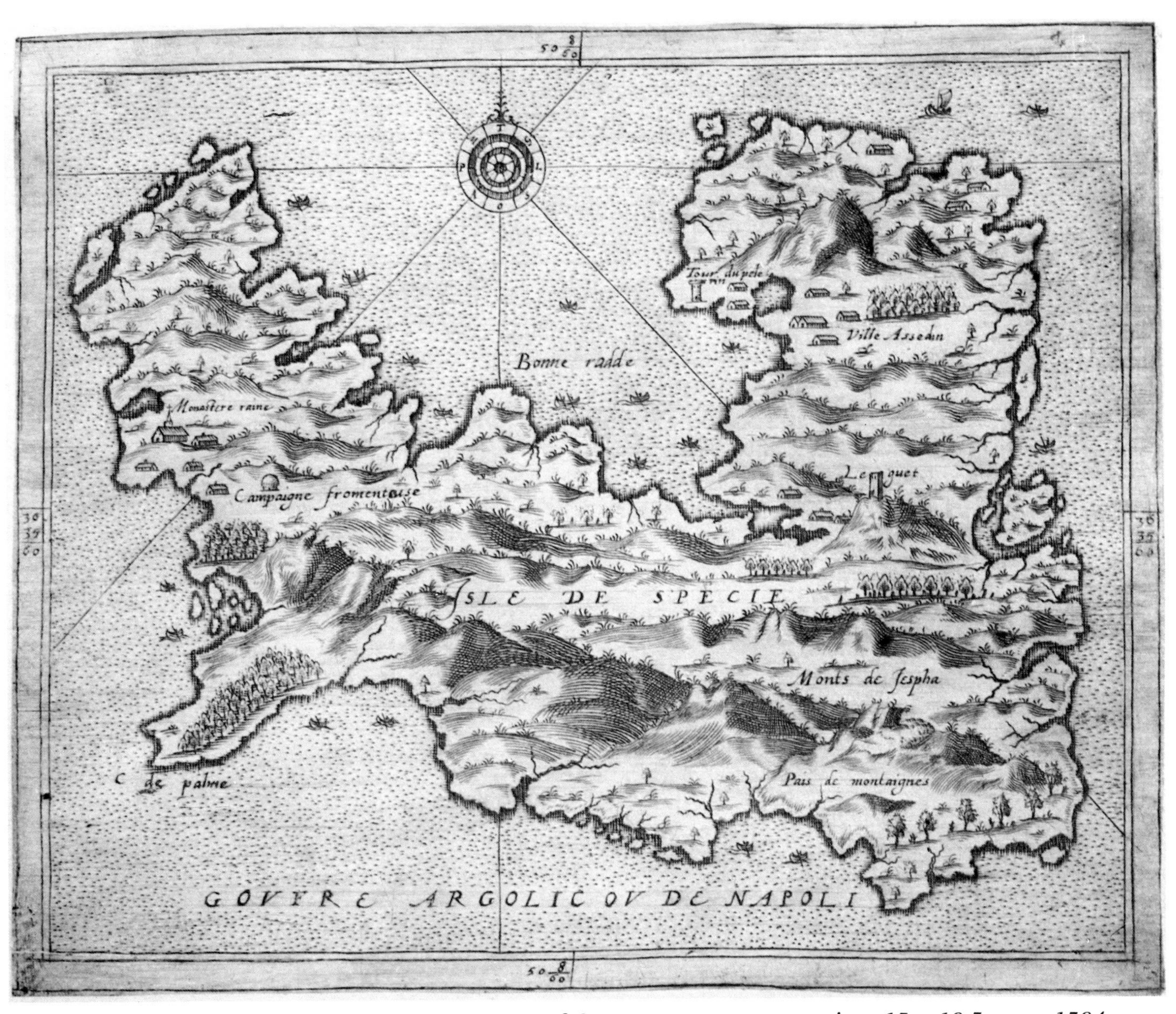

56. Anonymous: Map of Spetses, copper engraving, 15 × 18.5 cms, 1584

Jacopo Gastaldi (1500-1565): one of the major Venetian cartographers and cosmographers. He drew more than forty maps, which went through repeated editions between 1544 and 1570 and which were included in the atlas produced by the Venetian publisher Lafreri. He also drew 34 maps for the 1548 edition of Ptolemy.

57. *J. Gastaldi: Map of Greece of* c. *1575*

Septentrio
MAR MAGGIORE
ROMANIA
THIQVES
IAMBOLI
MAR DE MARMORA
Constatino polis
Scutari
GOLFO DE CONTESA
GOLFO DE MONTE SANTO
GOLFO DE SALONICHI
GOLFO DE ASPROSA
GOLFO DE MARIZA
GOLFO DE CARIDIA
BECSANGIAL
Mare
STALIMINE
ARCHIPELAGO
Aegeum
SCIRO
METELIN
SARCVM
SMIRNE
GOLFO DE NEGROPONTE
GOLFO DE LEPANTO
GOLFO DE ENGIA
GOLFO DE NAPOLI
SIO
SAMO
NICARIA
ANDRI
NICSIA
Milo
Stampalia
Scarpanto
C. Matapan
Cerigo
pars
Oriens
Meridies

58. *G. Rosaccio: Map of Karpathos, copper engraving, 10 × 17.5 cms, 1598*

Guiseppe Rosaccio (1530-1620): Florentine cosmographer and cartographer, the author of *Viaggio da Venetia, a Constantinopoli per mare e per terra... in Venetia*, 1598. This book was a sort of travellers' guide for those wishing to go from Venice to Constantinople and the Holy Land. It was illustrated with numerous maps of the Aegean islands and engravings of various scenes. The author described all the stops on the journey – whether by sea or by land – and notes the distances between them, in miles. He also gives placenames and the rivers, mountains, and products of each area. On the maps he marks churches, monasteries, mills, castles, mountains and even trees, and refers to harbours, bays and capes without going into any great detail.

59. G. Rosaccio: Map of Patmos, copper engraving, 10 × 7.5 cms, 1598

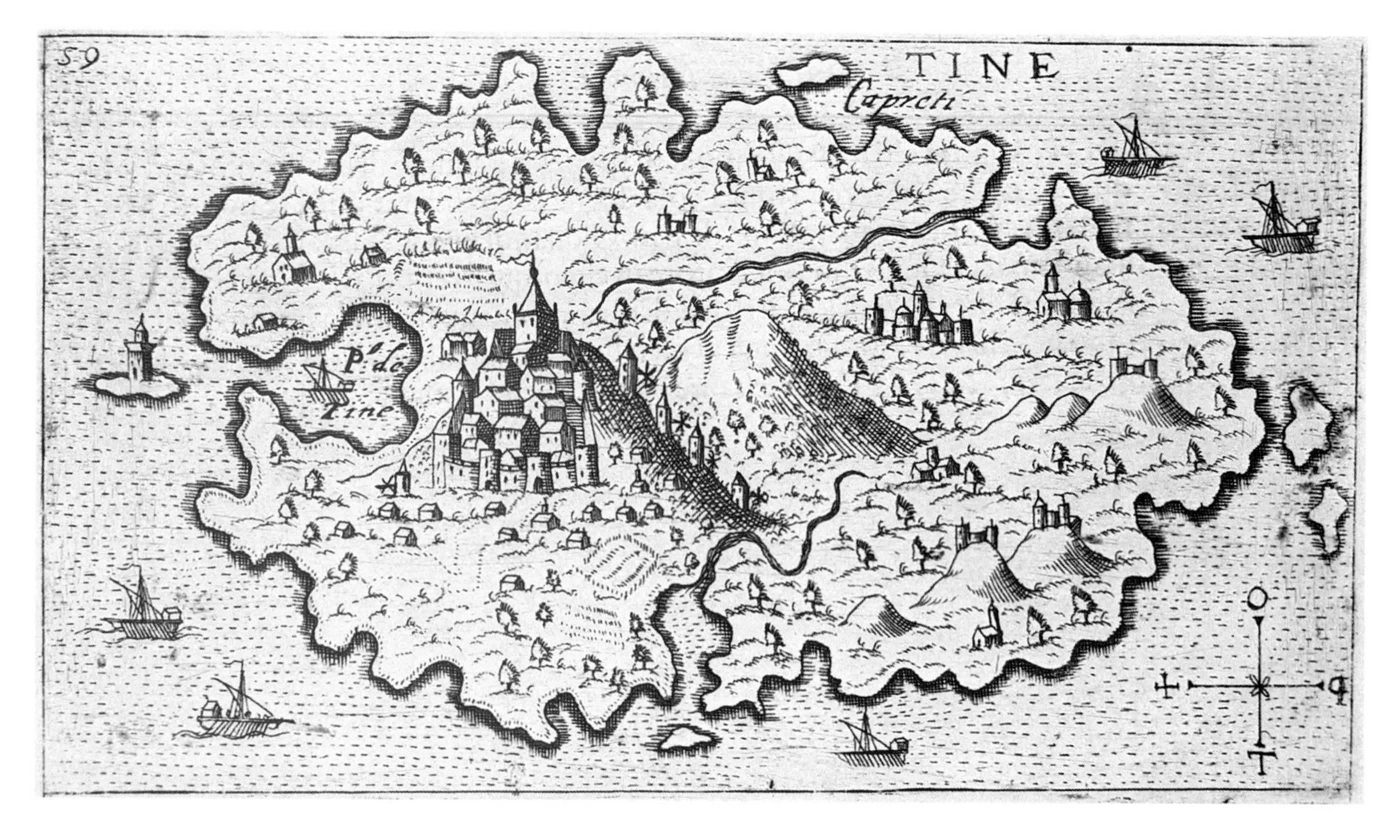
59
TINE
P. de Tine

NEGROPONTE
Cauo Montoso
Tolitada
Strocha
Sfara
Politica
Oreo
Lisso
Lipso
Loreo
Mandigo
Cupasi
Caualeni
Litar
Motone
Atchene

62.G. Rosaccio: Map of Skyros, copper engraving, 10 × 17 cms, 1598

60. G. Rosaccio: Map of Tinos, copper engraving, 10 × 17 cms, 1598
61.G. Rosaccio: Map of Euboea, copper engraving, 10 × 17 cms, 1598

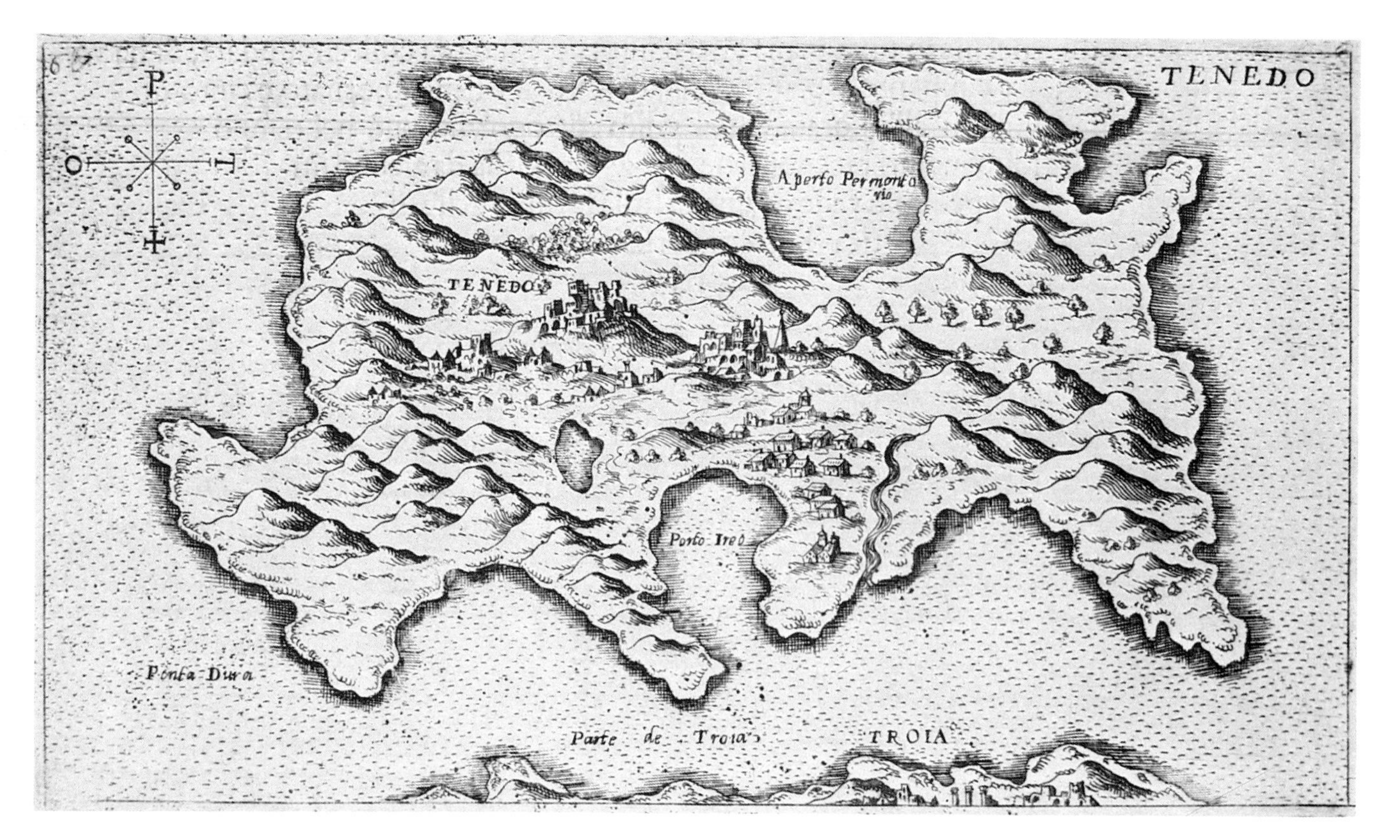
TENEDO
Aperto Permonta
rio
TENEDO
Porto Ireo
Ponta Dura
Parte de Troia
TROIA

ZEA INSVLA
Cholfeto Saluo
Schogeto
Pormontorio
Aqua amata
ZEA
Terapoli
Cauo aspro Permontorio

Gerardus Mercator (1512-1594): geographer, cartographer and mathematician. Mercator was born at Rupelmonde in Flanders, and studied at Louvain with Gemma Frisius, who inspired in him a love of map-making and geography. His religious convictions – he was a Protestant – led him to move, in 1552, to Duisburg in Germany, where he died. Mercator's main contribution to cartography lies in the projection which bears his name and which was first used in his map of the World in 1569. In 1578, Mercator published Ptolemy's *Geography*, which was a great publishing success. But it was Mercator and his friend and contemporary Ortelius who managed to rid the science of geography of the spectre of Ptolemy. In 1554 Mercator published the first large map of Europe, on six leaves, and in 1564 he completed his map of the British Isles.

His atlas *(Atlas sive Cosmographicae Meditationes)* was published in sections. The first contained 51 maps of Germany, France and Belgium, the second (23 maps) dealt with Italy and Greece and the third and last, published posthumously, depicted the rest of the world in 36 maps. Among the features of Mercator's cartography we may note the exact dimensions of the areas mapped, the measurement of distances, and the correct positioning of the various geographical features.

63. G. Rosaccio: Map of Tenedos, copper engraving, 10 × 17 cms, 1598
64. G. Rosaccio: Map of Kea, copper engraving, 10 × 16.5 cms, 1598

65(a). G. Mercator: Map of Greece, copper engraving, 48 × 31 cms,
66(b). G. Mercator: Map of Crete, with the islands of Corfu, Zakynthos, Melos, Naxos, Santorini, Karpathos, hand-coloured copper engraving, 48 × 34 cms, 1590

a

Nova Totius GRÆCIÆ descriptio.

b

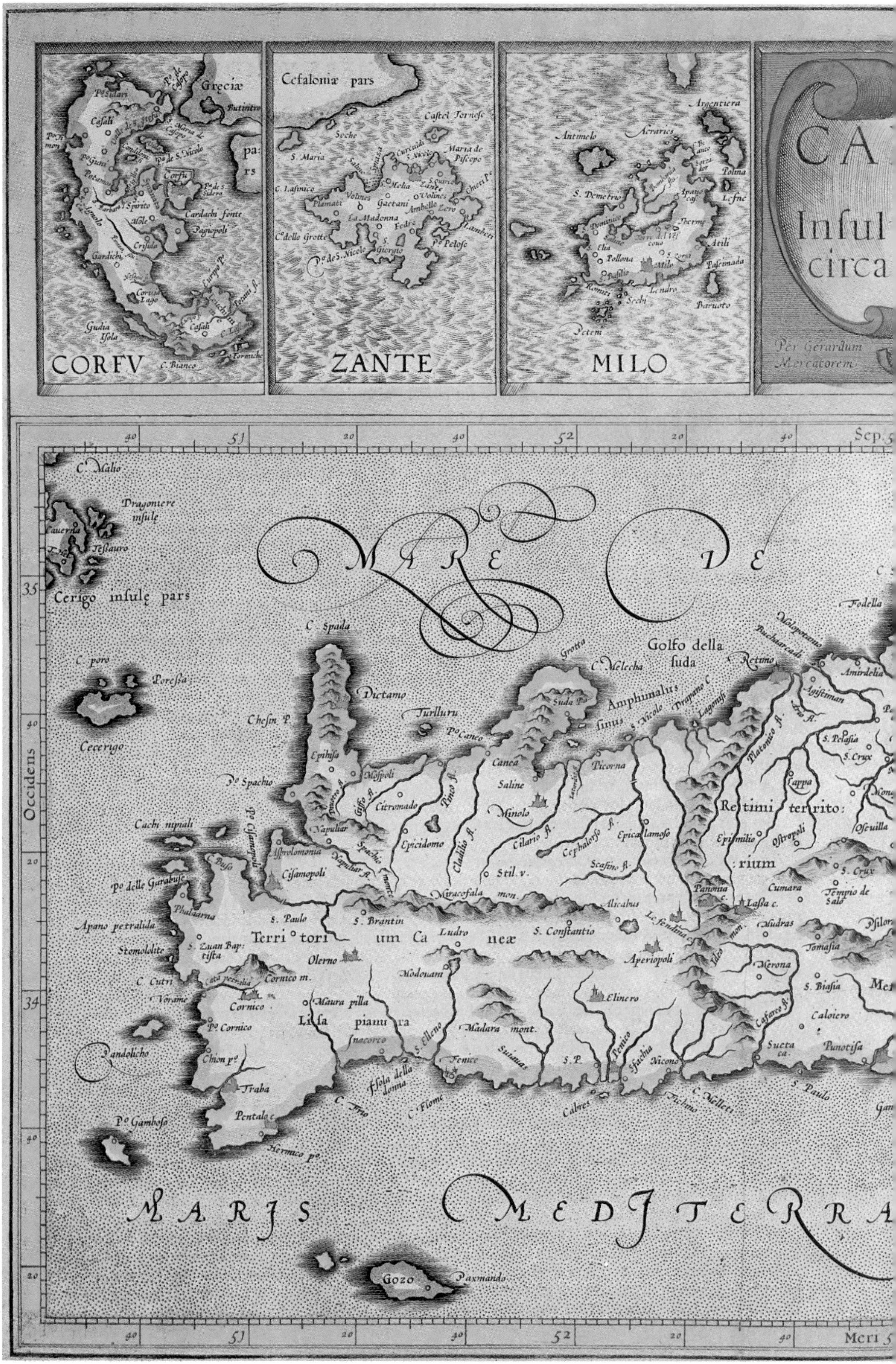
CORFU
ZANTE
MILO
Greciæ
pa: rs
Cefaloniæ pars
Castel Tornese
Argentiera
Antimelo
S. Demetrio
Insul
circa
Per Gerardum Mercatorem
MARE DE
Dragoniere insule
Cerigo insule pars
Occidens
C. Spada
Dictamo
Golfo della suda
Amphimalus sinus
Retimi territo: rium
Territori um Ca neæ
MARIS MEDITERRA
Gozo
Paxmando
Cecerigo
Lissa pianura
Madara mont.
Cornico
Traba
Pentalo c
Fodella
Meri
Sep.

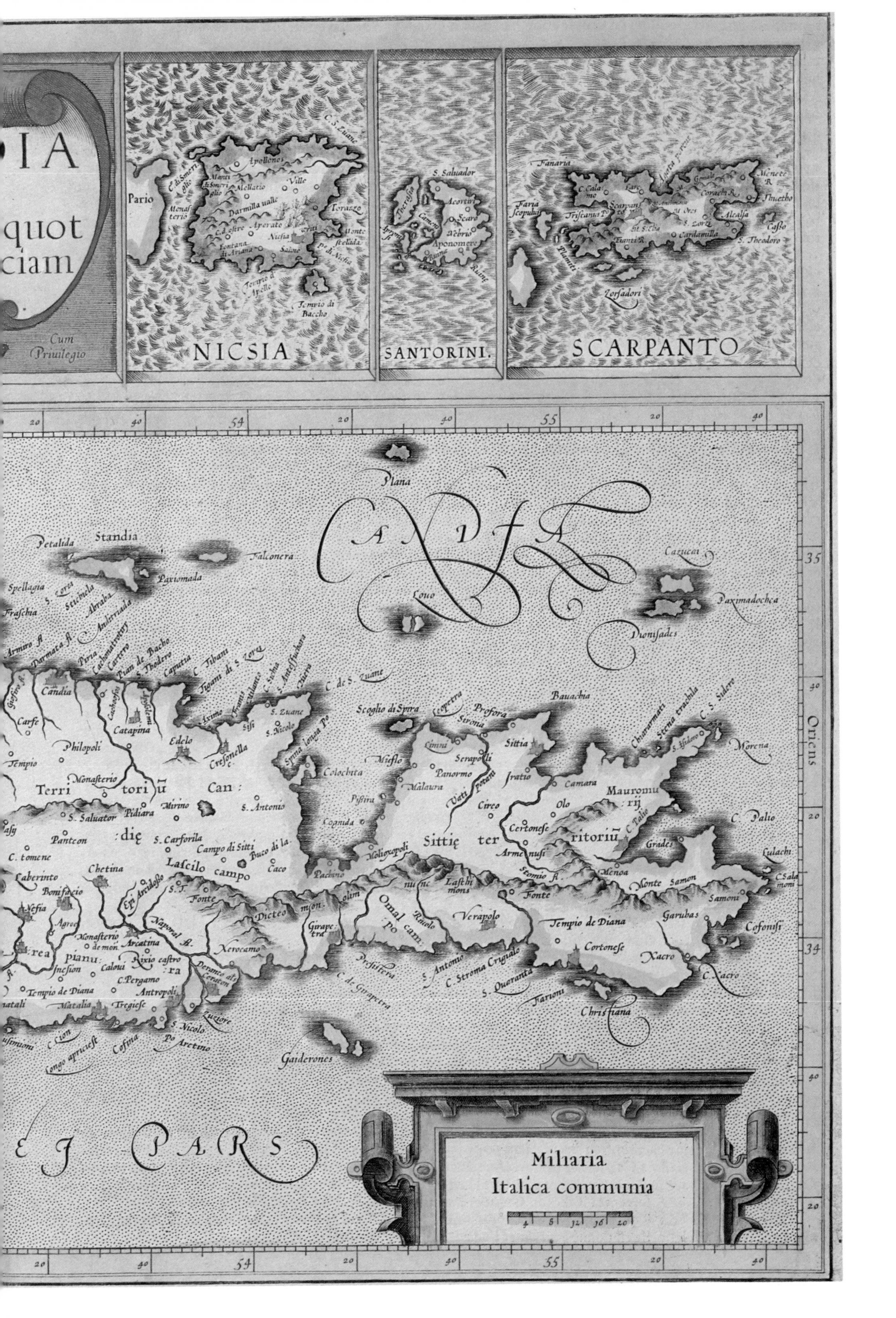

IA
quot
ciam
Cum Priuilegio
NICSIA
Pario
Apollonos
Ville
Darmilla ualle
Triti
Salone
Tempio di Baccho
SANTORINI.
S. Saluador
Acorini
Scaro
Aponomere
SCARPANTO
Fanaria
Faria Scopulus
Scarpant
Ores
Alcassa
S. Theodoro
Cassio
Cardamilla
Zorsadori
Plana
CANDIA
Lono
Standia
Petalida
Falconera
Paximada
Caticai
Paximadochca
Dionisades
Spellagia
Fraschia
Candia
Catapina
Edelo
Philopoli
Tempio
Terri tori u Can:
S. Saluator
Pidiara
Mirino
S. Antonio
Panteon
S. Carforila
Campo di Sitti
Buco di la. Caco
Lascilo campo
C. tomene
Laberinto
Chetina
Bonifacio
Nesia
Agros
Monasterio de mon.
Arcatina
Rixio castro
pianu
Caloui
C. Pergamo
Tempio de Diana
Antropoli
Matalia
Tregiese
S. Nicolo
Po Aretino
Cofina
Scoglio di Spira
Scopetra
Profora
Sirona
Bauachia
C. de S. Zuane
S. Zuane
S. Nicolo
Colochita
Miesso
Panormo
Serapolli
Sittia
Cognida
Molinopoli
Pachino
Sittię ter ritoriū
Camara
Mauromu rij
Olo
Certonese
Armenusi
C. Palio
Grades
Lulachi
Menoa
Monte Samon
Samoni
C. Salamoni
Fonte
Dicteo mon.
Girapetra
Omal cam po
Verapolo
Tempio de Diana
Garubas
Cofonisi
Cortonese
Xacro
C. Xacro
C. de Girapetra
S. Antonio
C. Stroma Crigialo
S. Quaranta
Farioni
Christiana
Gaiderones
Xerocamo
Oriens
E I PARS
Miliaria
Italica communia
4 8 12 16 20
20 40 54 20 40 55 20 40
35 40 20 34 40 20

67. G. Mercator: Map of Cyprus, with the islands of Lemnos, Chios, Mytiler

uboea, Kythera, Rhodes, hand-coloured copper engraving, 49 × 35.5 cms, 1606

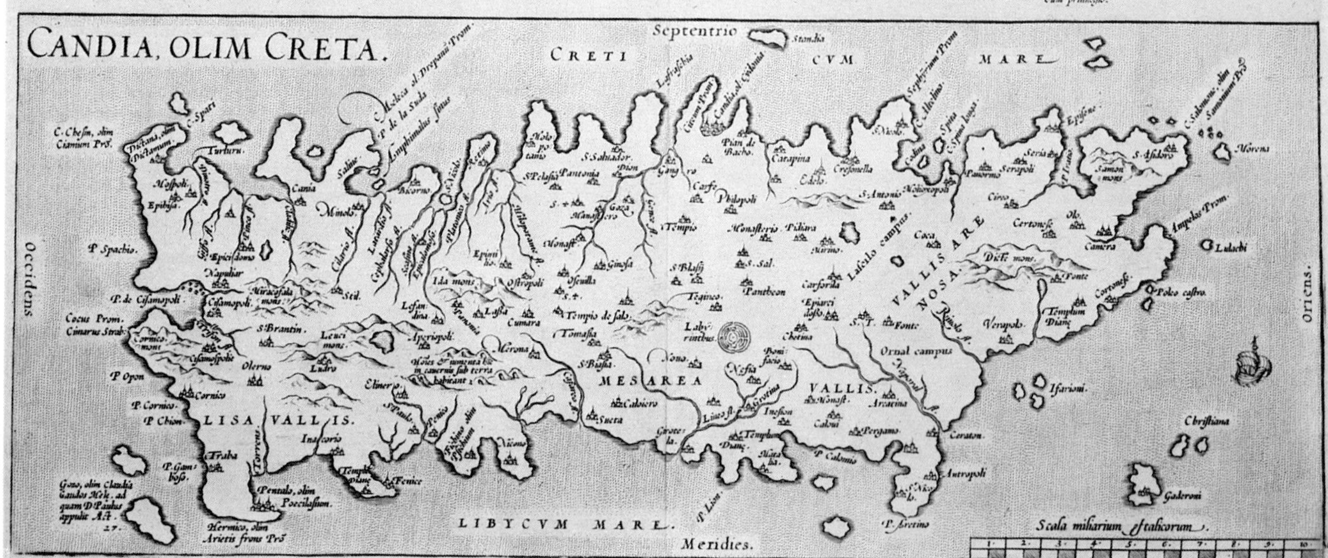

68. A. Ortelius: Map of Cyprus and Crete, copper engraving, 36.5 × 43.5 cms, 1570-1584

Abraham Ortelius (1527-1598): of German descent, Ortelius was born and died in Amsterdam. After studies in the Classics and mathematics, he travelled throughout Western Europe. His activities as a cartographer and publisher of maps also extended to the painting of maps, and he was influenced by Mercator, another of the first scientific mapmakers. In 1570 Ortelius published the first modern atlas, entitled *Theatrum Orbis Terrarum,* which went through repeated editions from then until 1612. In its initial form, the atlas consisted of 70 maps printed on 53 leaves. Supplemen-

69. A. Ortelius: Map of Crete, hand-coloured copper engraving, 7.5 × 10.5 cms, 1603

tary maps were gradually added to the original corpus, under the title of *Additamentum Theatri Orbis Terrarum.* The maps of Ortelius include many of the Aegean islands – Crete, Lemnos, Rhodes, Samos, Chios, and others. The Cyprus maps of 1573 and 1584 give the island its correct shape and exact proportions, along with details of its coastline. Crete was mapped along the intersecting lines of the winds, a relic of the medieval portolan maps. Among other works of Ortelius are maps of Egypt (1565), Asia (1567), Spain (1570) and the Holy Roman Empire (1571).

Nikolaos Sofianos: Corfiot man of letters who lived in Italy. Under the influence of the trend towards increased interest in classical antiquity during the 16th and 17th centuries, he published a map entitled "'Ελλάς" (1543, 1552). Sofianos took as his models in this the ancient geographers – Herodotus, Strabo and Ptolemy. In 1570, an alphabetical list of the place - names on Sofianos' map was published by Lafreri in Rome, under the title *Nomina Antiqua et Recentia Urbium Graeciae*. Ortelius, in the first editions of his *Theatrum Orbis Terrarum* (1570), made use of similar lists publishing the *Synonimia Geographica* in 1578 and the *Thesaurus Geographicus* in 1587.

70. A. Ortelius: «Ἑλλάς – Graecia Sophiani», hand-coloured copper engraving, 35 × 50 cms, 1579

PONTUS EUXINUS
AEGAEUM PELAGUS
ICARIUM PELAGUS
PROPONTIS
LYCIUM MARE
PAMPHYLIUM MARE
CARPATHIUM MARE
GALATIAE
BITHINIA
PONTUS ET
THRACIA
CRETA
RHODUS
CHIOS
LESBOS
LEMNOS
EUBOEA
ASIA
MYSIA MINOR
MYSIA MAIOR
TROAS
PHRYGIA MAYOR
CARIA
LYCIA
PAMPHILIA
PISIDIA
ARGOLICUS SINUS
LACONICUS SINUS
ORIENS
MERIDIES
Mil. Germ.
Mil. Gall.
Mil. Ital.
Stadia
51
52
53
54
55
56
57
58
59
60
61
62
63

SEPTEMTRIO.

CANDIA

C. Sansono. Petalida Standia Paxiomada. Fodella Atalli Frasch Palio castro. Retimo Agisti man. C. Melecha Grotta Turlluru. Porto della Suda Isola S. Nicolo. La pietra Canea. Citromado Saline C. Drapano Asprosomo ma. Cachi nipiali. Porto della Garabusa Spachia m. RETIMI TERR. TERRITORIVM DIAE. TERRITORIVM CANEAE. Apano petralida Stomoso lite. S. Zuan Bamitta S. Paulo Alicabus. S. Constantio. Modo uani Madara m. Mudras Psiloriti m. C. Tomene Candia. C. Cutri. Cata petralia. Maura pilla Campo Messarea Beluedere Cara Cadra MESSA REA. Pandolicno S. Ellen Sfachia Isola S. Paulo. Stramatali Ganda palla. Gaudo. Cabo S. Georgio Isola della Bona C. Frio Armiro fiu. Giofiro fiu. Darmata fl.

OCCIDENS.

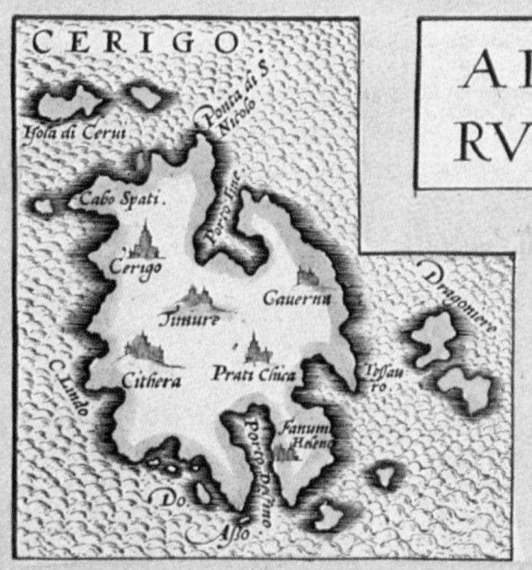

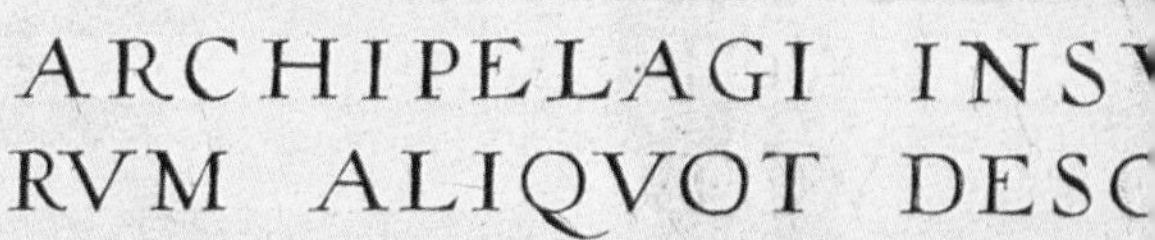

MERIDIES.

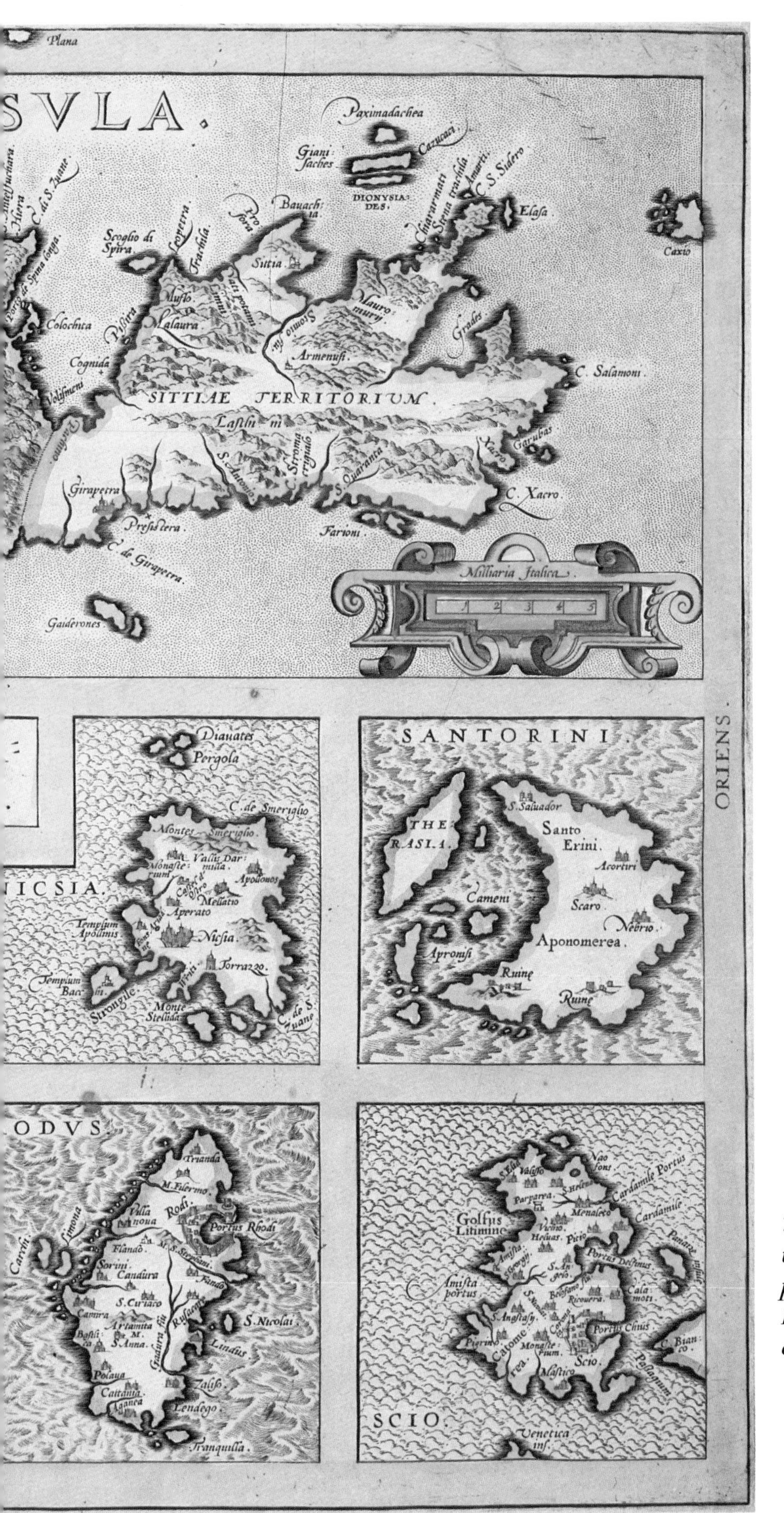

71. A. Ortelius: Map of Crete, with the islands of Mytilene, Kythera, Karpathos, Santorini, Melos, Lemnos, Euboea, Rhodes, Chios, hand-coloured copper engraving, 36 x 50 cms, 1584

CYPRI INSVLAE NOVA DESCRIPT. 1573.
SEPT
OCCIDENS.
MER
C. Cormachitti
C. Limniti.
C. Eleni.
C. S. Pifano
Diorigo
Sirianocari
PAPHIA
AMATHVSIA
Olympus Mons
Trodisi.
Prodromo.
Melandra.
De Chico.
Maconda.
Marmica.
Crotiri.
Trimitusa
Poli.
Potamios
Podrinio.
Merouili.
Coli.
Ferra.
Drusia.
Timochrini.
Guardia
Igna.
Rodes.
Feletra.
Strombi.
Amar.
Anuio.
Ara.
S. 2.
Chrisonera.
Cleri ca.
Chlima
Baffo olim Paphos.
Capo Bianco.
Pisseri
Auadimo.
Piramati.
Mandalati.
Cata.
Simbali
Cosole.
Acrotiri.
S. X.
Capo de le Gate
Limisso.
Alomano.
Pendaia.
Petra.
Agrolaco
Coraci.
Tenebria.
Cataforo.
Dribmo.
Calina.
Golata.
Marato.
Leno.
Cardama.
Caridac.
Filoga.
Saica.
Chiliaco.
S. 2.
Euresti
Siria.
Chiuida.
Zabata
S. Chitino.
Critiui.
Mesatiunda.
Pasula.
S. Ermi.
Limati.
Monag.
Dore.
Cagna.
Trimichini
S. Costantino.
S. Quant.
Orongo.
Labano.
Limisouchio.
Pirgo.
Pendamia.
Marin.
Dasilipotamo.
S. Marino.
Calauato.
Ville.
Alouanza.
Dafno.
Astagonia.
Agra.
Vala.
Agitho.
Ora.
Sasona
Diosimaco.
S. Andrea.
Capura.
Piatanista.
Arbrina.
S. Armi.
Cananía.
Liuadi.
Machen.
Calopanaia.
Dipotamia.
Pudino.
S. 2.
Diesto.
Livi.
Saradidi.
Synagora.
Aza.
Astimi.
Filato
Cascalo.
Patedi.
Pahicori.
S. Marina.
Mitida.
Fluso.
Limnia.
S. Pifani.
Melopni.
Agita.
Liniu.
Potami.
Stodori.
Peristeri.
Pardini.
Margasa.
Morso.
Ariati.
Tenari.
Kichita.
Bartha.
Ognocori.
Crusulin.
Chora.
Vasili.
Oritis.
Sarno.
Capuri.
Asomato.
Sisipo.
Larma.
Gambili.
Matag.
Muasi.
Dumatori.
Blosi.
Vnchito.
Corinia.
Vasilico.
LA
S. Todoro.
S. Eleni.
Pomo.
Cremidi
Ierunt.
S. Barbara
S. Zuani
Alexandreta.
Lefre.
Lubelico.
Vorisa.
Critu.
Sarca.
Aspreia.
Pendalitoria.
Arsos.
Vassa.
Galatiu.
Lassa.
Papitiu.
Nani.
Miglia
Salamina
Vrtelia.
S. Cusma.
Leruasa.
Marona.
Homedos.
Schlinica.
Corimaci.
Diachinisa
Pocan.
Risato.
Patra.
Terra
Arcimat.
Amogna.
Clora.
Mantata.
Suarnara.
Athlia
Coni.
Facoa.
Iolu.
Peati.
Sima.
Lurumu.
S. Sidro.
Eurati.
Pelatusa.
Chio.
Iaglia.
Crusoco.
Erico.
Milliaria Italica.
5. 10. 15. 20. 25.
5. 10. 15. 20.
5. 10. 15. 20.

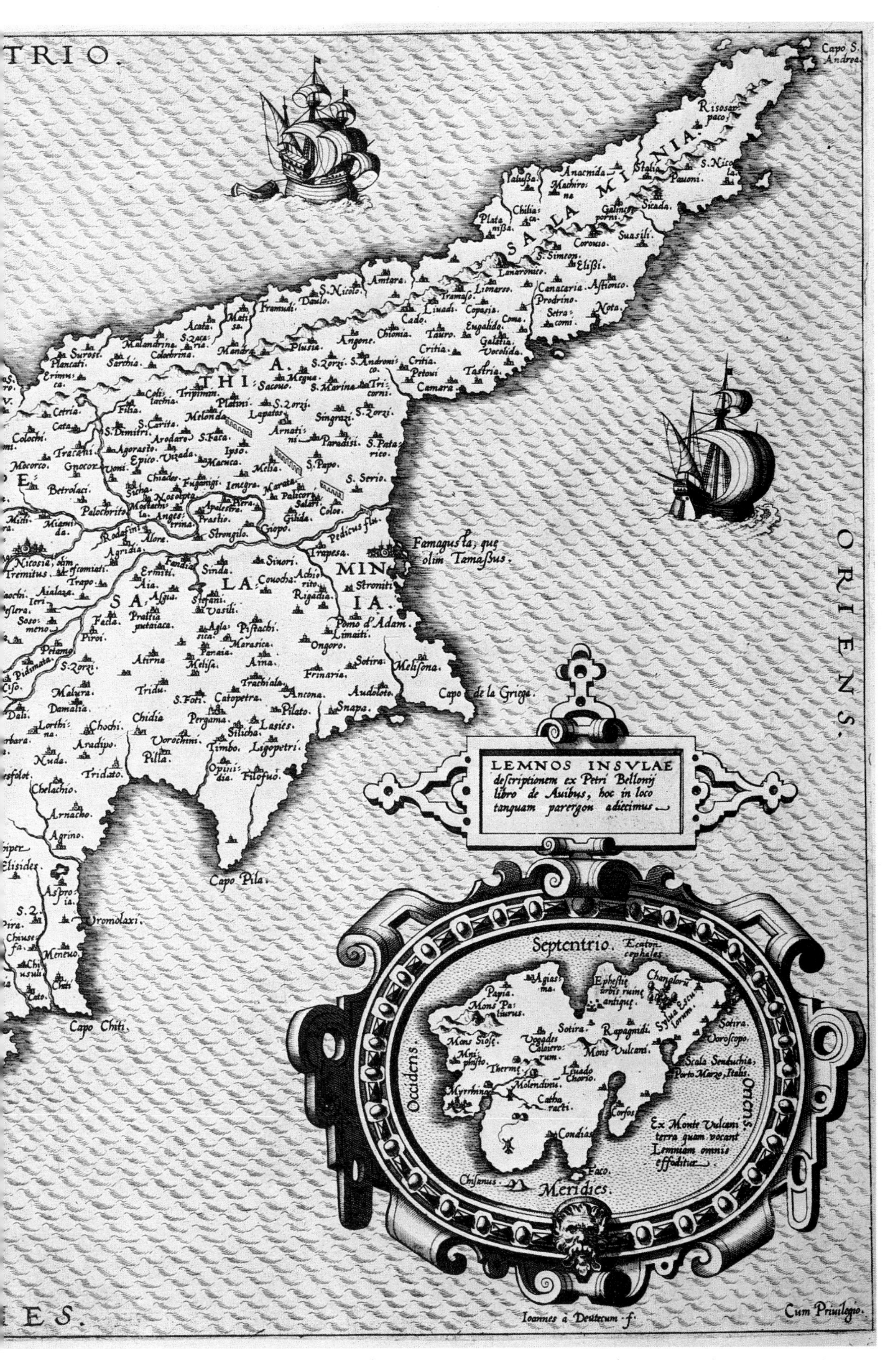

72. A. Ortelius: Map of Cyprus with Lemnos, copper engraving, 35 × 49 cms, 1573

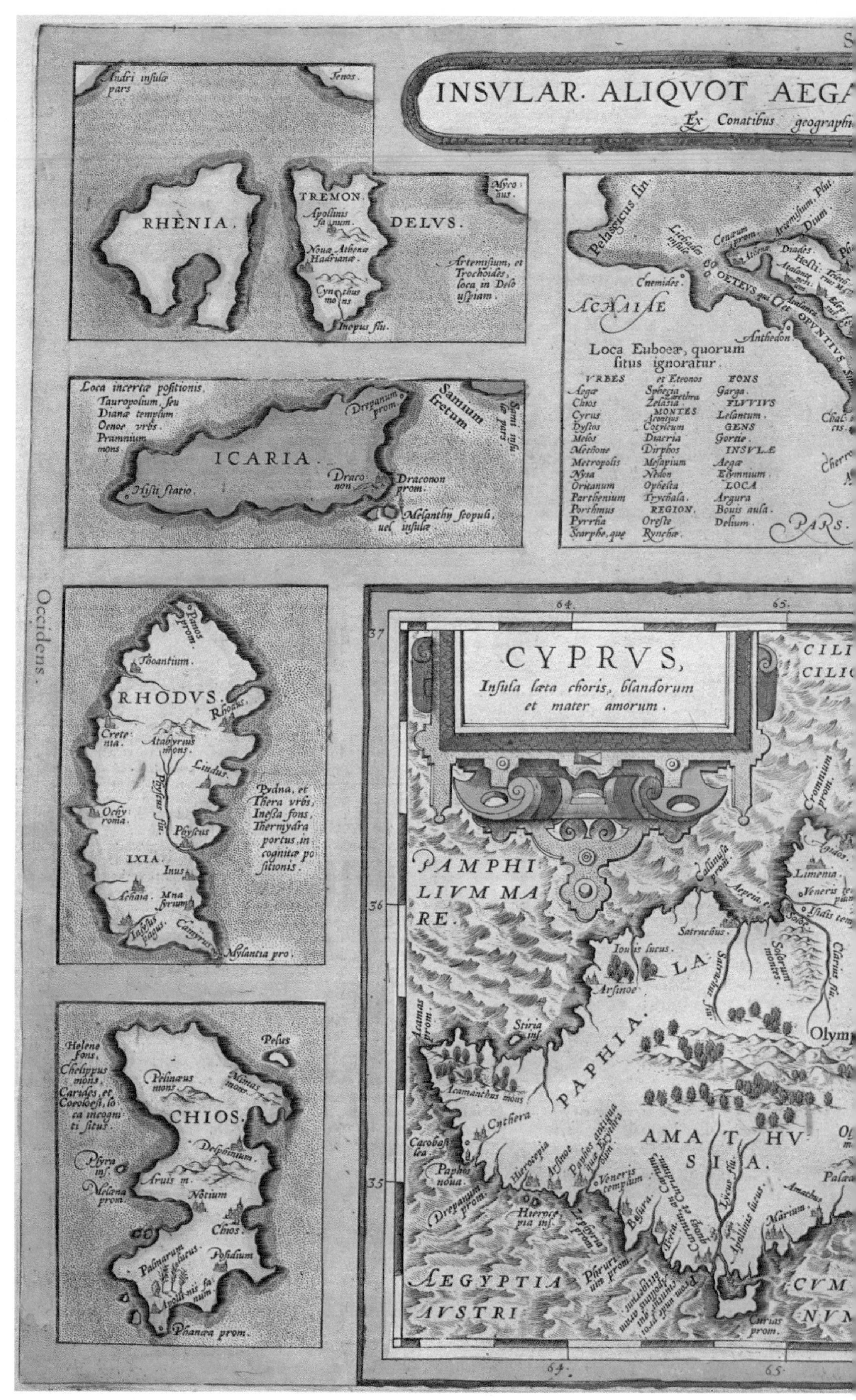

73. A. Ortelius: Map of Cyprus, with the islands of Delos, Ikaria, Rhodes, Chios, Eubo

mos, Kea, Kos, Lesbos, Lemnos, hand-coloured copper engraving, 43 × 49 cms, 1584

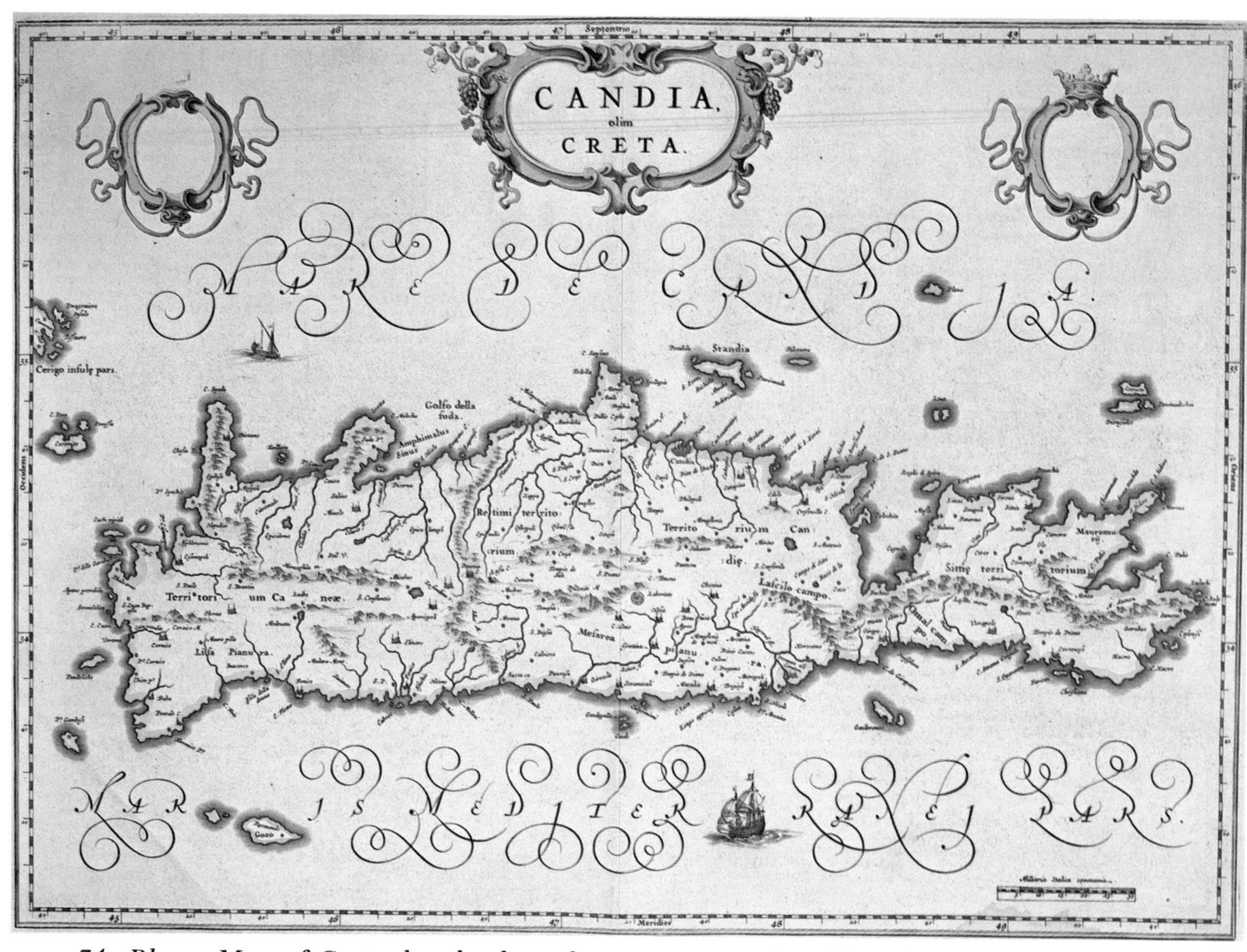

74. Blaeu: Map of Crete, hand-coloured copper engraving, 38 × 53 cms, after 1640

The Blaeu family (Jans Zoon, Janssonius, Johnson, Alcmarianus, Caesius) were cartographers, publishers and book-sellers in Amsterdam. The firm was founded by Willem (1571-1638), who produced maps of Holland, Spain and the continents. In 1608 he published the naval atlas *Licht der Zeevaert.* He bought 37 plates from Hondius in 1629, and published his first atlas of the continents. Willem had two sons, Joan (1596-1637) and Cornelius (1610-1648), who worked with him on the completion of the *Atlas Blaviane* (6 volumes) and the *Atlas Major* (9 volumes). In 1627, a fire destroyed the firm's printing works. Blaeu was official cartographer to the Dutch East India Company.

75. Blaeu: Map of Cyprus, hand-coloured copper engraving, 38 × 51 cms, 1635

HELLAS seu GRÆCIA VNIVERSA. AUTORE J. Laurenbergio.
Septentrio
Meridies
Occidens
DACIÆ PARS.
ILLYRI PARS.
THRACI
MACEDONIA
THESSALIA
ACHAIA
PELOPONNESUS
GOLFO DI VENETIA.
La Bocca del Golfo di Venetia.
MARE MEDITERRANEO
IONIUM PELAGUS.
CORINTHIACUS SINUS hod. Golfo de Lepanto
PELAGICUS SINUS.
ARGOLICUS SINUS.
LACONICUS SINUS.
Messeniacus Sinus.
CYPARISSIUS SINUS.
STRYMONICUS SINUS Golfo di Contessa.
SINGITICUS SINUS Golfo de Monte Santo.
Thermaicus Sinus Golfo di Salonichi.
Leucadia ins. hod. Santa Maura.
Cephalenia quæ et Samos et Samos hod. Cefalonia.
Zacynthus hod. Zante.
Phæacia qui et Corcyra ins. hod. Corfu.
EUBŒA Ins. quæ et Macris et Abantias.
NEGROPONTE
ALBANIA
EPIRUS
AETOLIA
ACARNANIA
BOEOTIA
ATTICA
PHOCIS
DORIS
LOCRIS
ARCADIA
LACONICA
MESSENIA
ARGOLIS
CORINTHIA
SICYONIA
ACHAIA PROPRIA
MAGNESIA
PHTHIOTIS
CHALCIDICE
PIERIA
MYGNIA
EMATHIA
LYNCESTIS
CASSIOPEA
THESPROTIA
DOLOPIA
CHAONIA
ORESTIS
CASTIS Regio
TAULANTIA
CHIMERA
CANINA
SARONICUS MARE
Sciro.
Cithera.

Johannes Wilhelm Lauremberg (1590-1658): writer, mathematician and historian, born at Rostock. His first known map is that of the Duchy of Mecklenburg, included in the atlases of Blaeu in 1630 and of Hondius in 1633. Lauremberg is most famous, however, for his maps of ancient Greece, brought together in the *Atlas Graecia Antiqua* of 1656. Lauremberg himself never visited Greece, but was familiar with the work of the great map-makers of the age and was influenced by Mercator and Ortelius.

76. J. Lauremberg: Map of Greece, hand-coloured copper engraving, 56 × 47 cms, 1700

77. J. Lauremberg: Map of the southern Aegean with the Cyclades, hand-coloured copper engraving, 48 × 57 cms, 1638

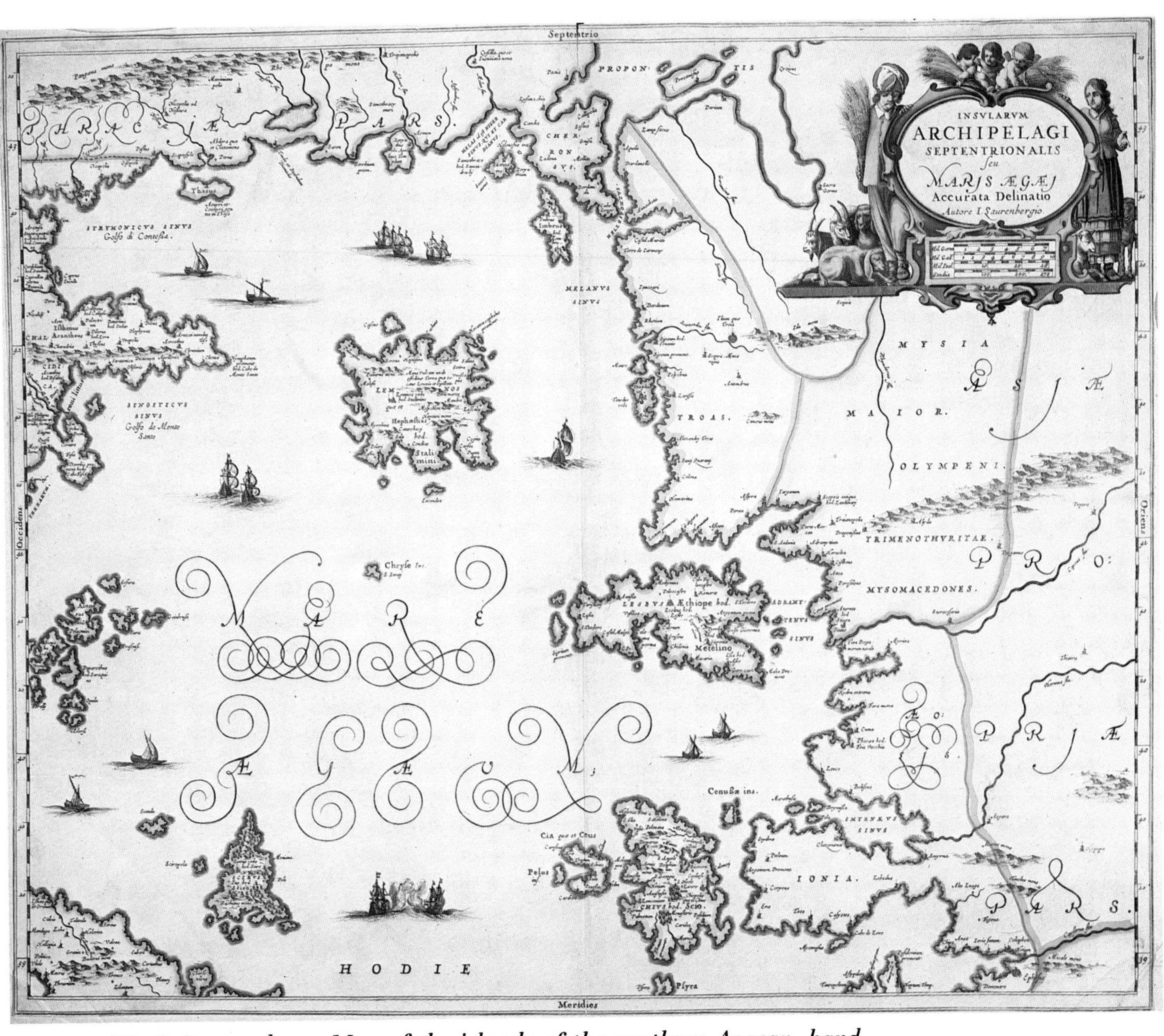

78. J. Lauremberg: Map of the islands of the northern Aegean, hand-coloured copper engraving, 48 × 57 cms, 1638

Marco Boschini (1613-1678): Venetian painter, engraver and cartographer, the author of two books referring to Greece. The first of these, entitled *L' Arcipelago con tutte le isole..*, was printed at the Nicolini works in Venice in 1658. It contains a map of the Aegean – included in this book – accompanied by a descriptive text and 48 more detailed maps of the islands. Most of the maps and the greater part of the text were taken from earlier works by Buondelmonti, Bordone and Porcacchi.

Boschini's other work, *Il regno tutto di Candia*, covers Crete and was published in 1651. The book, a large volume, contained 61 engravings including the map of Crete published here. The ground morphology is shown with particular care, and the names of bays, capes, coastal towns and regions are marked. Most of the engravings are detailed views of castles and harbours, and the book also includes an accurate reconstruction of the Turkish siege of Herakleio.

Boschini also wrote a handbook for artists under the title *La Carta del Navegar Pittoresco*, published in Venice in 1660, which related the history of Venetian art from Giambellino to Tintoretto.

79. M. Boschini: Map of the Aegean Sea, copper engraving, 31 × 25 cms, 1658

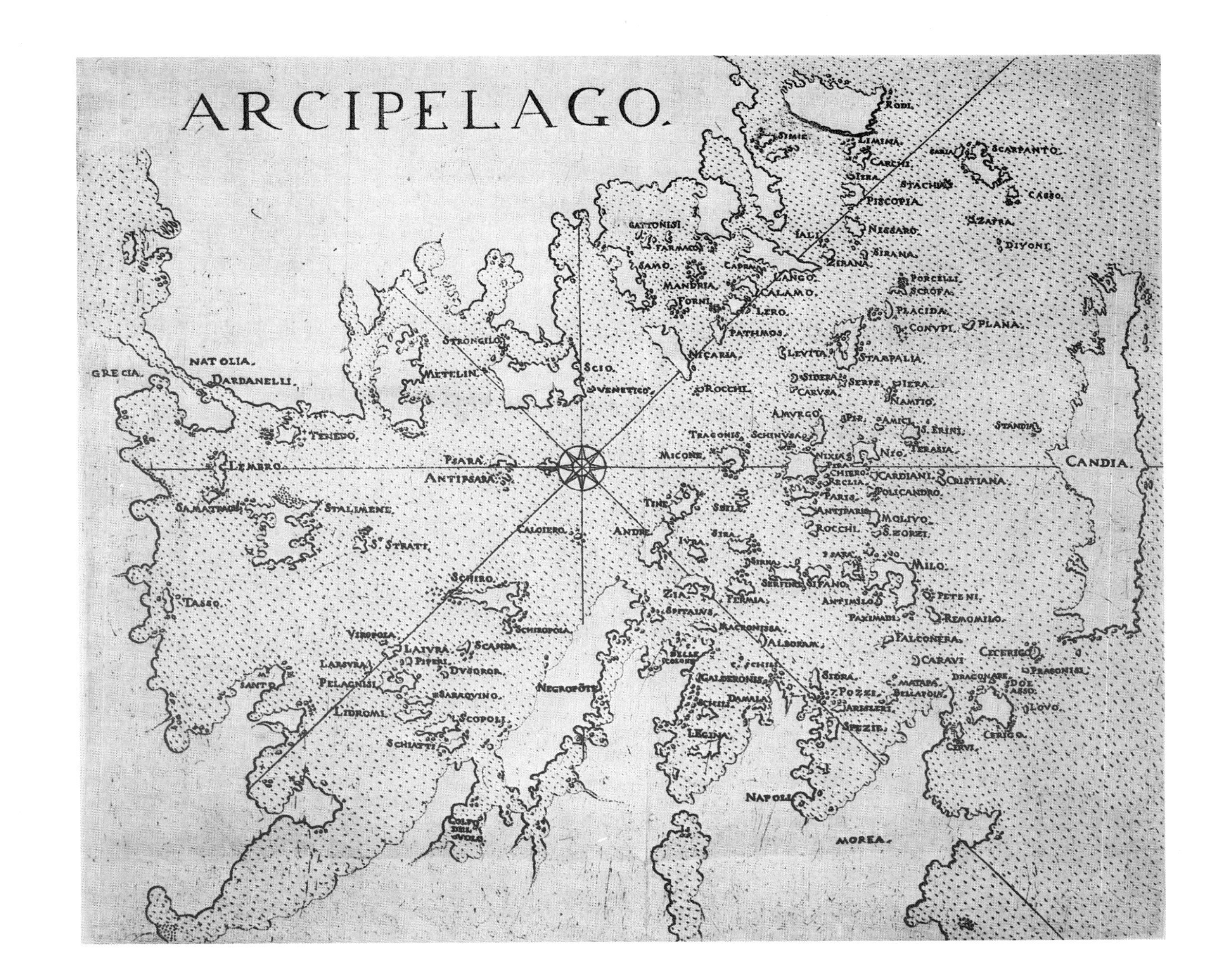
ARCIPELAGO.
GRECIA.
NATOLIA.
DARDANELLI.
TENEDO.
LEMBRO.
STALIMENE.
S. STRATI.
TASSO.
SCHIRO.
SCHIROPOLA.
SCANDA.
NEGROPÕTE.
STRONGILO.
METELIN.
SCIO.
VENETICO.
PSARA.
ANTIPSARA.
CALOIERO.
ANDRE.
TINE.
MICONE.
NICARIA.
SAMO.
MANDRIA.
FORNI.
CALAMO.
LERO.
PATHMOS.
LEVITA.
STAMPALIA.
RODI.
LIMINA.
SCARPANTO.
PISCOPIA.
NISSARO.
SIRANA.
CASSO.
ZAFFRA.
DIVONI.
PORCELLI.
SCROFA.
PLACIDA.
CONVPI.
PLANA.
NIO.
AMVRGO.
ROCCHI.
TRACONIS.
SCHINVSA.
NIXIA.
CARDIANI.
CRISTIANA.
POLICANDRO.
PARIS.
ANTIPARIS.
MOLIVO.
S. ZORZI.
MILO.
PETENI.
REMOMILO.
ZIA.
FERMIA.
SERFINI.
SIFANO.
ANTIMILO.
FALCONERA.
CARAVI.
CECERIGO.
SIDRA.
POZZE.
SPEZIE.
CERIGO.
CERVI.
LOVO.
CANDIA.
NAPOLI.
MOREA.

80. M. Boschini: Map of Cre

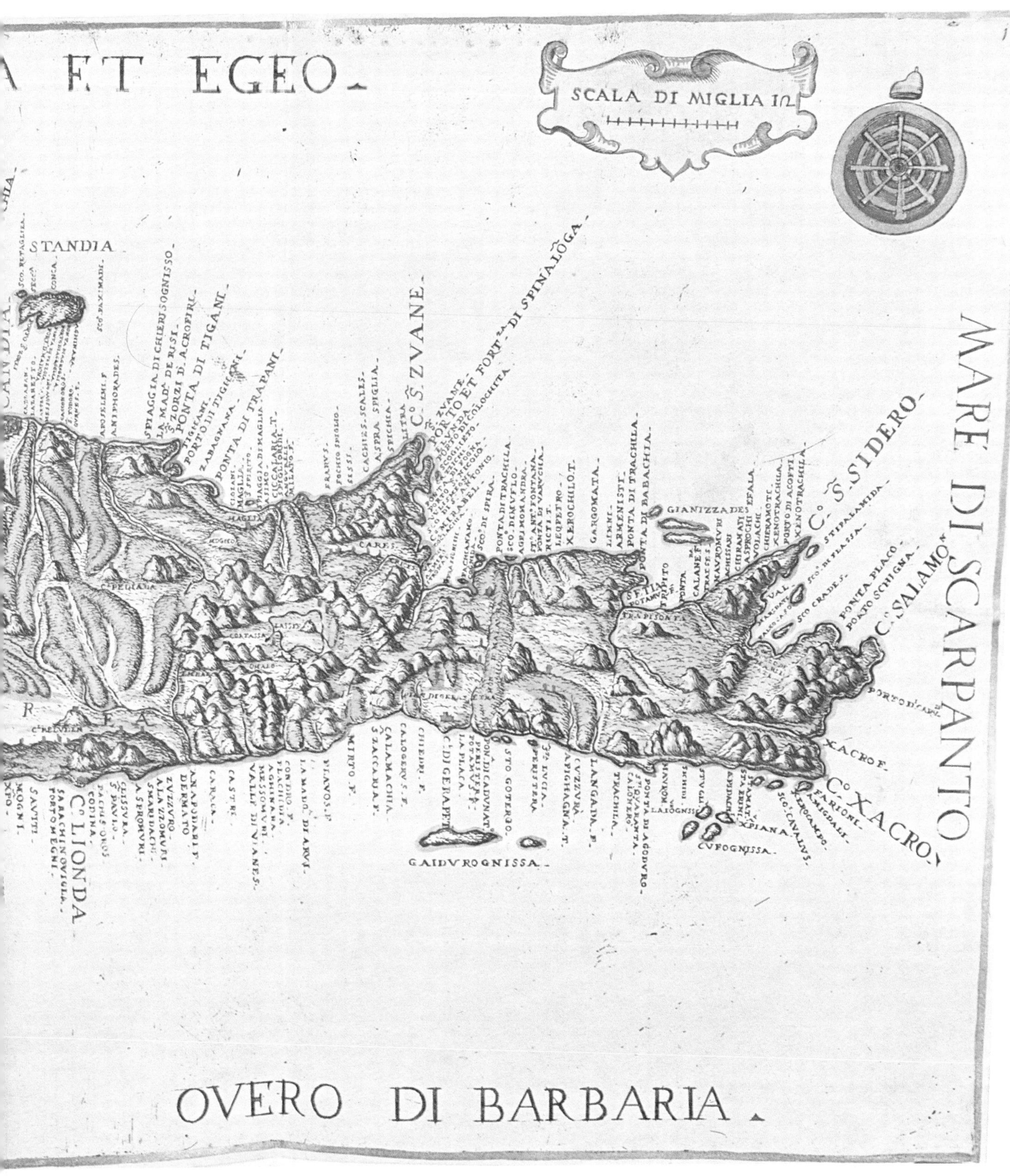

× 31 cms, copper engraving, 1651

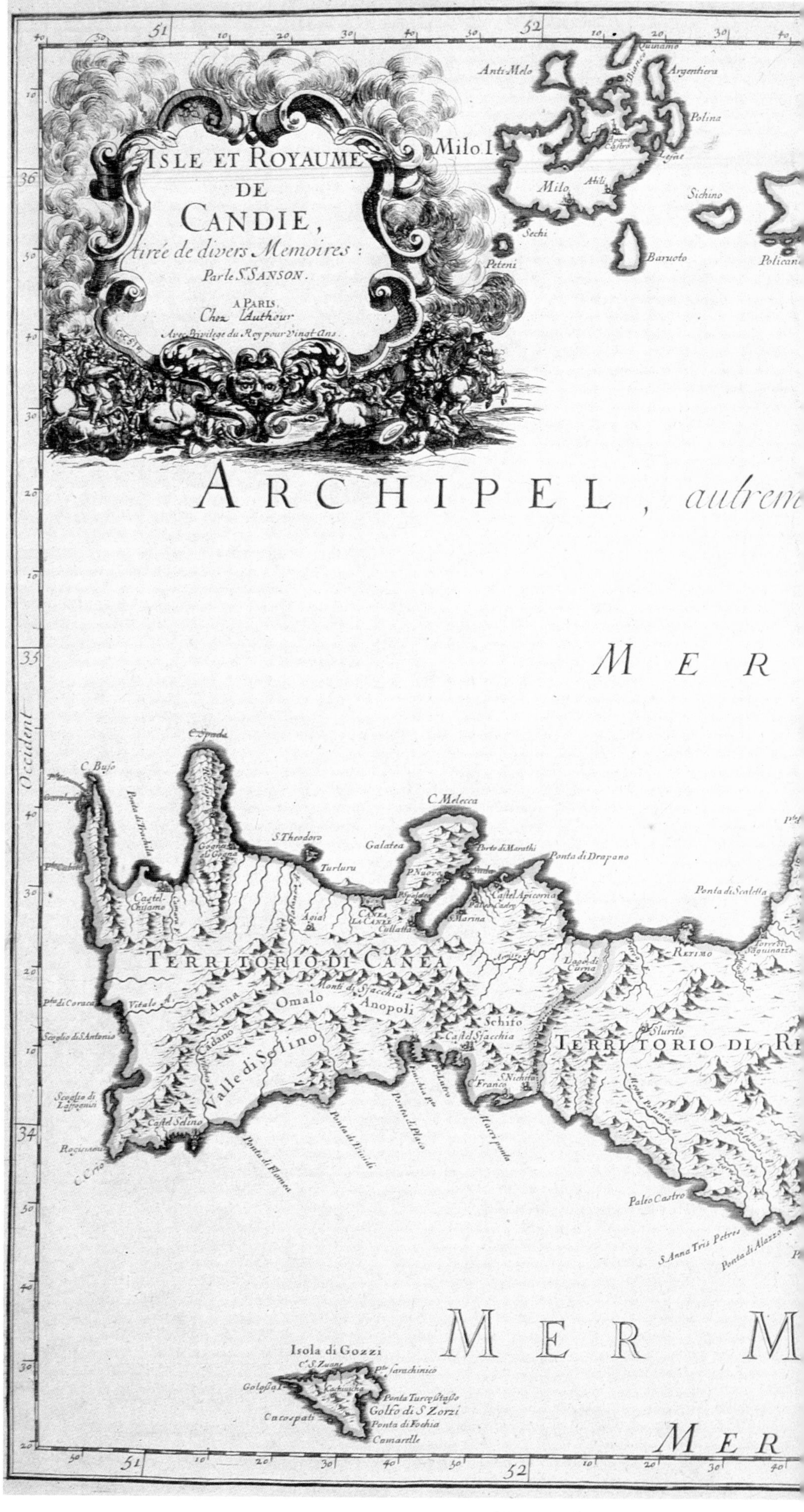

81. N. Sanson: Map of Cre

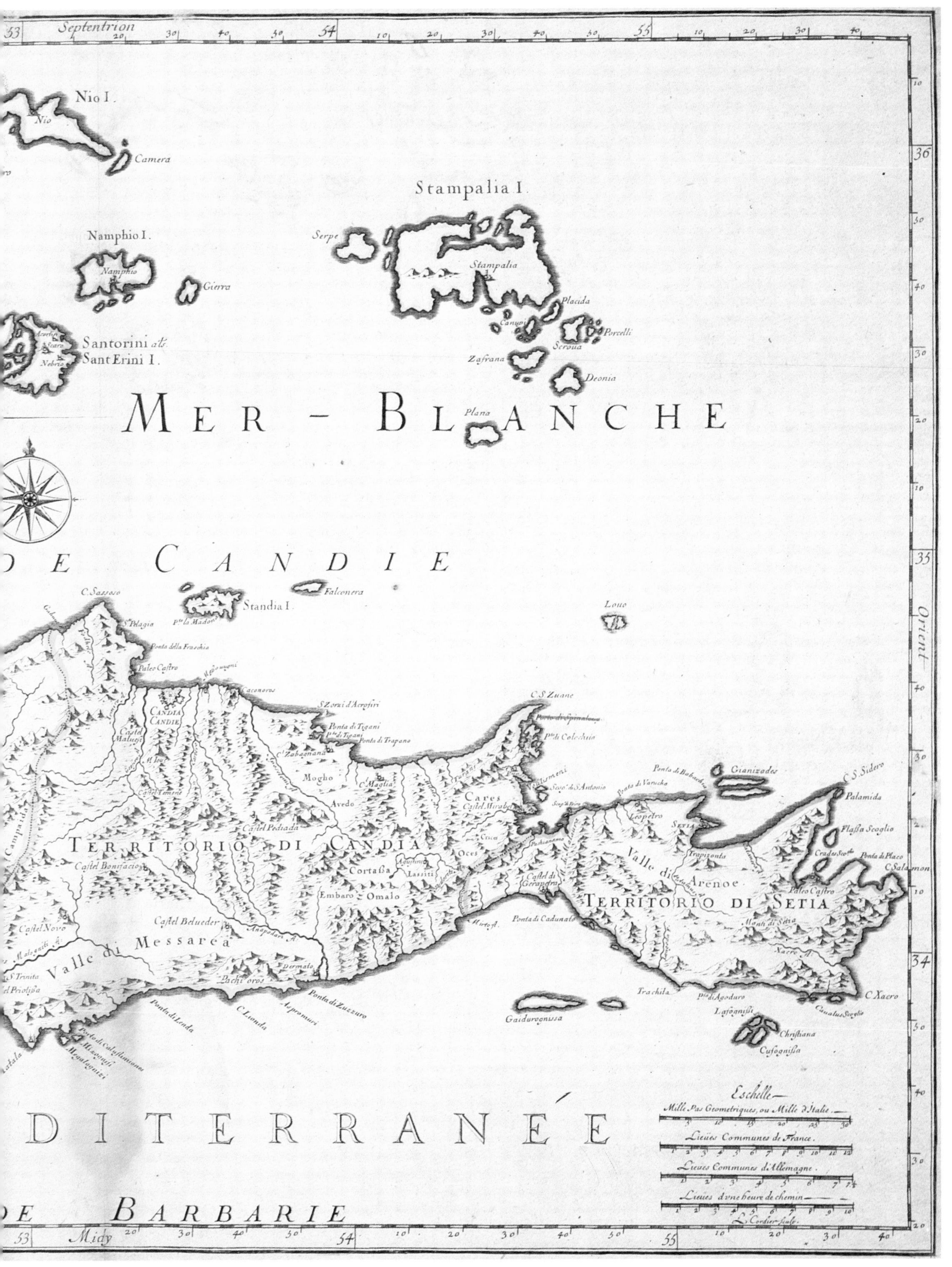

oper engraving, 39 × 55 cms, 1658

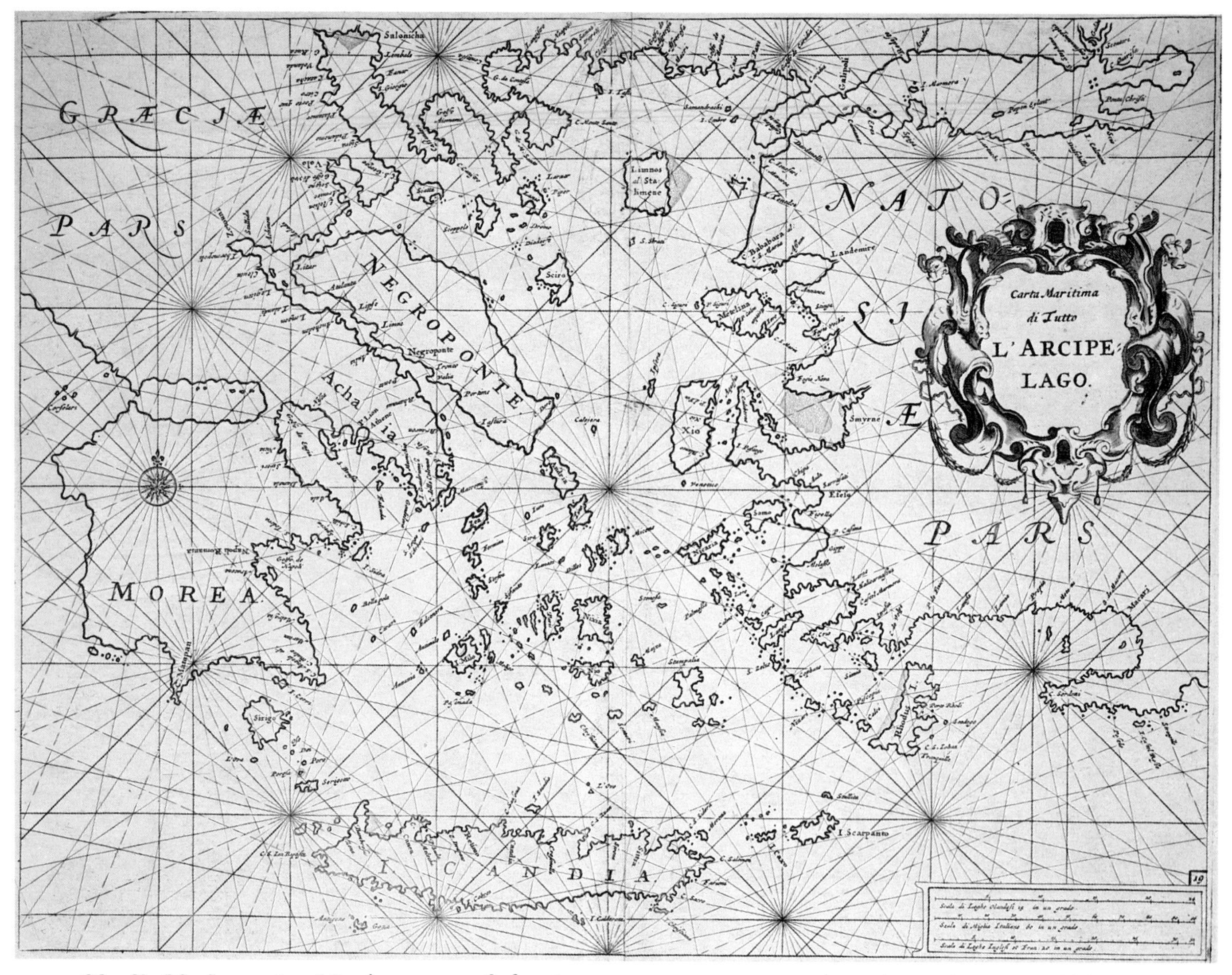

82. F. M. Levanto: Marine map of the Aegean, copper engraving, 40 × 53 cms, 1664

Nicolas Sanson (1600-1667): generally thought of as the father of the French 17th century school of map-making. Sanson published an atlas of France (1644), world atlases and another atlas under the title *Cartes Générales de toutes les Parties du Monde* (1658), containing 82 large maps. He was assisted by his son Nicolas (1626-1648), who was responsible, among other works, for a map of Russia. After Sanson's death, the firm was run by his sons Guillaume and Andrien, who published the atlas *Neptune François* in 1693. After 1670 the firm's map-making material was taken over by Herbert Jaillot.

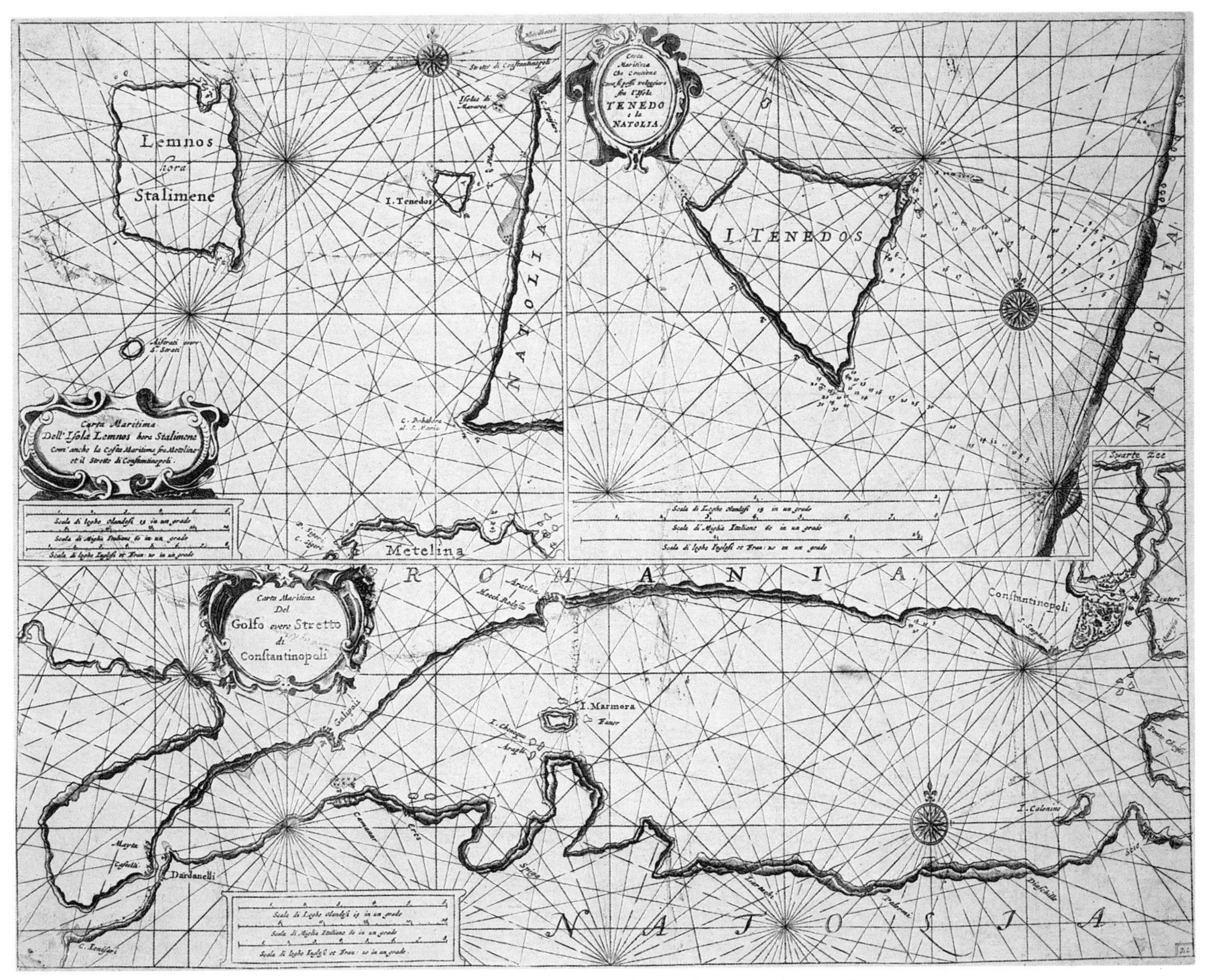

83. F. M. Levanto: Marine map of Tenedos, Asia Minor, Lemnos, Mytilene, and the straits of Constantinople, copper engraving, 39.5 × 51 cms, 1664

Francesco Maria Levanto: a cartographer from Genoa, Italy, Levanto published a *Prima Parte dello Specchio del Mare*, in 1664, containing 14 naval charts of the Greek islands and the Aegean Sea. The work was reprinted in 1698 by V.M. Coronelli.

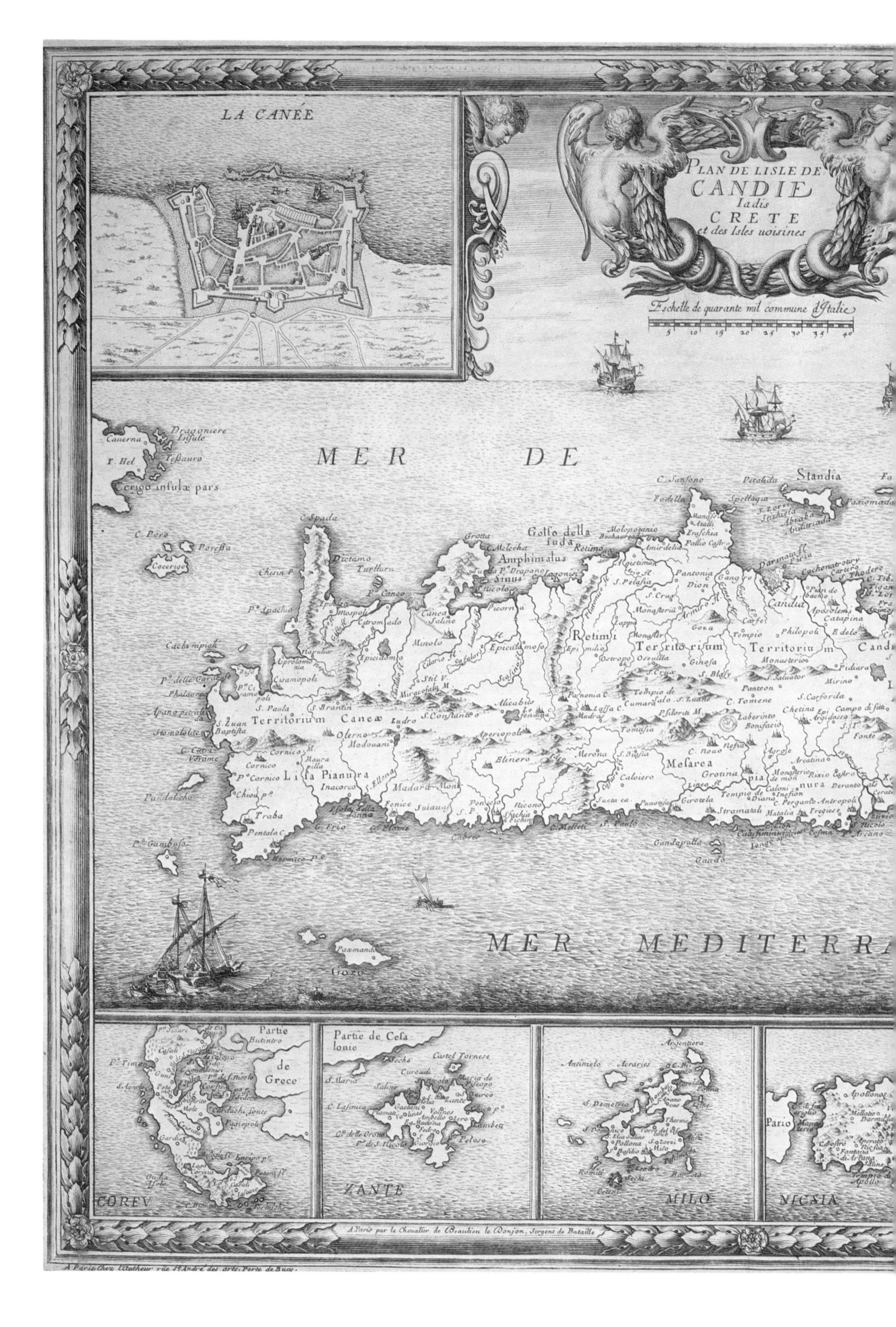
LA CANÉE
PLAN DE LISLE DE CANDIE Iadis CRETE et des Isles uoisines
Eschelle de quarante mil commune d'Italie
MER DE
MER MEDITERRA
Territorium Caneæ
Retimi Territorium
Candia
Partie de Cefalonie
Partie de Grece
COREV
ZANTE
MILO
NICSIA
A Paris par le Chevalier de Beaulieu le Donjon, Sergent de Bataille
A Paris Chez l'Autheur rue St André des arts, Porte de Bucy.

Sebastian de Pontault, Chevalier de Beaulieu (1613-1674): engineer in the French Army. Among his works: *Conquêtes de Louis le Grand* (1643-84) and *Villes de France* (1694).

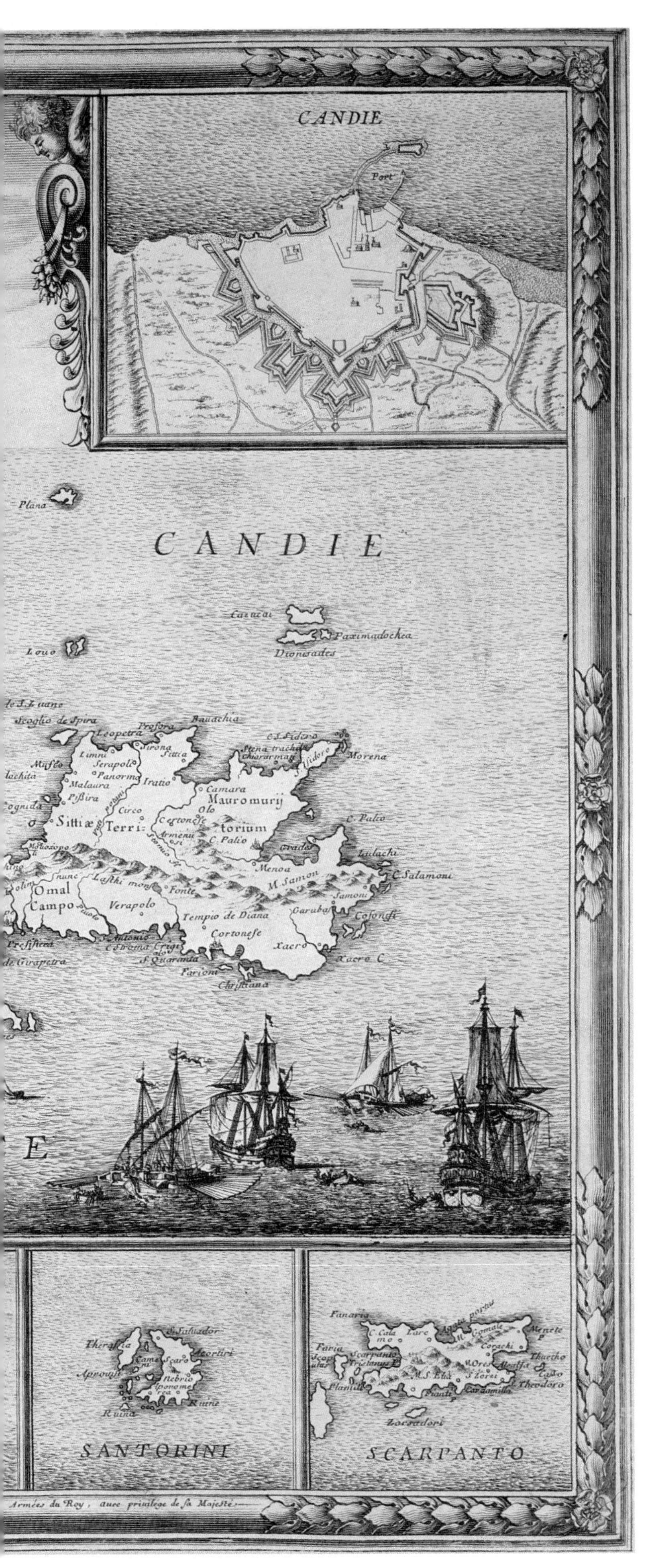

84. *S. de Beaulieu: Map of Crete, with the islands of Corfu, Zakynthos, Melos, Naxos, Santorini, Karpathos, copper engraving, 50 × 42 cms, 1674*

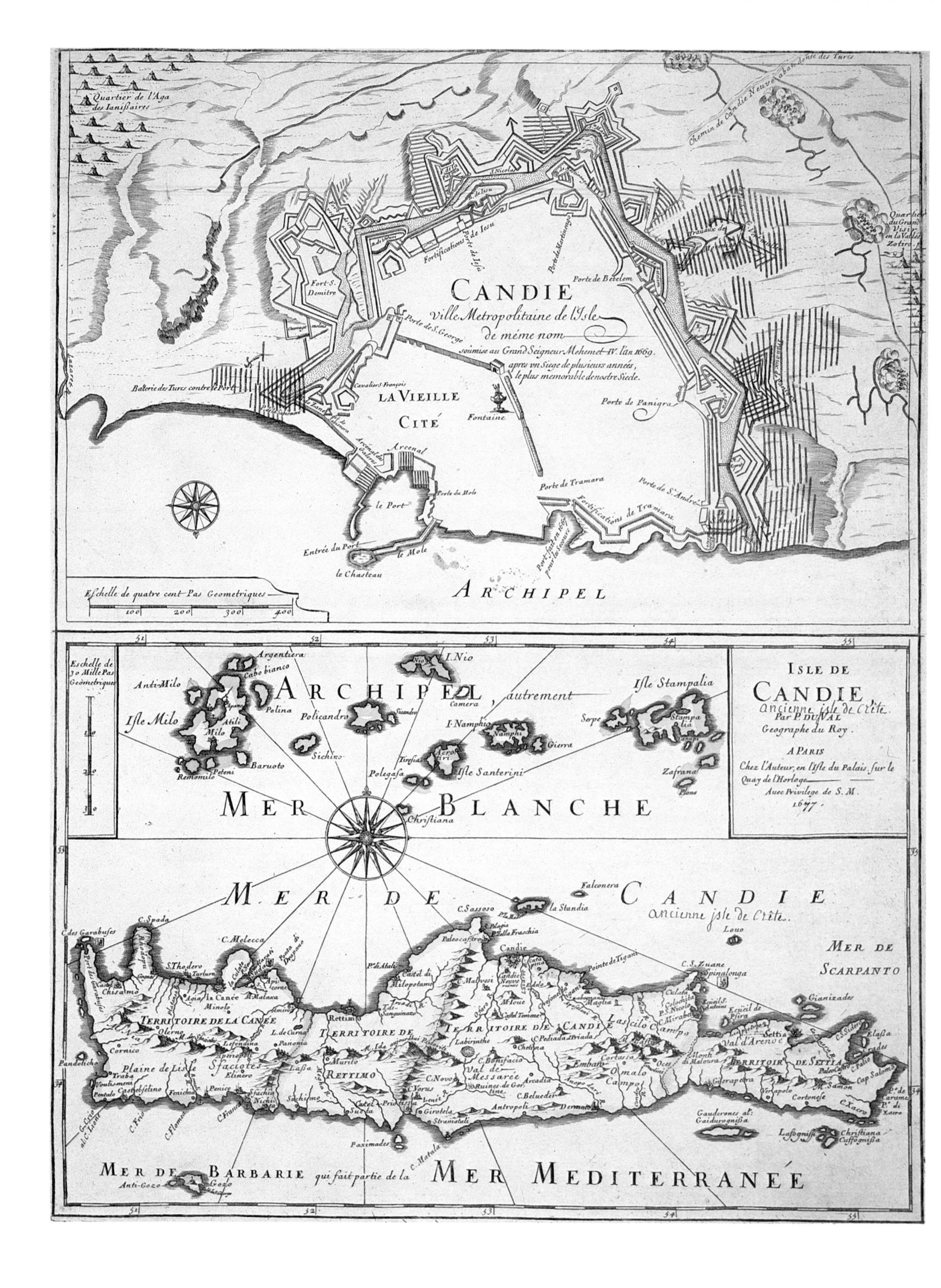
Quartier de l'Aga des Ianißaires
CANDIE
ville Metropolitaine de l'Isle de méme nom
soumise au Grand Seigneur Mehemet IV. l'an 1669. apres vn Siege de plusieurs années, le plus memorable de nostre Siecle.
Fort S. Demitre
Porte de S. George
Fortifications de Iesu
Porte de Betelem
Baterie des Turcs contre le Port
Cavaliers François
LA VIEILLE CITÉ
Fontaine
Porte de Panigra
Arcenal
Porte du Mole
le Port
Porte de Tramara
Porte de S. André
Fortifications de Tramara
Entrée du Port
le Mole
le Chasteau
Eschelle de quatre cent Pas Geometriques
100 200 300 400
ARCHIPEL
Chemin de Candie Neuve
Eschelle de 30 Mille Pas Geometriques
ARCHIPEL, autrement
MER BLANCHE
Isle Milo
Anti-Milo
Argentiera
Cabo bianco
Polina
Policandro
Sichino
I. Nio
Camera
I. Namphio
Isle Santerini
Isle Stampalia
Christiana
ISLE DE CANDIE
anciennε isle de Crête
Par P. DUVAL Geographe du Roy.
A PARIS Chez l'Auteur, en l'Isle du Palais sur le Quay de l'Horloge
Avec Privilege de S. M. 1677.
MER DE CANDIE
anciennε isle de Crête.
Falconera
MER DE SCARPANTO
C. Spada
C. Melecca
C. S. Zuane
Spinalonga
TERRITOIRE DE LA CANÉE
TERRITOIRE DE RETTIMO
TERRITOIRE DE CANDIE
TERRITOIR DE SETTIA
Plaine de Lisle
Sfaciotes
Val de Messaree
Omalo Campo
Lascito Campo
Val d'Arenoe
Candie
Rettimo
Labirinthe
Paximades
Gauderones al: Gaidurognißa
Christiana Cuffognißa
MER DE BARBARIE qui fait partie de la MER MEDITERRANÉE
Gozo
Anti-Gozo
51 52 53 54 55

Pierre du Val (1618-1683): geographer to the King of France and pupil of Sanson. Among his publications: *Cartes de Géographie* (1662), *Le Monde ou la Géographie Universelle* (1662), *Diverses Cartes* (1677), *Géographie Universelle* (1682).

Van Keulen: leading family of Dutch cartographers and publishers, whose members were active in the trade for some two hundred years. The firm was founded by Johannes van Keulen (1654-1715). In 1680 he published a *Zee Atlas*, with a text and 38 maps by Clas Jansz Vooght, which was an immediate success. This first edition was followed up by five more within the space of nine years, including versions in French and English. In 1683 van Keulen published a *Zee Fakkel*, and ten years later managed to buy out one of his main rivals, the firm of Hendrik Doncker the Elder. Both works – the *Zee Atlas* and the *Zee Fakkel* – went through numerous expanded and revised editions. Johannes van Keulen retired in 1704, and was succeeded in the business by his son Gerard (1678-1727), who was a mathematician as well as an engraver and publisher. Although Gerard died quite young, he had time to revise his father's atlas and to add new maps of unusually large dimensions, which he published in an edition of 180 maps in 1710. In 1710, too, he was appointed hydrographer to the Dutch East Indies Company. Among other members of the family were Johannes van Keulen the younger, who revised the *Zee Fakkel* and added important maps of Africa, Asia and Australia, Gerard Hulst van Keulen, and Cornelius Buys van Keulen. The last representative of the clan was Gerard Hulst van Keulen van de Velde, after whom the firm passed into other hands. In 1885, all its stock was auctioned off and scattered throughout the world.

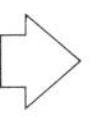

85. P. du Val: Map of Crete, hand-coloured copper engraving, 51.5 × 39.5 cms, 1677

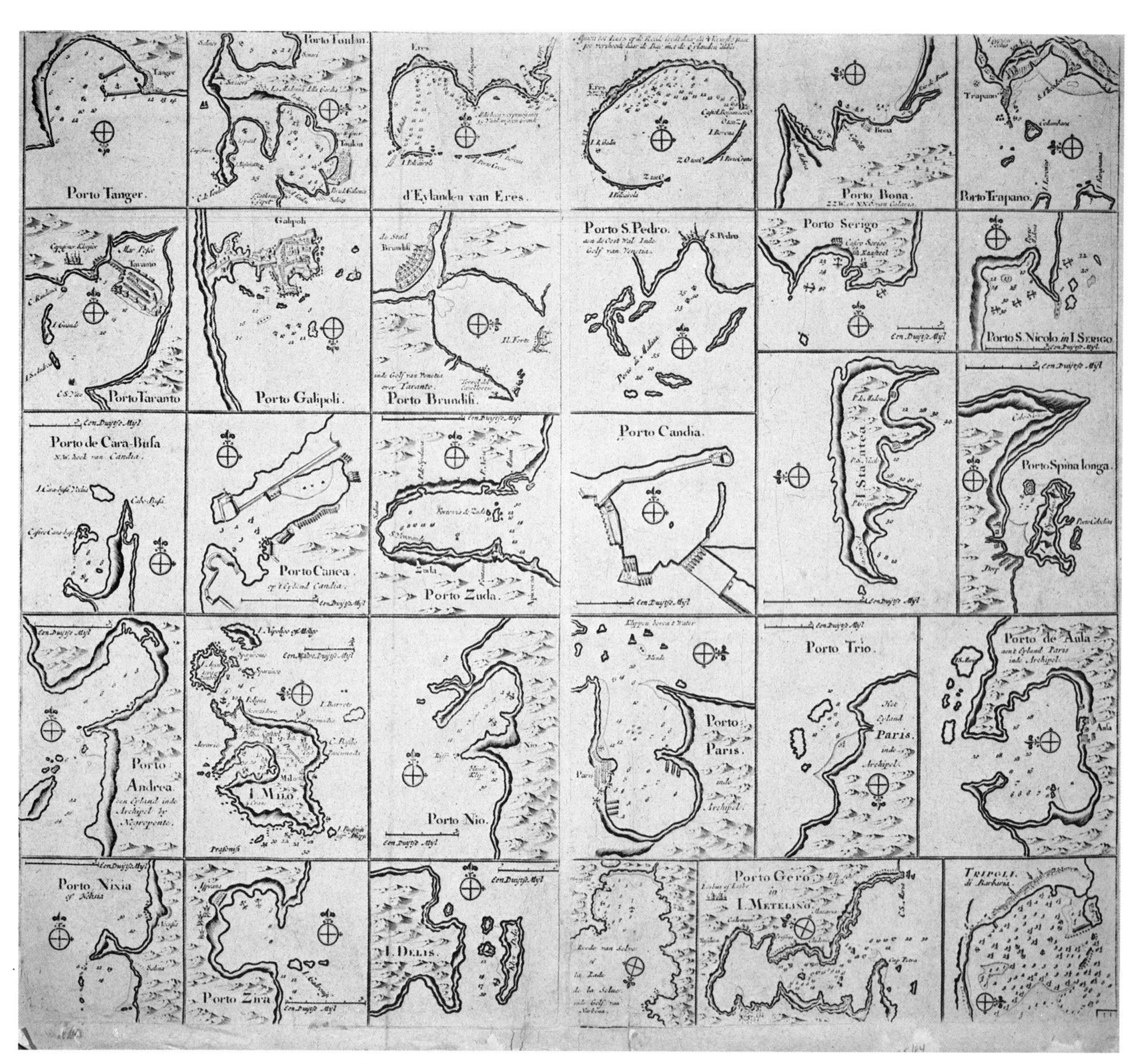

86. Van Keulen: Harbour chart of the islands of the Aegean , copper engraving, 51 × 58 cms, 1680

87. Van Keulen: Map of the islands of the Aegean, copper engraving, 59 × 51 cms, 1680

MACEDONIA
ROMANIA
Mygnia
Amphaxitis
Emathia
Chalcidica
Pieria
Magnesia
THESSALIA
Phthiotis
Golfo van Zeiton
Opunti
Bœotia
Megaris
Attica
ACHAIA
I. Lemnos
Scio
ARCHIPELLAGUS
MARE DI NICARIA
MOREA
BRASSO DE MEYN
C. Matapan
I. SERIGO
I. Milo
Nio
I. Stampalia
MARE DI CANDIA
CANDIA
MIDDELANDSCHE ZEE
PASKAART Van de
ARCHIPELAGUSCHE EYLANDEN.
Naaukeurig opgestelt.

CANEA
INSULA CANDIA
Ejusque FORTIFICATIO edita per F. de Wit
5 10 15
Milliaria Germanica communia.
MARE DE
CERIGO INS:
Standia
CANEA
CANDIA
Nova Candia
TERRITORIUM
RETIMO
Lisa
Pianura
Masarea
MARIS MEDITERRANEI
GOZO
SPINA LONGA
RETIMO
Gedruckt tot Amsterdam by Frederick de Wit

Frederick de Wit (1610-1698): Dutch cartographer and publisher. He founded his firm in 1648 and was succeeded in it by his son, also named Frederick. The firm produced a series of world atlases: *Atlas Minor* (1670), *Zee Atlas* (1675), *Atlas Major* (1690), and others. In 1706, the firm was taken over by P. Mortier and later by J. Covens and C. Mortier.

88. F. de Wit: Map of Crete framed by its fortresses, hand-coloured copper engraving, 46 × 55 cms, 1680

Exactissima totius
ARCHIPELAGI
nec non
GRÆCIÆ
TABULA
in qua omnes subjacentes
Regiones et Insulæ
distincte ostenduntur per
NICOLAUM VISSCHER
Amstelo-Bat.
SERVIÆ PARS
BULGARIÆ PARS
GOLFO DI VENETIA.
La Bocca del Golfo di Venetia
MARE MEDITERRANEUM
IONIUM PELAGUS
MACEDONIA
EPIRUS
THESSALIA
ACHAIA
PELOPONNESUS
MOREA
Thermaicus Sinus Golfo di Salonichi
PELAGICUS SINUS
STRYMONICUS SINUS Golfo di Contessa
CORINTHIACUS SINUS bod. Golfo de Lepanto
SARONICUS MARE
ARGOLICUS SINUS bod. Golfo de Napoli
LACONICUS SINUS bod. Golfo de Colochina
Messeniacus Sinus Golfo de Coron
CYPARISSIUS SINUS bod. Golfo de l'Arcadia
EUBOEA Ins. qui et Macris et Abantias Salonike
NEGROPONTE
Cephalonia
Leucadia ins. bod. Santa Maura
Zacynthus bod. Zante
Cythera Isola Cerigo
Phæacia qui et Corcyra ins. bod. Corfu
Milliaria Italica Communia
Milliaria Germanica Communia

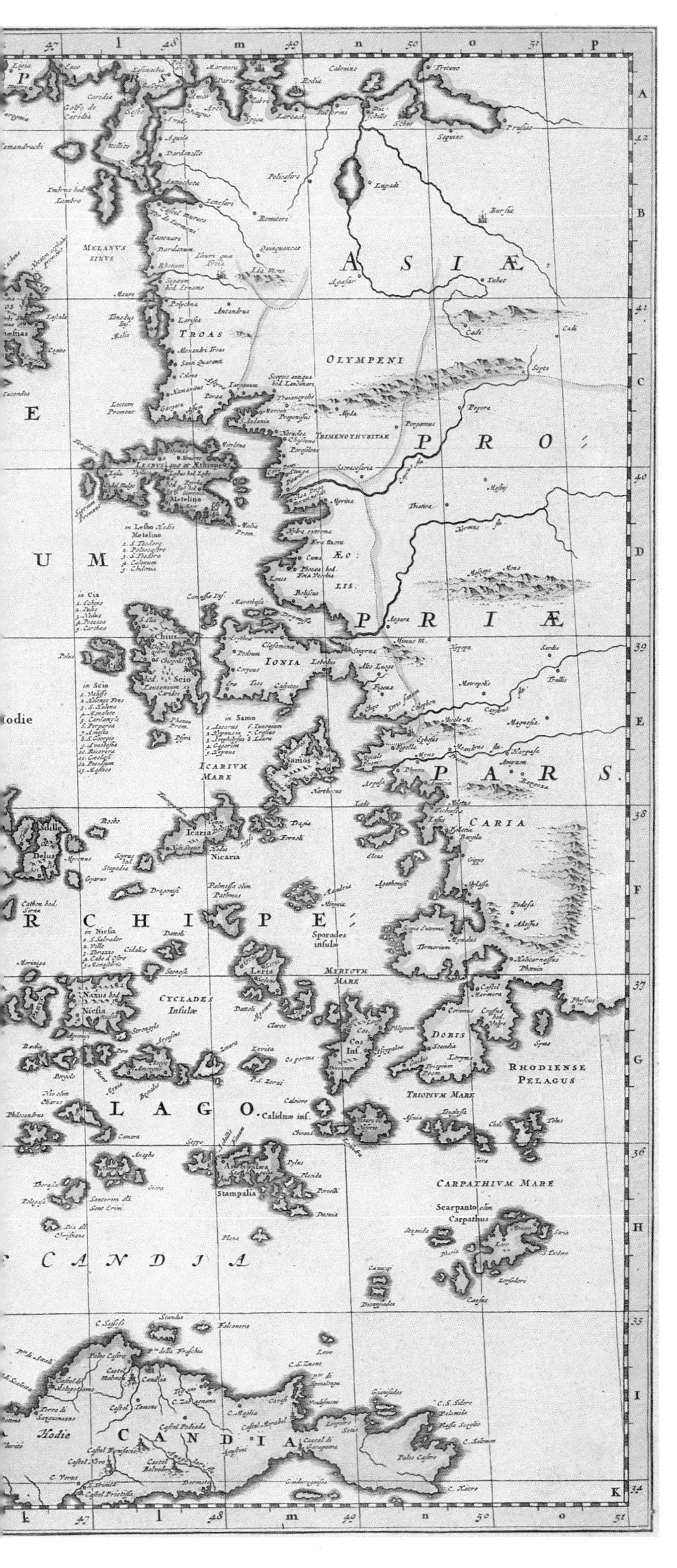

Visscher: a Dutch family of Amsterdam whose members were engravers and map publishers.

The family was founded by Claes Jansz(oon) (1587-1652), also known as Piscator. In the beginning, Claes worked for Hondius, and later set up his own business, in which he was succeeded by his son Nicolaes (1618-1679) and then by his grandson, who bore his name (1649-1702). The Visscher firm was very active in the publishing world, issuing a number of large maps and atlases, among which were the *Atlas Contractus* (1657), the *Atlas Minor* (1682-1716), the *Atlas Major* (1702) and the *Atlas Nova* (1638-1661).

89. N. Visscher: Map of the Aegean Sea, copper engraving, 50 × 46 cms, 1682

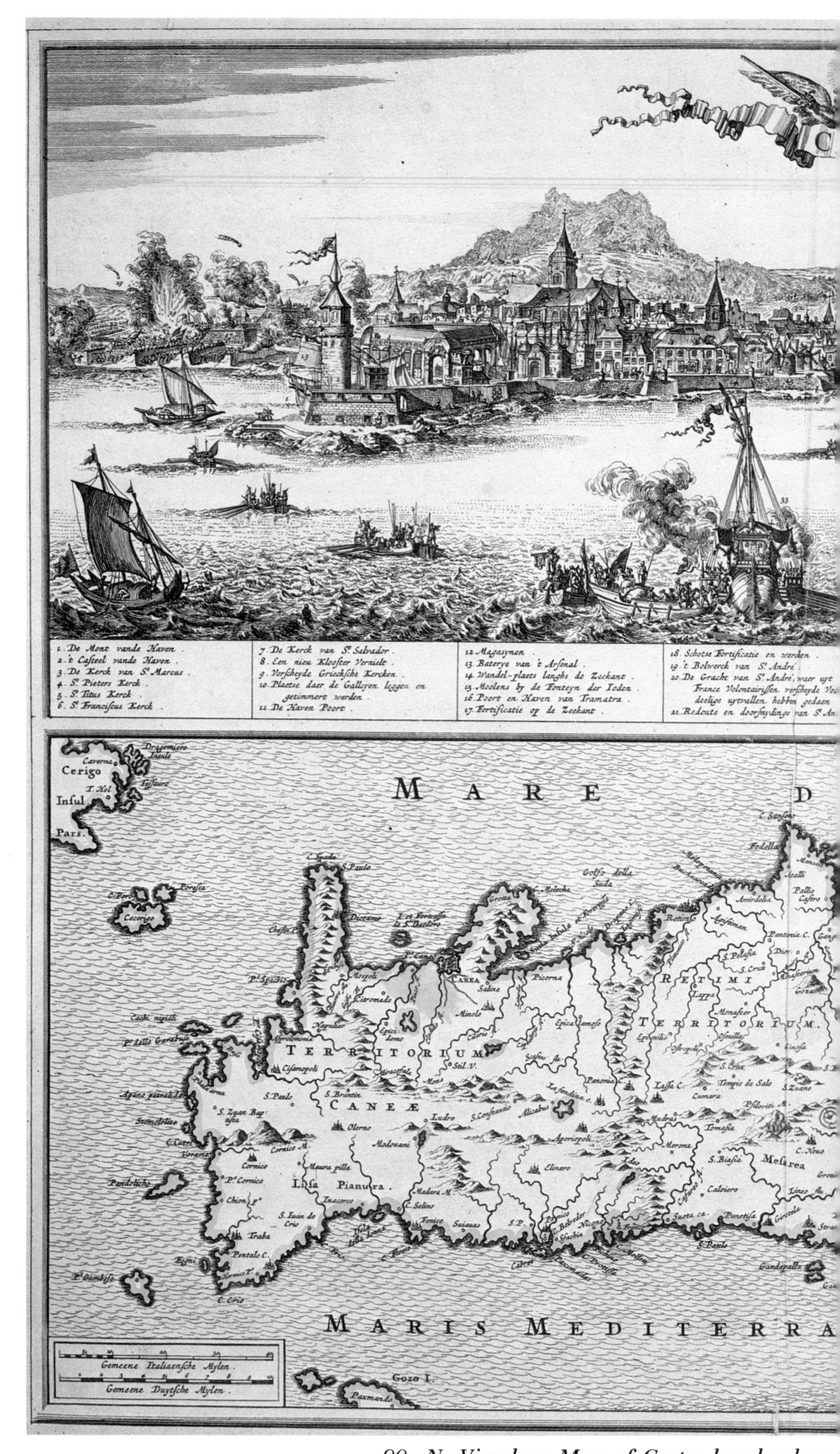
1. De Mont vande Haven .
2. 't Casteel vande Haven .
3. De Kerck van S.t Marcus .
4. S.t Pieters Kerck .
5. S.t Titus Kerck .
6. S.t Franciscus Kerck .
7. De Kerck van S.t Salvador .
8. Een nieu Klooster Vernielt .
9. Verscheyde Griecksche Kercken .
10. Plaetse daer de Galleyen leggen en getimmert werden .
11. De Haven Poort .
12. Magasynen .
13. Baterye van 't Arsenal .
14. Wandel-plaets langhs de Zeekant .
15. Moolens by de Fonteyn der Ioden .
16. Poort en Haven van Tramatra .
17. Fortificatie op de Zeekant .
18. Schotse Fortificatie en werken .
19. 't Bolwerck van S.t André .
20. De Gracht van S.t André, waer uyt
France Volontairissen verscheyde Voo
deelige uytvallen hebben gedaen
21. Redoute en doorsnydinge van S.t An
Cerigo
Insul
Pars.
Cecorigo
MARE D
Canea
TERRITORIUM
CANEÆ
RETIMI
TERRITORIUM.
Mesarea
MARIS MEDITERRA
Gozo I.
Paxmando
Gemeene Italiaensche Mylen .
Gemeene Duytsche Mylen .

90. N. Visscher: Map of Crete, hand-colour

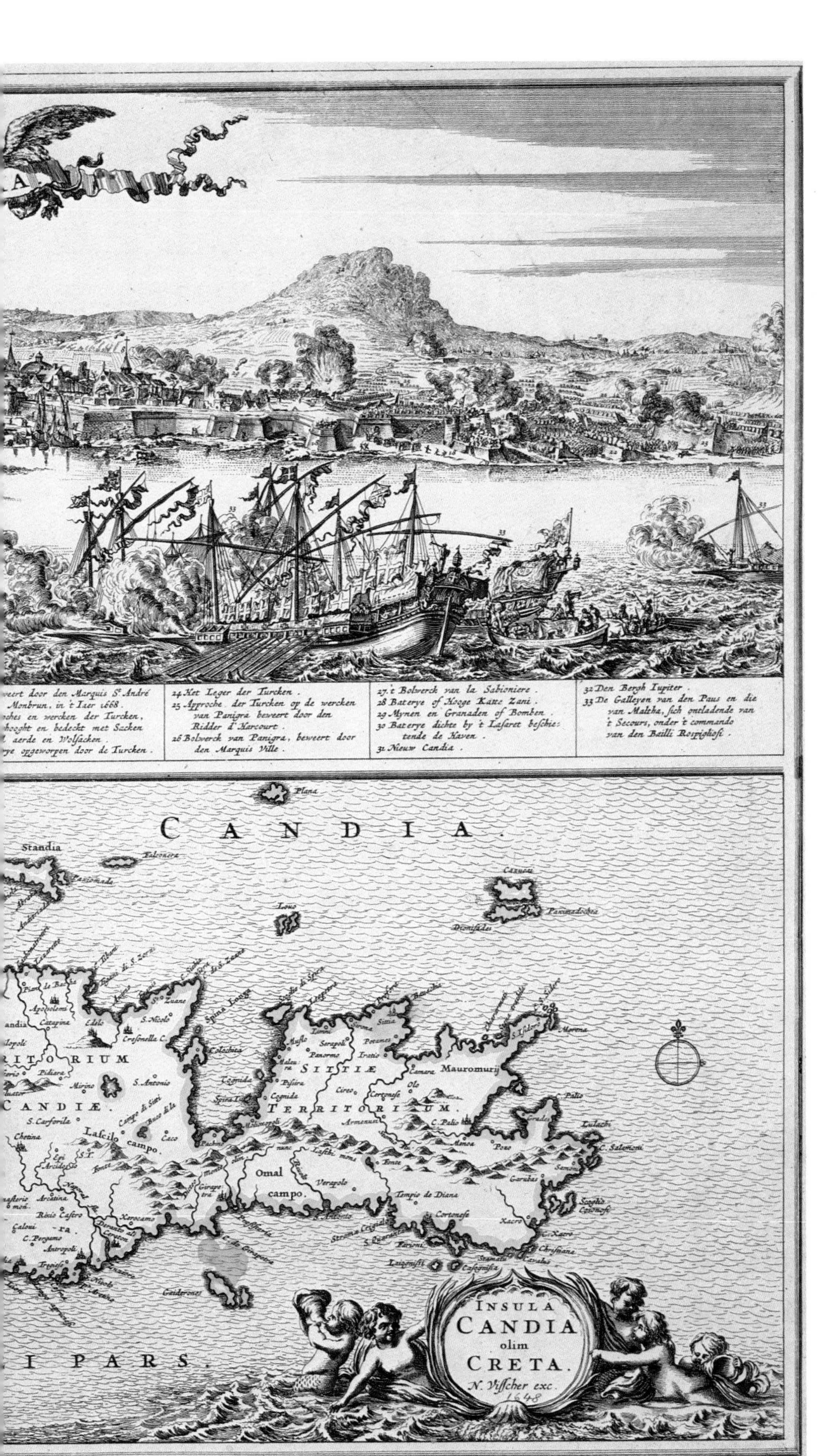
24 Het Leger der Turcken.
25 Approche der Turcken op de wercken van Panigra beweert door den Ridder d'Harcourt.
26 Bolwerck van Panigra, beweert door den Marquis Ville.
27. 't Bolwerck van la Sabioniere.
28 Baterye of Hooge Katte Zani.
29 Mynen en Granaden of Bomben.
30 Baterye dichte by 't Lasaret beschietende de Haven.
31 Nieuw Candia.
32 Den Bergh Iupiter.
33 De Galleyen van den Paus en die van Maltha, sich ontladende van 't Secours, onder 't commando van den Bailli Rospigliosi.
Plana
CANDIA.
Standia
Dionisades
SITTIÆ
TERRITORIUM.
Mauromurij
Omal campo.
Lasciti campo.
INSULA CANDIA olim CRETA.
N. Visscher exc.
1648
PARS.

pper engraving, 41.5 × 51 cms, 1682

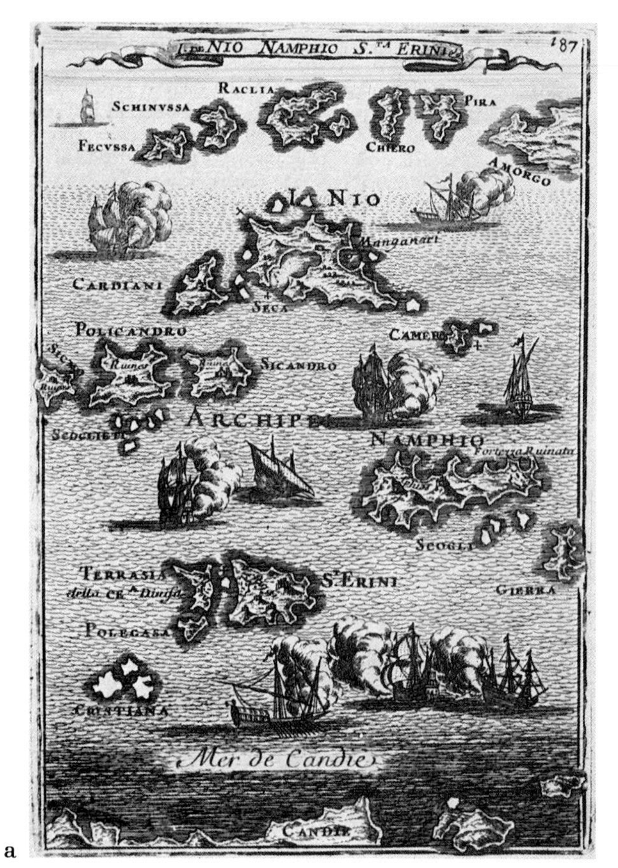

a

Alain Manesson Mallet (1603-1706), French engineer who served in the Portuguese army and later under Louis XIV. In 1683 he brought out a work entitled *Description de l' Univers* from which the maps shown here are taken. The book was in five volumes, and contained maps of the islands, views of cities and plans. It was published in German in 1688.

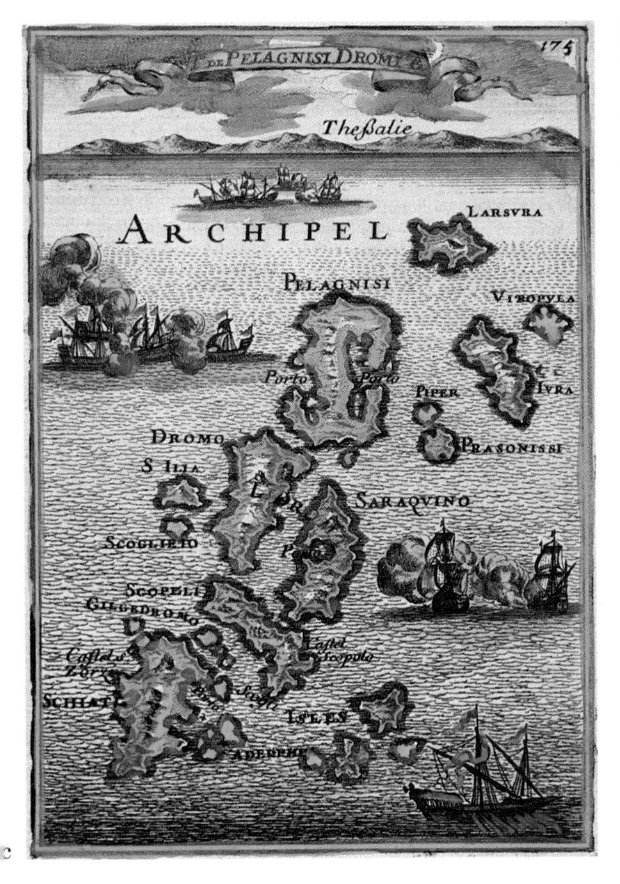

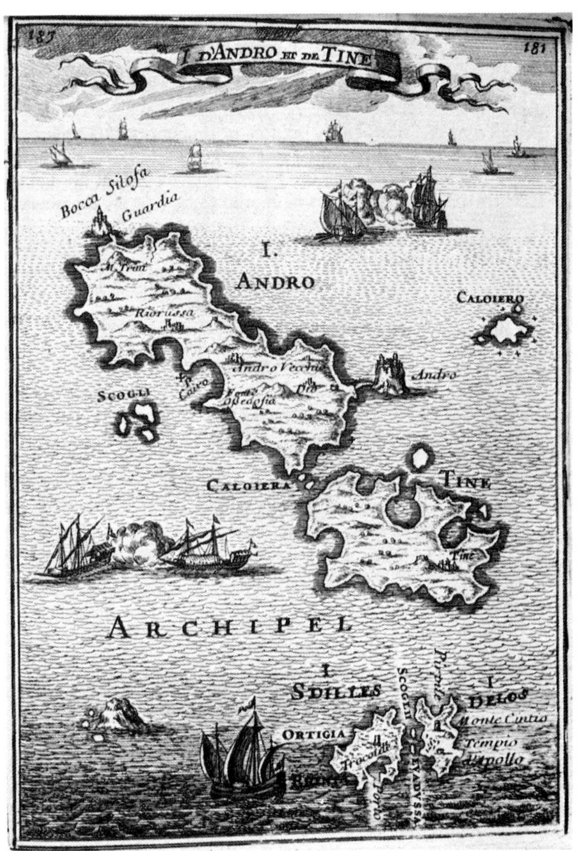

91(a). A. M. Mallet: Map of the islands of Ios, Anafi, Santorini, copper engraving, 15 × 10.5 cms, 1683
92(b). A. M. Mallet: Map of the islands of the eastern Aegean, copper engraving, 14 × 10 cms, 1683
93(c). A. M. Mallet: Pelagonisi and Alonnisos, copper engraving, 13 × 10 cms, 1683
94(d). A. M. Mallet: Map of the islands between Andros and Tinos, copper engraving, 15 × 10.5 cms, 1683

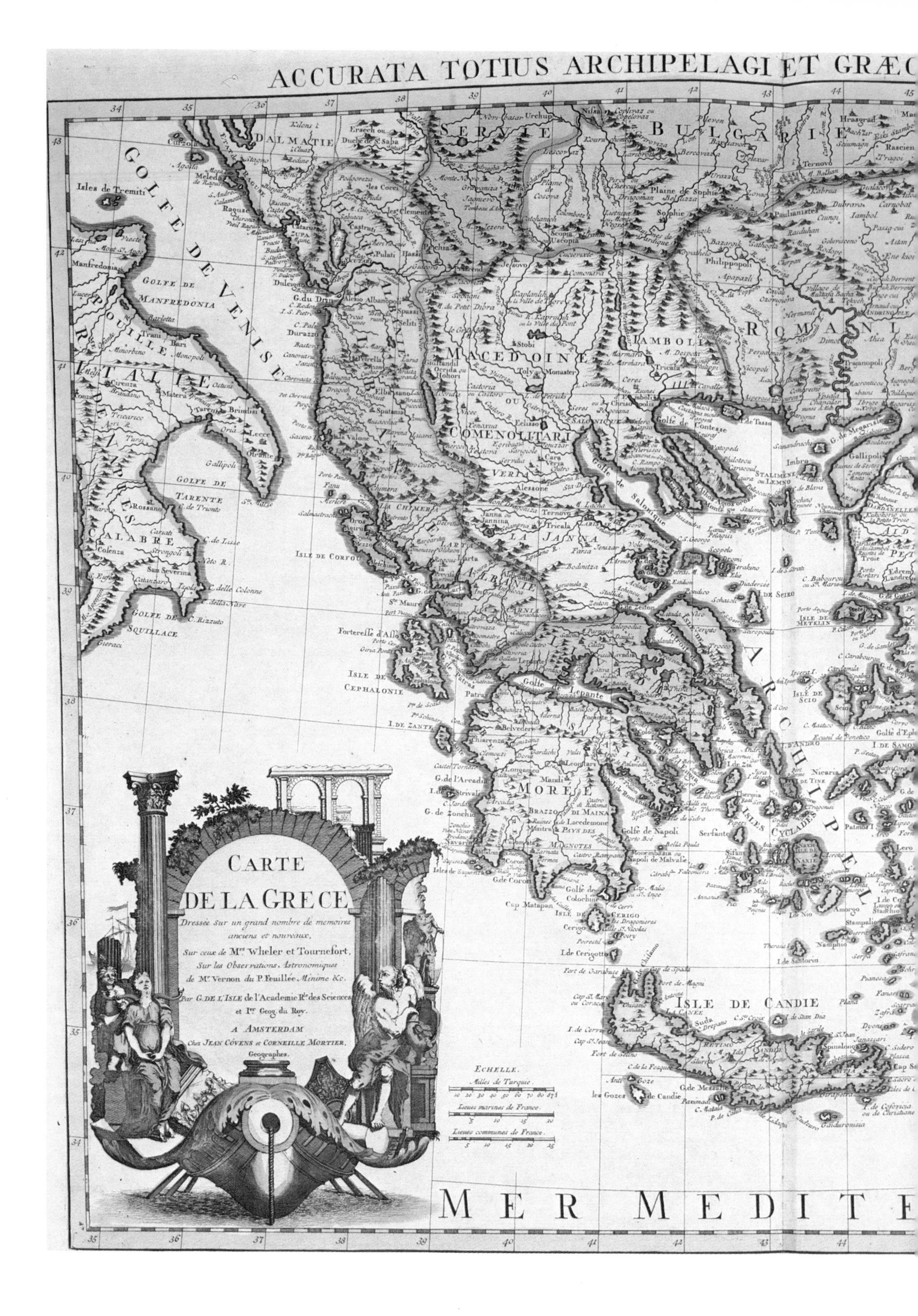
ACCURATA TOTIUS ARCHIPELAGI ET GRÆC
CARTE DE LA GRECE
Dressée sur un grand nombre de memoires anciens et nouveaux,
Sur ceux de Mrs. Wheler et Tournefort,
Sur les Observations Astronomiques de Mr. Vernon du P. Feuillée Minime &c.
Par G. DE L'ISLE de l'Academie Rle. des Sciences et Ier Geog. du Roy.
A AMSTERDAM
Chez JEAN COVENS et CORNEILLE MORTIER, Geographes.
ECHELLE.
Milles de Turquie.
Lieues marines de France.
Lieues communes de France.
MER MEDITE
GOLFE DE VENISE
ITALIE
MACEDOINE
ARCHIPEL
MOREE
ISLE DE CANDIE
ROMANIE
BULGARIE
SERVIE
DALMATIE
ALBANIE

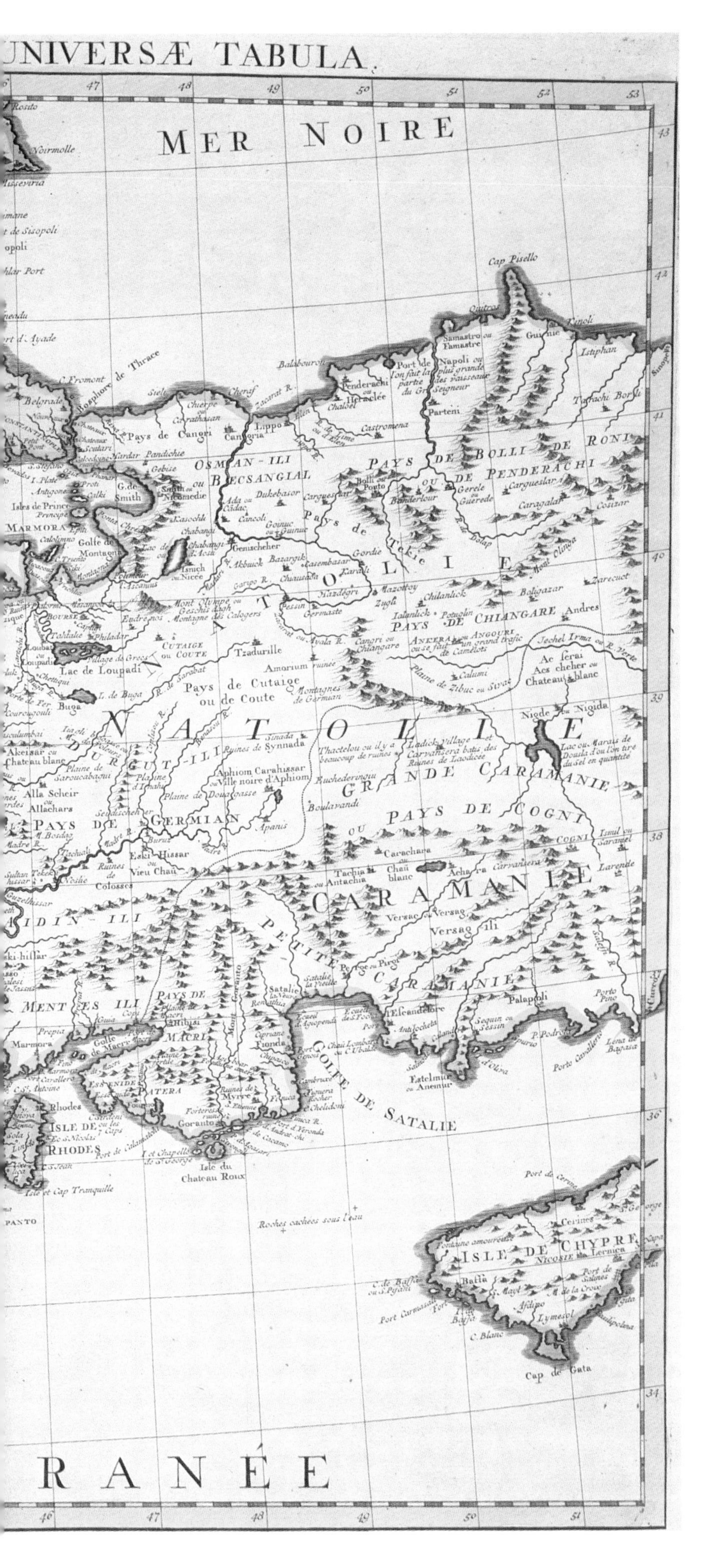

Guillaume de l' Isle or Delisle (1675-1726): a pupil of Cassini, he became known with his *Recueil d' Observations* of 1693. This was followed by maps of Asia, Africa and Europe, and a world map (1700). His total output amounted to some 100 maps, which were brought together in a volume published after his death by a number of firms: J. Covens and P. Mortier (Amsterdam, 1733), G. Abrizzi and Q. Girol (Venice, two volumes, 1740 and 1750), and his brother-in-law Philippe Buache, in France, in 1789.

95. G. Delisle: Map of Greece and the Aegean, hand-coloured copper engraving, 45 × 58 cms, 1683-1761

Giacomo Cantelli da Vignola (1643-1695): cartographer from Modena. Among his works are a four-leaf map of France (1691 and 1694), a map of Italy (1695), and of Brandenburg (1687). The map of the Aegean included here is from his *Mercurio Geografico* (1688), which also contained maps of Greece, Macedonia, Epirus, and the Peloponnese.

96. Giacomo Cantelli da Vignola: Map of the Aegean Sea, copper engraving, 55 x 43 cms, 1685

ARCIPELAGO MAR EGEO
con le coste del Medesimo
e l'ISOLE che in esso si ritrouano
descritto, con l'accrescim.to di uarie notizie
da Giacomo Cantelli da Vignola
Su l'esemplare delle Carte migliori
e con la direzione delle più accreditate
Relazioni
dato in Luce da Gio. Giacomo de Rossi
dalle sue Stampe in Roma alla Pace
con P. del S.P.
1685.
MACEDONIA
ROMANIA
MAR di MARMORA et PROPONTIS
Settentrione
Mezzo giorno
Ponente
Levante
IANNA
LIVADIA
ISOLA DI NEGROPONTE EVBOEA
SACCANIA
ANATOLIA o ASIA MINOR
MARE DI NICARIA
MARE DI MANDRIA
MARE DI SCARPANTO
ISOLA DI CANDIA ol CRETA
Golfo di Salonichi
Golfo di Contessa
Golfo di Monte Santo
Golfo d'Eno, ouero Golfo di Caridia o di Magarizo
Golfo d'Egina
Territorio di Canea
Territorio di Retimo
Territorio di Candia
Territorio di Setia
NOTE
M. Monte.
C. Capo.
P.ta Punta.
P. Porto.
fl. fiume.
S. Scoglio.
I. Isola.
L. Lago.
Scala di 60. Miglia Italiane

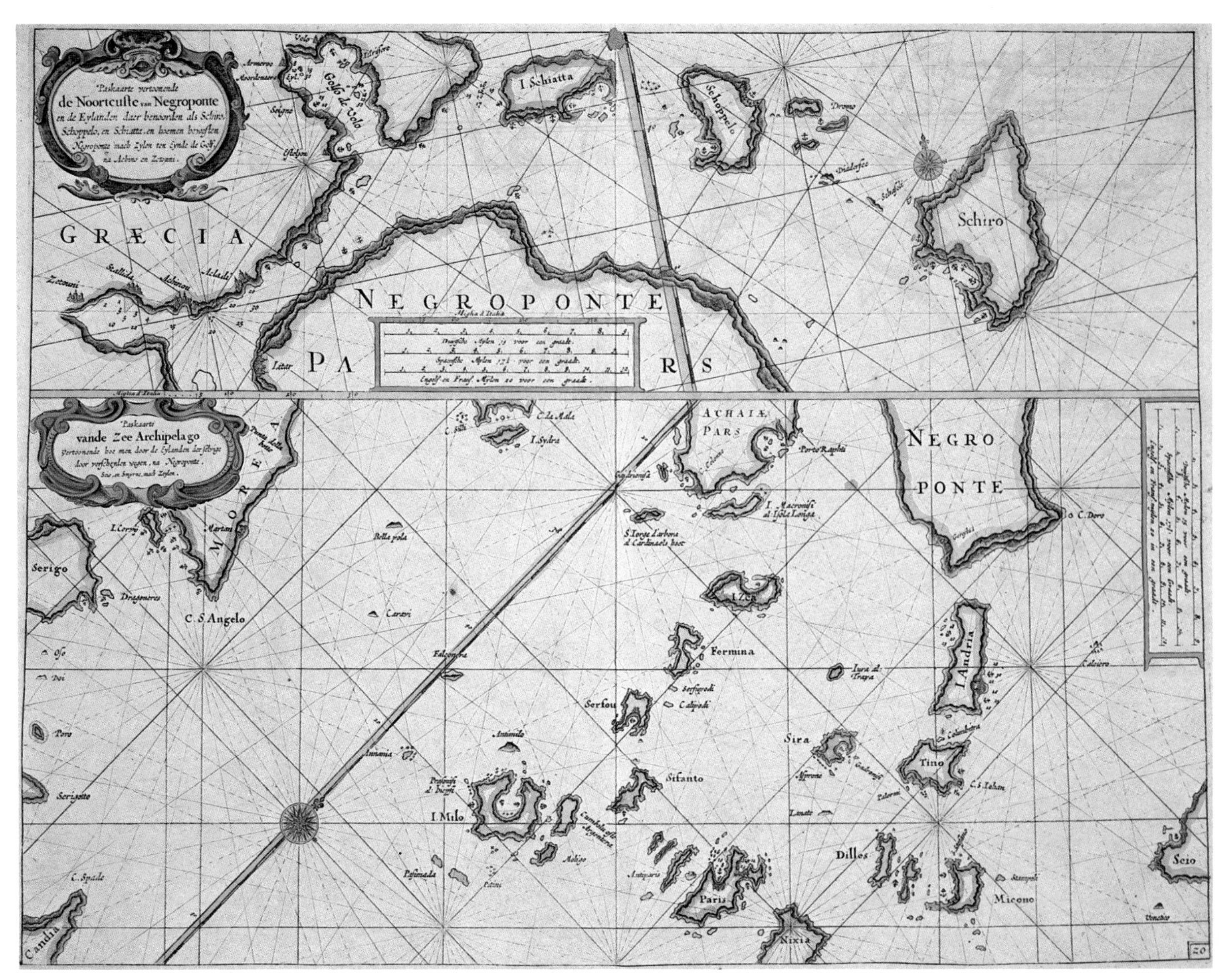

97. J. Robinj: Marine map of Euboea, Skyros, Skopelos, Skiathos, hand-coloured copper engraving, 52 × 40 cms, 1683

Jacobus Robinj (died *c.* 1710): Dutch hydrographer, painter and publisher, who lived at Amsterdam and worked for the van Keulen firm. Among his works are the *Zee Atlas* published in 1683 and again in 1688 and 1689 and the *Atlas de la Mer* of 1696.

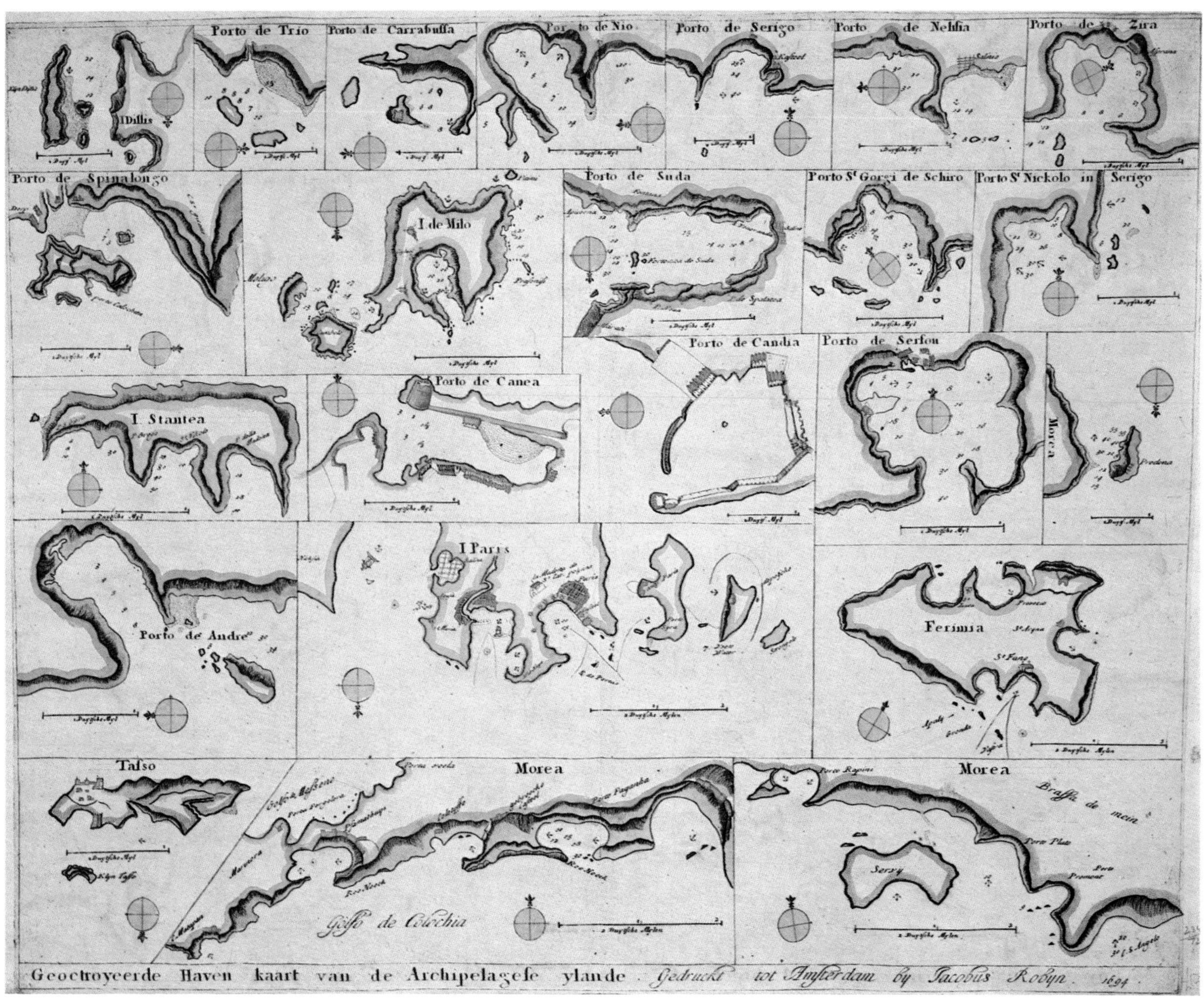

98. J. Robinj: Harbour chart of the islands of the Aegean, hand-coloured copper engraving, 42 × 53 cms, 1694

GRÆCIÆ PARS
Salonicha
Fanar
G. de Contessa
I. Tasso
C. Monte Santo
Limnos al. Stalimene
Scoppelo
Dromo
Diadorse
S. Sirati
Sciro
C. Sigiri
NEGROPONTE
Negroponte
Tronzo
Valia
Portimo
Tastura
Achaia
Calojera
Andria
Zea
Fermina
Sira
Serfou
Sifanto
Micono
Dilles
Nixia
Stenosa
Maixa
Nio
L. Milo
Pasimada
Bella pola
I. Sidra
Napoli Romania
Golfo de Napoli
MOREA
C. Matapan
I. Cervi
Sirigo
Oso
Doi
Poro
L'Ova
Perosa
Serigotto
C. Spade
I. Standia
L'Ovo
C.S. Ioan Baptista
Canea
Retimo
Candia
CANDIA
I. Calderoni
Antigozo
Gozo

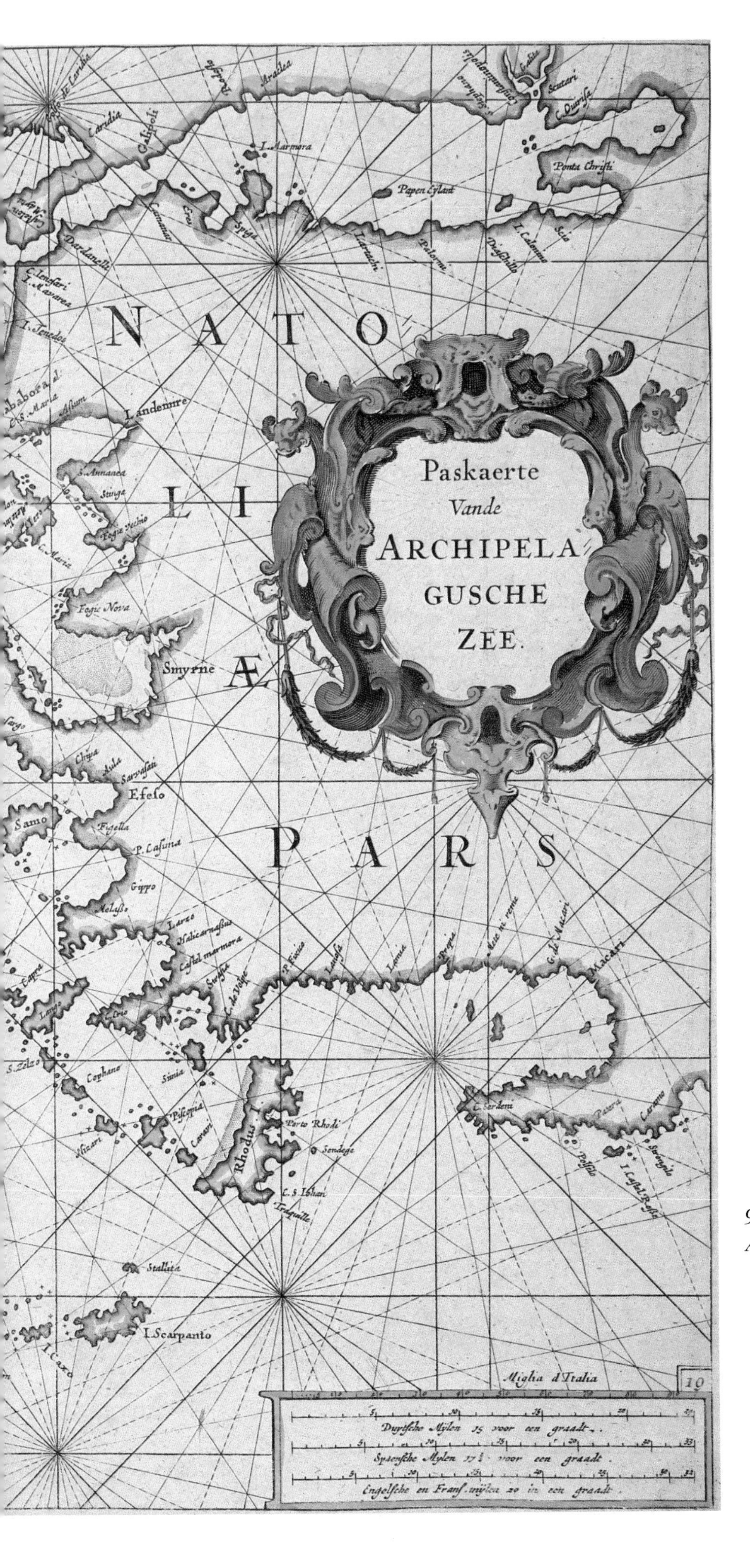

99. J. Robinj: Map of the Aegean, hand-coloured copper engraving, 40 × 51.5 cms, 1683

100. Map of the Aegean, copper engraving, 14 × 17 cms, 1686

The map of the Aegean (no. 100) forms part of the *Archipelagus Turbatus* (1686) and is the work of an unknown cartographer. The work, in sixteenmo, was issued by the German publisher Jacob Enderling during a war between Venice and Turkey. The map was reprinted in the same publisher's *Der hohe Berg Olympus...* (Augsburg, 1688).

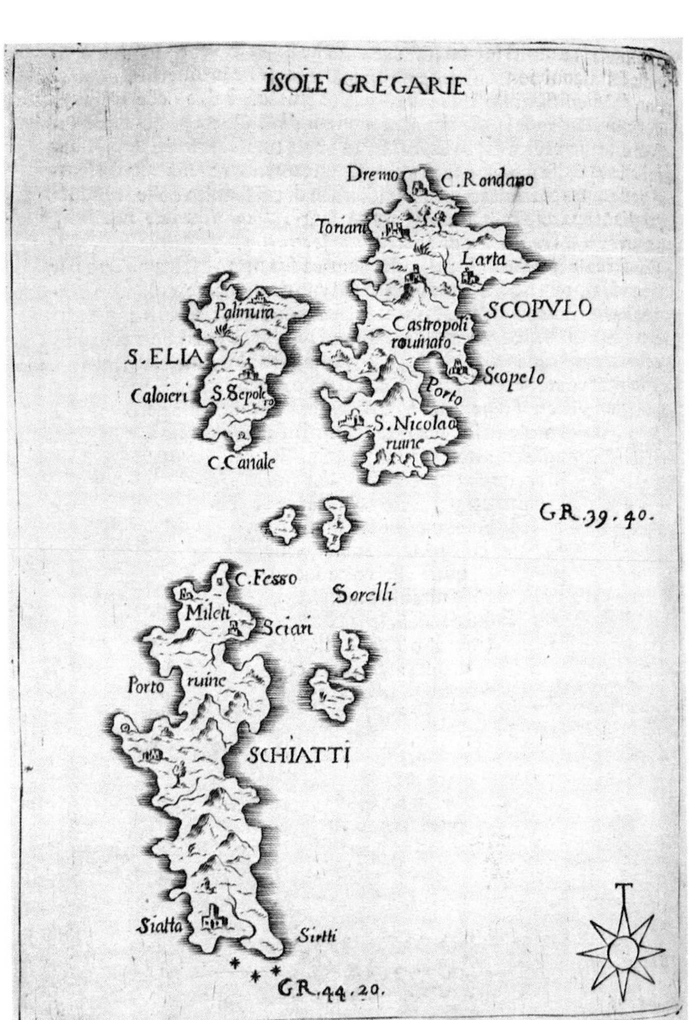

101. F. Piacenza: Map with the islands of Kalogeros and Kinaros, copper engraving, 17 × 12.5 cms, 1688
102. F. Piacenza: Map of the Sporades, copper engraving, 17.5 × 15 cms, 1688

Francesco Piacenza: Napolitan geographer who, in 1688, published at Modena a work entitled *L' Egeo redivivo o'sia chorografia dell' Arcipelago*. Dedicated to Duke Francesco II of Modena, the book contained 62 maps of the Greek islands and a map of the Aegean. Piacenza was influenced by earlier cartographers, and especially by Marco Boschini, in his drawing and in his choice of names.

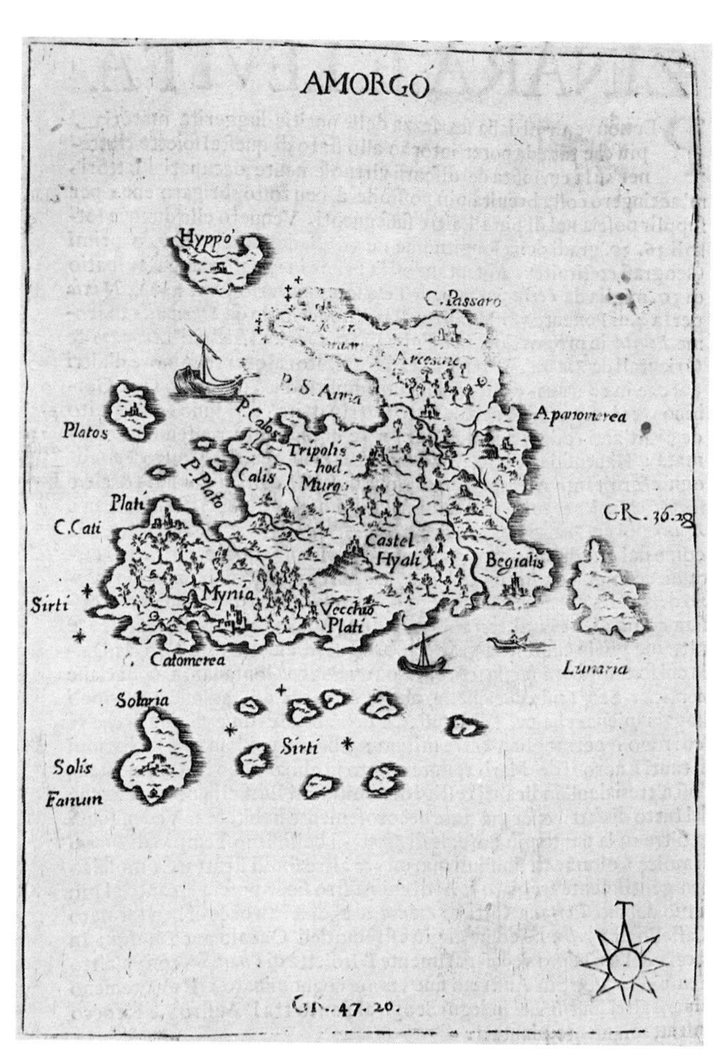

103. F. Piacenza: Map of Amorgos, copper engraving, 17 × 12.5 cms, 1688

104. F. Piacenza: Map of Mykonos, copper engraving, 17 × 13 cms, 1688

105. F. Piacenza: Map of the Aegean, copper engraving 18,5×14 cms, 1688.

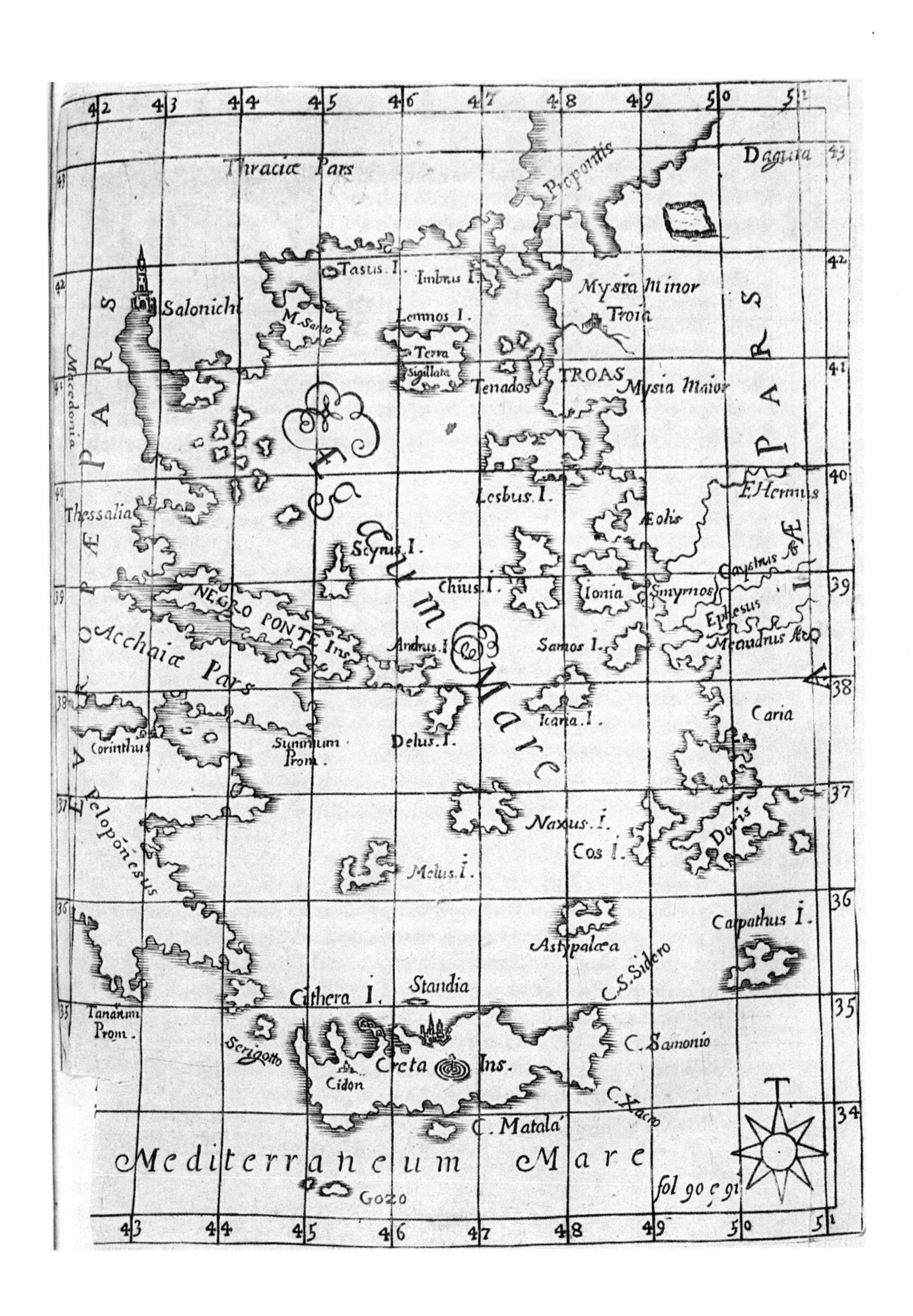
Thraciæ Pars
Propontis
Dagiua
Tasus. I.
Imbrus I.
Mysia Minor
Troia
Salonichi
M. Santo
Lemnos I.
Terra Sigillata
Tenados
TROAS
Mysia Maior
Macedonia
Lesbus. I.
F. Hermus
Thessalia
Æolis
Scyrus I.
Caystrus
Chius. I.
Ionia
Smyrnos
Ephesus
NEGRO PONTE Ins.
Andrus. I.
Samos I.
Meandrus
Acchaiæ Pars
Caria
Icaria. I.
Corinthus
Sunnium Prom.
Delus. I.
Naxus. I.
Cos I.
Doris
Peloponesus
Melus. I.
Carpathus I.
Astypalæa
C. S. Sidero
Cithera I.
Standia
Tanarum Prom.
C. Samonio
Serigotto
Creta Ins.
Cidon
C. Xacro
C. Matala
Mediterraneum Mare
fol 90 e 91
Gozo

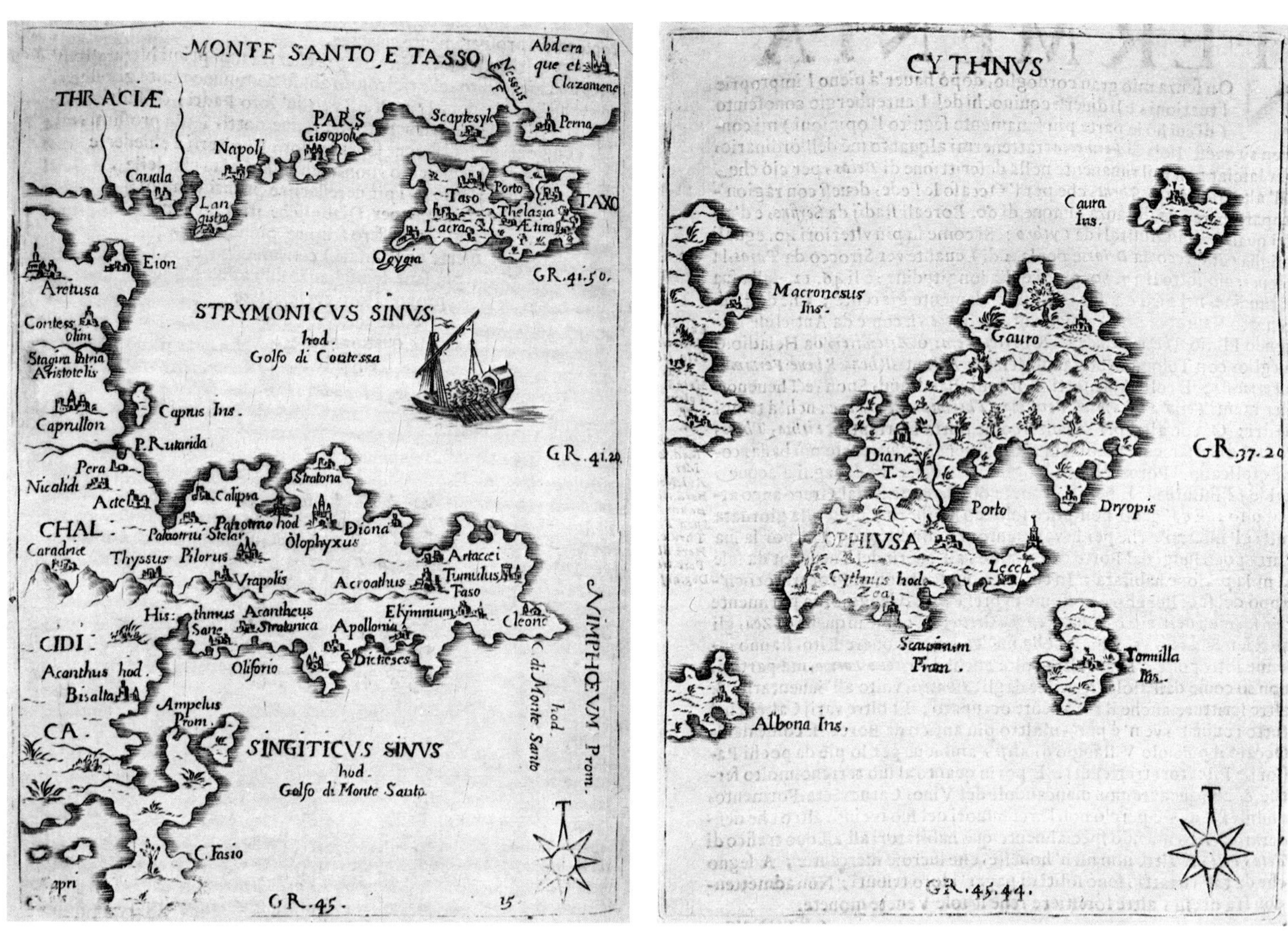

106. F. Piacenza: Mount Athos and Thasos, copper engraving, 17.5 × 12.5 cms, 1688
107. F. Piacenza: Map of Kythnos and Ophiousa, copper engraving, 17 × 12.5 cms, 1688

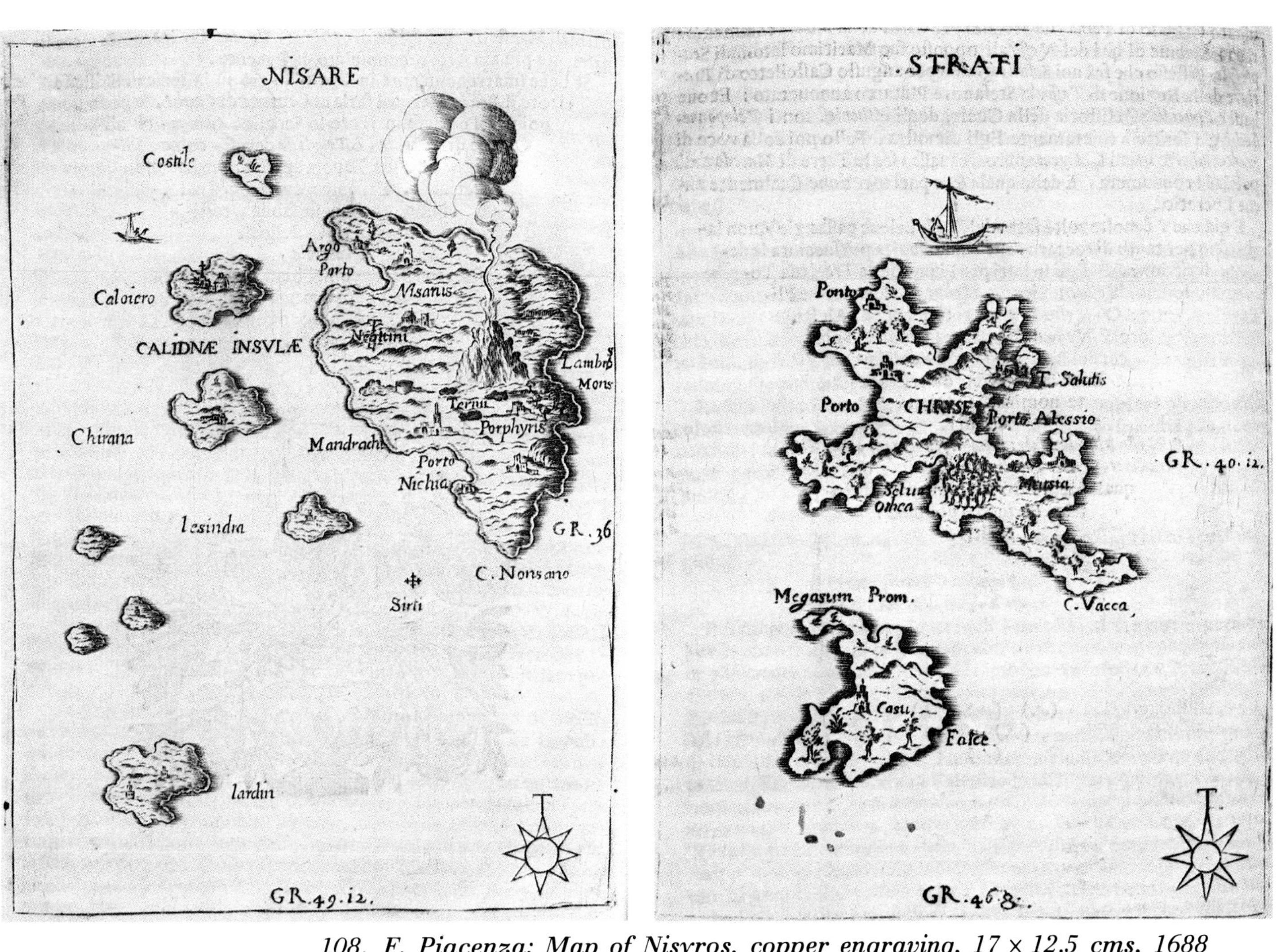

108. F. Piacenza: Map of Nisyros, copper engraving, 17 × 12.5 cms, 1688
109. F. Piacenza: Map of Ai Stratis, copper engraving, 17.5 × 15 cms, 1688

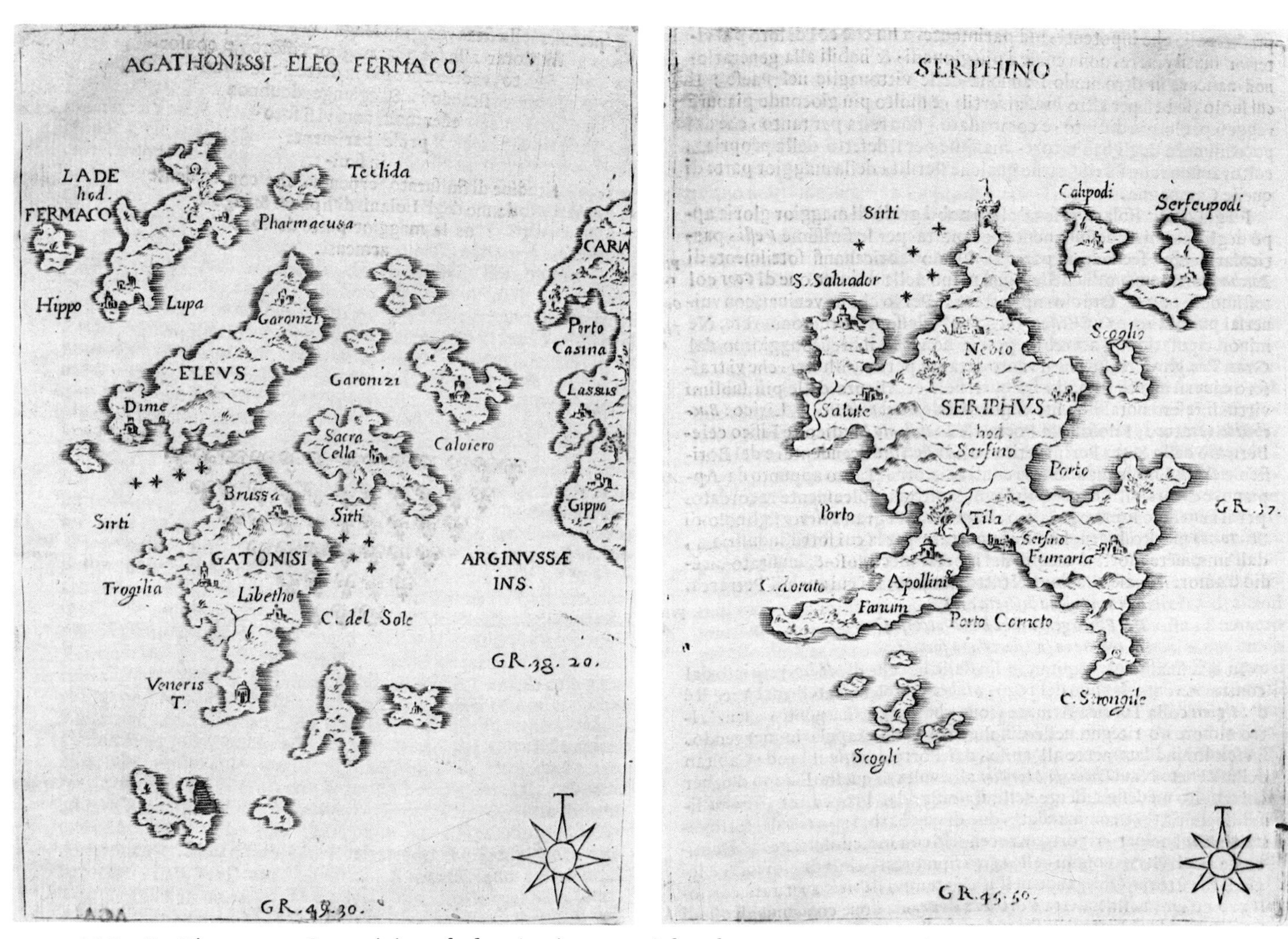

110. F. Piacenza: Gatonisi and the Arginouses islands, copper engraving, 17.5 × 13 cms, 1688
111. F. Piacenza: Map of Seriphos, copper engraving, 18.5 × 14 cms, 1688

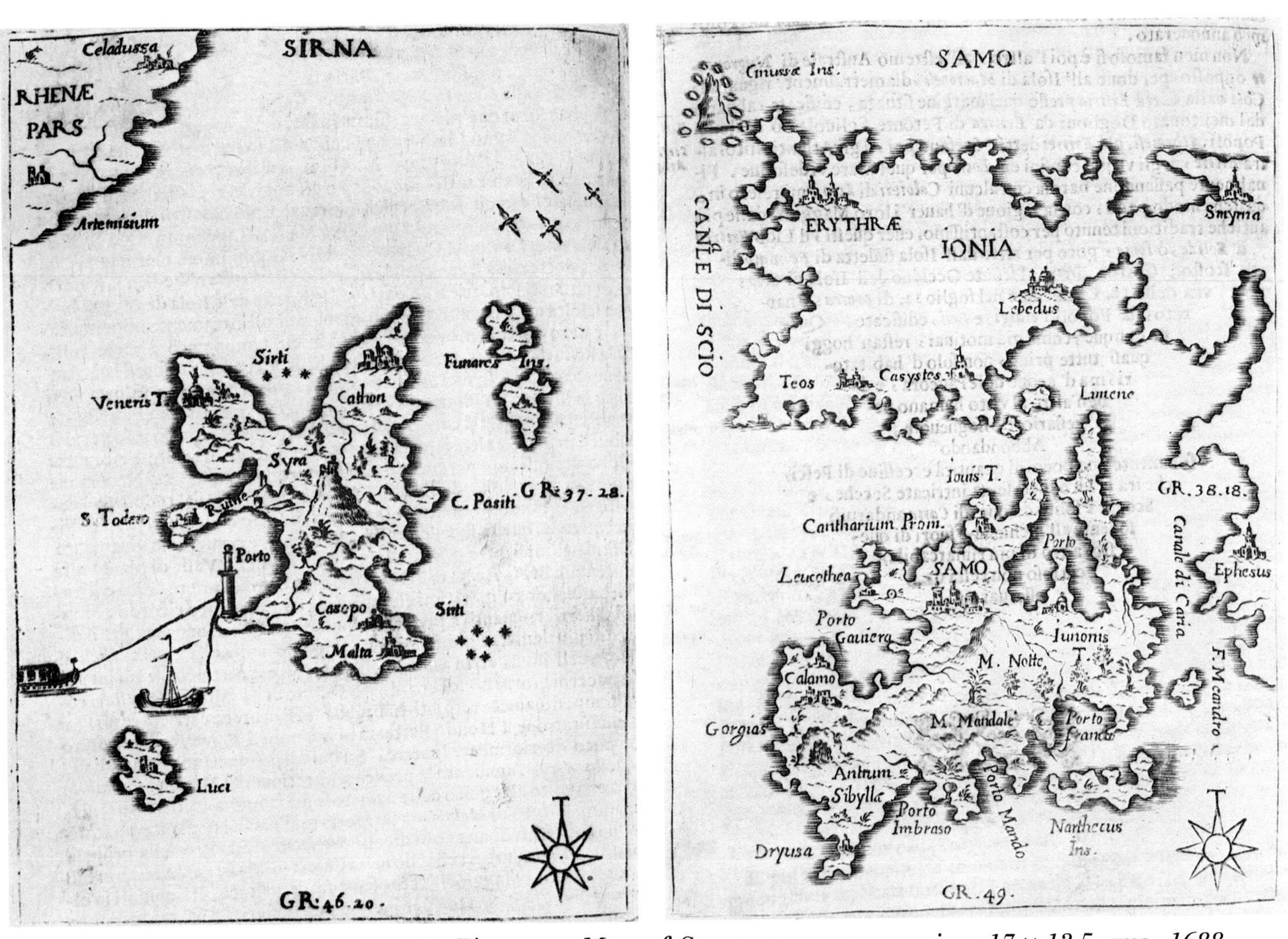

112. F. Piacenza: Map of Syros, copper engraving, 17 × 12.5 cms, 1688
113. F. Piacenza: Map of Samos, copper engraving, 17 × 13 cms, 1688

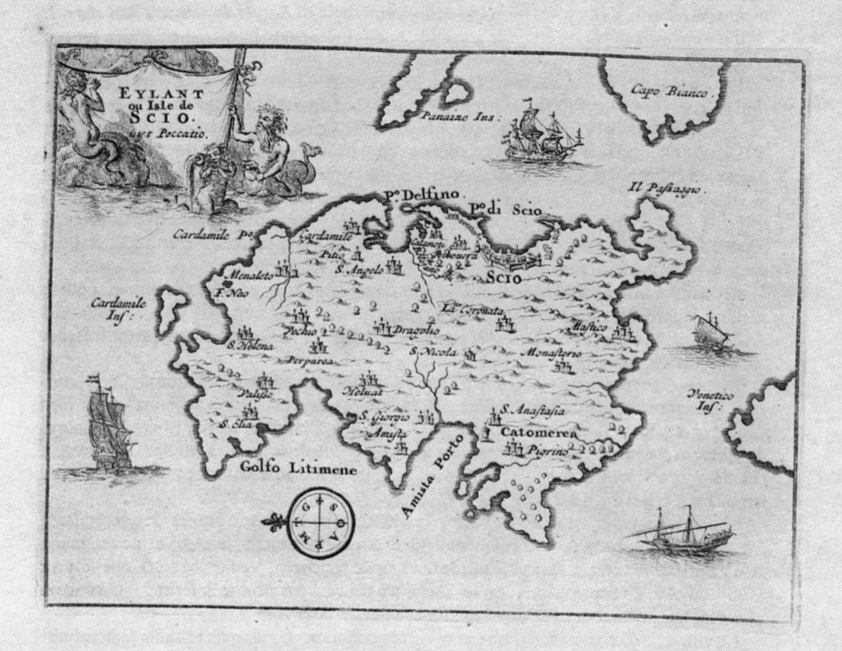

me à présent *Metelin*, vis-à-vis de l'ancienne ville d'*Erythre*, situëe sur la terre-ferme, & fort près ou à l'opofite de l'*Ionie*, Province de l'*Asie mineure*, dont elle n'est séparée que par un canal ou trajet étroit, entre les villes d'*Ephése* & de *Smyrne*.

Strabon fait le trajet de *Chios* à *Lesbos* de près de quatre-cents stades, & dit que le vent le plus-commode pour le faire est celui du Midi.

Elle a cent-vingt-trois miles d'Italie de circuit. Cependant il y a des Auteurs qui le font de douze, & d'autres de [1] soixante-trois miles plus-petit. *Strabon* lui donne neuf-cents stades de tour, en voguant autour de ses côtes.

Porcach. [1] Spon.

Pline le fait monter à cent-vingt-cinq-mille pas; mais *Isidore*, dans *Pline*, le fait de neuf-mille plus-grand. D'autres le posent de [2] cent-vingt-cinq lieuës d'Angleterre, ou de [3] trente de France.

[2] Sand. [3] Stokhovi

Elle est fort-élévée au dessus de l'eau, & s'étend en longueur du Septentrion au Midi.

On la divise en deux parties, dont l'une est apellée en Grec *Apanomerea*, ce qui signifie la partie haute, qui est situëe entre le Septentrion & l'Occident, & l'autre *Catomerea*, c'est-à-dire la partie basse, qui est situëe à l'opositede la précédente, un peu au dessous ou plus-bas.

Elle avoit anciennement une ville & un Château, apellé *Delphinium*, avec un bon port & une rade qui pouvoit bien contenir quatre-vingts-vaisseaux.

Strabon parle d'un port de *Chios* fort-profond, qu'il nomme *Phane*, mais dans *Ptolomée* & *Stephanus* on trouve un Cap désigné sous ce nom. Cependant il y peut avoir l'un & l'autre; car *Tite Live* nomm en un endroit *Phane* un port de *Chios*, & en un autre un Cap de cette île. Ce Cap est encore à présent nommé *Phanale* ou *Panale* par quelques Auteurs & par d'autres *Capo Masticho*. Le mot de *Phane* vaut autant à dire qu'*aparition*, parce qu'on conte qu'en cét endroit l'île de *Delos* commença à paroître à la Déesse *Latone*. *Strabon* met près de *Phane* un temple d'*Apollon* & un bois de palmiers.

Phane. Stephan.

Le même Auteur place, après le Cap de *Melene*, une contrée apellée* *Ariusie*, qui est rude, raboteuse, d'environ trente stades d'étenduë & qui n'a point de port; mais qui produisoit de son tems le meilleur vin de toute la Gréce.

* ou *Aruisie*. Herod.

La ville de *Chios* étoit une des douze villes de l'*Ionie*, de même que celle de *Samos*; mais elle

 étoit

Olfert Dapper (1636-1689). Flemish geographer for Amsterdam. In 1686 he published *Naukerige, Beschryving der Eilanden in de Archipel...*, a French translation of which came out in 1703, with the title *Description exacte des îles de l' Archipel...* Dapper himself never visited the places which he describes and depicts in his work. His sources were the works of well-known travellers and seamen's accounts. Of particular interest are his illustrations with copper engravings showing maps of the islands, islanders' costumes, plants and rare animals.

114. O. Dapper: Map of Chios, copper engraving, 1703

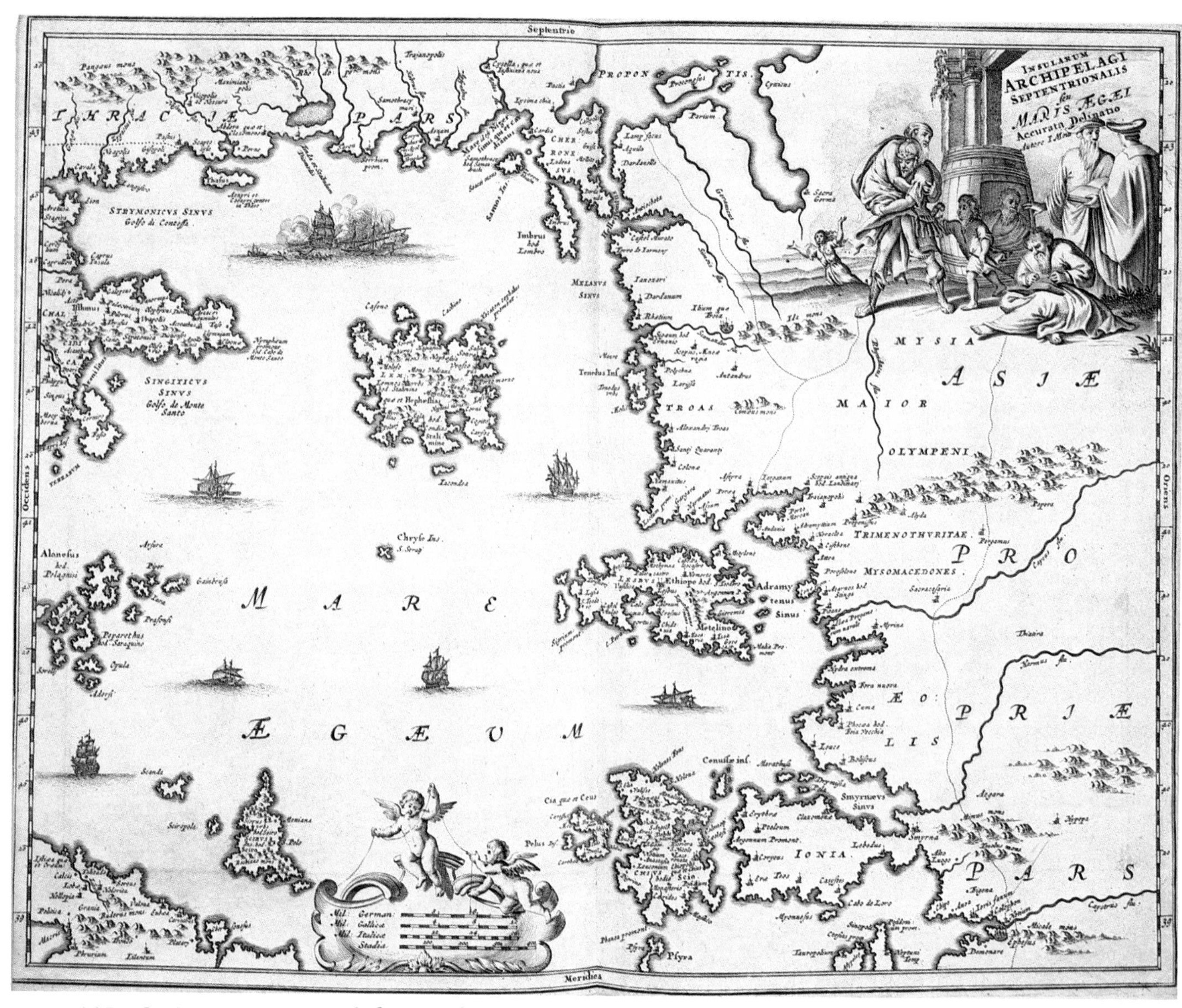

115. O. Dapper: Map of the northern Aegean, copper engraving, 36.5 × 30 cms, 1688

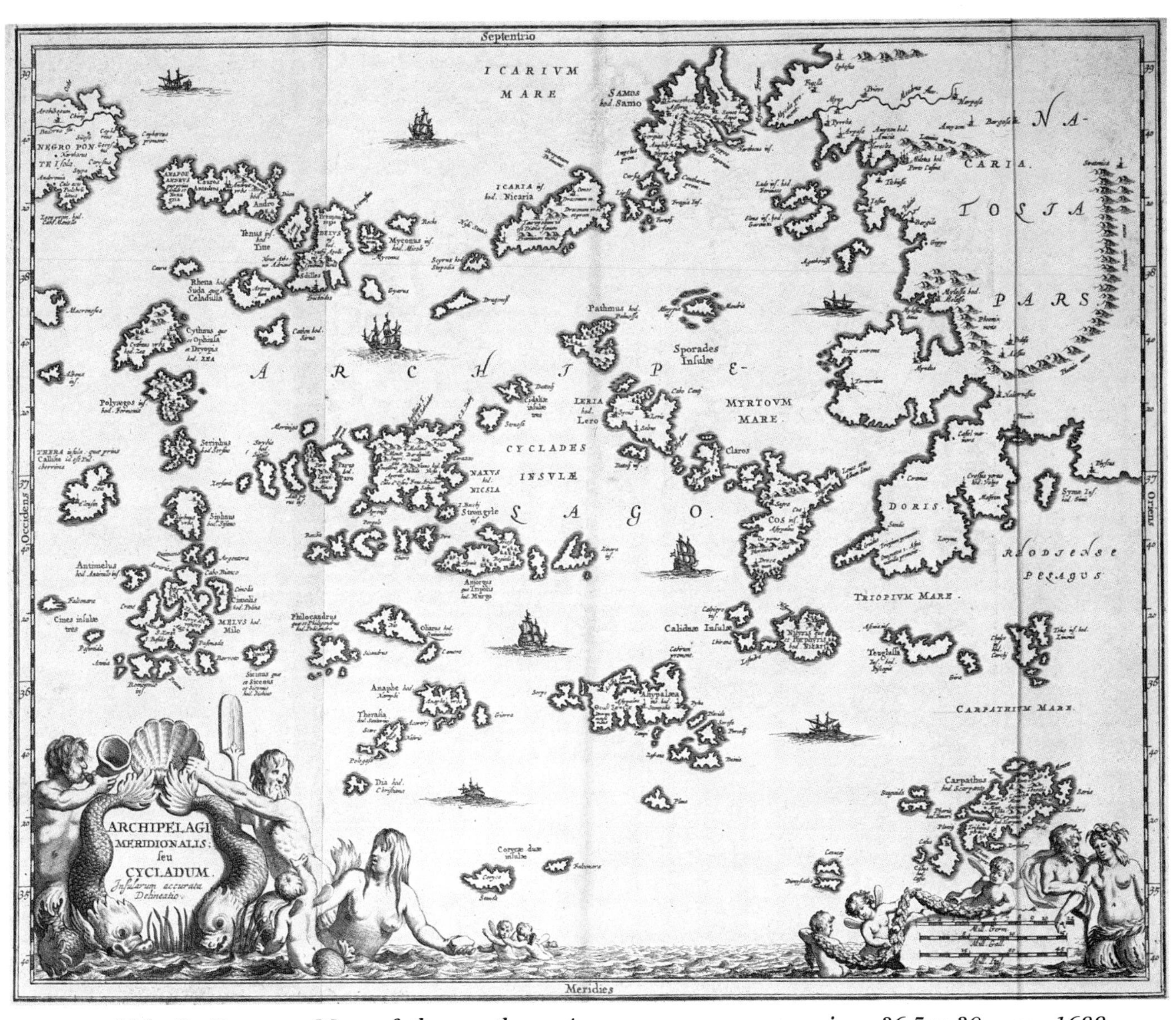

116. O. Dapper: Map of the southern Aegean, copper engraving, 36.5 × 30 cms, 1688

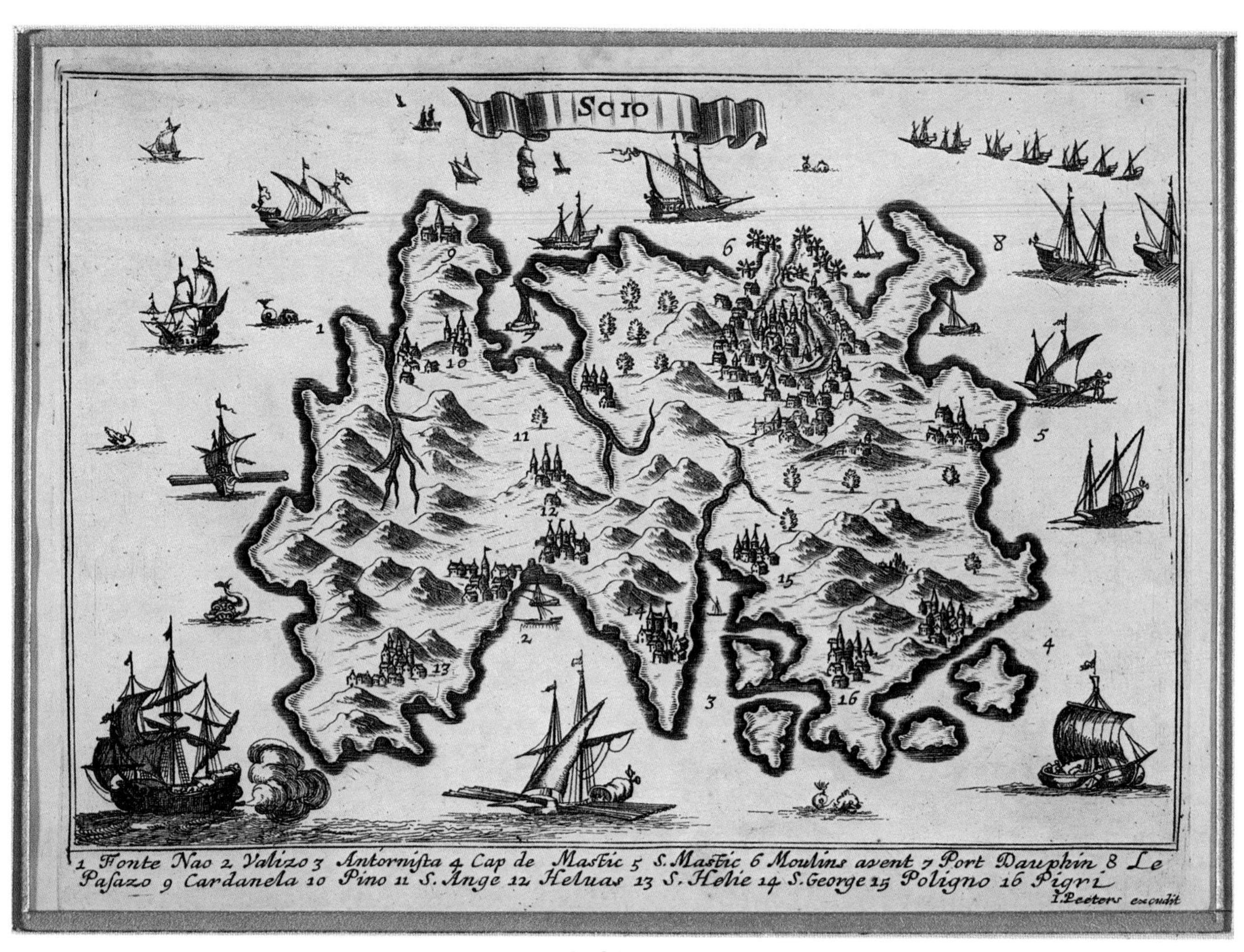

117. J. Peeters: Map of Chios, copper engraving, 13.5 × 20 cms, 1690

Jacobus Peeters (1637-1695): engraver and publisher, of Amsterdam. Maps of Cyprus, Tinos and Chios have survived from his *Description des principales villes, havres et isles du golfe de Venise... et des isles principales del' Archipel... 1690.* Apart from brief descriptive notes, the work contains 143 outstanding copper engravings, showing Greek cities and harbours and also containing maps of the Aegean islands. The book was dedicated to the Republic of Venice, shown on the title page as Mistress of the Mediterranean after its victory over the Ottoman Turks at the battle of Korone, 1685.

Also by Peeters was an *Atlas en abrégé* of 1692 and 1696.

118 J. Peeters: Map of Cyprus, copper engraving, 13.5 × 20 cms, 1690
119 J. Peeters: Map of Tinos, copper engraving, 13.5 × 20 cms, 1690

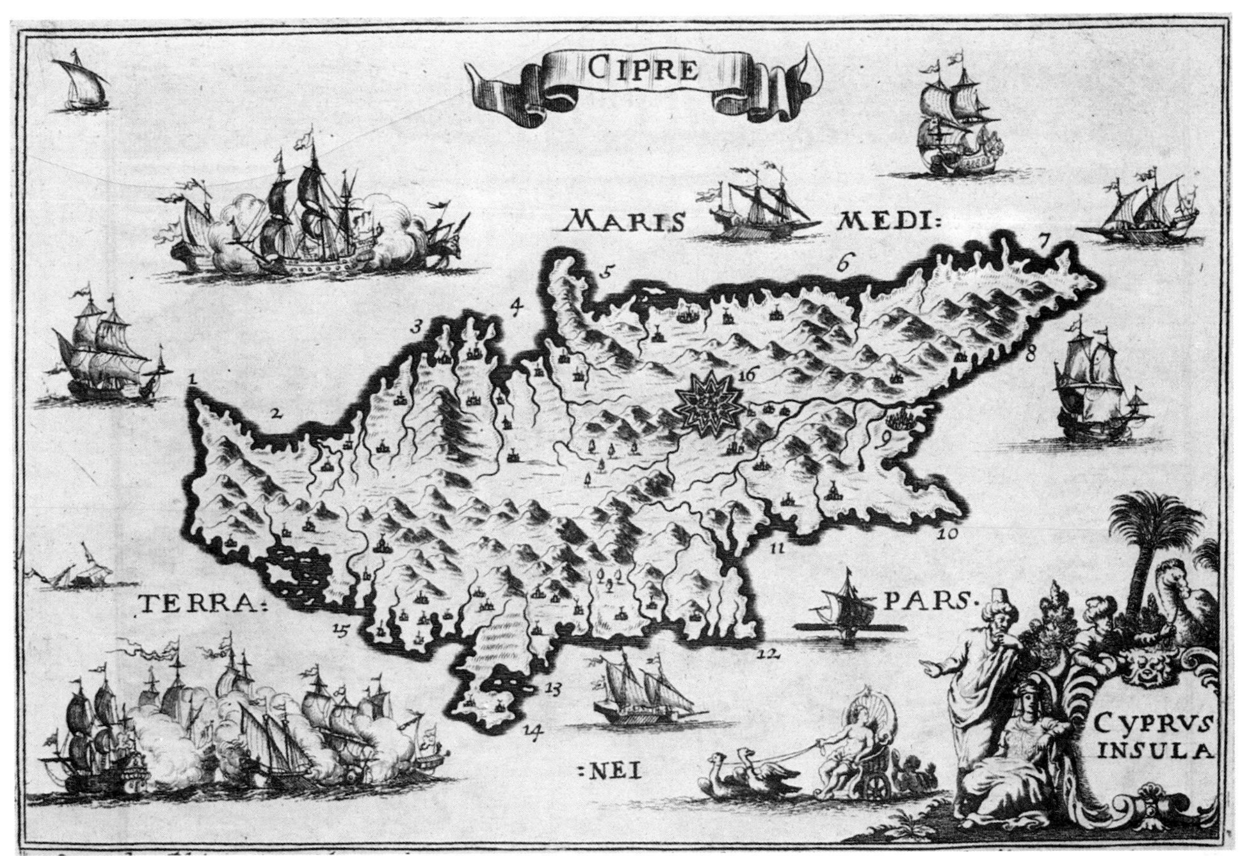
CIPRE
MARIS MEDI:
TERRA:
PARS.
:NEI
CYPRUS INSULA

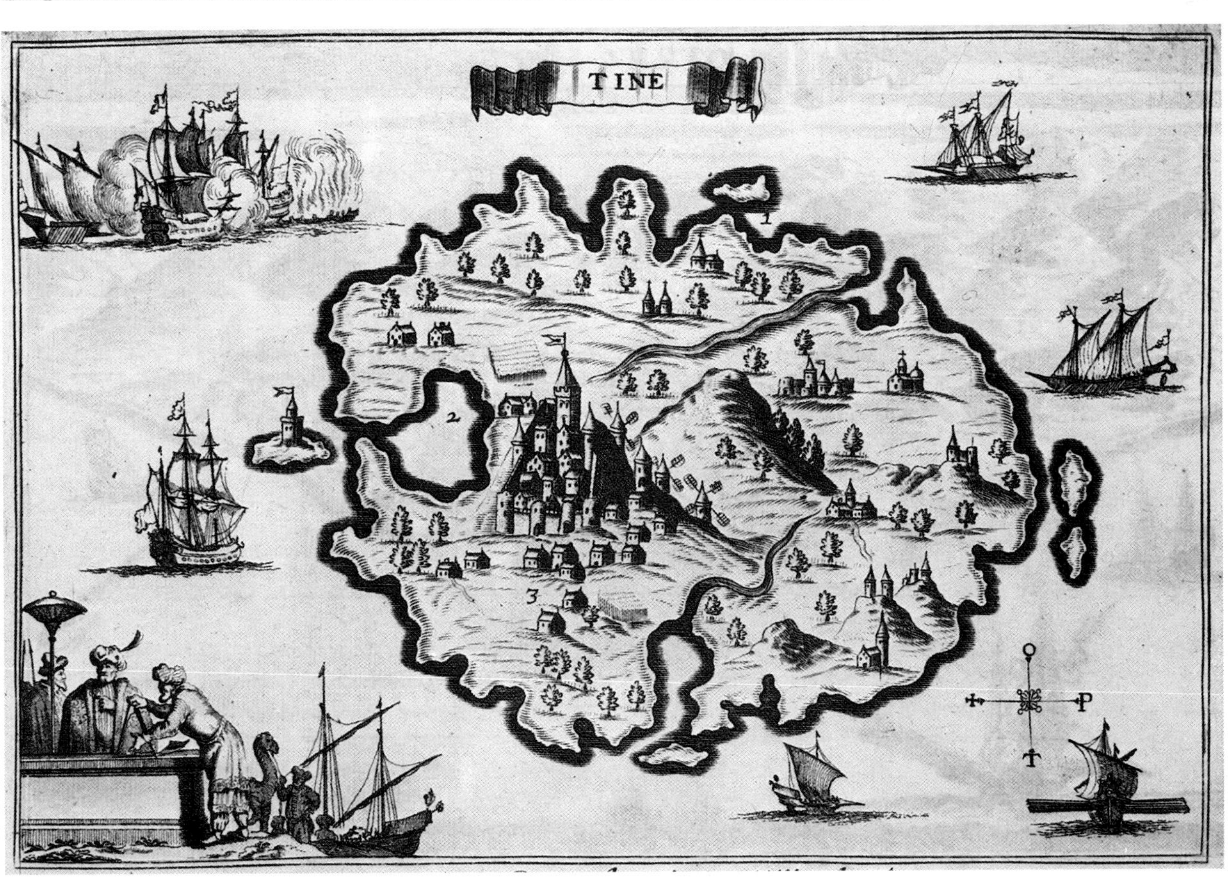
TINE

Prom. Pontadura, ed Apesfo. I Promontorj dell'Isola sono *Pontadura* à mezzo giorno, ed *Apesfo* à Maestro verso Settentrione, amendue elevati, ed alpestri dalla parte del Mare, mà dentro terra discendendo in amene Valli s'humiliano in delitiose pianure fertili d'ogni bene, in modo, che non solo basta al mantenimento degli Habitanti; mà ne sopravanza, e particolarmente Vini, e Moscati perfetti, da quali ritraggono utili considerabili, oltre il pagare col tratto di essi le solite rigorose contributioni a' Turchi, che godono anche i più dilettevoli divertimenti nella caccia de' Lepri, e delle Pernici, che in prodigiosa copia vi si trovano, ed invitano anche i Forestieri, qual' hor ve ne giungono à goderne. *Fertilità, e delitie.* Poco lungi dalla Città verso mezzo giorno si vedono le rovine dell'antica *Tenos* distrutta d'ordine d'Archelao, come riporta Nicostrato, ed ivi pur sono gli avanzi del gran Tempio di Nettuno, come alle Sponde Australi del Porto Reale quelle del Tempio d'Apollo. *Avanzi d'antichità pregiate.*

Trà le diverse Isolette, ed abietti Scogli, che sono d'intorno à quest'Isola, cospicue si rendono le *Maure*, ò *Macores*, hoggidì chiamate *Longestre*, e quattro di numero, benche Baudrand le metta due sole col nome di *Calydne*. La più vicina alla Natolia è *Sabalette*, dal Negro chiamata propriamente *Maure*. All'Occidente di questa *Oviaro*, ò *Oviaros*, dove sussistono riguardevoli avanzi d'un Tempio già consacrato ad Apollo, ed in cui à riporto di Nicostrato celebravansi ogni Olimpiade con gran dispendio i Giuochi Hecatesi. Al Ponente Maestro d'*Oviaro* giace *Lengrino*, ò *Forino*; & à Mezzo giorno di tutte *Lanura*, e *Martere*. Nicostrato dice, che servivano alle delitie della Nobiltà Trojana, mentre la prima non arriva ad essere trè miglia lontana da quelle Sponde, e poscia da ristretti Canali sono state una dall'altra divise; e soggiugne il medesimo, che i Greci affatto le rovinassero, perche non sussistessero memorie della Trojana grandezza. In effetto vi sono vestigie di gran fabbriche, e se il timore de' Corsari non li distraesse, vi stanzierebbero molti, che vi vanno à stare di passaggio per raccoglierví mele, di cui sono abbondantissime, e così pure i Pescatori, che vi passano dal *Tenedo*, e dall'Asia in certe stagioni per prendervi Delfini, che ci abbondano, e da essi ne cavano olio non solo per proprio uso, mà anche da vendere con molto profitto. *Canale del Tenedo abbondante di Delfini.*

C A L O J E R O.

Molte Isole col nome di Calojero. PIù d'un' Isoletta col nome di *Calojero* si trova nell'Arcipelago, parte comprese frà le Sporadi, parte trà le Cicladi, altre trà le Neutrali. Quella, che quì prendiamo à descrivere, viene da molti affermato, che sia una dell' *Isole Calidne*, che sono al numero di trè connumerate da Plinio, Strabone, Homero, ed altri frà le prime. *Isole Calidne.* Altri vogliono, che sia situata frà l'Isola d'Andro, ed il Capo d'Oro di Negroponte, stimandola l'Isoletta *Gyarus*, ò *Gyaros* da Strabone, e Plinio chiamata; da Paesani *Joura*, ò *Jura*; mà questo nome, che la distingue, ne fà anco dubitare. *Sito del Calojero.* *Opinioni diverse sopra il numero delle Calidne.* Dicono altri, che *le Calidne* fossero due sole, ponendole poco lungi dal *Tenedo*, verso la Natolia col nome di *Maure* chiamate. Vi è chi ne mette una sola nel Mare Mirtòo, frà Guido, e Stampalia, ch'il Bochart dice fosse chiamata *Calymnia* per l'abbondanza del mele, che vi si trova; poiche *Calymna* in lingua Fenicia vuol dire *Dulcis sedes*, ed in Hebreo *Chali-tina* significa *Dulcis rupes*. *Opinione del Laurembergio.* Il Laurembergio però, ed altri mettono *le Calidne* trà Nisiro, e Stanchiò, co' nomi di *Lisndra*, *Chirana*, e *Calojero*; e gli Atlanti vi aggiungono *Costile*.

Figura di Calojero. Stravagante è la figura di quest' Isoletta, poiche dal piede fino alla cima è tutta inaccessibile; e pure vi è, chi afferma havesse circa 12 miglia di circuito, e da' Francesi viene chiamata per ironia *le Bon Vieillart*, cioè il *Buon Vecchio*, perche cuoprendo coll'acque le sue radici, i Vascelli ingannati, credendo trovarvi sicuro l'approdo, vanno à perire trà que' duri scanni. *Nomi differenti.* Altri anche la nominano *Pania*, *Panagea*, *e Panaja*. S'inalza egli dunque dal Mare tutta scoscesa, dirupata, e grebanosa in modo, che per salirvi alcuni huomini divoti, che cercavano la solitudine, convennero aggrapparsi come Capri; mà nella cena trovata una cōmoda, e deliciosa pianura, pensarono di farvi stanza. *Suoi Diru-pi.* Alla metà dunque della sua altezza s'imaginarono mettere un' Argano con attaccarvi una Barchetta, dentro alla quale discendevano à procurare nell' Isolette vicine quello, ch'il Terreno alpestro non poteva provedere, e colla medesima risalivano. *Habitata da trè Romiti.*

Così per lungo tempo vi si mantennero trè soli Romiti, i quali per non essere da qualche invidia ingannati, havevano anche frà essi un contrasegno di sibilo stabilito, col quale quei, ch'andavano con la Barchetta limosinando, quando tornavano, facendosi conoscere, venivano accolti, e con la Barchetta rialzati. *Barchetta per salire nel Calojero.* Alcuni barbari Ladroni però, imaginandosi, ch'ivi potessero raccogliere delle ricchezze, s'ingegnarono à falsificare la Barca, gli Habiti, ed il fischio; e così verso la sera, in tempo, che sapevano dover ancora qualche poco tardare il Cercante al ritorno, in mentita divisa entrarono nella Barchetta, e tirati in alto, trucidarono i due poveri Romiti, e spogliato il luogo di quanto vi era, tornarono à discendere; mà mentre credevano ritornare alle loro Habitationi colla preda, con improvisa tempesta per giusto castigo del Cielo restarono ingojati dall'onde. *Come assassinati, e trucidati da alcuni Ladroni.* Così giunto il Cercante alla Barca, nè trovato chi lo rialzasse, restò per lungo tempo dishabitato. *Morte degli Assassini.* Vi ritornarono poi altri Romiti, come tuttavia vi sono, i quali vengono anche, come huomini di santa vita rispettati, servendosi pure questi dell' artificio della Barchetta per salire, e scendere; ed essendo nelle rupe di que' sassi nidi di grossi Falconi, si profittano colla preda di questi, e donandoli, ne ritraggono in ricompensa proviande per il loro alimento. *Altri Romiti tornarono à rihabitarvi.*

All' Austro di Andro è un'altra Isoletta, pure *Calojero* nominato, perche in picciolo Romitaggio vi si trattiene un Calojero. *Isole differenti col nome di Calojero.* Tolomeo chiamò *Atlantes Nesum* un' altra Isoletta al Promontorio Ceneo di Negroponte situata, ch'il Negro nominò *Calojero*, e da Baudrand tenuta l' *Atlante* di Plinio, hoggidì chiamata *Talanta* nell'Euripo. Altra ve n'è vicino à Tine, dove pure due Eremiti si trattengono, ed altra nel Canale frà la Caria, e l'Isole Arginusse; e per la quarta di Garbino verso Austro all' *Isola di Policandro* una di 5 miglia di circuito; mà deserta, e solo piena d'Uccelli, e Cervi. Al Maestro di Leria una simile habitata da un Calojero. Una dishabitata alla fronte Occidentale di Nixia. Finalmente all Austro di Dromivi è pure una vaga Isoletta, chiamata *Calojero* con Eremitaggio, e Chiesa officiata da trè, ò quattro Greci della medesima professione.

ISOLE

Vincenzo Maria Coronelli (1650-1718): born in Venice, and studied theology in Rome, where he was also taught Euclidian geometry and the ancient Greek writers. In 1680, he constructed two globes, one of the heavens and one of the earth, which he presented to the Duke of Parma. The globes made a great impression but also provoked violent reaction which led to their destruction. In 1681 Coronelli visited Paris, where he worked for three years at the court of Louis XIV and was awarded the title of Cosmographer. Returning to Venice in 1684, he founded the first Geographical Association, known as the Academy of Argonauts.

The wars between Venice and Turkey and his compatriots' victories had an influence on Coronelli, who designed and published many series of maps adorned with Venetian castles, cities and scenes of battle. In 1685, he was created Cosmographer of Venice.

The total oeuvre of Coronelli is enormous, and made use of the work of many artists. Among his most significant works: *Morea* (1687), *Atlante Veneto* (1690-96), *Corso Geografica Universale* (1692-94), *Isolario* (1696-7), *Specchio del Mare* (1698), *Singalente di Venezia* (1716).

120. V.M. Coronelli: page from the Isolario, *with the island Kalogeros, 1696*

121. V. M. Coronelli: Map of the northern Aegea

and-coloured copper engraving, 61 × 46 cms, 1696

122. V. M. Coronelli: Map of the southern Aegea

pper engraving, 61 × 46 cms, 1696

123. V. M. Coronelli: Map of Cyprus, copper engraving, 46 × 61 cms, 1696

Edward Wells (1667-1727): mathematician, geographer and theologian. His *New Set of Maps of Ancient and Present Geography* was published in 1700 and contains the map of the Aegean reprinted here. The book went through repeated editions until 1738.

124. E. Wells: Map of the Aegean and of Crete, copper engraving, 50 × 37 cms, 1700-1738

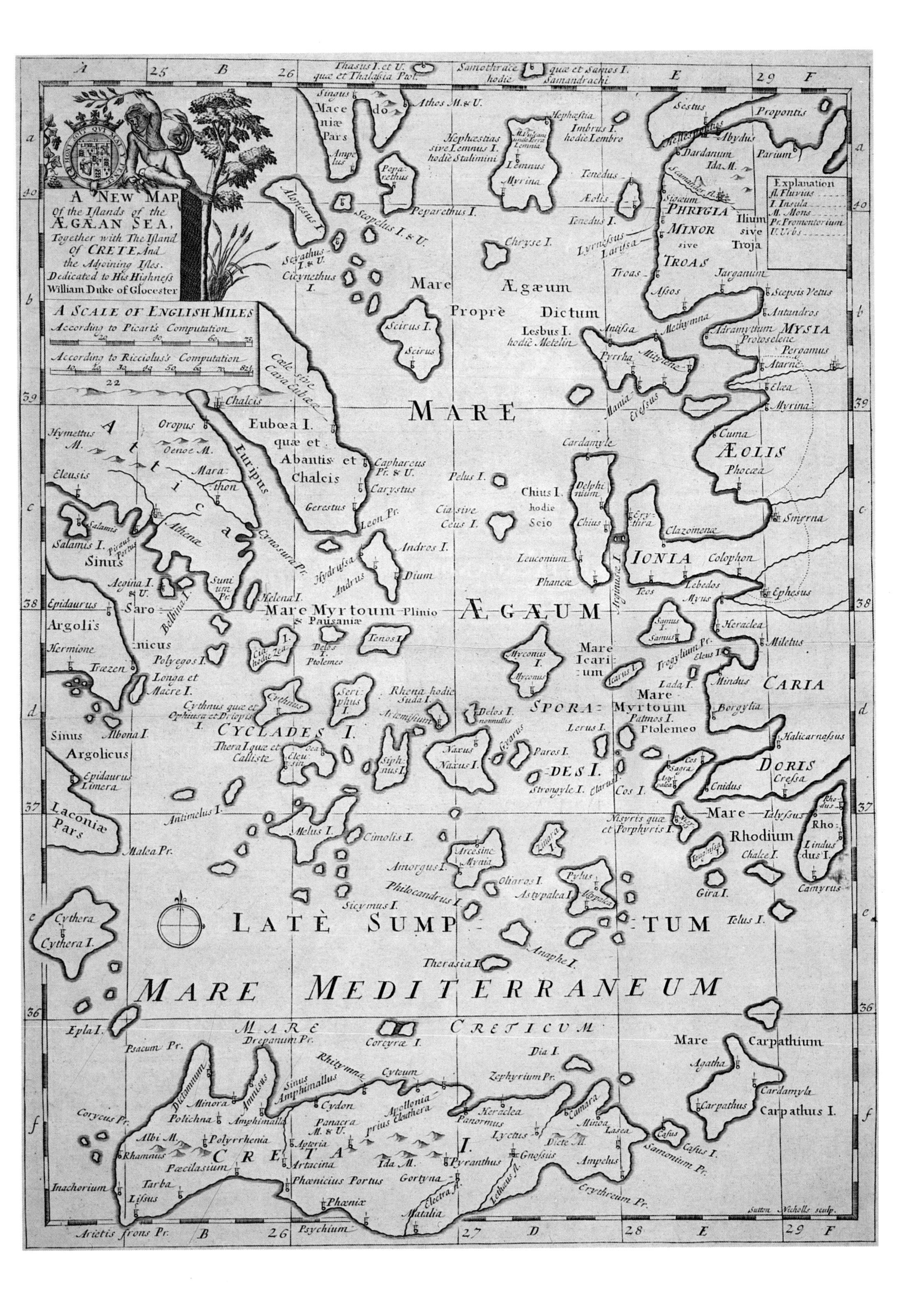
A NEW MAP
Of the Islands of the
ÆGÆAN SEA,
Together with The Island
Of CRETE And
the Adjoining Isles.
Dedicated to His Highness
William Duke of Glocester
A SCALE OF ENGLISH MILES
According to Picart's Computation
According to Ricciolus's Computation
Explanation
fl. Fluvius
I. Insula
M. Mons
Pr. Promontorium
U. Urbs
MARE
Mare Ægæum
Proprè Dictum
ÆGÆUM
Mare Myrtoum Plinio & Pausaniæ
CYCLADES I.
SPORADES I.
LATÈ SUMPTUM
MARE MEDITERRANEUM
MARE CRETICUM
Mare Carpathium
Mare Icarium
Mare Myrtoum Ptolemeo
Mare Rhodium
Attica
Euboea I. quæ et Abantis et Chalcis
PHRYGIA MINOR sive TROAS
MYSIA
ÆOLIS
IONIA
CARIA
DORIS
CRETA I.
Cythera I.
Carpathus I.
Sutton Nicholls sculp.

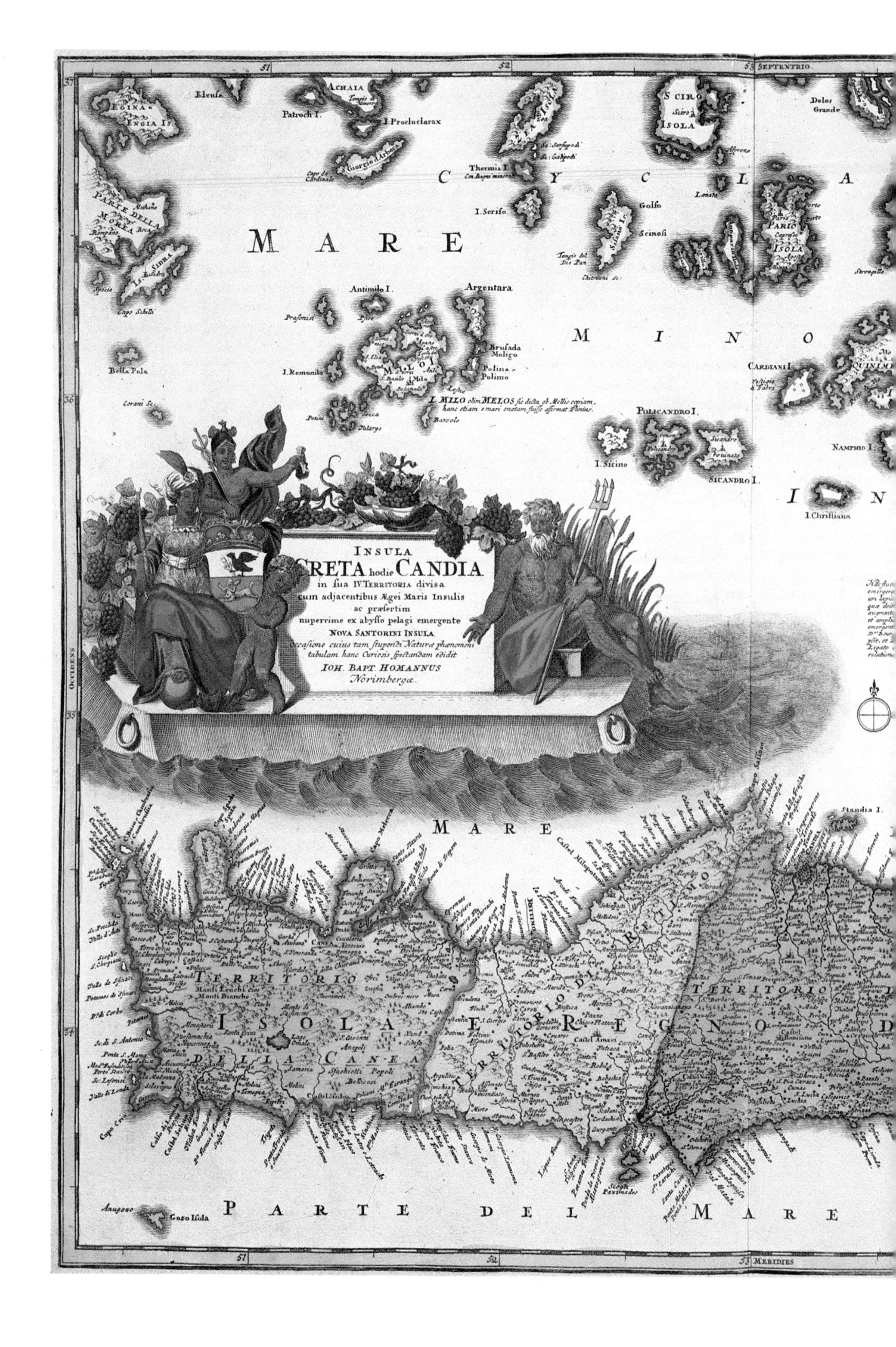
INSULA
CRETA hodie CANDIA
in sua IV. TERRITORIA divisa
cum adjacentibus Ægei Maris Insulis
ac præsertim
nuperrime ex abysso pelagi emergente
NOVA SANTORINI INSULA.
occasione cuius tam stupendi Naturæ phænomeni
tabulam hanc Curiosis spectandam edidit
IOH. BAPT. HOMANNUS
Norimbergæ.
SEPTENTRIO
MERIDIES
OCCIDENS
MARE
C Y C L A
M I N O
I N
MARE
P A R T E D E L M A R E
TERRITORIO
ISOLA
DELLA CANEA
TERRITORIO DI RETIMO
TERRITORIO
REGNO
ACHAIA
Eleusa
Patroch I.
I. Procluclarax
Thermia I.
I. Serifo
SCIRO
Sciro
ISOLA
Delos Grande
PARIO
ISOLA
Antimilo I.
Argentara
Brusada
Polina o Polimo
I. Remonilo
Bella Pola
CARDIANI I.
POLICANDRO I.
I. Sicino
SICANDRO I.
NAMPHIO I.
I. Christiana
I. MILO olim MELOS sic dicta ob Mellis copiam, hanc etiam e mari enatam fuisse affirmat Plinius.
Standia I.
CANEA
RETIMO
Gozo Isola
Anugovo

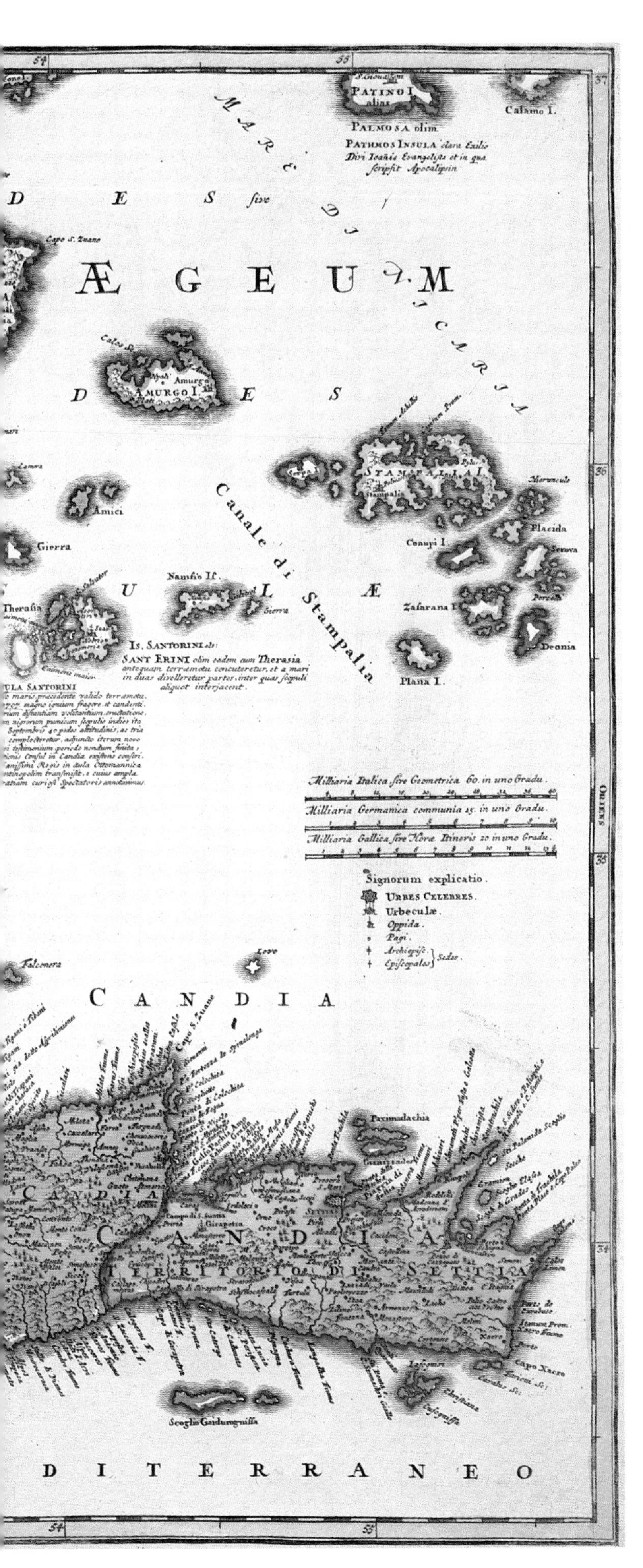

Johan Baptist Homann (1663-1724), engraver and paper merchant, was born at Kammlach and died at Nuremberg. He was geographer to the Holy Roman Emperor and a member of the Prussian Royal Academy of Sciences. His first atlas was published in 1704. Among his other works are: *Neuer Atlas*, 1707, *Grosser Atlas*, 1731, 1737, *Kleiner Atlas*, 1742 and *Atlas Homannianus*, 1762.

125. J. B. Homann: Map of Crete and the islands of the Aegean, on which is noted the eruption of the volcano of Santorini and the emergence of Palaia Kameni, hand-coloured copper engraving, 48 × 57 cms, 1702-1773

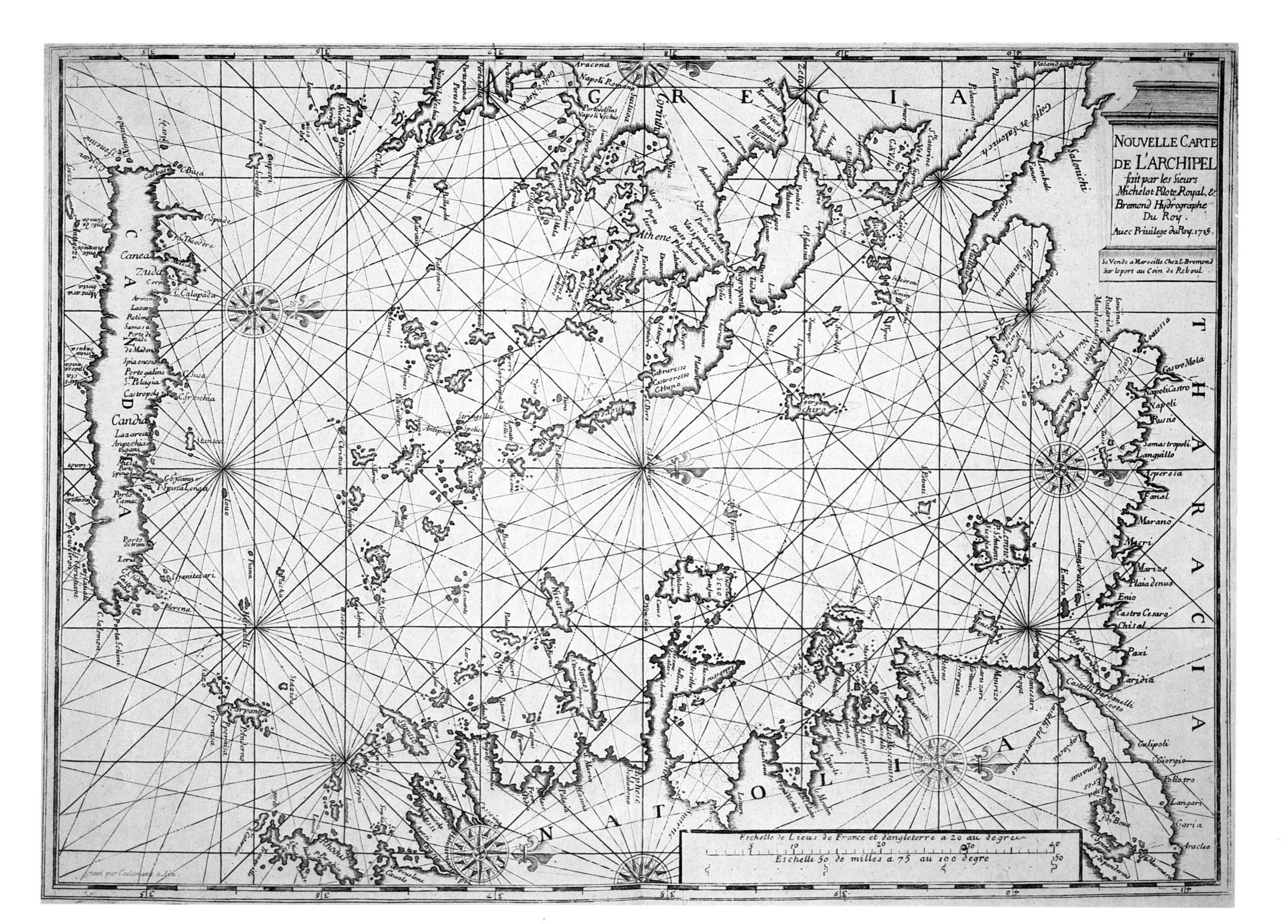
NOUVELLE CARTE
DE L'ARCHIPEL
fait par les Sieurs
Michelot Pilote Royal, &
Bremond Hydrographe
Du Roy.
Avec Privilege du Roy. 1715
Se Vend a Marseille Chez L. Bremond
sur le port au Coin de Reboul
GRECIA
THARACIA
NATOLIA
CANDIA
Eschelle de Lieus de France et d'angleterre a 20 au degre
Eschelle 50 de milles a 75 au 100 degre
grave par Coulemans a Aix
Salonichi
Golfe de Salonich
Lembale
Fanar
Corintho
Athene
Negroponte
Canea
Candia
Lemnos
Samandrachi
Embro
Troya
Castelli Dardanelli
Galipoli
Nicarie
Samos
Scio
Rhodus
Scarpanto
Nio
Naxia

John Seller (1664-1679): hydrographer to King Charles II and publisher of maps. His *English Pilot* was published in 1671, with maps of the Eastern Mediterranean, the Ionian Islands, the Aegean Islands, the Peloponnese, the Hellespont and Propontis. The work went through numerous editions until 1803 and was supplemented by John's descendent Jeremiah, also a hydrographer. Among other works by Seller are: *Atlas Maritimus* (1675), *Atlas Minimus* (1679), *Atlas Terrestris* (1680), *Atlas Contractus* (1690).

Henri Michelot: French naval captain; Laurent Bremond: royal hydrographer. In 1715, these two jointly published a map of the Aegean entitled *Nouvelle Carte del' Archipel Fait* (sic) *par les Sieurs Michelot Pilote Royal et Bremond Hydrographe du Roy. Se vendre à Marseille chez L. Bremond.* Another work was published in 1718: *Recueil de plusieurs plans des ports et rades de la mer Méditerranée.* This was reprinted in 1727-30, and an English version appeared in 1802.

126. H. Michelot - L. Bremond: Map of the Aegean, copper engraving, 63 x 46.5 cms, 1715-1726

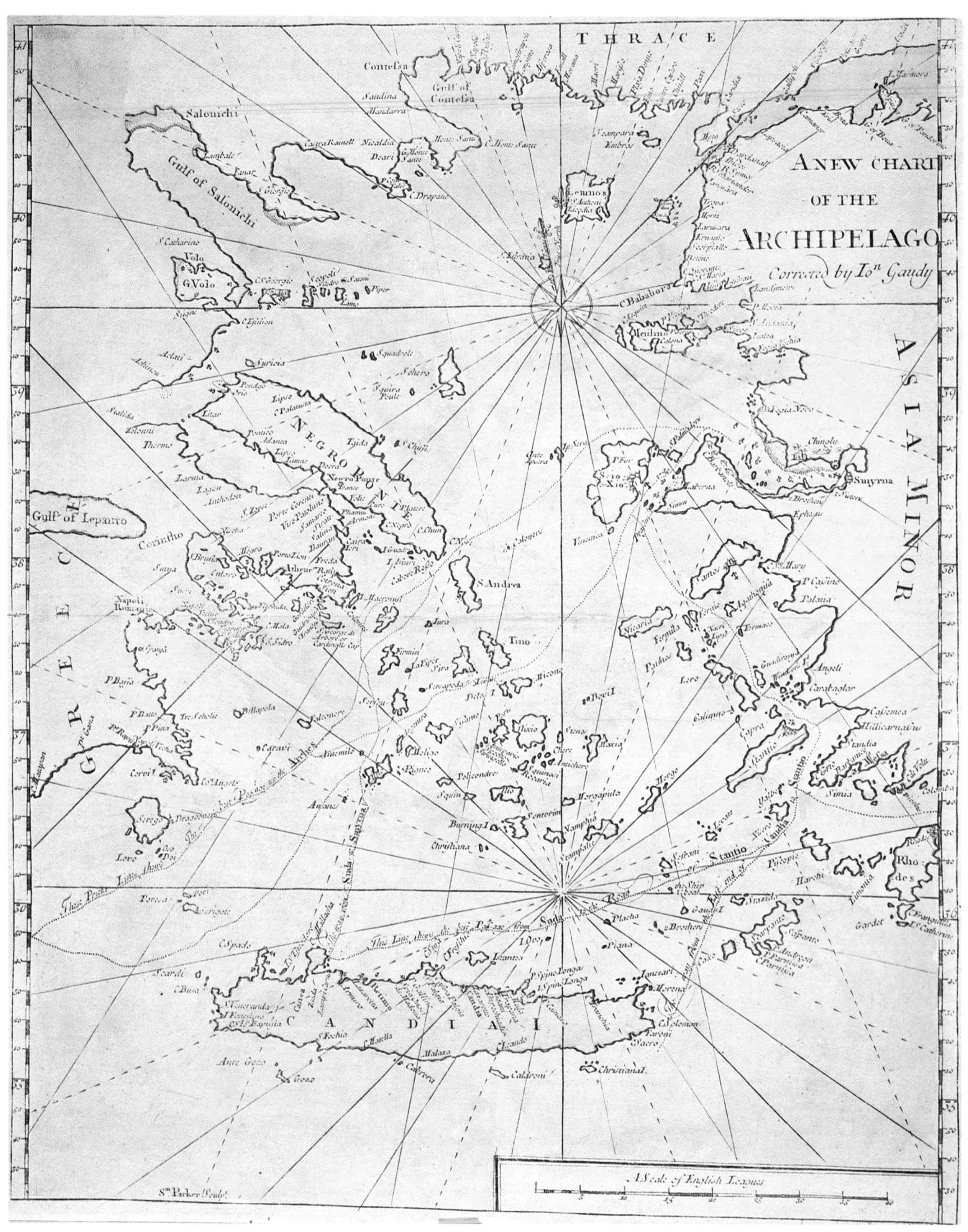

127. J. Seller: Map of the Aegean, hand-coloured copper engraving, 54 × 44 cms, 1716

128. F. Grognard: Map of the Aegean, copper engraving, 80 × 56.5 cms, 1745

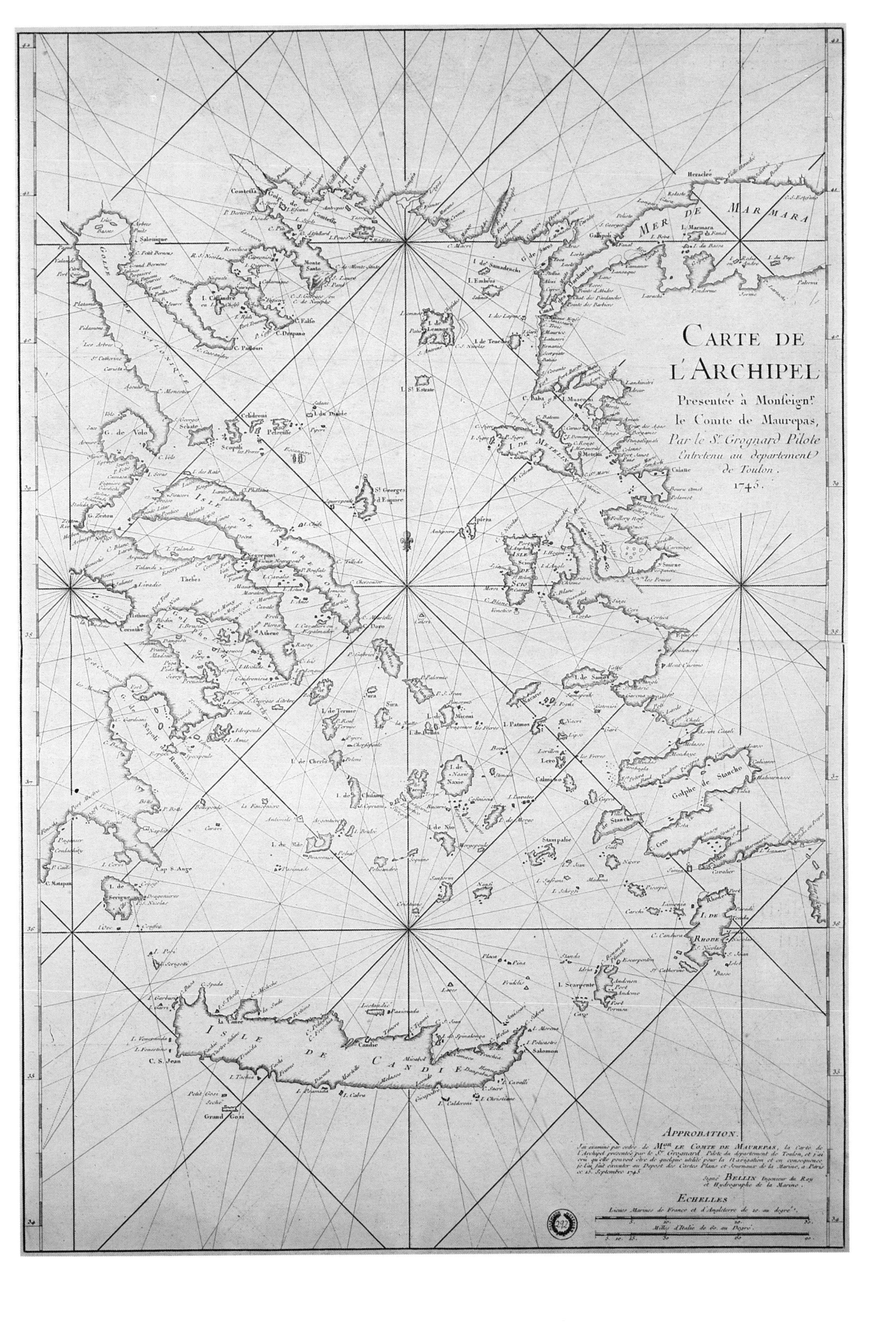
CARTE DE
L'ARCHIPEL
Presentée à Monseignr.
le Comte de Maurepas,
Par le Sr. Grognard Pilote
Entretenu au departement
de Toulon.
1745.
APPROBATION.
J'ai examiné par ordre de Mgr. LE COMTE DE MAUREPAS, la Carte de l'Archipel presentée par le Sr. Grognard Pilote du departement de Toulon, et j'ai cru qu'elle pouvoit être de quelque utilité pour la Navigation et en consequence je l'ai fait executer au Depost des Cartes Plans et Journaux de la Marine, à Paris ce 15. Septembre 1745.
Signé BELLIN Ingenieur du Roy et Hydrographe de la Marine.
ECHELLES
Lieues Marines de France et d'Angleterre de 20. au degré.
Milles d'Italie de 60. au Degré.
MER DE MARMARA
ISLE DE NEGREPONT
ISLE DE CANDIE
I. DE METELIN
Golphe de Stancho
I. DE RHODE
Monte Santo
Salonique
Gallipoli
Athene
Candie
Naxie
I. Patmos
Stampalie
I. de Samos

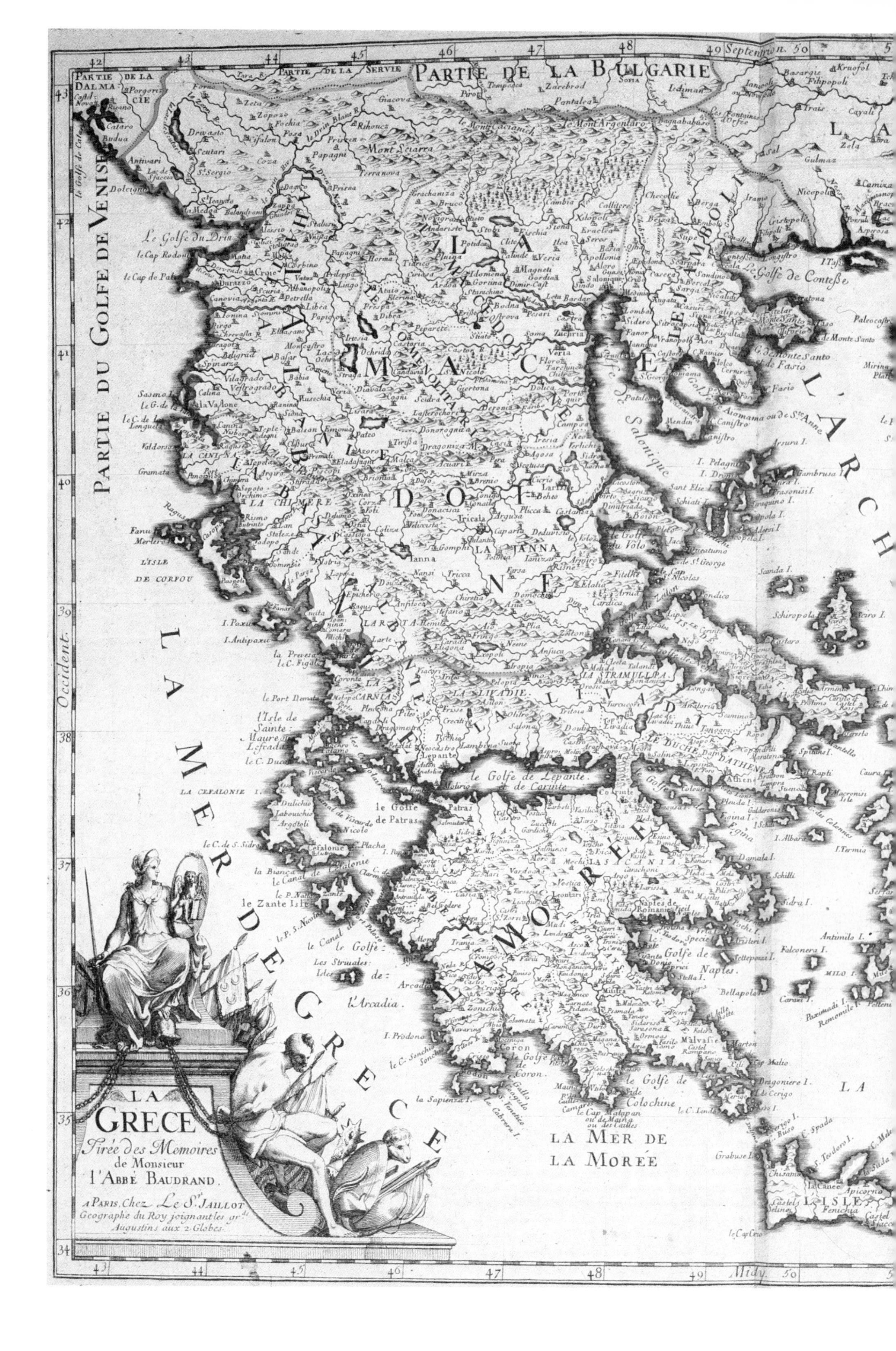
LA GRECE
Tirée des Memoires
de Monsieur
l'Abbé Baudrand.
A PARIS, Chez Le Sr. JAILLOT
Geographe du Roy joignant les grds.
Augustins aux 2 Globes.
PARTIE DE LA BULGARIE
PARTIE DE LA SERVIE
PARTIE DE LA DALMACIE
PARTIE DU GOLFE DE VENISE
LA MER DE GRECE
LA MER DE LA MOREE
LA MACEDOINE
L'ALBANIE
LA LIVADIE
LA MOREE
L'ISLE DE CORFOU
LA CEFALONIE I.
le Golfe de Lepante
le Golfe de Patras
le Golfe de Salonique
le Golfe de Contesse
le Golfe du Volo
Golfe de Naples
le Golfe de Coron
le Golfe de Colochine
Le Golfe du Drin
LA JANNA
LA CHIMERE
Septentrion
Midy
Occident

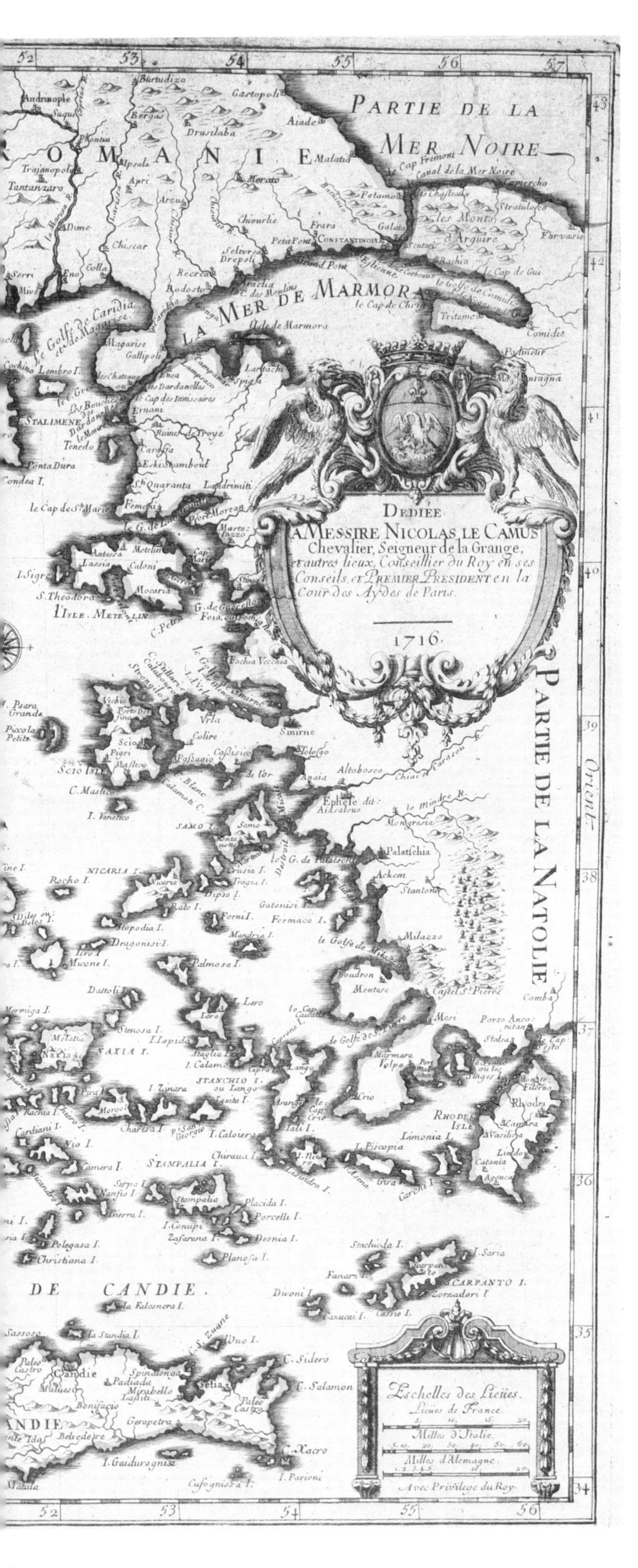

Abbé Baudrand (1633-1700): geographer to the King of France, published a map of Greece in 1688. Among other works: *Postes d' Italie* (1695), *Stato della Chiesa*, (published by Rossi, Rome, 1669), *Geografica* (1682).

129. M. A. Baudrand: Map of Greece, copper engraving, 46 × 54.5 cms, 1716

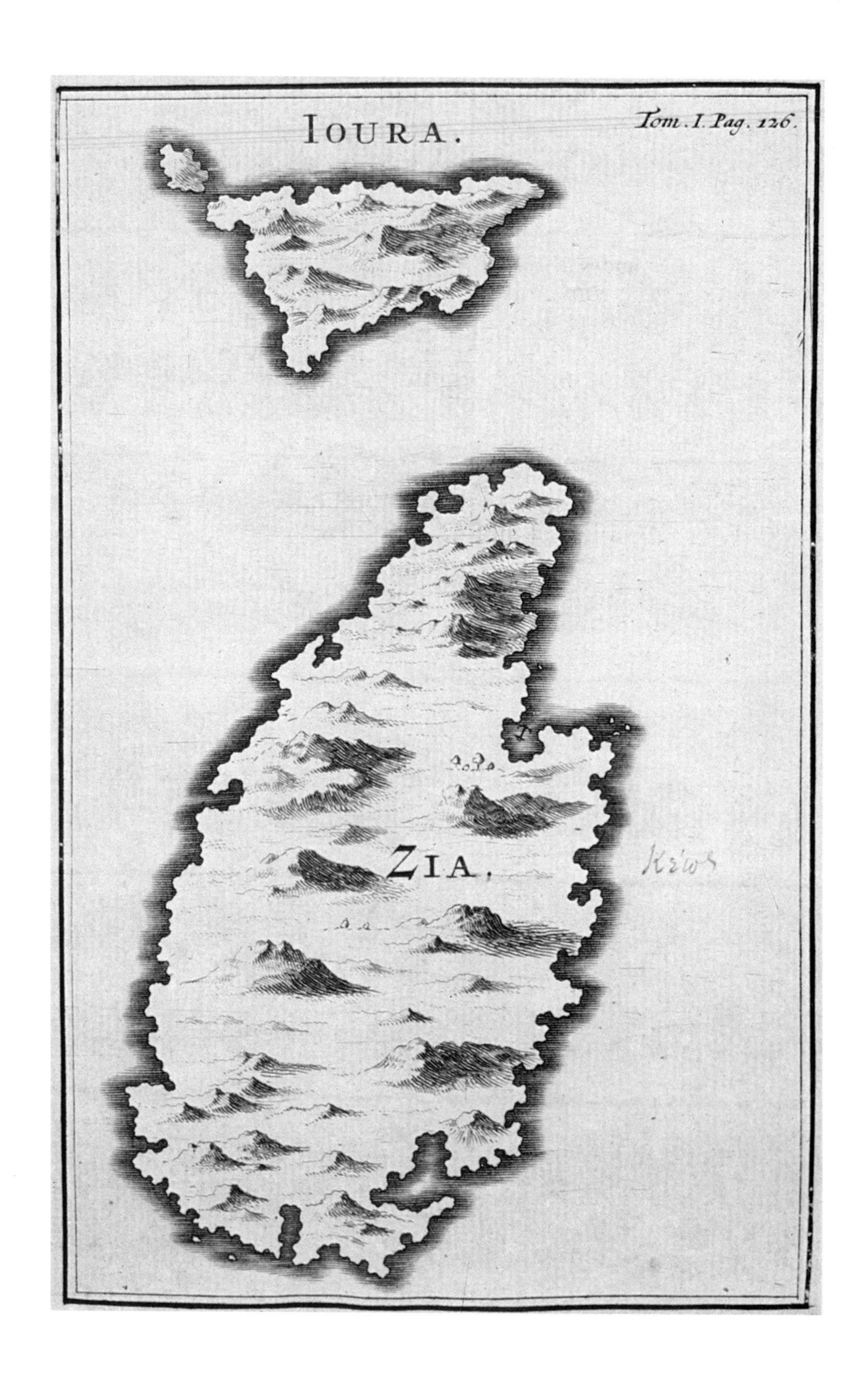
IOURA.
Tom. I. Pag. 126.
ZIA.

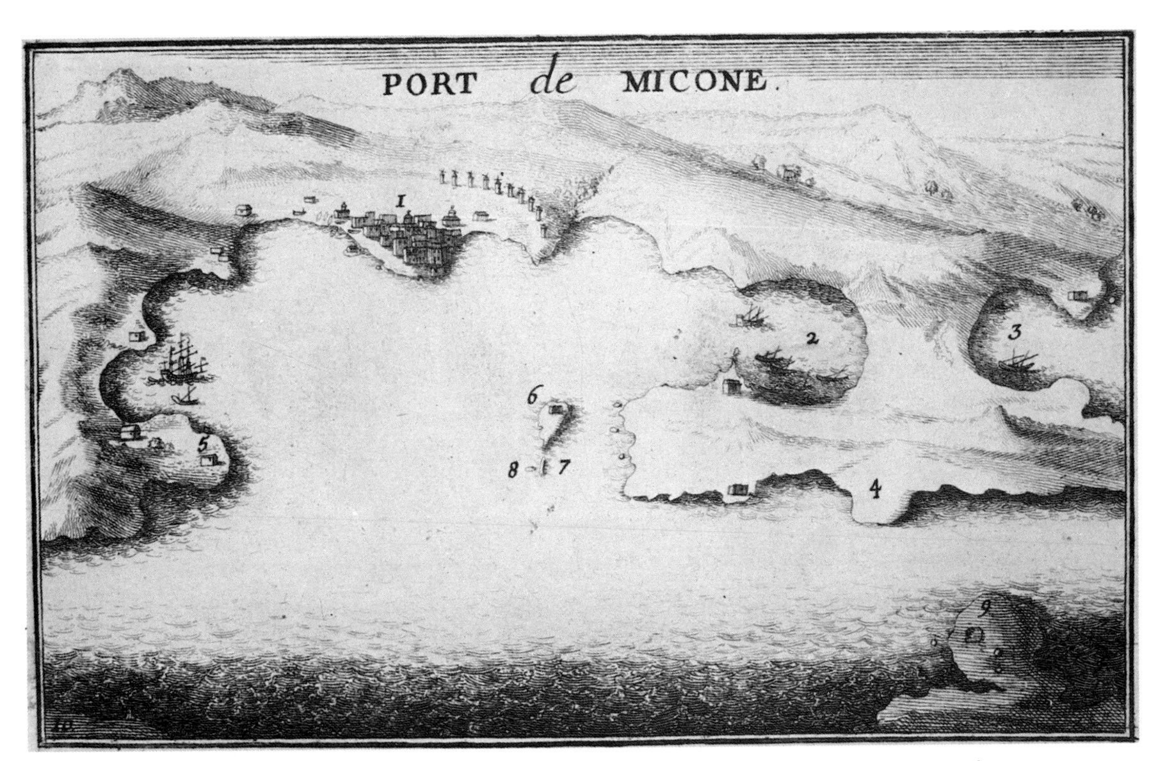

131. Pitton de Tournefort: The harbour of Myconos, copper engraving, 22 x 35 cms, 1717.

Pitton de Tournefort: French botanist, member of the Academy of Sciences. In 1700, acting on the orders of Louis XIV, he undertook an official mission to the Levant, the fruit of which was a two-volume work entitled *Relation d' un voyage du Levant,* first published in 1717. The first volume was devoted to the Greek islands of the Aegean, and the second to Turkey which is described as far as its easternmost frontiers. What makes Tournefort so important is that his work sees the birth of scientific research based on a study of living Greece. Observations are not restricted to botany; indeed, they deal mostly with the economy and administration of the islands, their ethnologica make-up, their customs and the various form of Turkish oppression. Tournefort was accompanied on his mission by the artist Audriet, who made on-the-spot drawings of harbours, scenes from daily life, plants and animals. These drawings were used to make the wonderful engravings with which the *Journey* is adorned.

130. Pitton de Tournefort: Map of Kea and Yaros, copper engraving, 16 x 10 cms, 1717

MACEDONIA
THESSALIÆ
GRECIÆ PARS
ACHAYA
Salonicha
Golfo di Salonichi
Golfo di Aiomama
Golfo di Contessa
Golfo di Monte Santo
Golfo di Asperosa
Golfo di Volo
Golfo di Zitoun
Golfo di Patrasso
Golfo di Lepanto
Golfo di Engia
Golfo di Napoli di Romania
Golfo di Coron
Athene
Negro Ponte
Lemnos
Schiro
Sciatti
Schopoli
Andros
Tino
Sira
Zea
Milo
Micono
Nio
Amorgo
Candia
Canea
Retimo
CERIGO
MARE ÆGEUM
ARCHIPELAGO
MARE DI CANDIA
MARE MEDI
Hodie

Pieter Vander Aa (1659-1733): publisher and book-seller from Leiden. He published a series of atlases which included the *Atlas Nouveau* (1700), the *East and West Indies* (1707, in 28 volumes) and the *Galerie Agréable du Monde* (1729, in 66 volumes). A total of 100 copies of this last work were sold, and from it come the maps of the Aegean shown in this book.

132. P. Vander Aa: Map of the Aegean with all the islands and the coastline which borders it, hand-coloured copper engraving, 44 × 50.5 cms, 1729

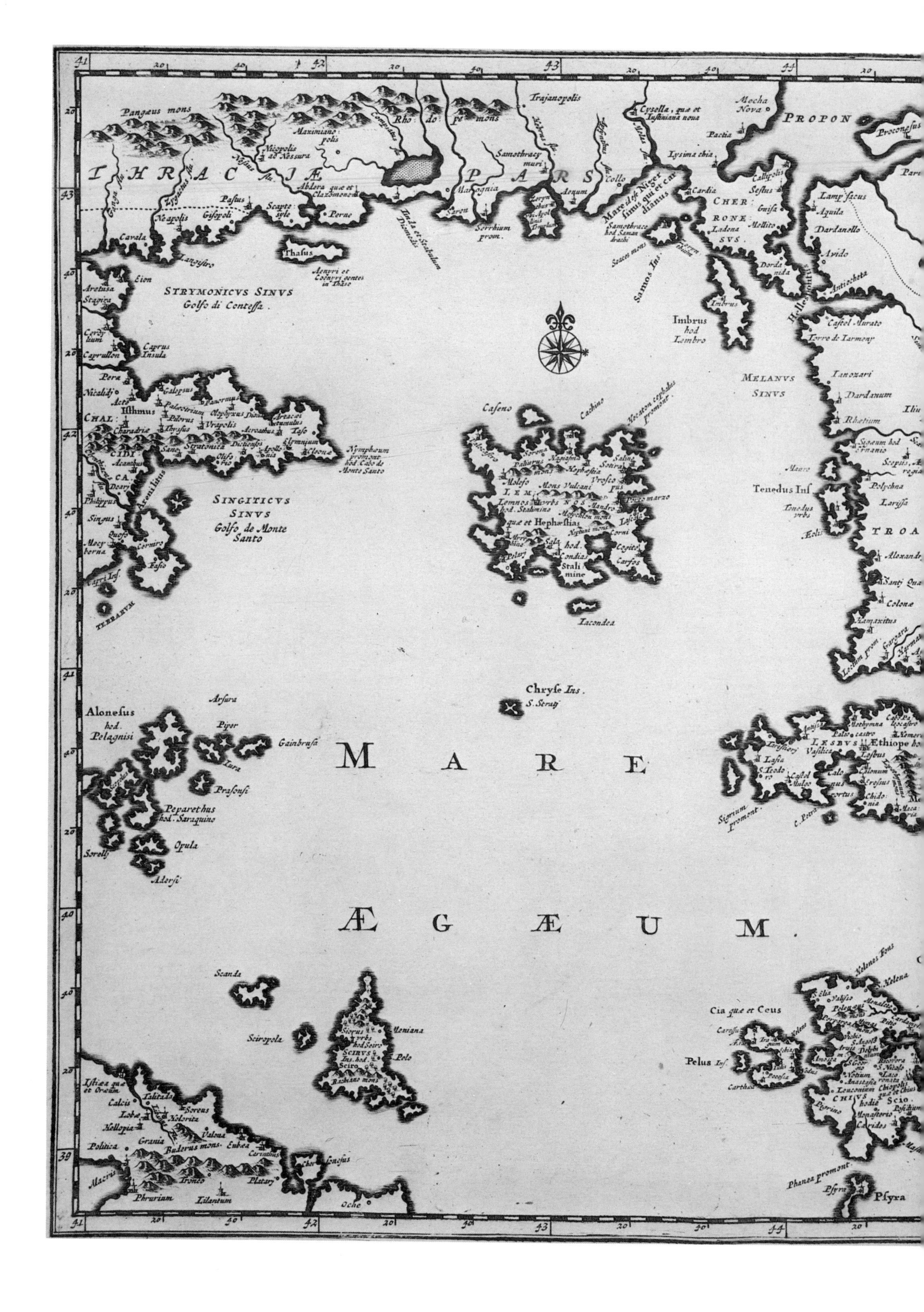

MARE
ÆGÆUM.
THRACIÆ PARS
Pangæus mons
Rhodope mons
Trajanopolis
PROPON
Proconesus
Maximiano polis
Nicopolis ad Nessura
Abdera quæ et Clazomenæ
Neapolis
Cavala
Scaptesyle
Perne
Thasus
Maronia
Serrhium prom.
Samothracy muri
Cardia
Lysima chia
Pactia
Mecha Nova
CHERRONESUS
Sestus
Madito
Lampsacus
Aquila
Dardanello
Avido
Antiocheta
Imbrus hod Lembro
Samos Ins.
STRYMONICUS SINUS
Golfo di Contessa
Eion
Aretusa
Stagira
Caprus Insula
Caprullon
Pera
Isthmus
CHAL CIDI CA
Stratonica
Cleonæ
Nymphæum promont. hod. Cabo de Monte Santo
SINGITICUS SINUS
Golfo de Monte Santo
Singus
Mecyberna
Capri Ins.
Caseno
Cachino
LEMNOS
Stalimine
Lacondea
MELANUS SINUS
Castel Murato
Ianozari
Dardanum
Rhætium
Sigeum hod Granaio
Polychna
Larissa
Tenedus Ins.
Tenedus urbs
TROA
Alexand
Colonæ
Hamaxitus
Lectum prom.
Chryse Ins. S. Strati
Arsura
Alonesus hod. Pelagnisi
Piper
Gainbrusa
Lura
Prasonsi
Peparethus hod. Saraquino
Sorelli
Opula
Adorsi
LESBUS
Methymna
Ethiope
Sigrium promont.
C. Petro
Scanda
Sciropola
SCIRUS Ins. hod. Sciro
Meniana
Pelo
Cia quæ et Ceus
Pelus Ins.
Carthæa
Melanes Pons
Melena
CHIUS Scio
Caridos
Phanea promont.
Psyra
Istiæa quæ et Oræum
Calcis
Lobæ
Mellopia
Politica
Valona
Buderus mons.
Eubœa
Cerinthus
Platay
Phrurium
Lilantum
Oche
Macris

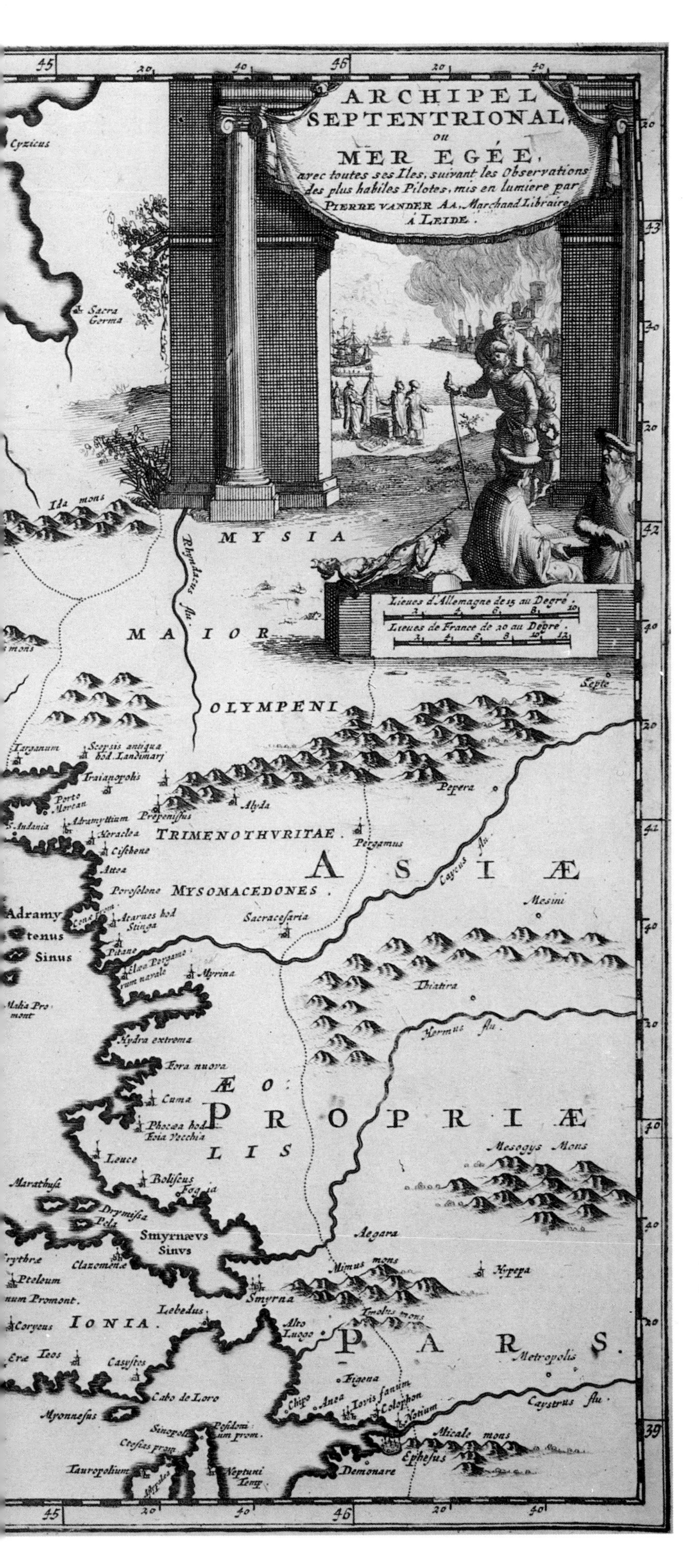

133. P. Vander Aa: Map of the northern Aegean, copper engraving, 28.5 × 36 cms, 1729

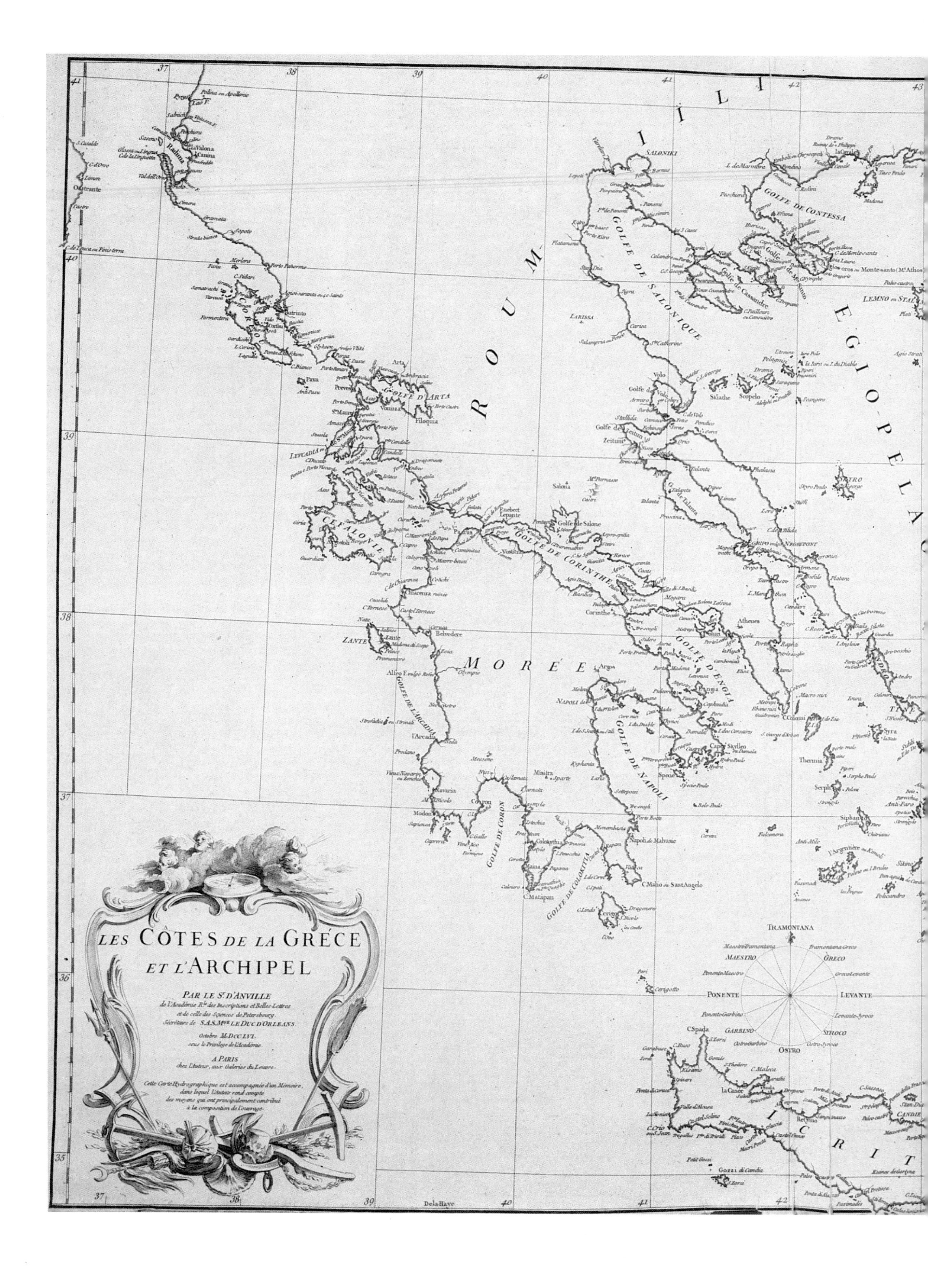
LES CÔTES DE LA GRÉCE
ET L'ARCHIPEL
PAR LE S.r D'ANVILLE
de l'Académie R.le des Inscriptions et Belles-Lettres
et de celle des Sciences de Petersbourg.
Sécrétaire de S.A.S.M.gr LE DUC D'ORLEANS.
Octobre M.DCC LVI.
sous le Privilege de l'Académie.
A PARIS
chez l'Auteur, aux Galeries du Louvre.
Cette Carte Hydrographique est accompagnée d'un Mémoire,
dans lequel l'Auteur rend compte
des moyens qui ont principalement contribué
à la composition de l'ouvrage.
De la Haye
ROUM-ILI
MORÉE
GOLFE DE SALONIQUE
GOLFE DE CORINTHE
GOLFE D'ENGIA
GOLFE DE NAPOLI
GOLFE DE CORON
GOLFE DE COLOKITIA
GOLFE DE CONTESSA
GOLFE D'ARTA
CEFALONIE
ZANTE
LEUCADIA
SALONIKI
LARISSA
Athenes
Corinthe
Napoli de Malvasie
C. Matapan
TRAMONTANA
MAESTRO
GRECO
PONENTE
LEVANTE
GARBINO
SIROCO
OSTRO
la Canée
Retimo
CANDIE

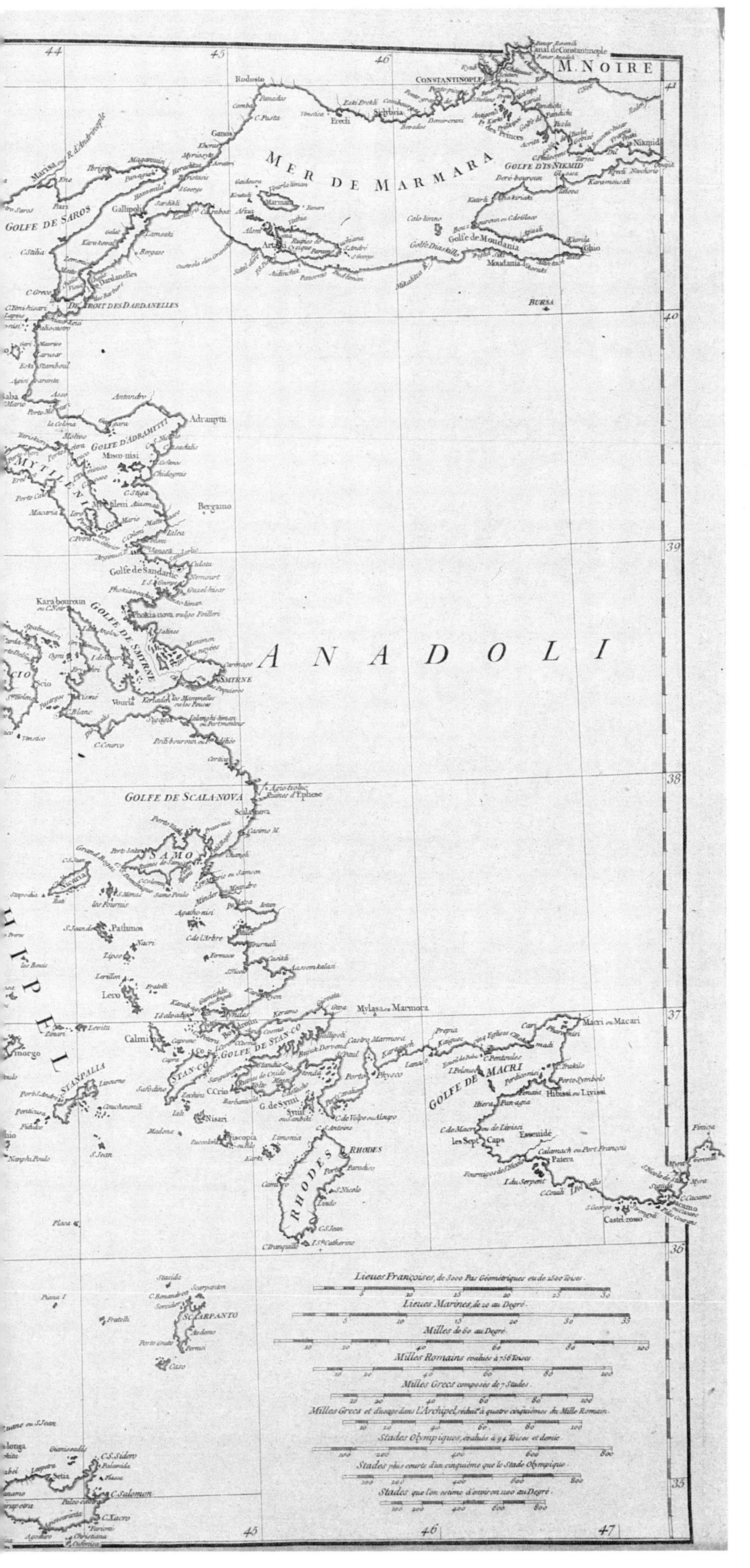

J.B.B. D' Anville (1697-1782): major French geographer and cartographer, with more than 200 maps to his credit. He produced maps of France (1719), North America (1746), South America (1748), Africa (1749), Asia (1751), an *Atlas de la Chine* (1737), and a *General Atlas* which was repeatedly reprinted between 1737 and 1780. The maps of Greece and the Aegean in this book are from that Atlas. D' Anville was elected to the Academy in 1773.

134. J. B. B. d' Anville: Map of the coasts of Greece and the Aegean, copper engraving, 70 x 55 cms, 1756

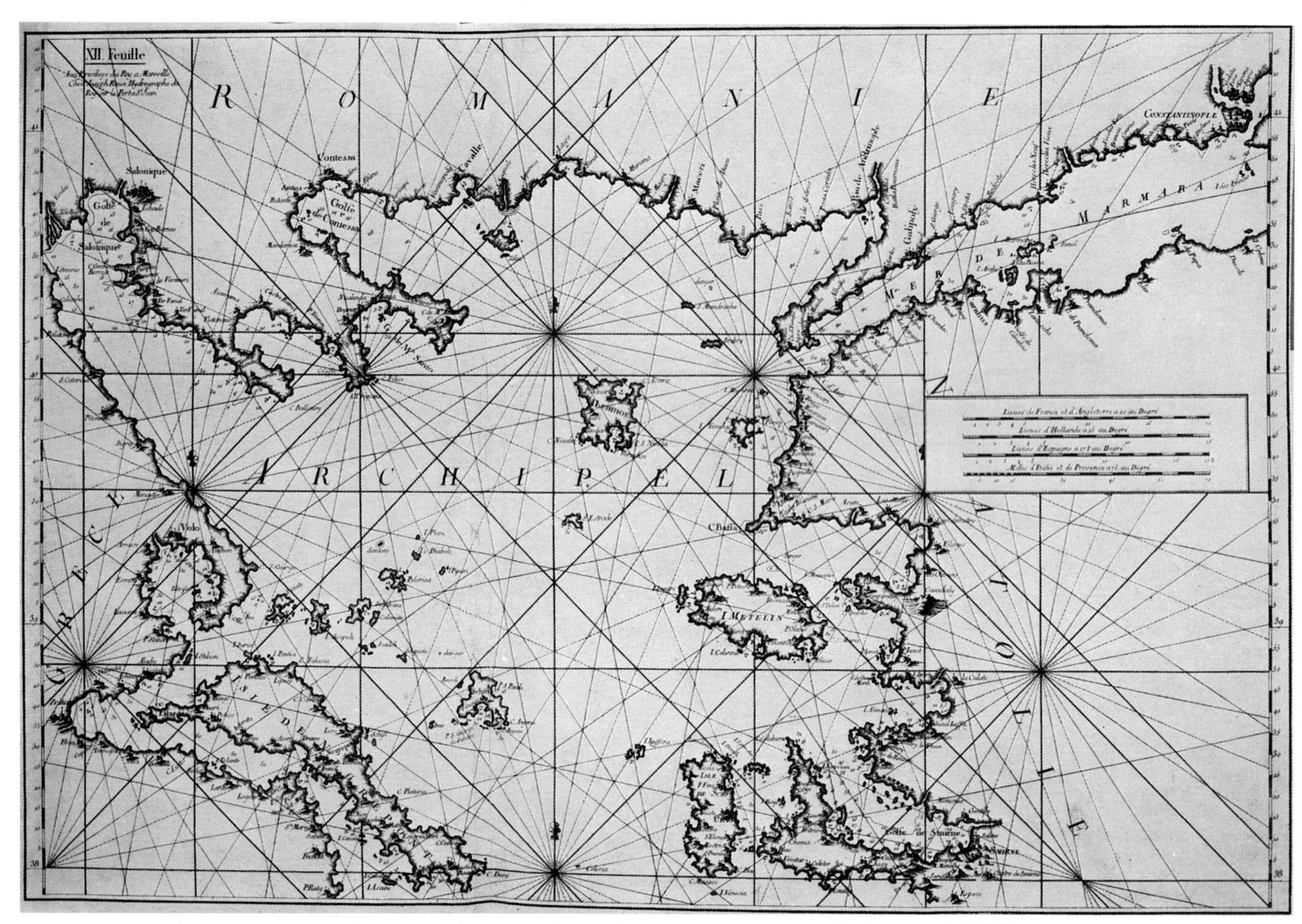

135. J. Roux: Map of the northern Aegean, copper engraving, 83 × 55 cms, 1764

Joseph Roux: French hydrographer to the King, published a 12-leaf map of the Aegean in 1764. Two of the leaves show the North and South Aegean. His *Recueil des Principaux Plans des Ports et Rades de la Méditerranée* (1764) contained numerous maps of the Aegean islands. Among other works: *Costes de Provence* (1770), *Golfe de Lyon* (1771).

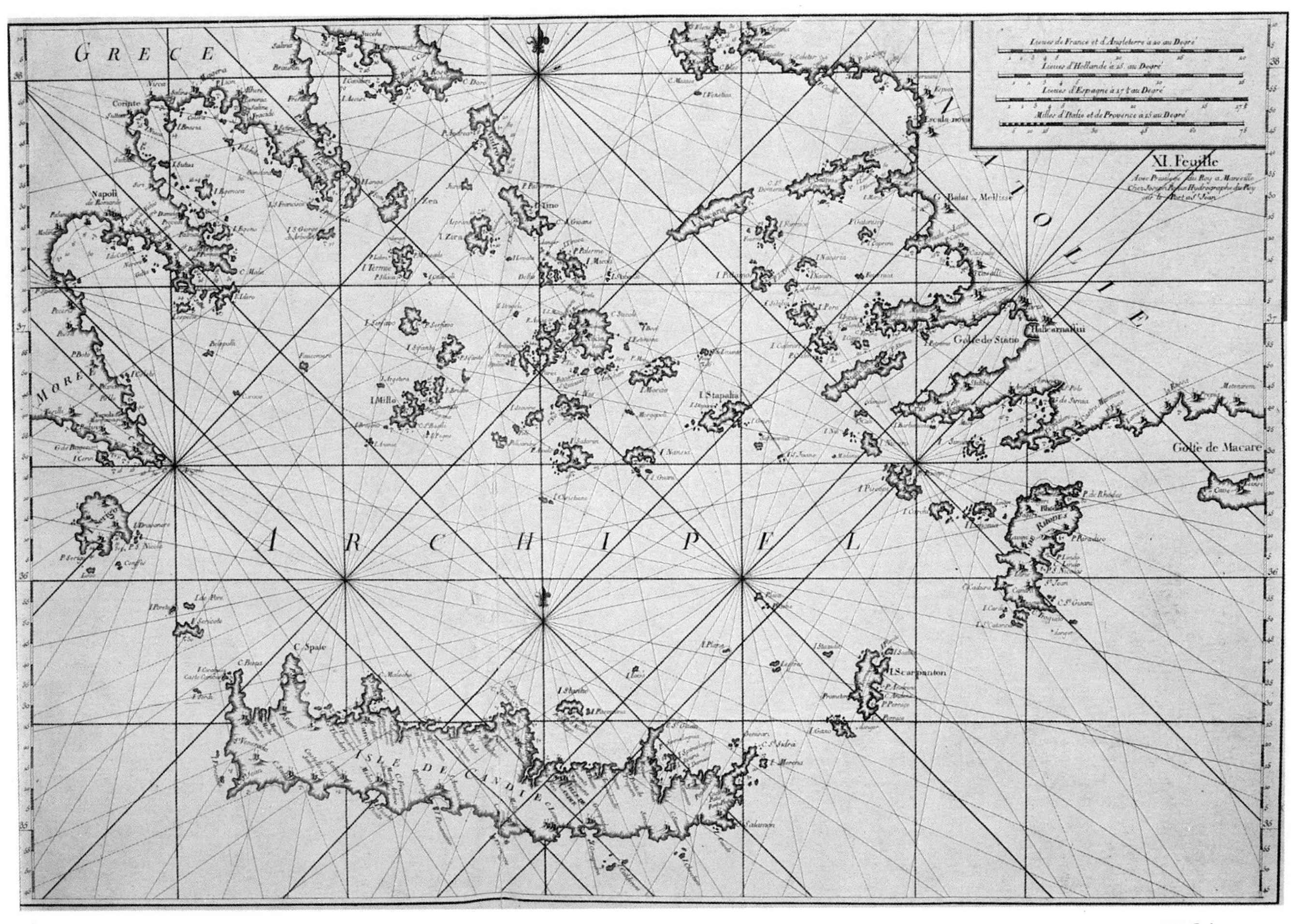

136. J. Roux: Map of the southern Aegean, copper engraving, 83 × 55 cms, 1764

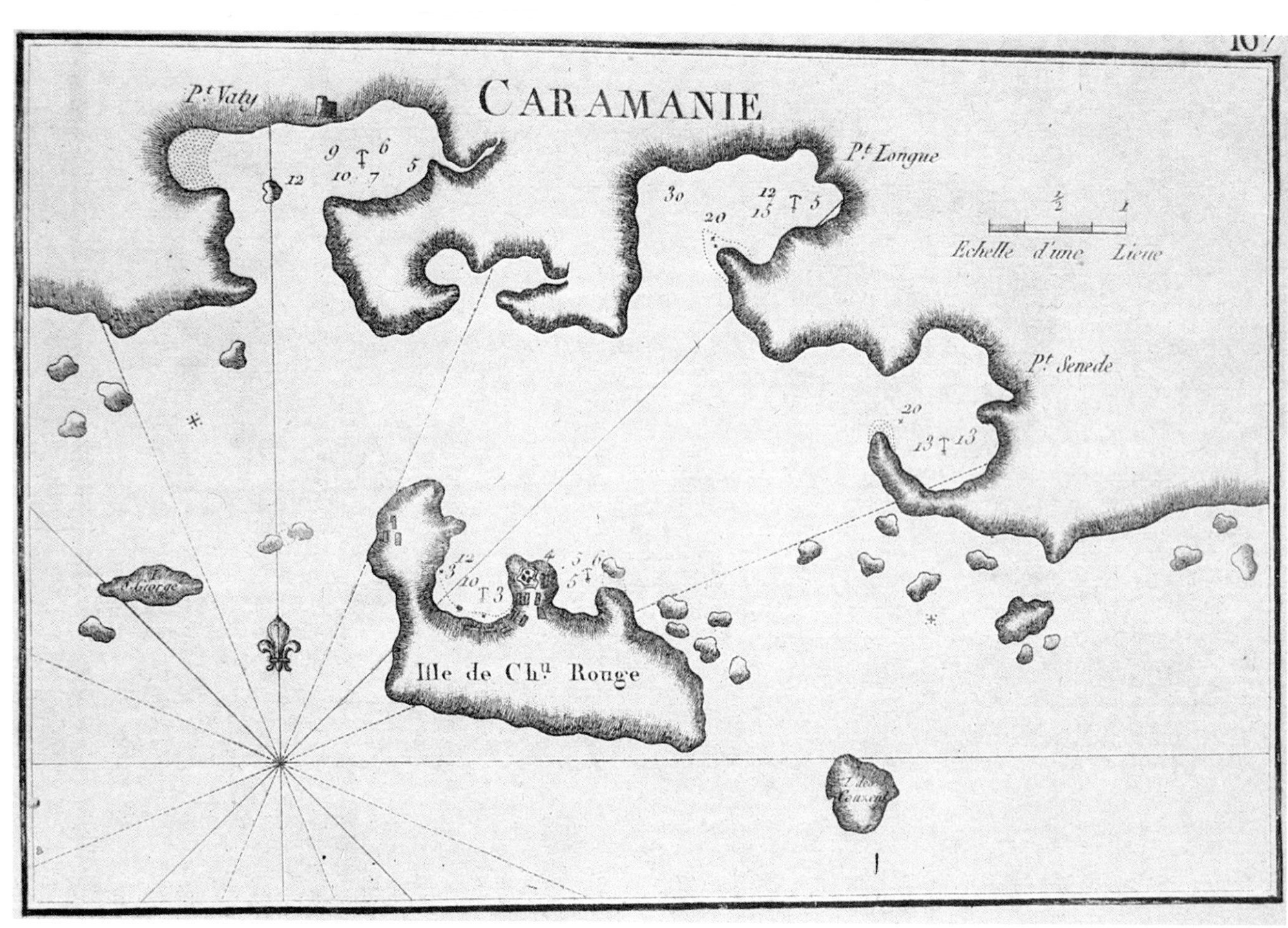

137. J. Roux: Map of Kastellorizo, copper engraving, 13 × 18 cms, 1764

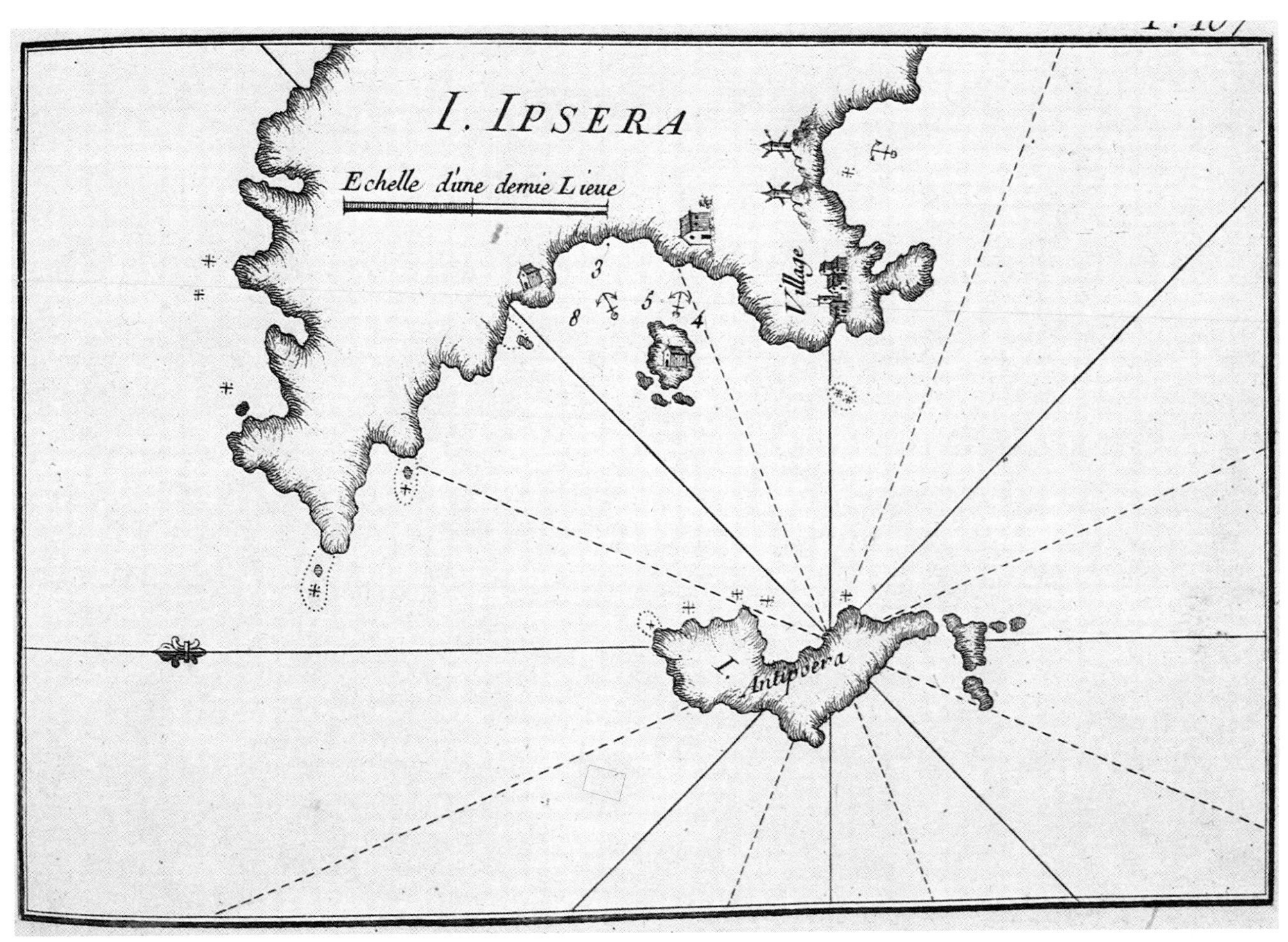

138. J. Roux: Map of Psara, copper engraving, 12.5 × 19 cms, 1764

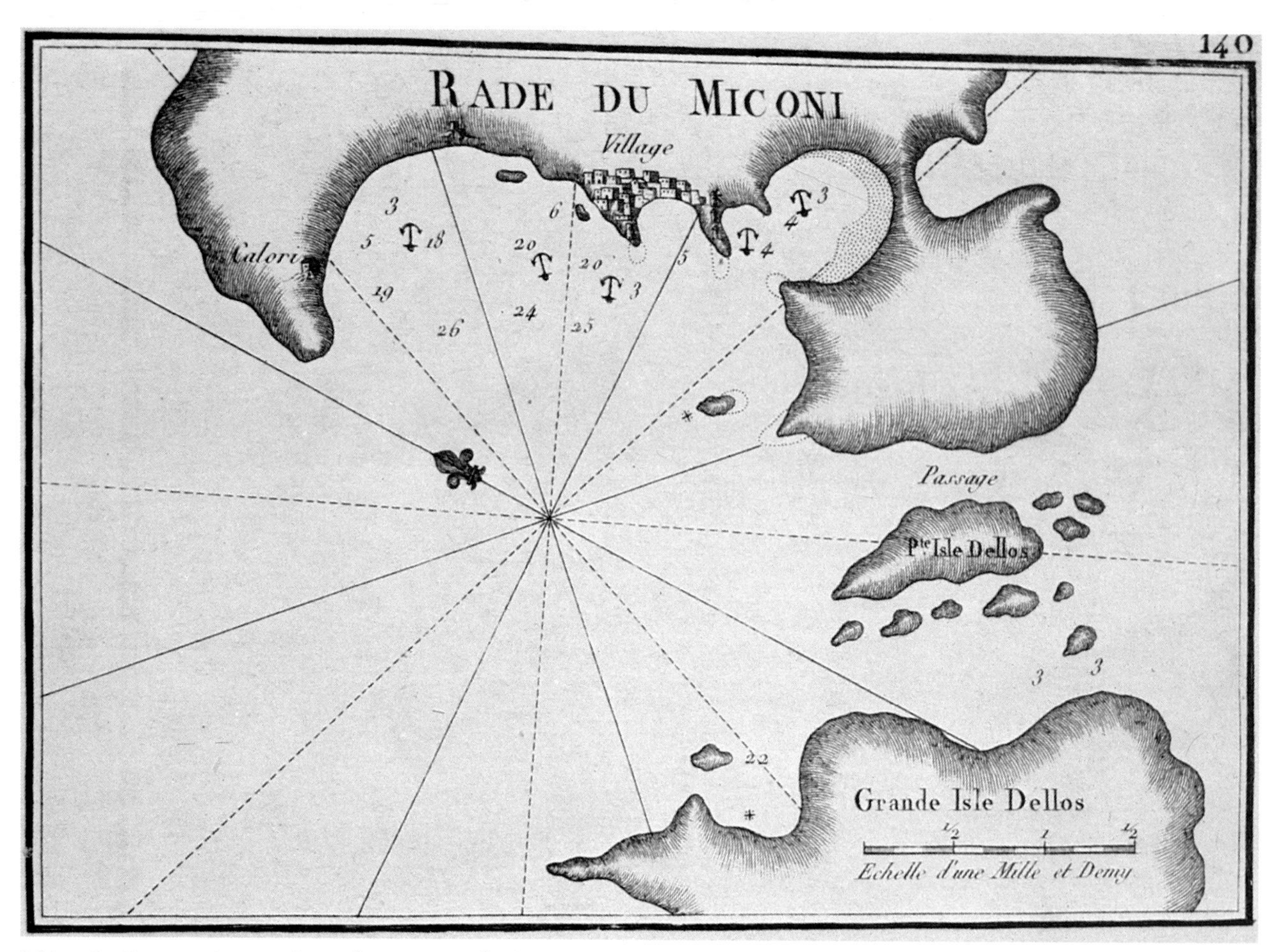

139. J. Roux: Bay of Mykonos and the island of Delos, copper engraving, 13 × 18 cms, 1764

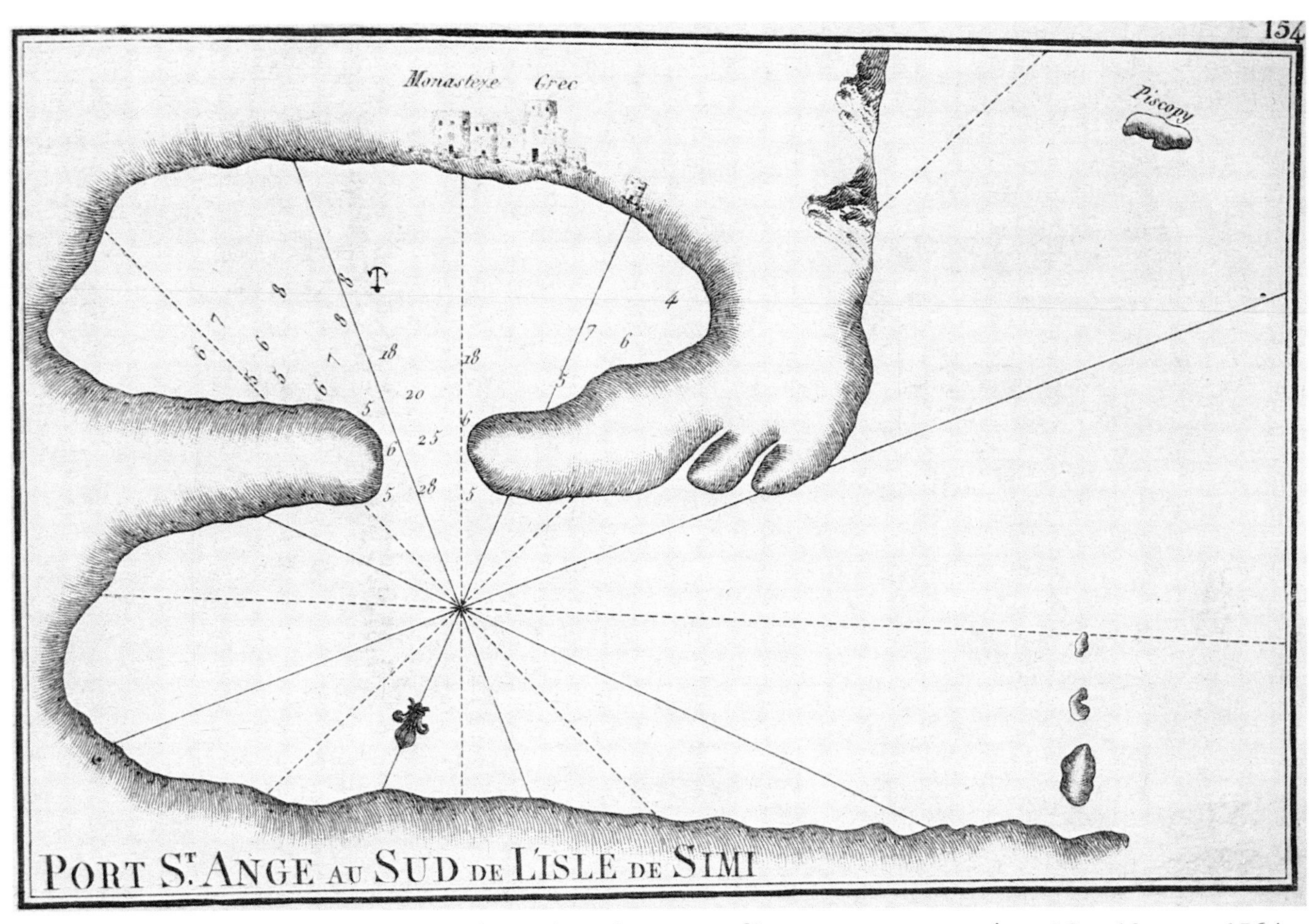

140. J. Roux: Symi and part of the Asia Minor coastline, copper engraving, 13 × 18 cms, 1764

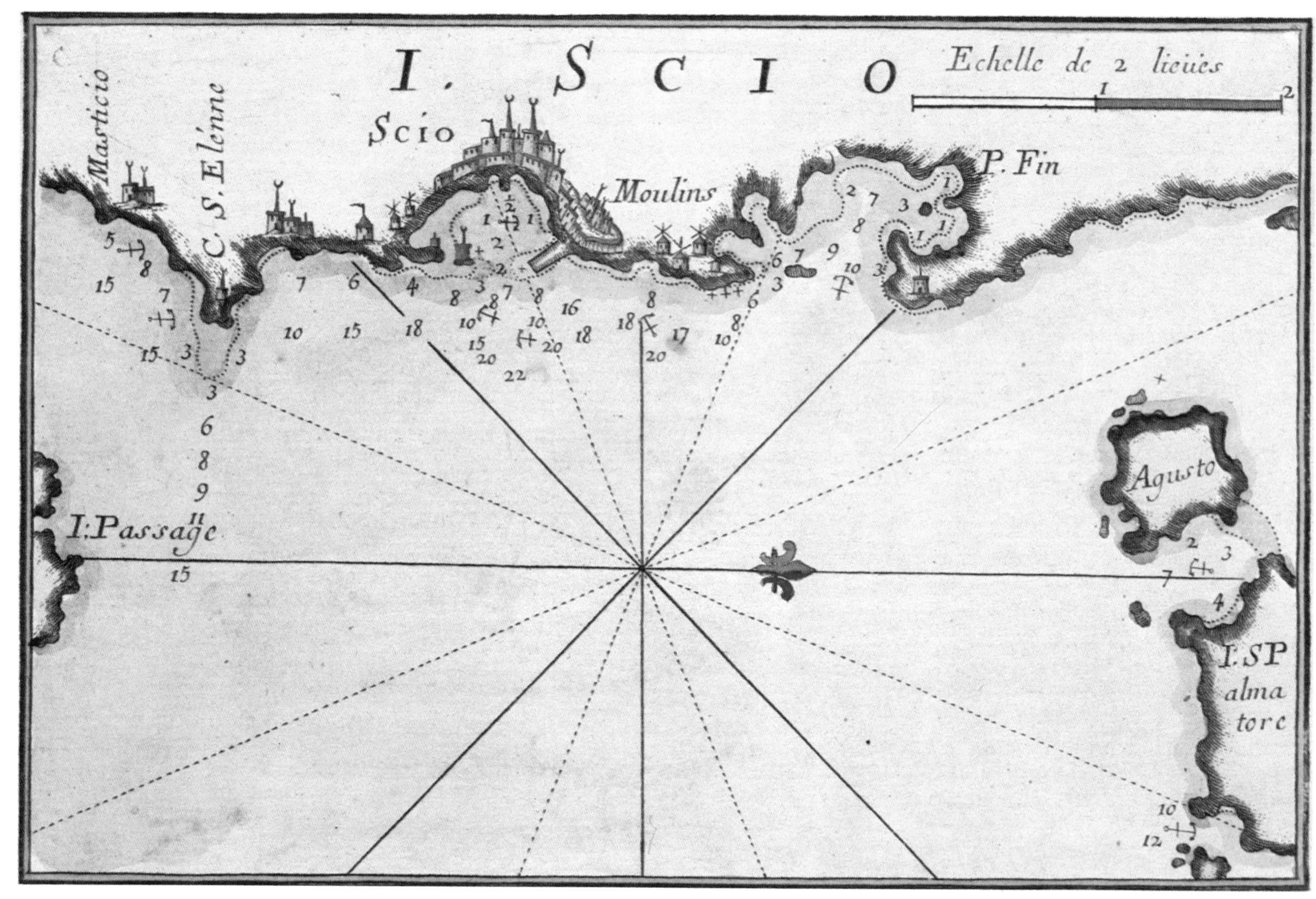

141. J. Roux: Map of Chios, copper engraving, 13 × 18 cms, 1764

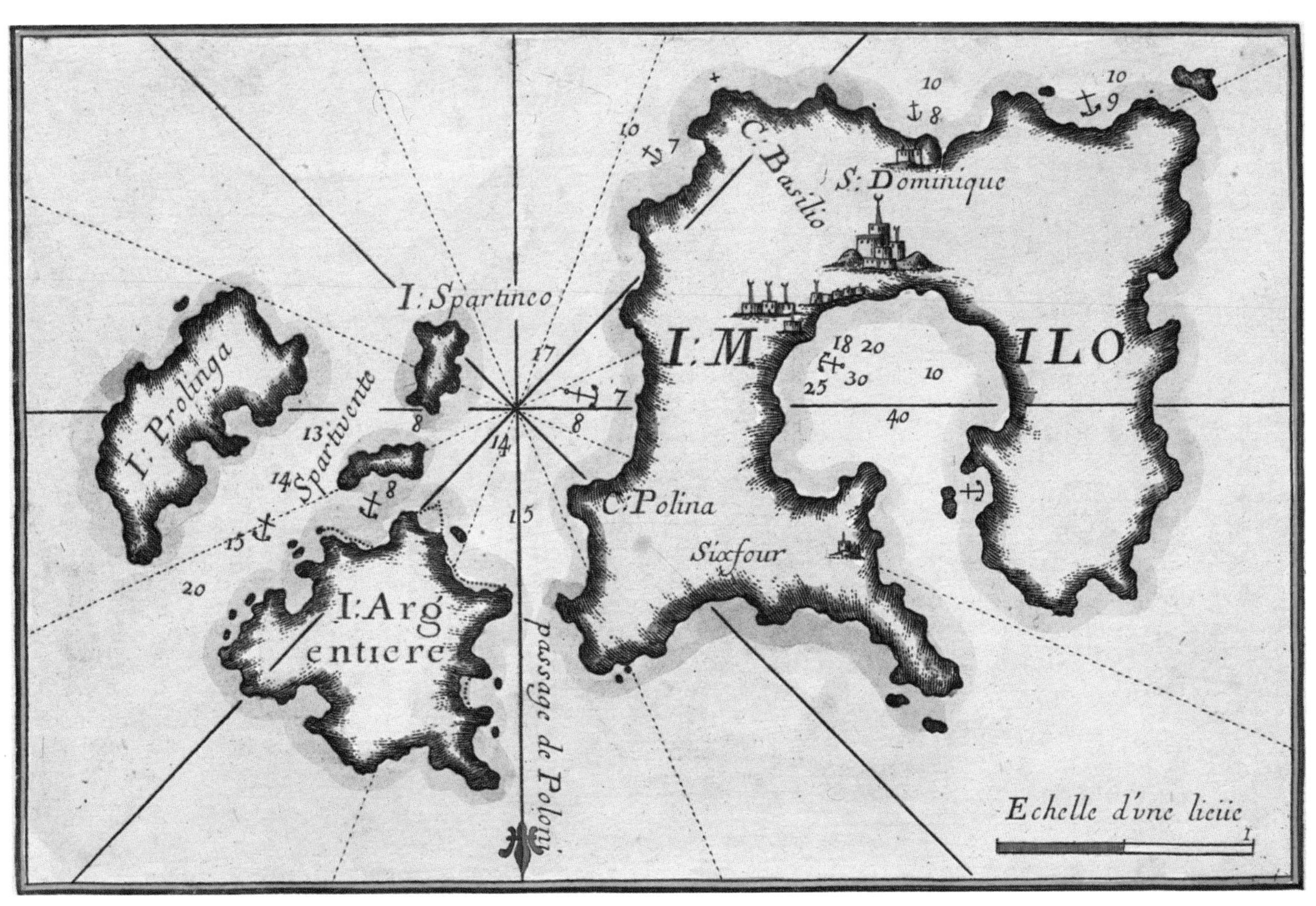

142. J. Roux: Map of Melos, copper engraving, 13 × 18 cms, 1764

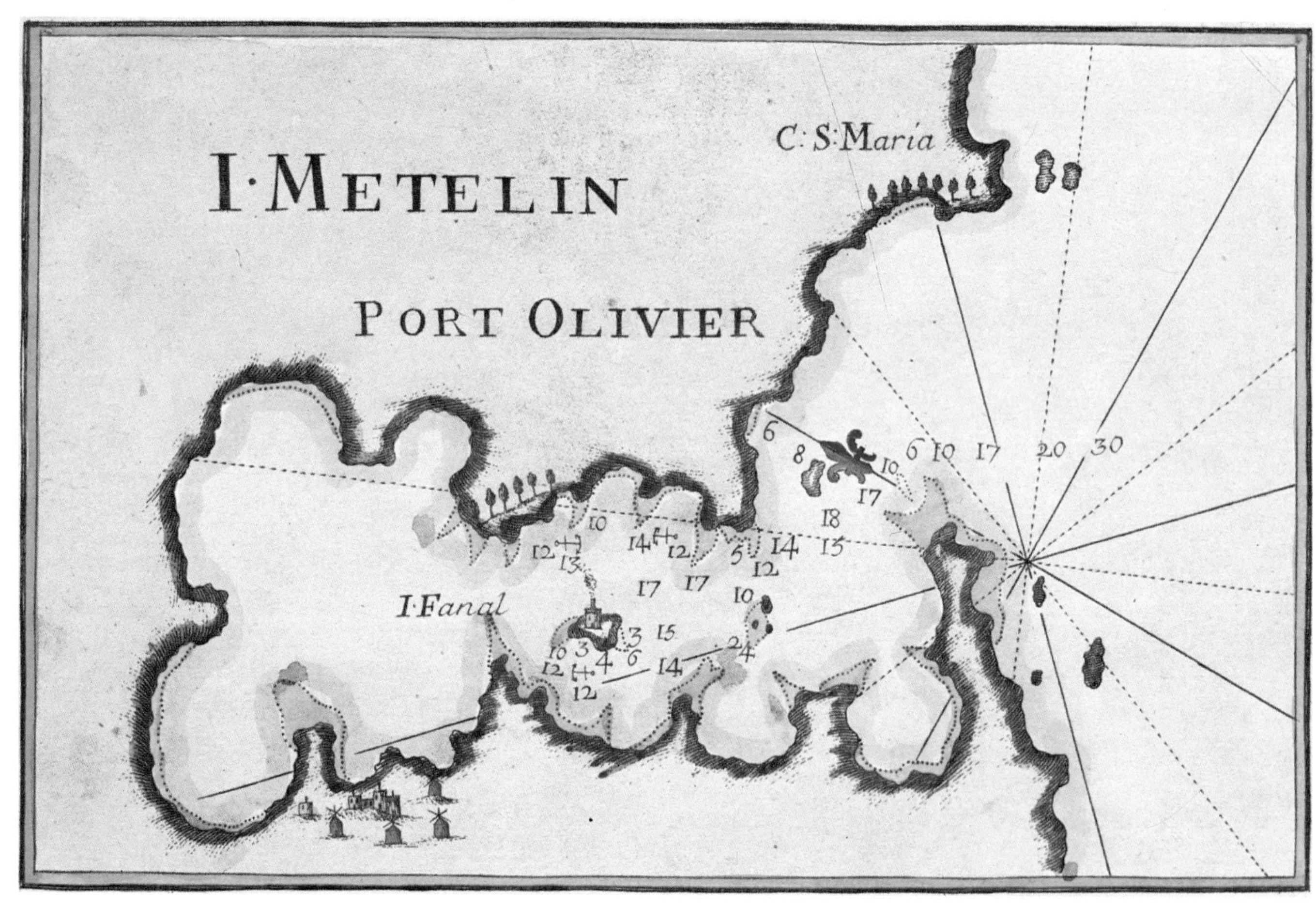

143. J. Roux: The Gulf of Yeras, Mytilene, copper engraving, 13 × 20 cms, 1764

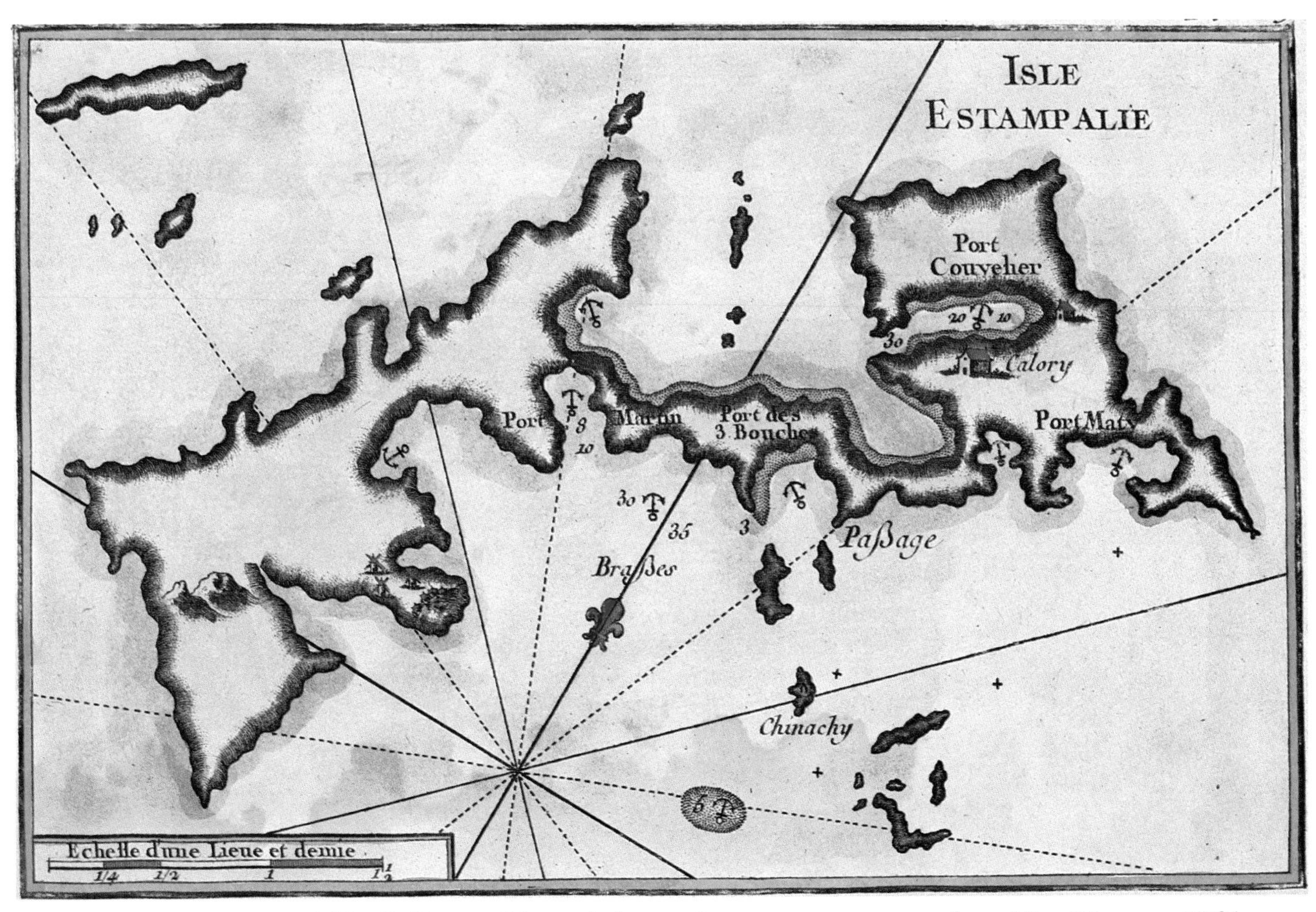

144. *J. Roux: Map of Astypalaea, copper engraving, 13 × 20 cms, 1764*

GREECE,
ARCHIPELAGO
AND
PART OF ANADOLI
By L. S. DE LA ROCHETTE,
MDCCXC.
LONDON.
Published for WILL.M FADEN,
Geographer to the KING.
January 1st 1791.
In this Map, or rather Geographical Essay,
Morea and the adjacent parts are delineated according to
the Drawing of the German Engineer Velmer von Bottmersdorf in the Venitian
Service, a Curious Manuscript obligingly communicated by some late Traveller,
to whom also we owe a multitude of New and interesting Details
in the several districts of Greece, Macedonia &c.
as well as in the Archipelago,
and on the Western and Southern Coasts of Anadoli.
For the Country round Athens, or Ancient Attica; the Passes of
the Thermopylae and of the Valley of Tempe, with the
Surrounding Parts; and for the Isles of Zant & Negroponte,
Use has been made of the Papers of Mr. Stuart.
The Ancient Names are underlined
as Lectone.
GULF OF VENICE
ALBANIA
MACEDON or COMENOLITARI
THESSALY JANNA
GREECE
LIVADIA
IONIAN SEA
ISLE OF CORFU
GULF OF LEPANTO
MOREA
SEA OF SAPIENZA
EGIO-PELAGO
ISLE OF EGRIPO vulgo NEGROPONTE
ARCHIPELAGO
CYCLADES
Turc. AK-DEGNIZ
CRITI or ISLE OF CANDIA
MEDITERRANEAN
Longitude East of London.

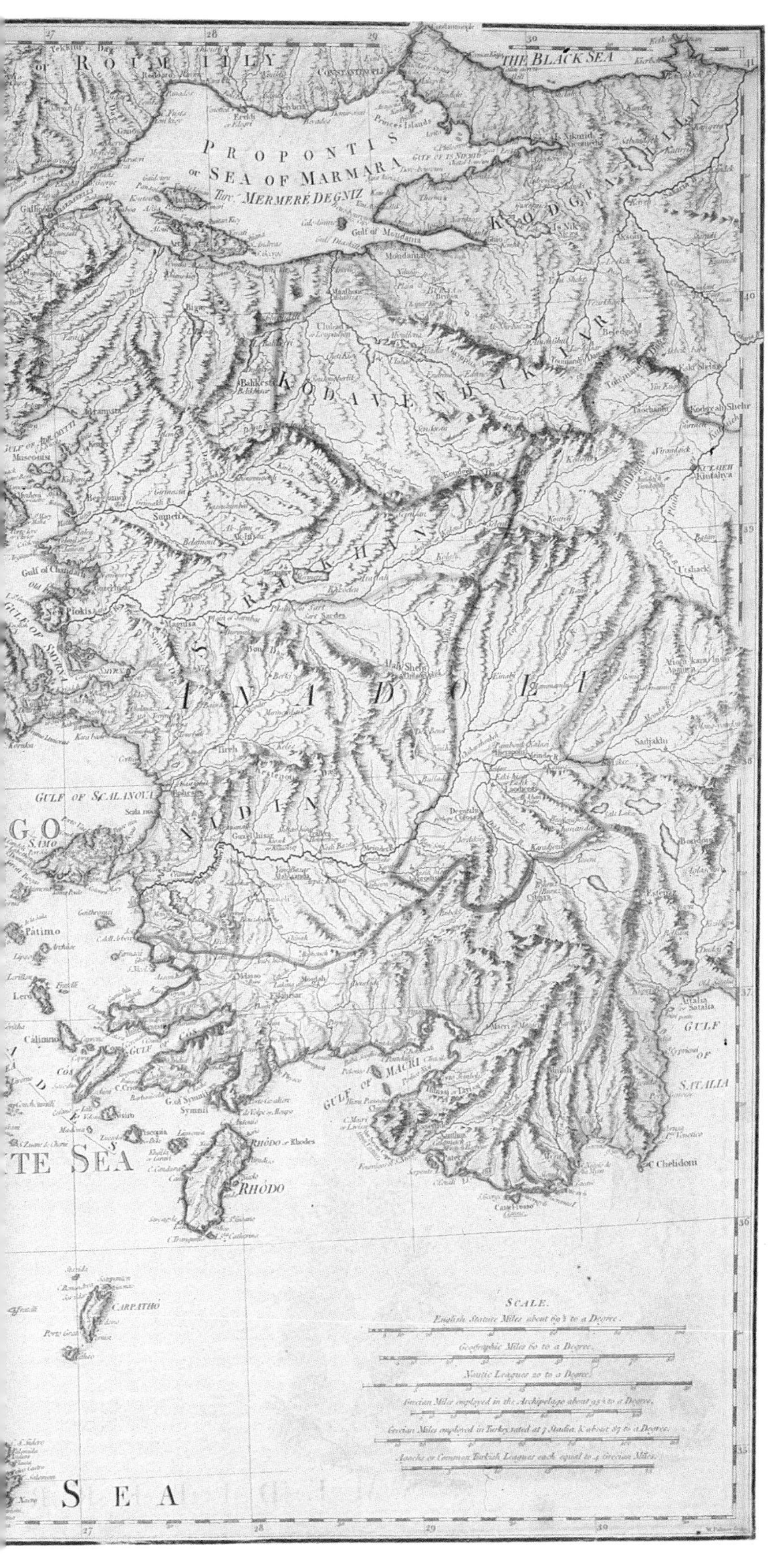

L.S. de la Rochette (1731-1802): map-maker and engraver, who worked with geographer W. Faden on the *General Atlas* published in 1791. De la Rochette's work on Greece formed part of the *Antiquities of Athens* published by J. Stuart in 1794.

145. L.S. de la Rochette: Map of Greece, the Aegean and Asia Minor, copper engraving, 53 × 75 cms, 1791

LA GRECE
ET
SES ISLES
Pour le Voyage du Jeune Anacharsis
Par M BARBIÉ DU BOCAGE
Longitude du Méridien de l'Observatoire de Paris.
MACÉDOINE
ILLYRIE
TAULANTIENS
LYNCESTIDE
EPIRE
THESSALIE
CHALCIDIQUE
Golfe Thermaique
Golfe de Piérie
MER IONIENNE
CEPHALLENIE
CORCYRE
Leucade
Zacynthe
Ambracie
Golfe d'Ambracie
ACHAIE
ARCADIE
ARGOLIDE
MESSENIE
LACONIE
PELOPONESE
BEOTIE
Athenes
Corinthe
Sicyone
Argos
Sparte
Megalopolis
Messène
Olympie
Delphes
Thèbes
Chalcis
Andros
Tenos
Syros
Ceos
Egine
Paros
Melos
Siphnos
Cythère
Cythere I.
Golfe de Messène
Golfe de Laconie
MER DE MYRTOS
CYCLADES
MER DE CRETE
Pella
Apollonie
Olynthe
Scopelos
Scyros
Halonese
Peparethe
Thasos
Athos
Thera
Gortyne
Cydonie
Lyctos
Gandos
Ægilie
Epidamne

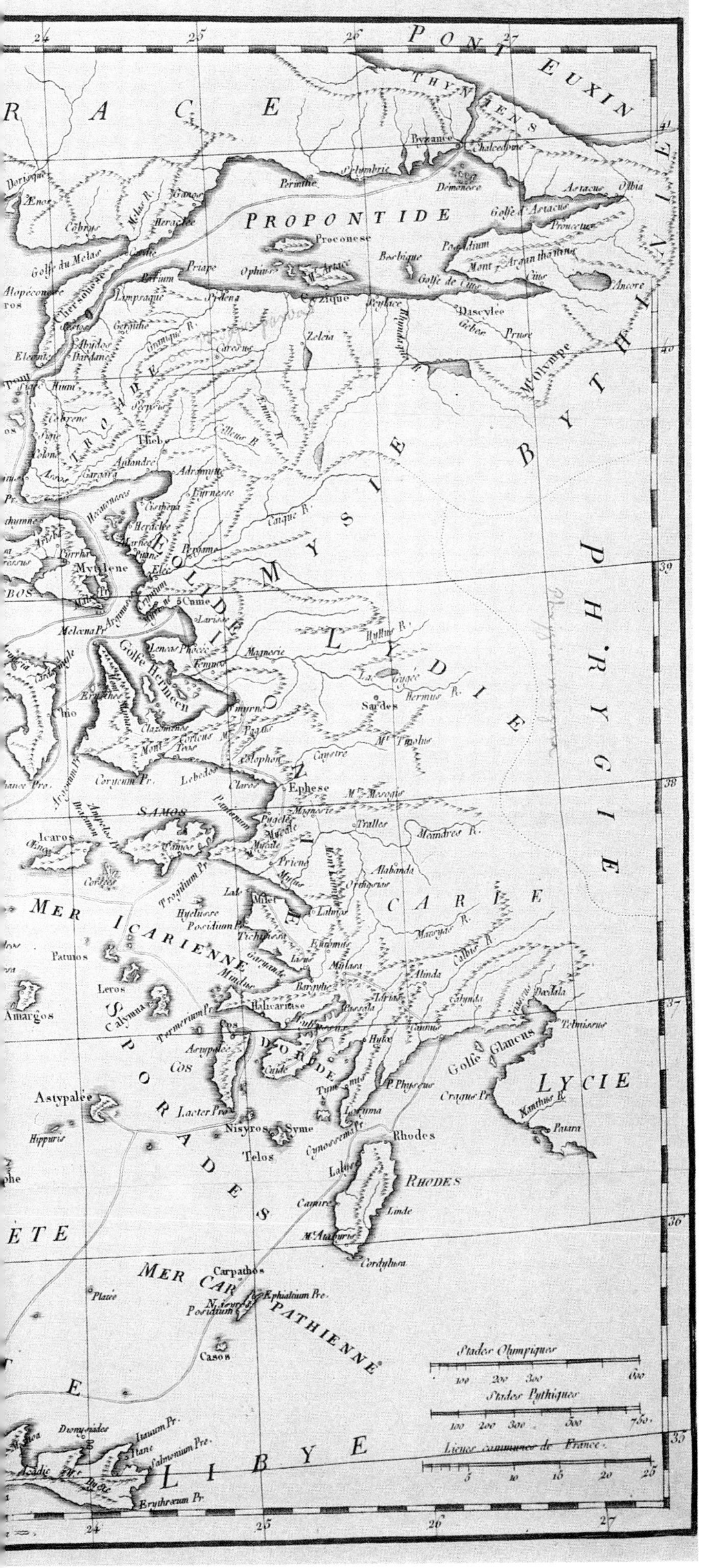

Jean Denis Barbié du Bocage (1760-1826): major French geographer and cosmographer, one of the founder-members of the Paris Geographical Association and pupil of the great d' Anville. Bocage drew the maps in the *Voyage du Jeune Anacharsis* (1781-88) and corrected the *Hémisphères* of d' Anville of 1786. Among other works: *Recueil de Cartes Géographiques* (1791), *Plan de Constantinople* (1822), *Mer des Indes* (1811).

146. Barbié du Bocage: Map of Greece and its islands, copper engraving, 42 × 35 cms, 1791

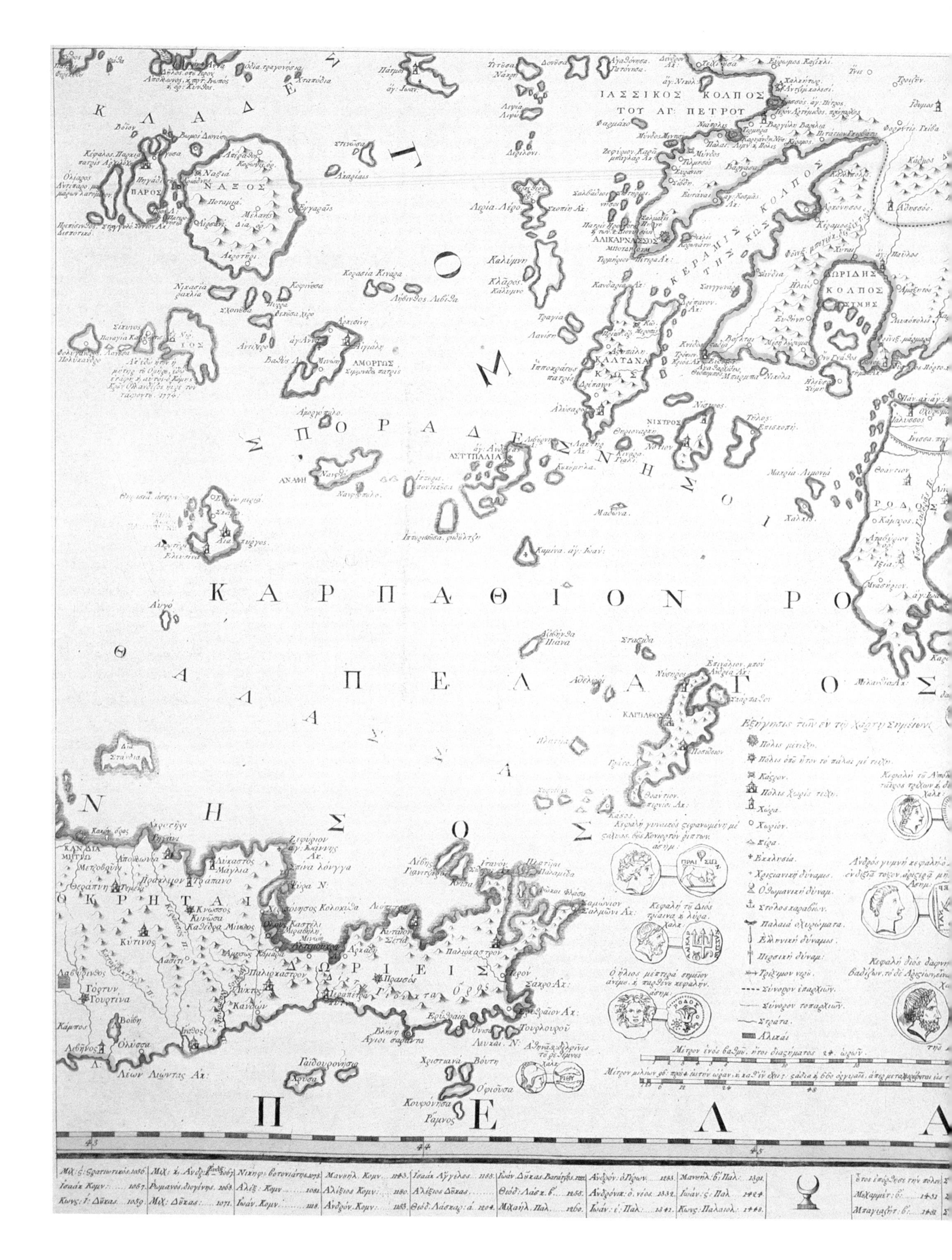
ΙΑΣΣΙΚΟΣ ΚΟΛΠΟΣ
ΤΟΥ ΑΓ: ΠΕΤΡΟΥ
ΝΑΞΟΣ
ΠΑΡΟΣ
ΑΜΟΡΓΩΣ
ΑΣΤΥΠΑΛΙΑ
ΑΛΙΚΑΡΝΑΣΣΟΣ
ΚΑΛΥΔΝΑ
ΝΙΣΥΡΟΣ
ΔΩΡΙΔΗΣ ΚΟΛΠΟΣ
ΡΟΔΟΣ
ΚΑΡΠΑΘΟΣ
ΚΑΡΠΑΘΙΟΝ
ΚΡΗΤΑΙ
ΔΩΡΙΕΙΣ
Κνωσσός
Κύτινος
Γόρτυν
Πραισός
Ἱεράπετρα
Ἐξήγησις τῶν ἐν τῷ χάρτῃ σημείων
Πόλις μετὰ τείχους.
Κάστρον.
Χώρα.
Χωρίον.
Ἐκκλησία.
Χριστιανικὴ δύναμις.
Στόλος.
Ἑλληνικὴ δύναμις.
Περσικὴ δύναμις.
Σύνορον ἐπαρχιῶν.
Στράτα.
Ἀλικαί.

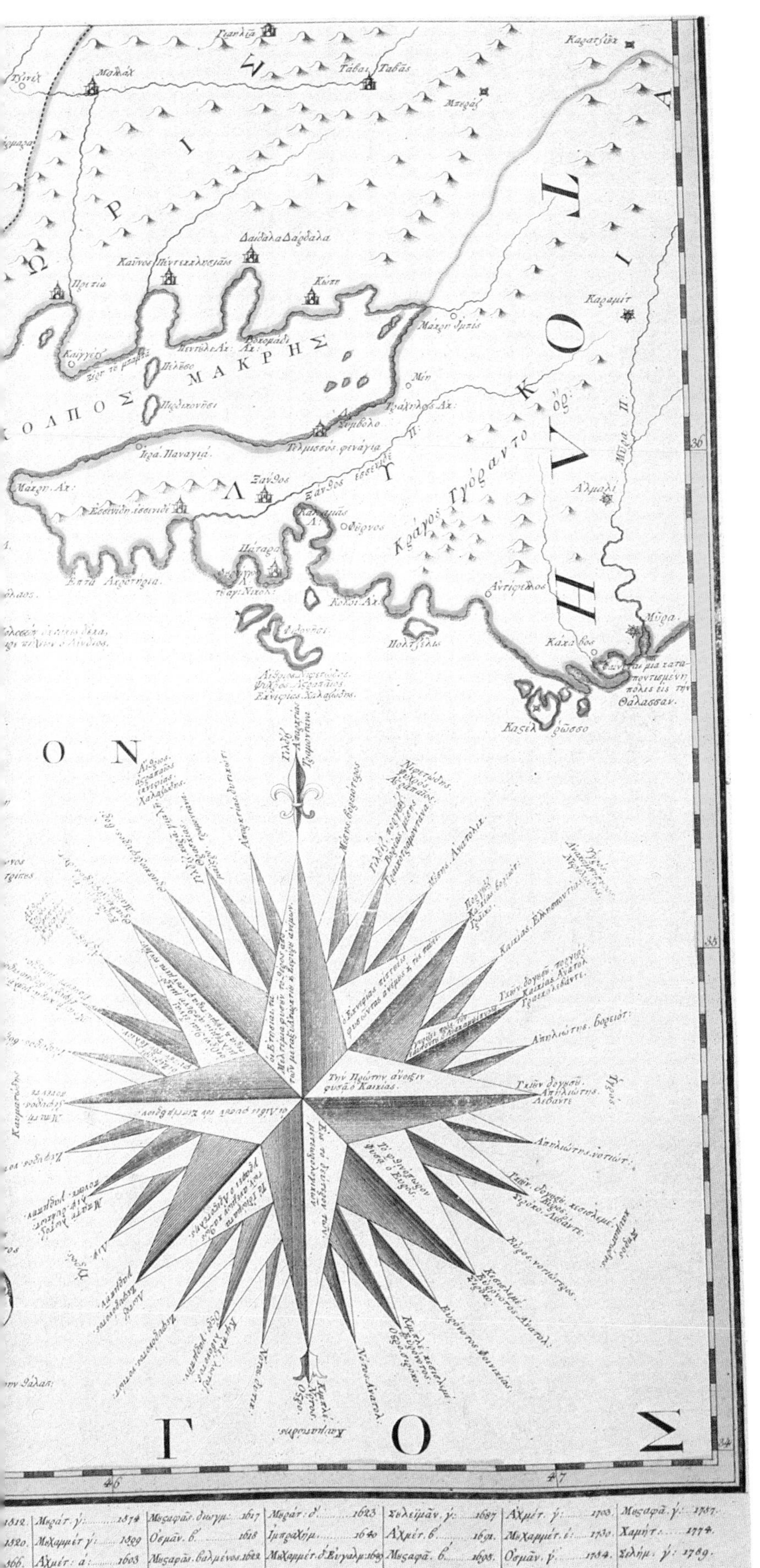

The 'Charta of Greece' of Rhigas Pherraios is a map of enormous dimensions, covering the area from the Carpathians and the Danube to Crete and from the Adriatic to the Black Sea and Bithynia in Asia Minor. It was printed in Vienna, in 1797, and split into 12 leaves, each measuring 205 × 205 cms. The map was engraved by Müller.

The first leaf, entitled *Ἐπιπεδογραφία τῆς Κωνσταντινουπόλεως (The Ground Plan of Constantinople)*, was published separately in late 1796. The remaining 11 leaves depicting the rest of the area were then printed, and together with the Ground Plan make up the twelve-leaf Charta of Greece, 1797. This monumental work of cartography was intended to awake the national feelings of the enslaved Greeks and other peoples of the Balkans. Rigas Pherraios' map contains a wealth of historical references and information: dates of battles, victories over the barbarians, lists of the Emperors of Byzantium, ancient coins, ancient inscriptions and ancient names, which are placed next to their modern equivalents.

147. Leaf from the Map of Rigas Ferraios, 205 × 205 cms, 1797

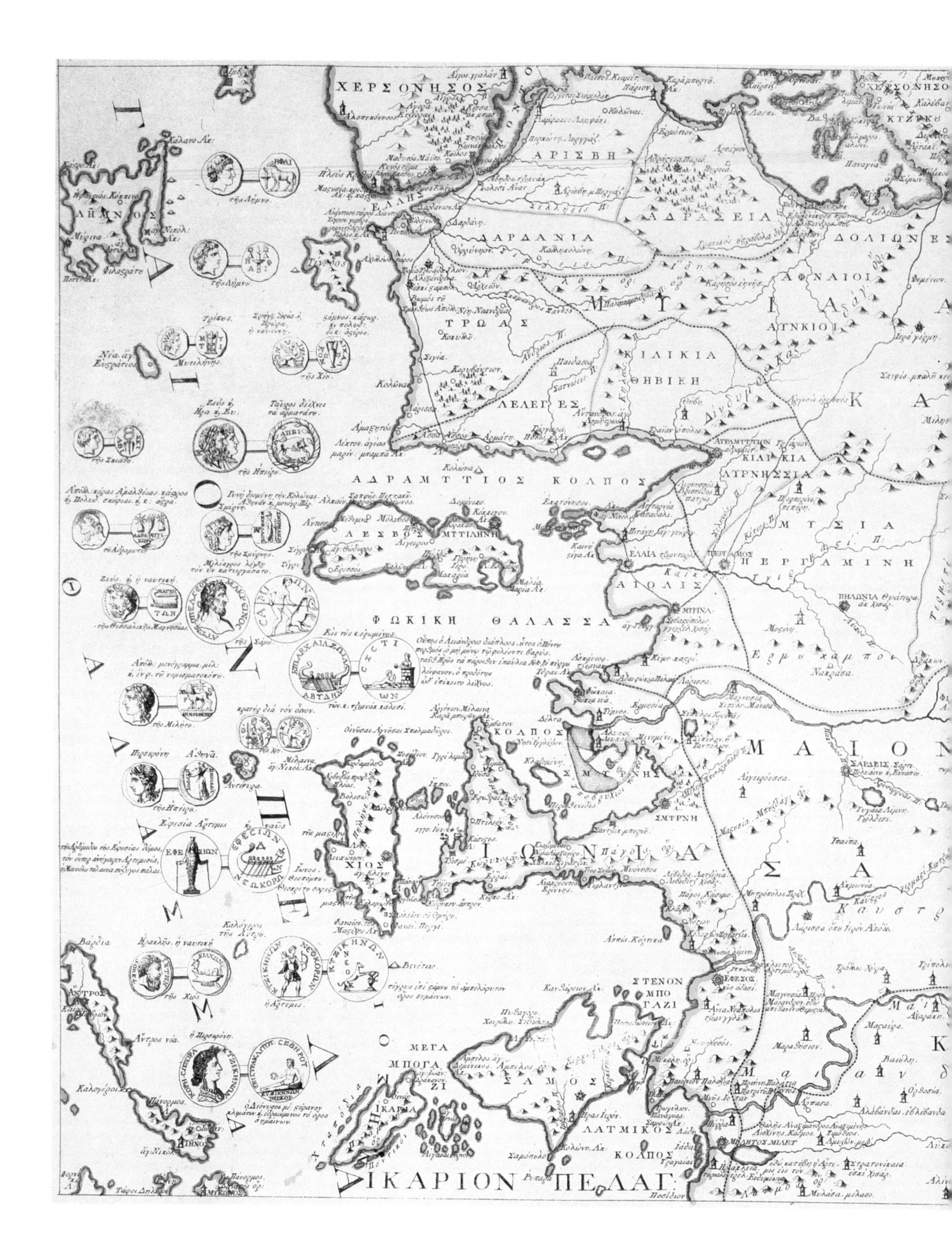

ΧΕΡΣΟΝΗΣΟΣ
ΑΡΙΣΒΗ
ΑΔΡΑΣΕΙΑ
ΔΑΡΔΑΝΙΑ
ΑΦΝΑΙΟΙ
ΤΡΩΑΣ
ΚΙΛΙΚΙΑ
ΘΗΒΙΚΗ
ΛΕΛΕΓΕΣ
ΑΔΡΑΜΥΤΤΙΟΣ ΚΟΛΠΟΣ
ΛΕΣΒΟΣ
ΜΥΤΙΛΗΝΗ
ΦΩΚΙΚΗ ΘΑΛΑΣΣΑ
ΑΙΟΛΙΣ
ΠΕΡΓΑΜΟΣ
ΠΕΡΓΑΜΙΝΗ
ΜΥΣΙΑ
ΣΜΥΡΝΗ
ΧΙΟΣ
ΙΩΝΙΑ
ΕΦΕΣΟΣ
ΣΤΕΝΟΝ ΜΠΟΓΑΖΙ
ΜΕΓΑ ΜΠΟΓΑΖΙ
ΣΑΜΟΣ
ΙΚΑΡΙΑ
ΛΑΤΜΙΚΟΣ ΚΟΛΠΟΣ
ΙΚΑΡΙΟΝ ΠΕΛΑΓ.
ΛΗΜΝΟΣ
ΕΦΕΣΙΩΝ
ΚΥΖΙΚΗΝΩΝ

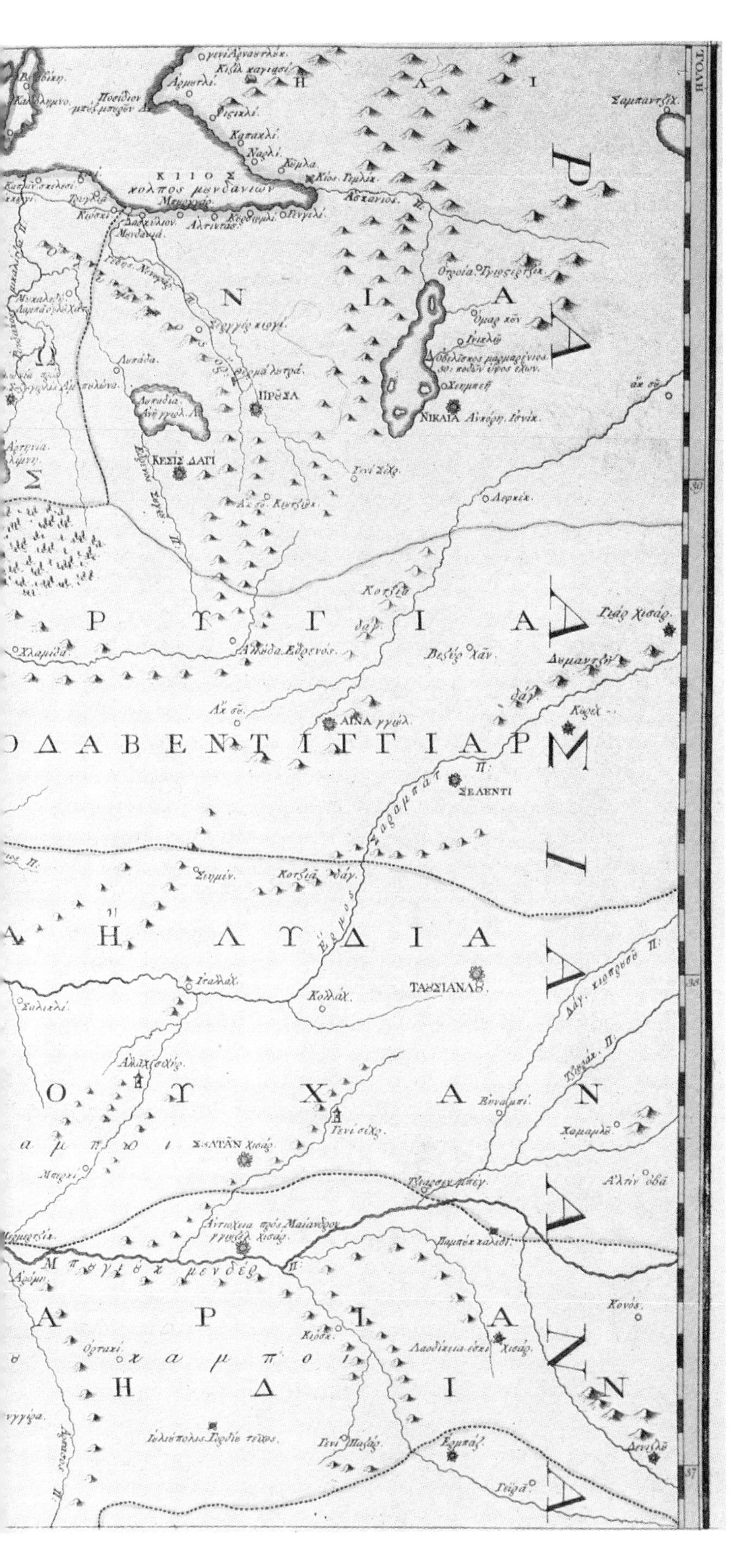

148. *Leaf from the Map of Rigas Ferraios, 205 × 205 cms, 1797*

M.G.F.A. Comte de Choiseul Gouffier (1752-1819): French diplomat, ambassador to Constantinople from 1784-1792 and author of the famous *Voyage pittoresque de la Grèce* (1782-1822). This massive work was adorned with outstanding engravings on a variety of subjects executed by the greatest masters of the period. The work also contained some maps of the Aegean. Gouffier visited the Aegean islands, the Greek cities of Asia Minor, Pergamum, Troy, Thrace and Mount Athos. He himself drew a map of the Mediterranean (1776), a map of the island of Paros and a map of Delos.

149. Choiseul Gouffier: Map of Lemnos, Imbros and Samothrace, copper engraving, 38.5 × 26.5 cms, 1809

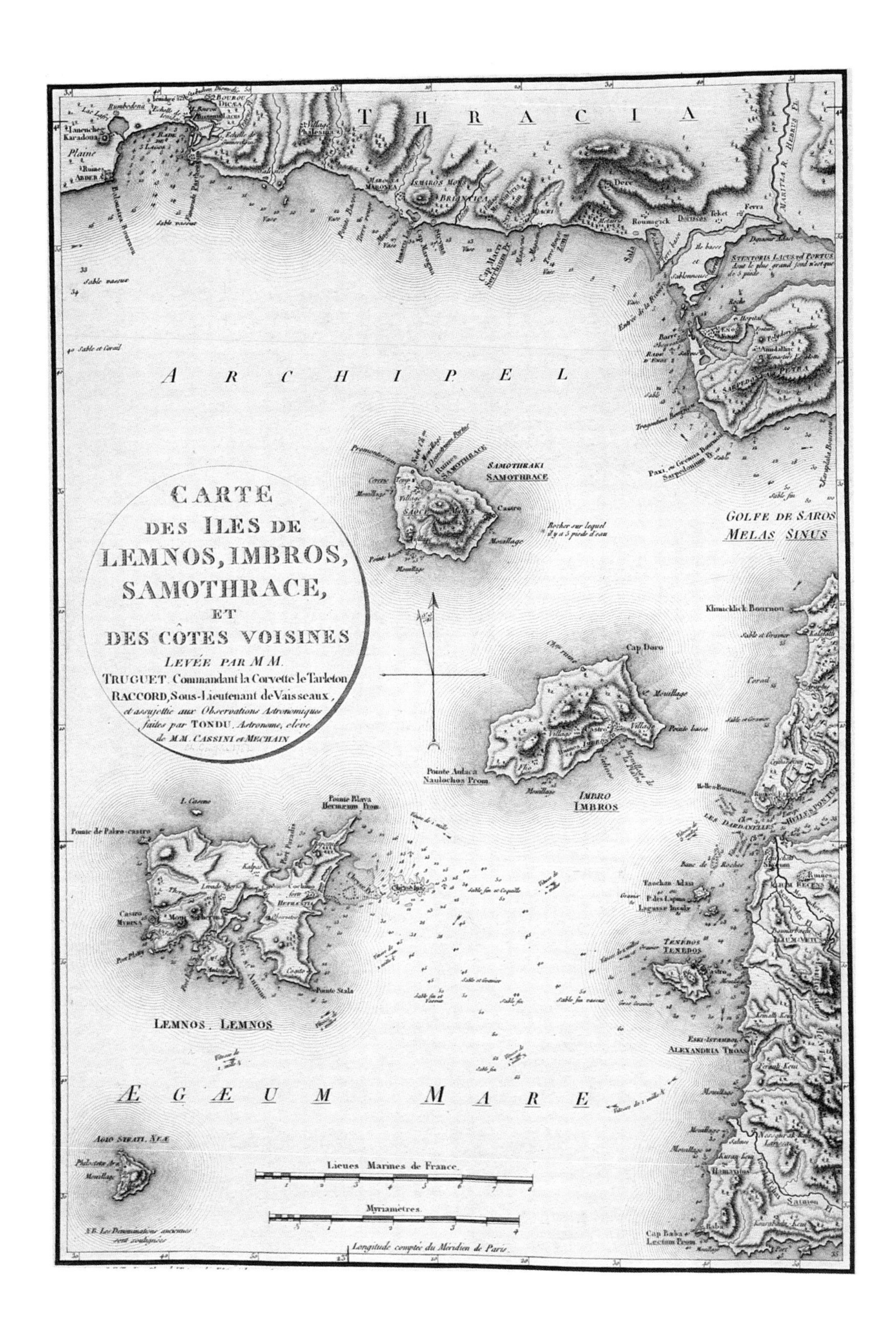
CARTE
DES ILES DE
LEMNOS, IMBROS,
SAMOTHRACE,
ET
DES CÔTES VOISINES
LEVÉE PAR M.M.
TRUGUET, Commandant la Corvette le Tarleton
RACCORD, Sous-Lieutenant de Vaisseaux,
et assujettie aux Observations Astronomiques
faites par TONDU, Astronome, élève
de M.M. CASSINI et MECHAIN
THRACIA
ARCHIPEL
SAMOTHRAKI
SAMOTHRACE
GOLFE DE SAROS
MELAS SINUS
Cap Doro
IMBRO
IMBROS
LEMNOS. LEMNOS
TENEDOS
ÆGEUM MARE
Lieues Marines de France
Myriamètres
Longitude comptée du Méridien de Paris

150. *Choiseul Gouffier: Map of Greec*

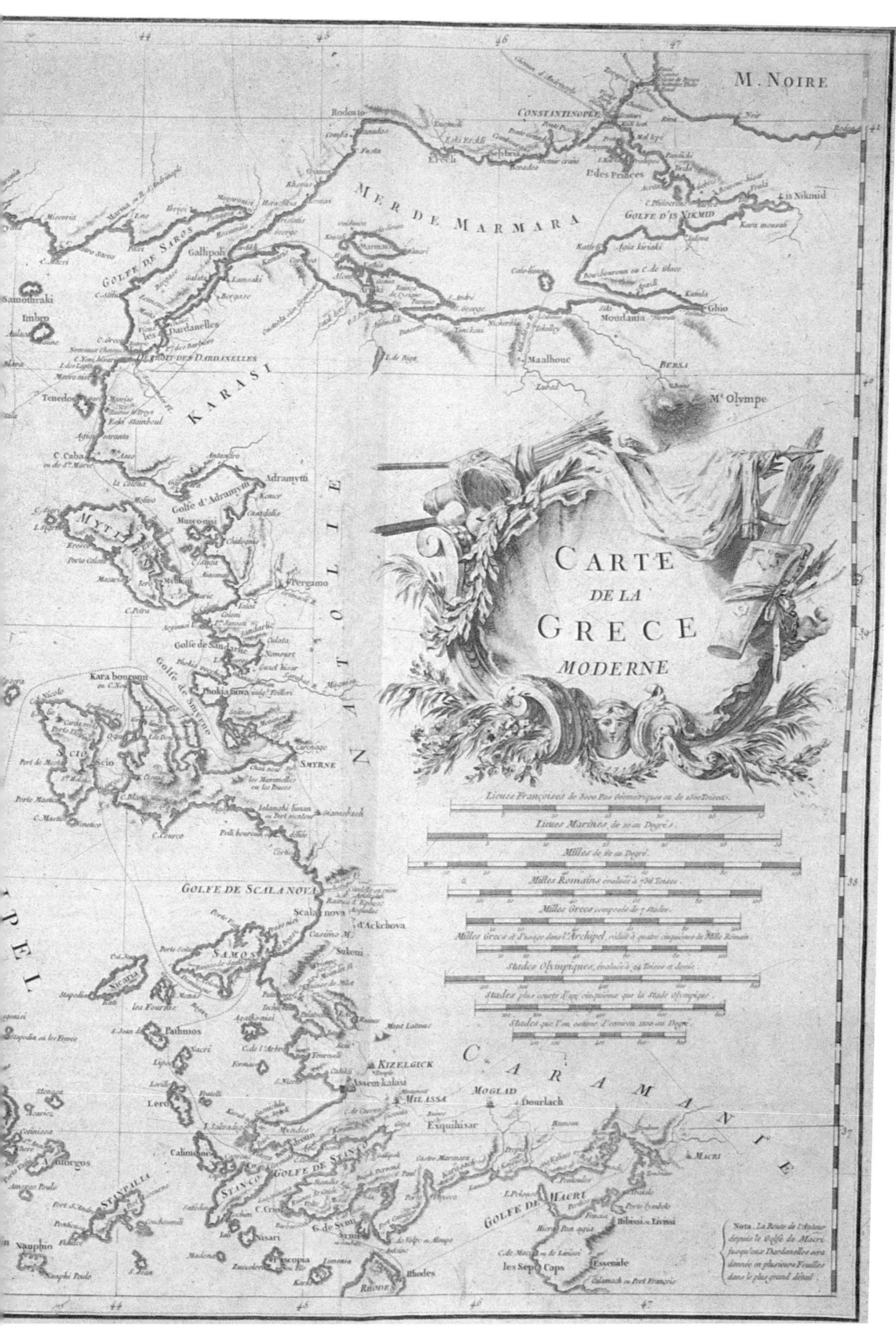

pper engraving, 43 × 61.5 cms, 1782

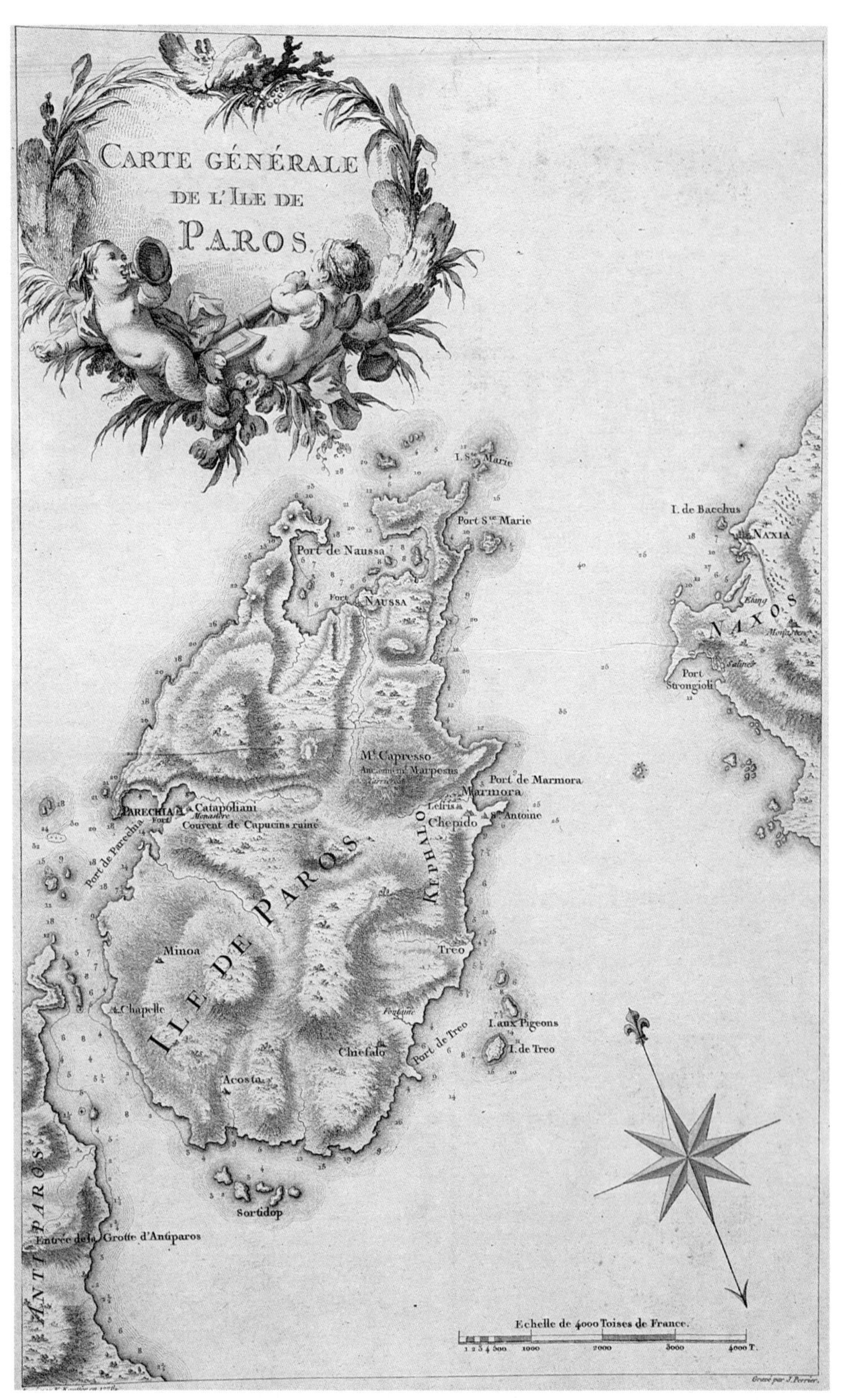

151. *Choiseul Gouffier: Map of Paros, copper engraving, 34 × 21 cms, 1782*

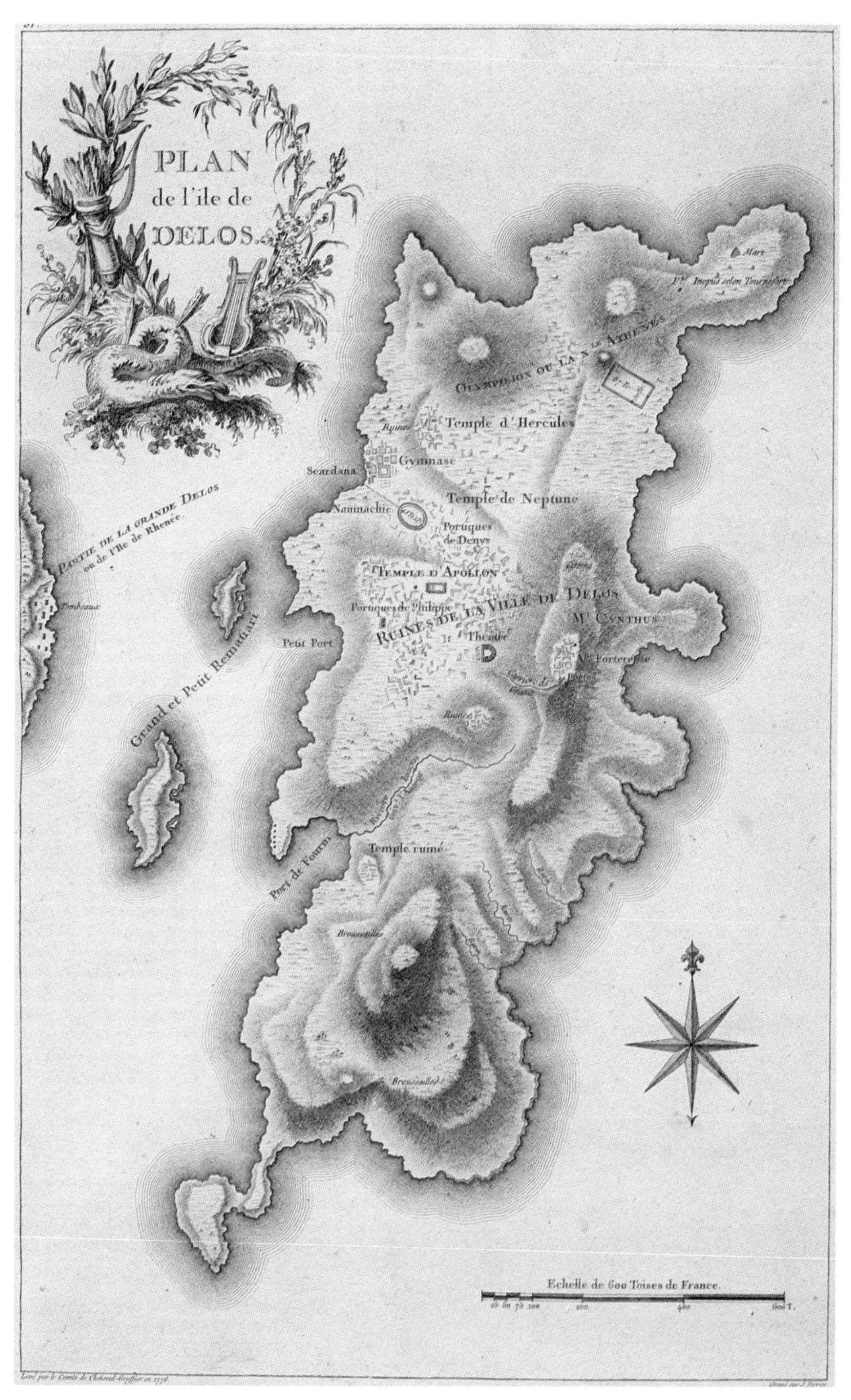

152. *Choiseul Gouffier: Map of Delos, copper engraving, 34.5 × 21 cms, 1782*

Captain Nikolas Kefalas: from Zakynthos, son of a sailor, author of works intended to convey to his compatriots his theoretical knowledge of navigation and travel on the open sea. In 1817, he published his *Θαλάσσιος Ὁδηγία (Guide to the Sea)* at Vienna, using material taken from English, French and Italian sources but also including information gathered by the Captain himself on his voyages. This book was followed by *Θαλάσσιος Νομοθεσία (Maritime Law)* and *Χάρτης Μαύρης και Μεσογείου Θαλάσσης (Maps of the Mediterranean and the Black Sea)*. He published a *Χάρτης της Μεσογείου Θαλάσσης και του Αιγαίου Πελάγους (Map of the Mediterranean and the Aegean)* in 1818. Kefalas dedicated all these works to the Government of the Ionian Islands, which, however, refused to accept the dedication.

153. Map of the Aegean drawn by Captain Nikolas Kefalas of Zakynthos, 98 × 66 cms, 1818

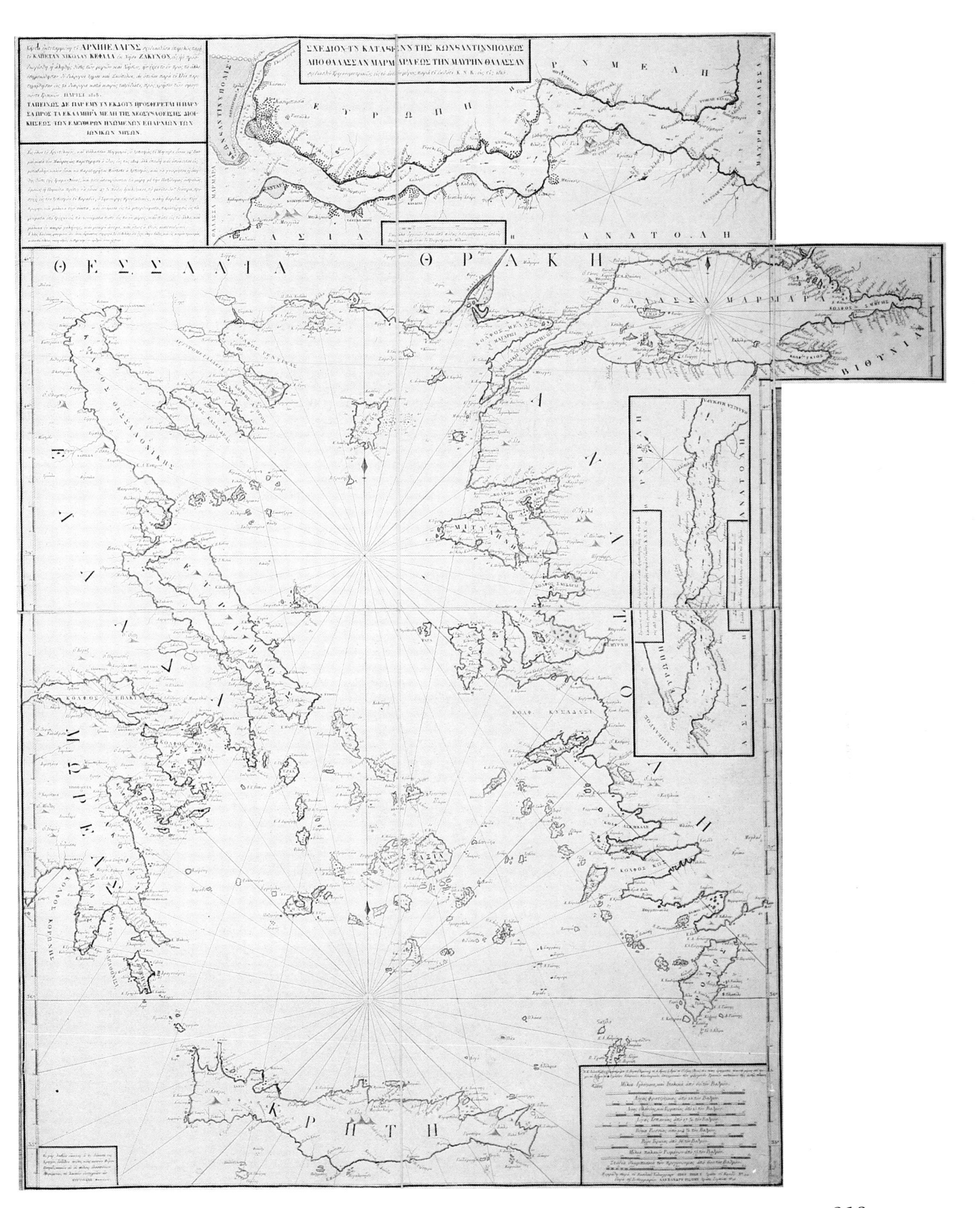
ΣΧΕΔΙΟΝ ΤΥ ΚΑΤΑΒΕΝΝ ΤΗΣ ΚΩΝΣΑΝΤΙΝΠΟΛΕΩΣ
ΑΠΟ ΘΑΛΑΣΣΑΝ ΜΑΡΜΑΡΑ ΕΩΣ ΤΗΝ ΜΑΥΡΗΝ ΘΑΛΑΣΣΑΝ
ΡΥΜΕΛΗ
ΕΥΡΩΠΗ
ΑΣΙΑ
ΑΝΑΤΟΛΗ
ΘΕΣΣΑΛΙΑ
ΘΡΑΚΗ
ΘΑΛΑΣΣΑ ΜΑΡΜΑΡΑ
ΒΙΘΥΝΙΑ
ΚΟΛΠΟΣ ΘΕΣΣΑΛΟΝΙΚΗΣ
ΚΟΛΠΟΣ ΚΑΣΣΑΝΔΡΑΣ
ΚΟΛΠΟΣ ΑΔΡΑΜΥΤΙ
ΜΙΤΥΛΗΝΗ
ΚΟΛΠΟΣ ΕΠΑΚΤΟΥ
ΚΟΛΠΟΣ ΑΘΗΝΑΣ
ΜΩΡΕΑΣ
ΚΟΛΦ. ΚΥΣΑΔΑΣΙ
ΚΡΗΤΗ
ΡΟΔΟΣ

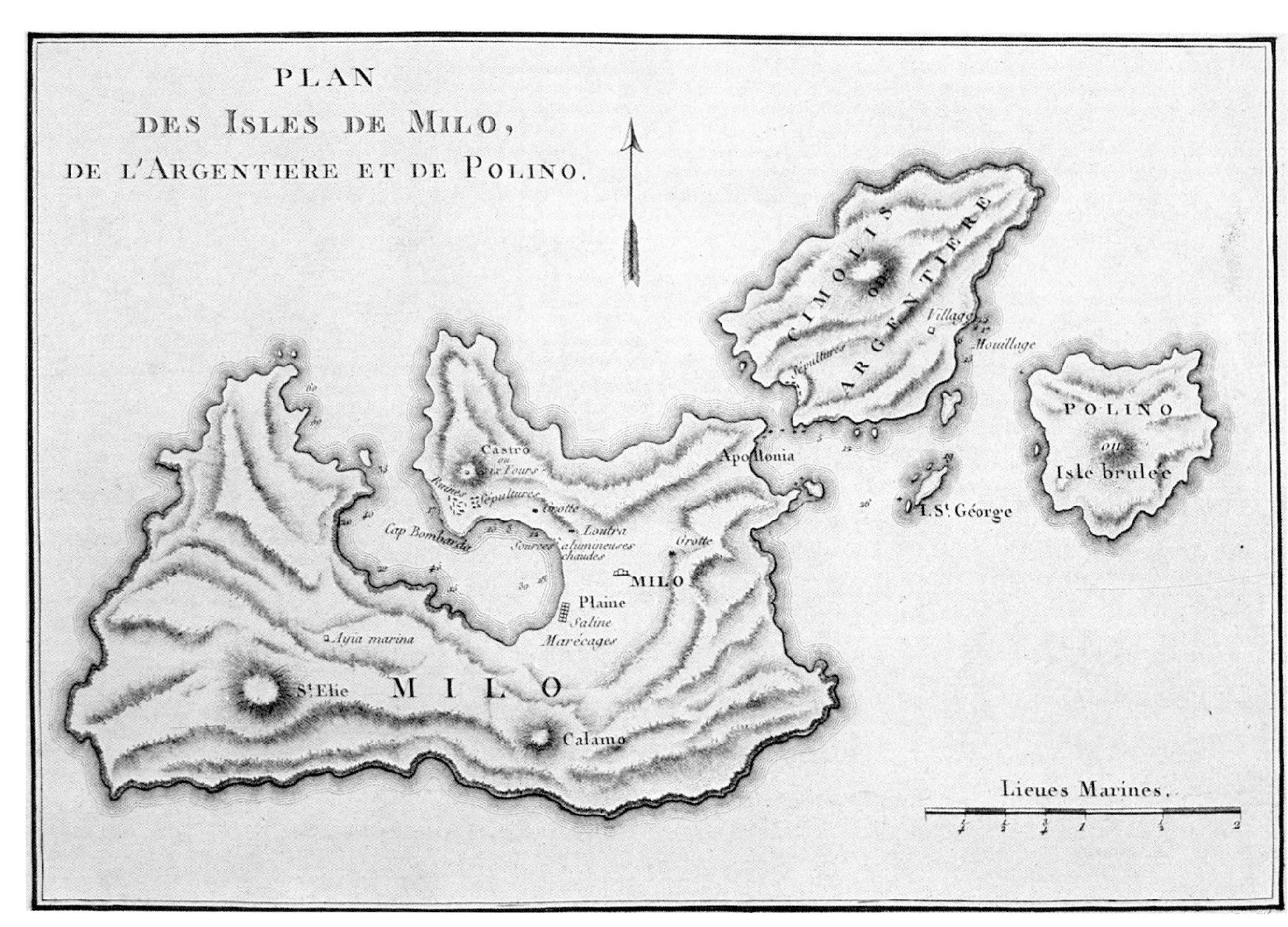

154. G.A. Olivier: Map of Melos, Kimolos and Polyvos, copper engraving, 17 × 24 cms, An IX

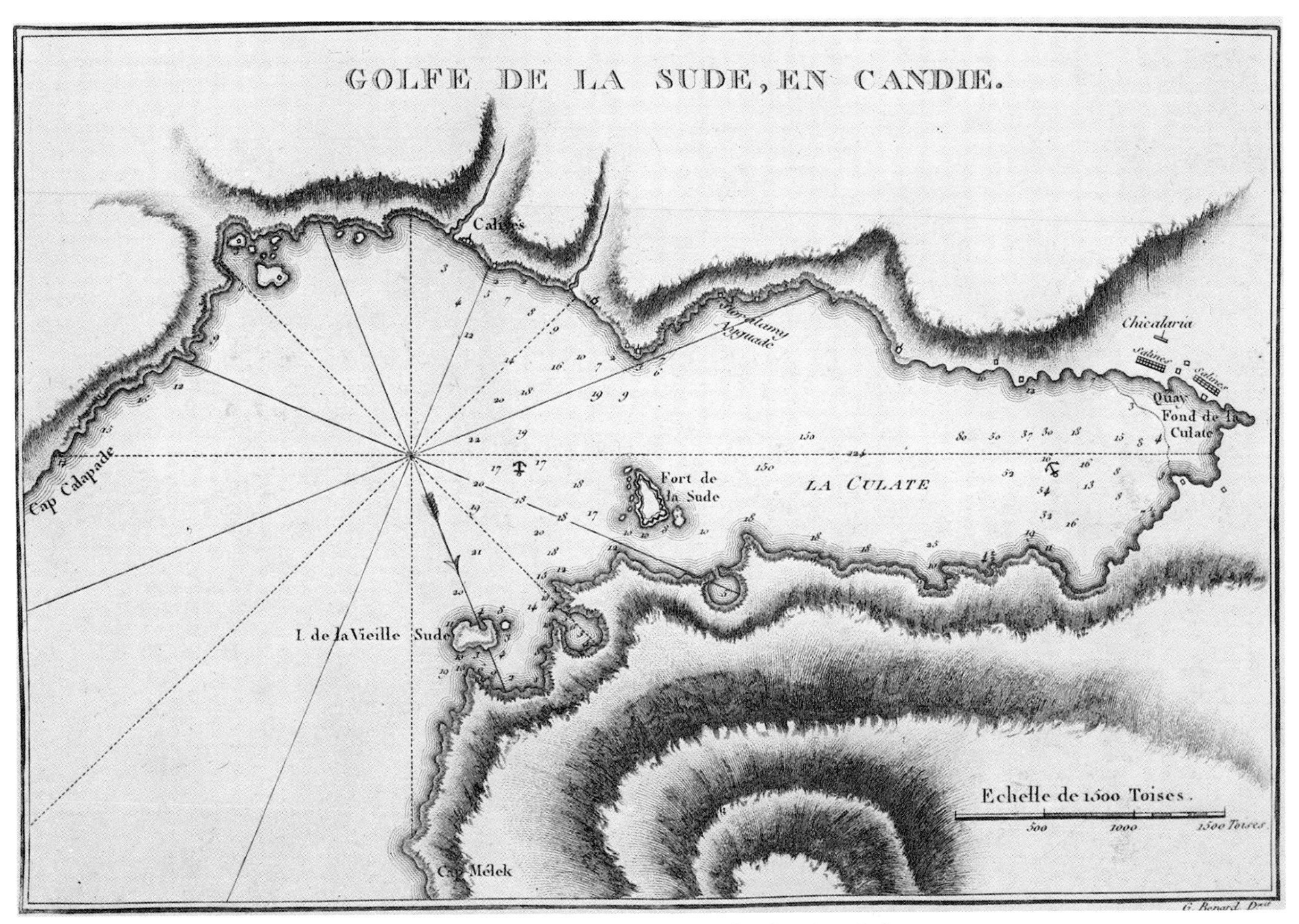

155. G. A. Olivier: Souda Bay, Crete. Drawn on the basis of the survey conducted in 1738 by French naval engineer Leroi, copper engraving, 16.5 × 24 cms, An IX.

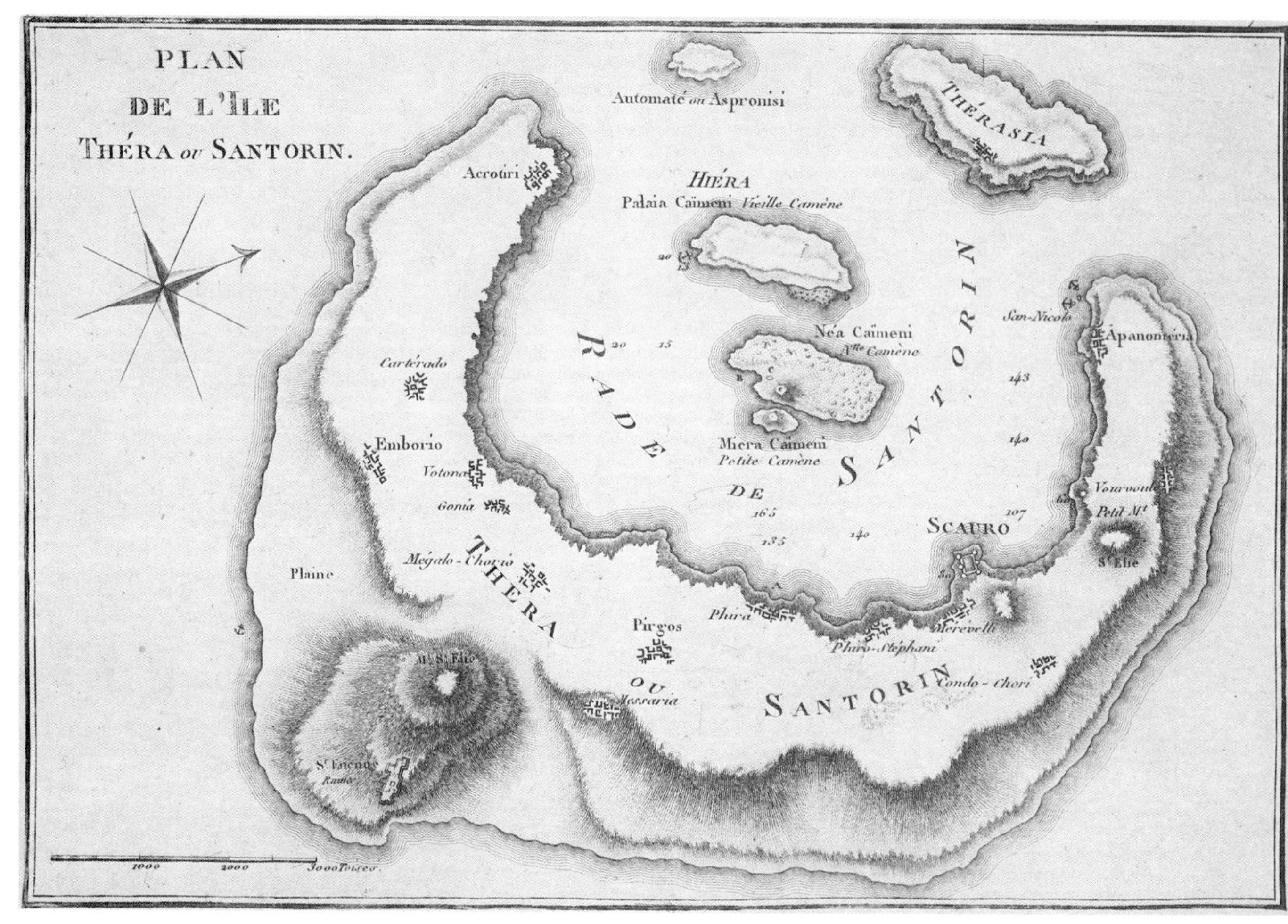

156. G. A. Olivier: Map of Santorini, copper engraving, 16.5 × 24 cms, An IX.

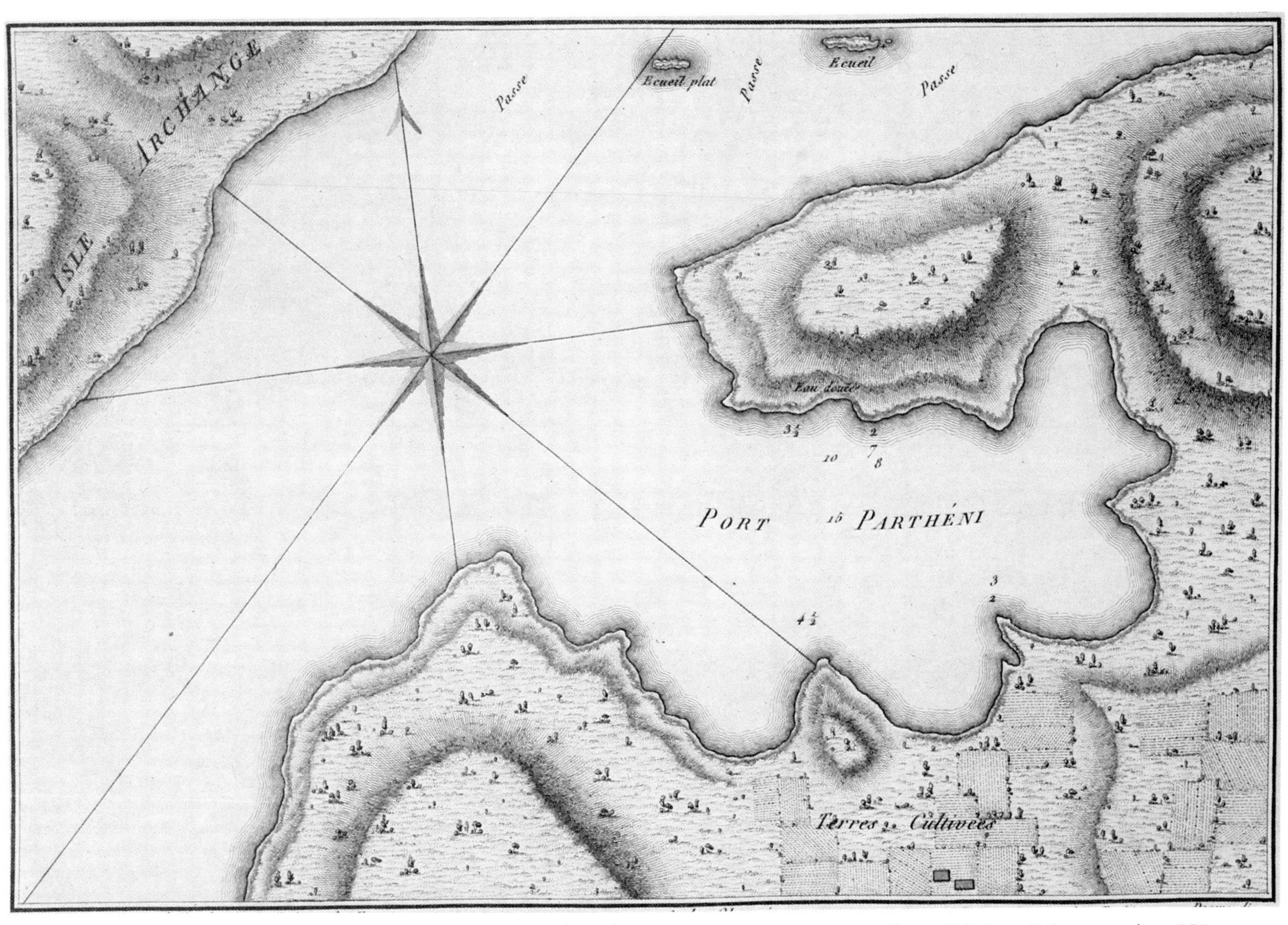

157. G. A. Olivier: Partheni, Leros, copper engraving, 16.5 × 24 cms, An IX.

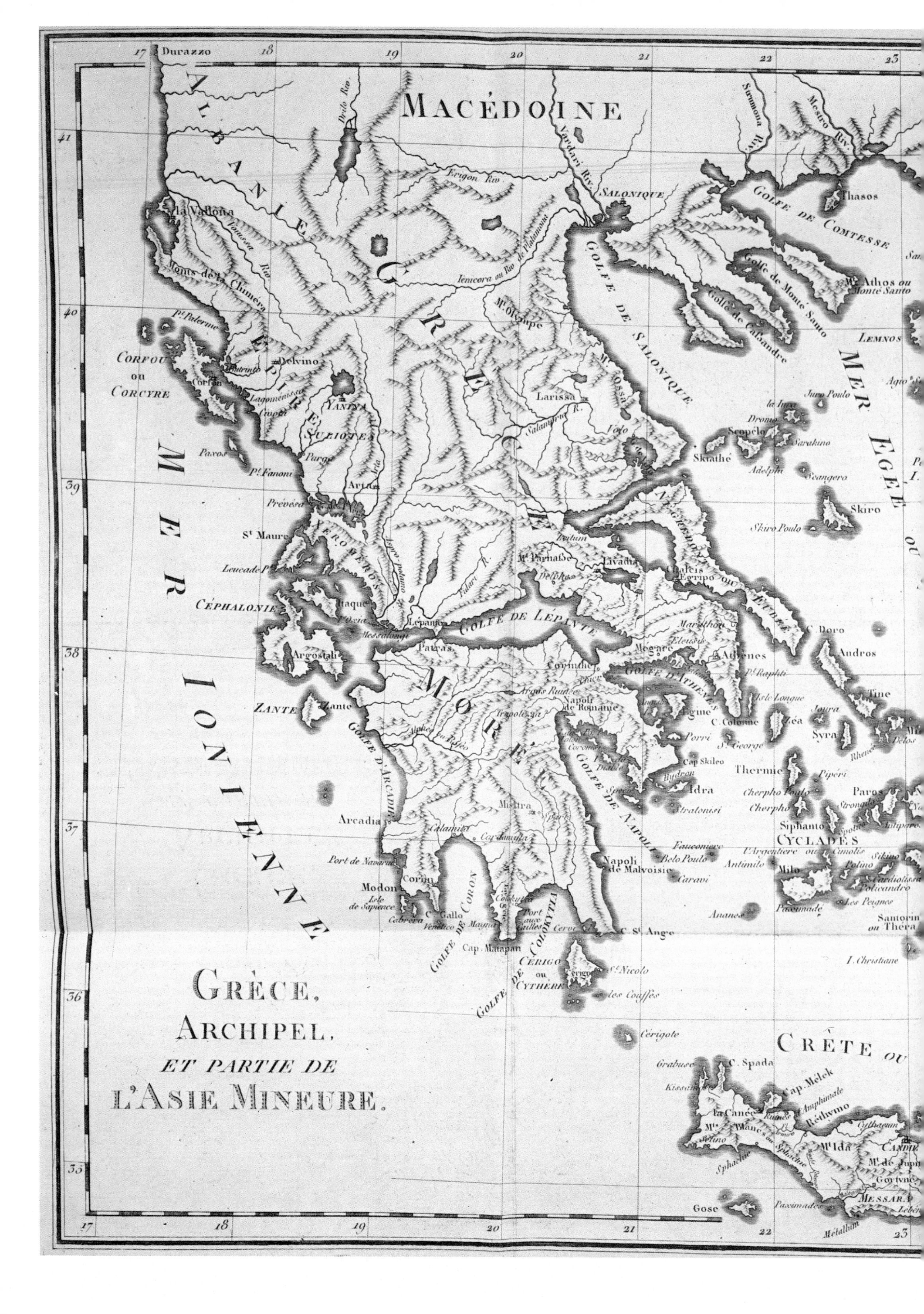
GRÈCE,
ARCHIPEL,
ET PARTIE DE
L'ASIE MINEURE.
MACÉDOINE
ALBANIE
GRÈCE
ÉPIRE
MORÉE
MER IONIENNE
MER EGÉE
CRÈTE OU
CYCLADES
Durazzo
Salonique
Golfe de Salonique
Golfe de Comtesse
Golfe de Monté Santo
Golfe de Cassandre
Mt. Athos ou Monté Santo
Thasos
Lemnos
Larissa
Mt. Olympe
Mt. Ossa
Corfou ou Corcyre
Corfou
la Vallona
Delvino
Yanina
Suliotes
Parga
Paxos
Arta
Prévésa
St. Maure
Leucade
Céphalonie
Argostoli
Itaque
Zante
Lépante
Golfe de Lépante
Messalongi
Patras
Corinthe
Mt. Parnasse
Livadia
Chalcis
Egripo ou Eubée
Marathon
Megare
Athènes
Golfe d'Athènes
C. Colonne
Napoli de Romanie
Golfe de Napoli
Golfe d'Arcadie
Arcadia
Port de Navarin
Modon
Coron
Golfe de Coron
Mistra
Napoli de Malvoisie
C. St. Ange
Cap. Matapan
Cerigo ou Cythère
Cérigote
Golfe de Colokytia
Skiathé
Scopélo
Skiro
C. Doro
Andros
Tine
Syra
Zéa
Thermie
Idra
Milo
Siphanto
Santorin ou Théra
Grabuse
C. Spada
Cap. Mélek
La Canée
Rétimo
Mt. Ida
Candie
Gose
Messara

158. G. A. Olivier: *Map of Greece, the Aegean, and part of Asia Minor, drawn on the basis of the maps of Barbié du Bocage and Choiseul Gouffier, but with alterations and corrections which were the fruit of on-the-spot investigation, copper engraving, 34 × 43 cms, An IX.*

159. Benoist: Map of t

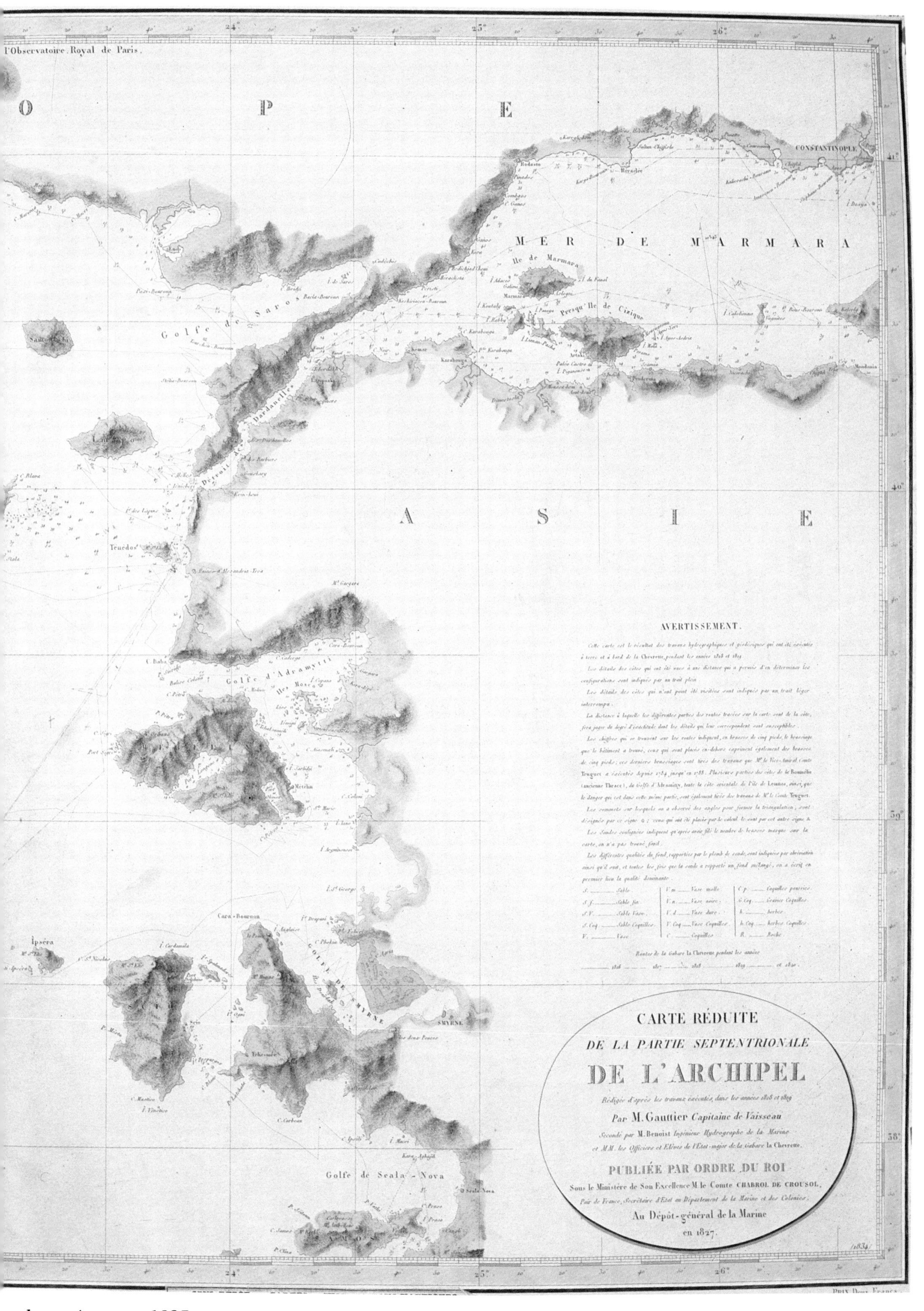

orthern Aegean, 1827

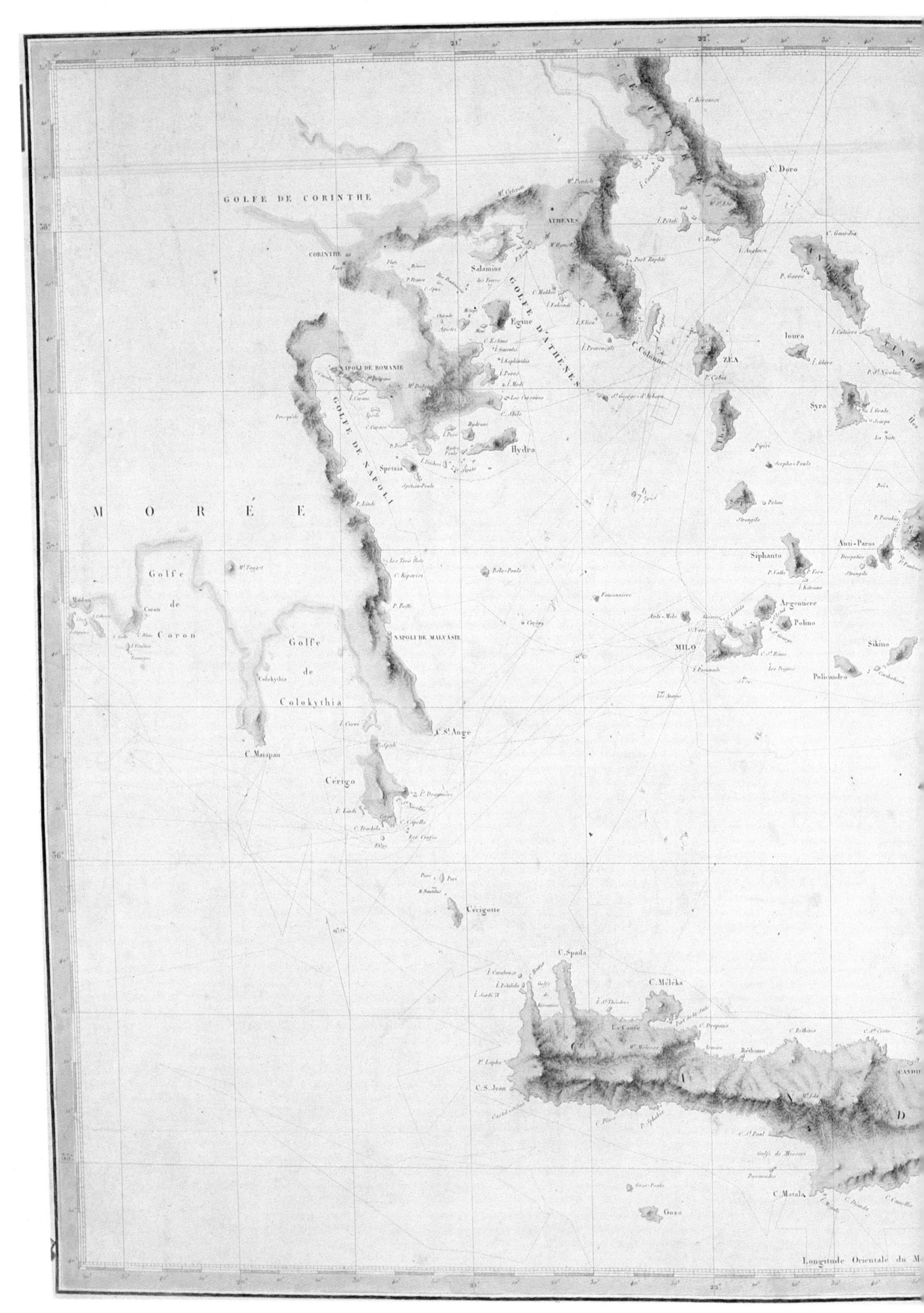

160. Benoist: Map of th

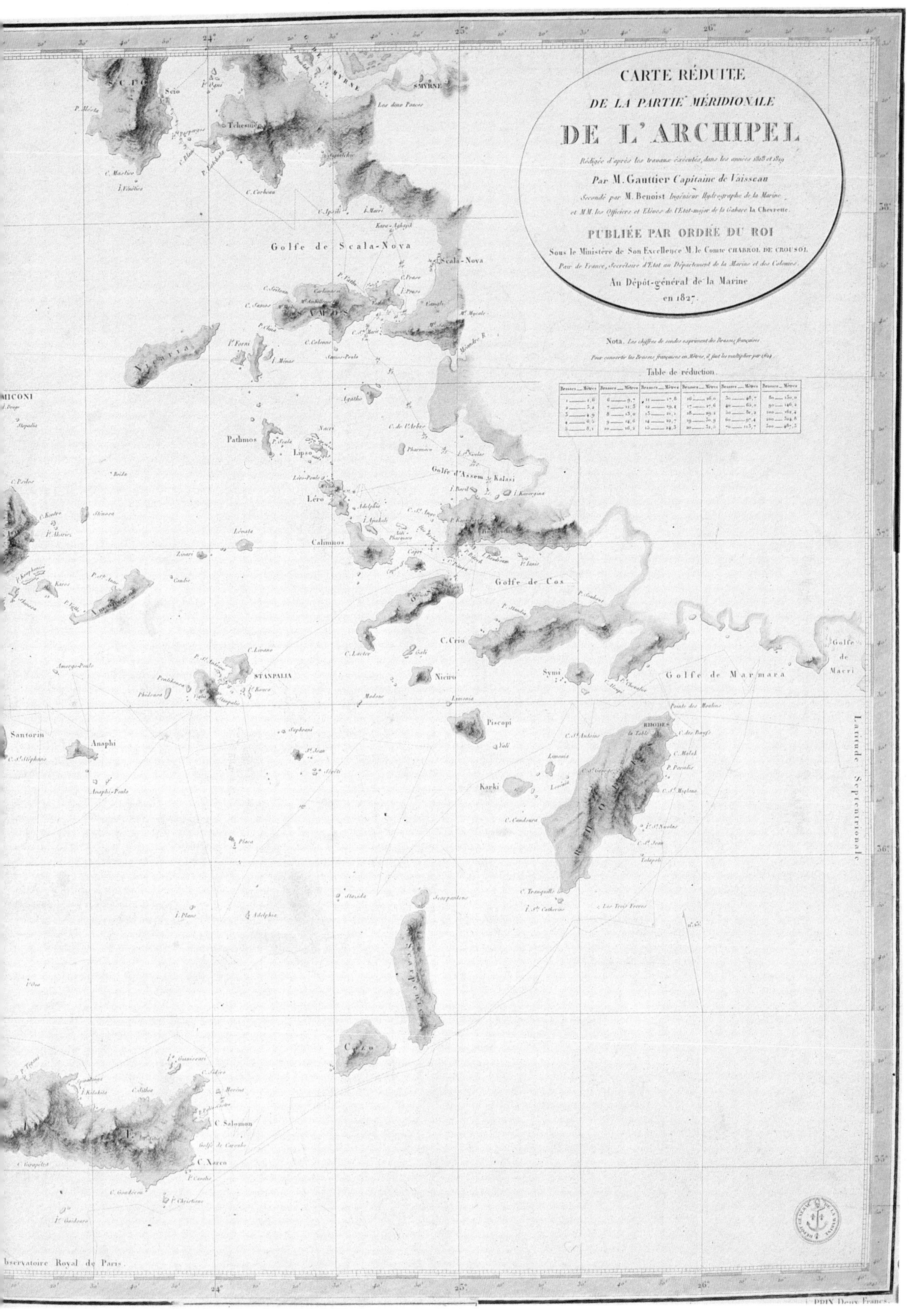

Brasses — Mètres	Brasses — Mètres	Brasses — Mètres	Brasses — Mètres	Brasses — Mètres	Brasses — Mètres
1 — 1,6	6 — 9,7	11 — 17,8	16 — 26,0	30 — 48,7	80 — 130,0
2 — 3,2	7 — 11,3	12 — 19,4	17 — 27,6	40 — 65,0	90 — 146,2
3 — 4,9	8 — 13,0	13 — 21,1	18 — 29,2	50 — 81,2	100 — 162,4
4 — 6,5	9 — 14,6	14 — 22,7	19 — 30,9	60 — 97,4	200 — 324,8
5 — 8,1	10 — 16,2	15 — 24,3	20 — 32,5	70 — 113,7	300 — 487,3

…uthern Aegean, 1827

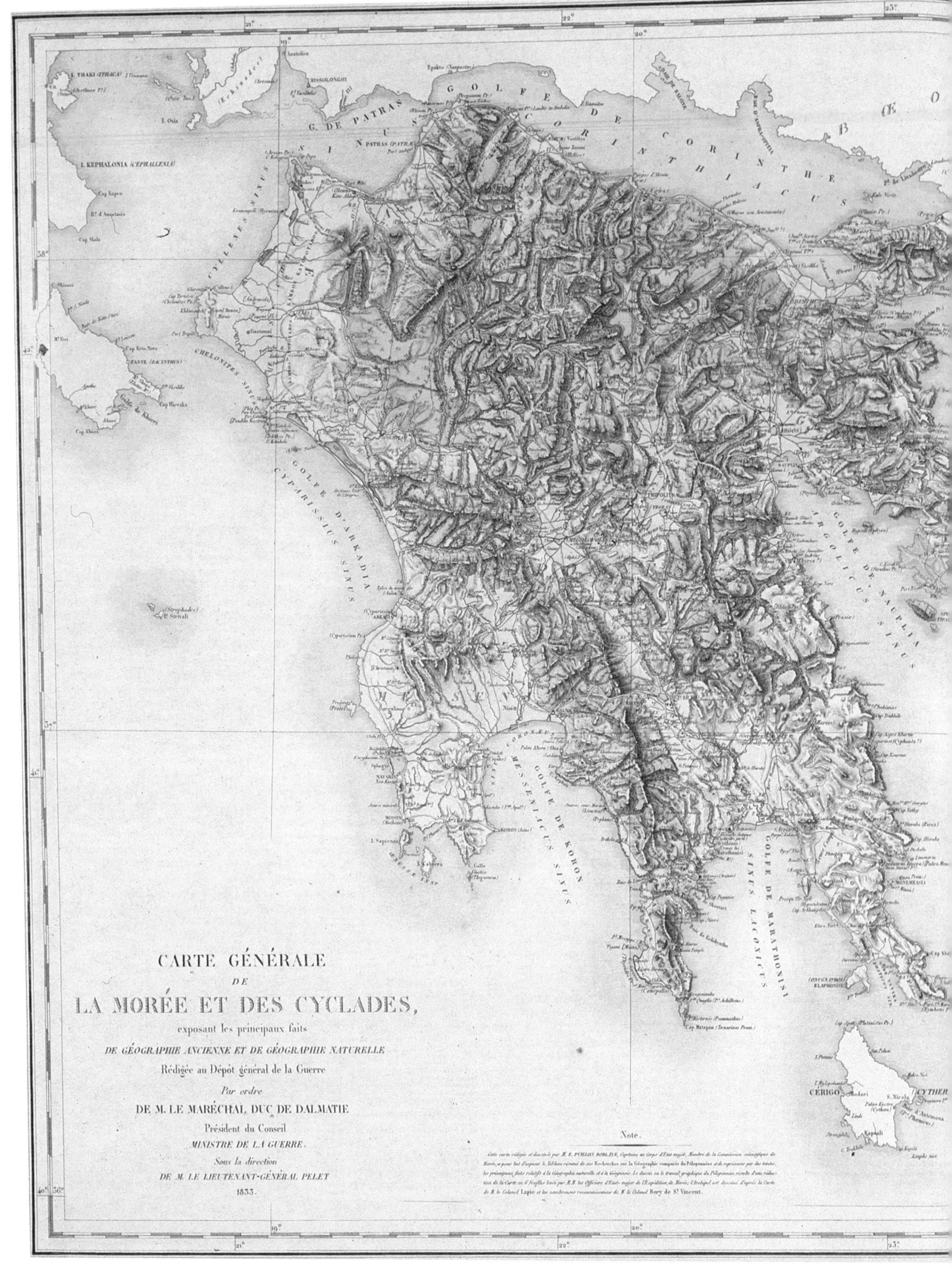

161. Map of the Peloponnese and the Cyclades, by the Frenc

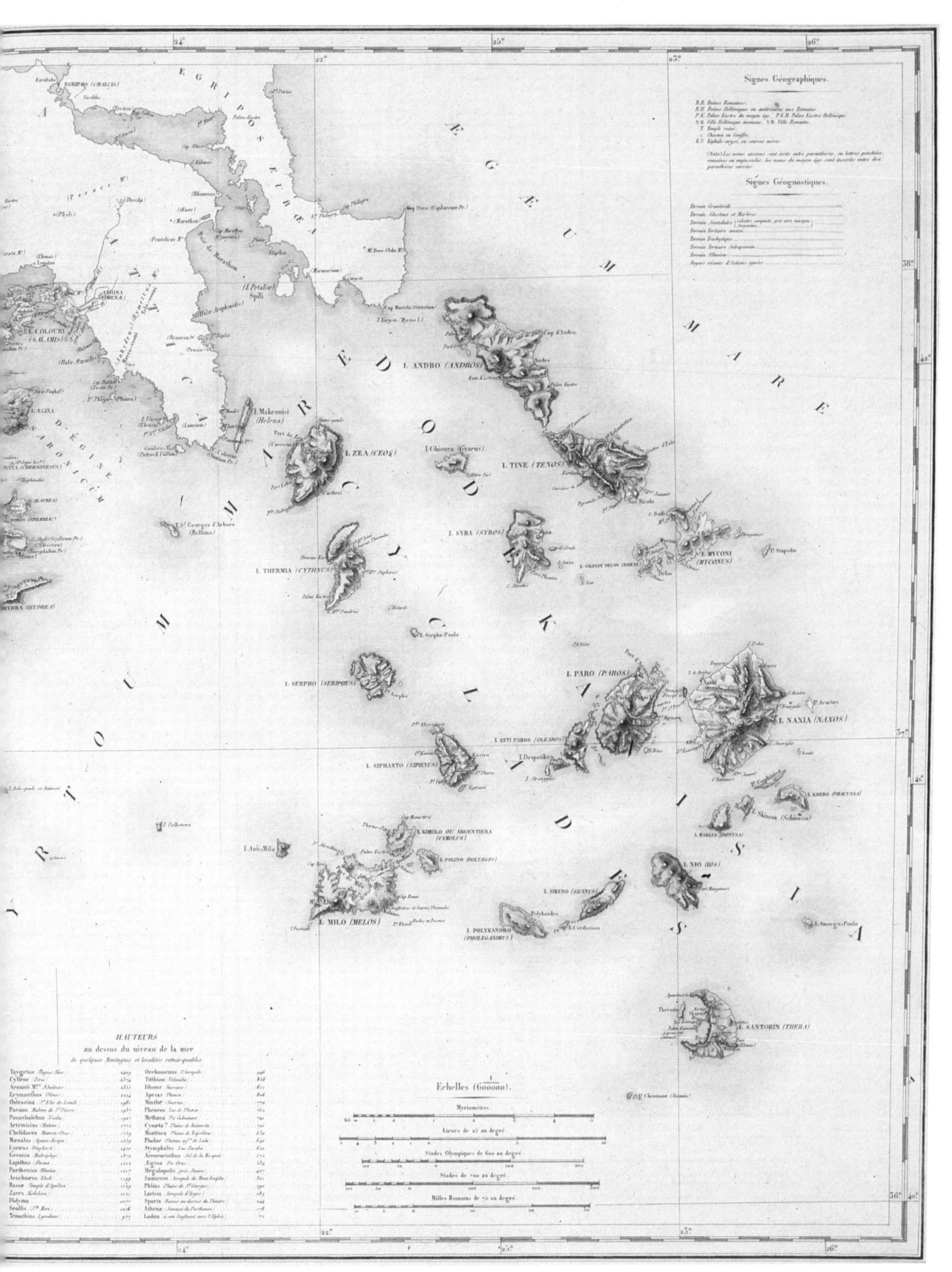

...ission to the Morea, copper engraving, 49 × 77 cms, 1833

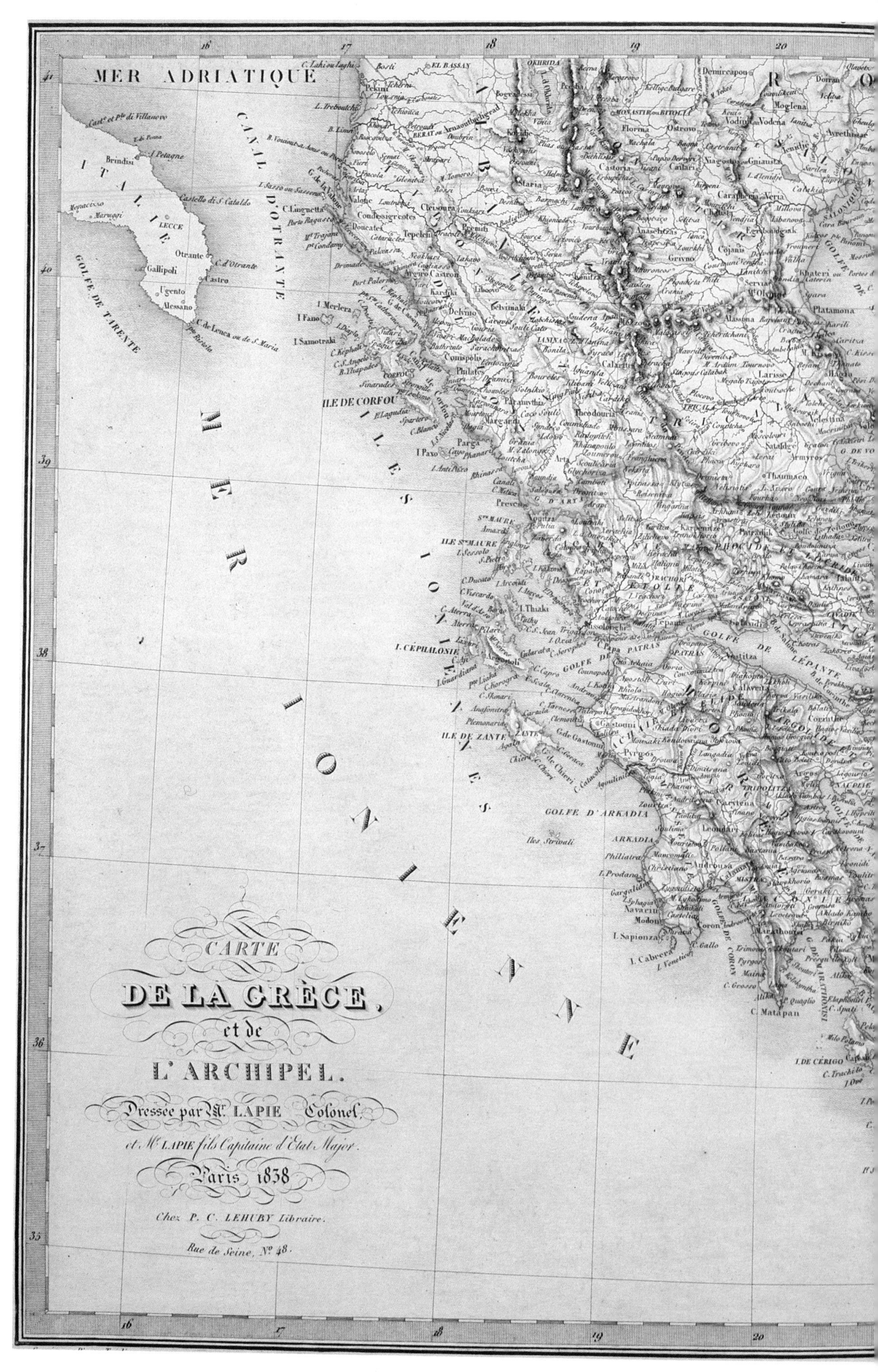

162. Lapie: Map of Greece a

e Aegean, 40 × 55 cms, 1838

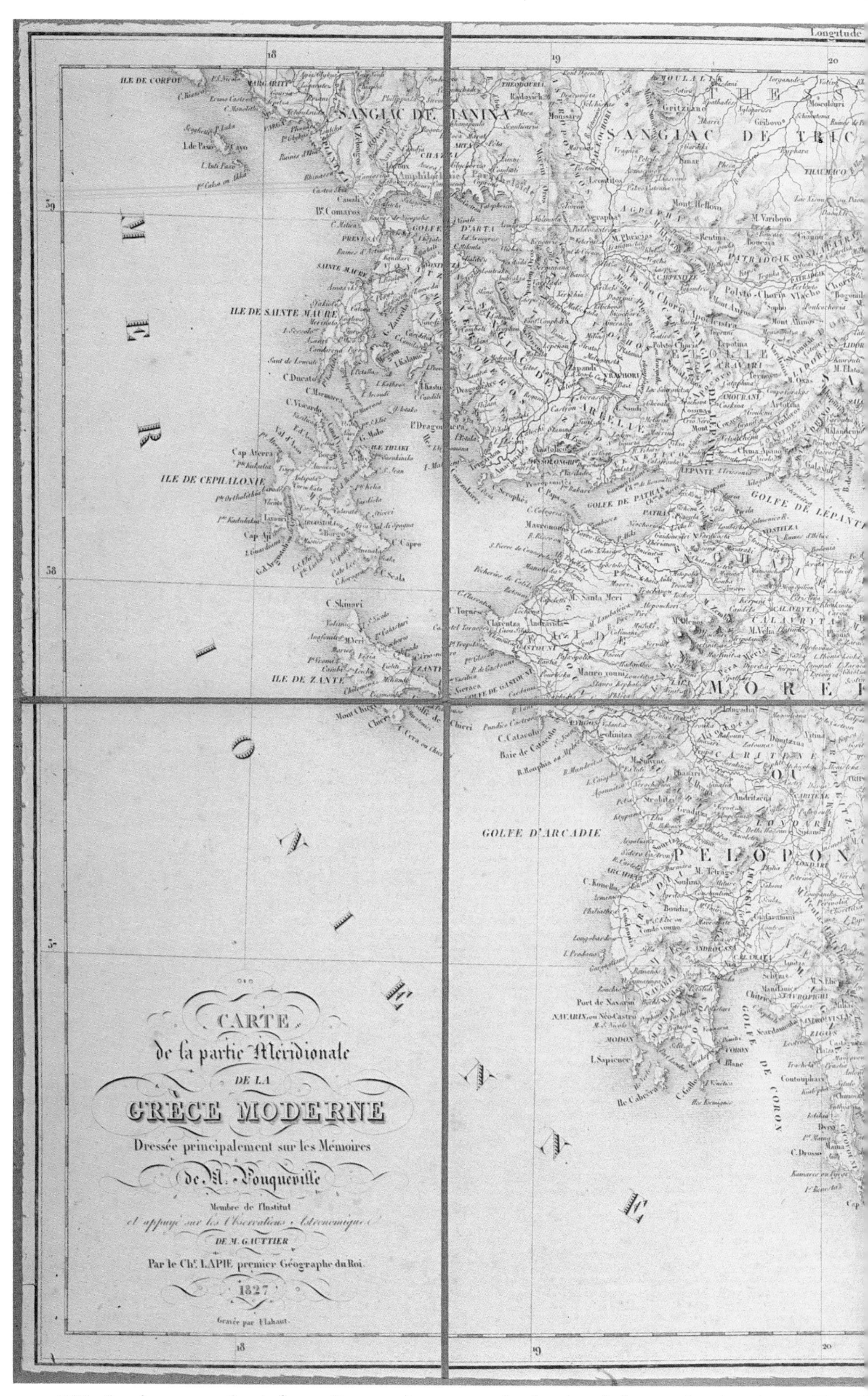

163. Lapie: map of southern Greece drawn on the basis of the work of Pouqueville an

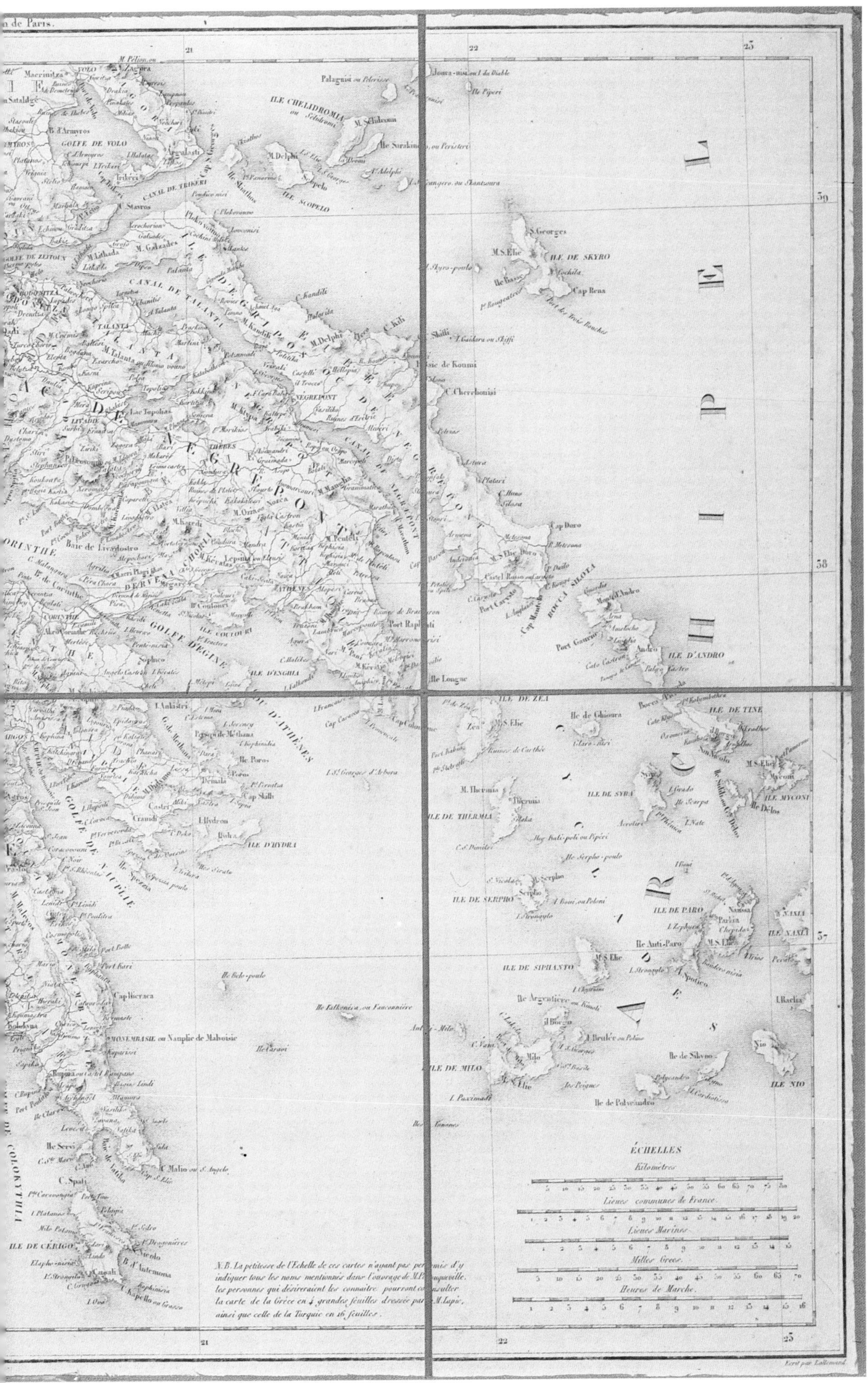

he astronomical observations of P. Gauttier; copper engraving, 40 × 54 cms, 1827.

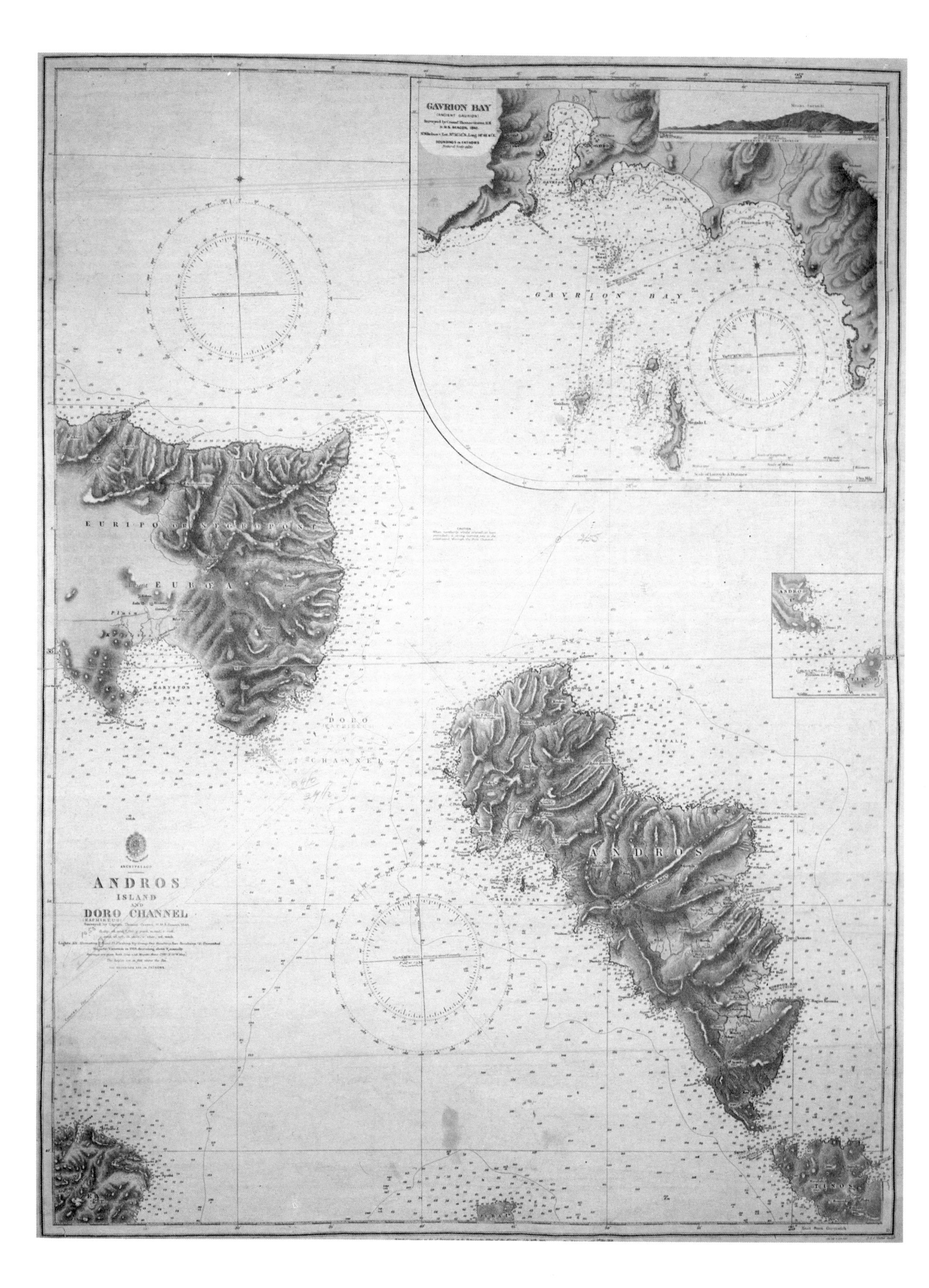
GAVRION BAY
(ANCIENT GAURION)
H.M.S. BEACON
SOUNDINGS in FATHOMS
GAVRION BAY
EURIPO or NEGROPONT
EUBŒA
DORO
CHANNEL
ANDROS
GAVRION BAY
VITALI BAY
TINOS
ARCHIPELAGO
ANDROS
ISLAND
AND
DORO CHANNEL
(KAPHIREUS)
THE SOUNDINGS ARE IN FATHOMS

165. *W. Smith: Map of the Aegean, 39 × 31 cms, 1843.*

164. *British Admiralty chart of Andros, 83 × 63 cms, 1844.*

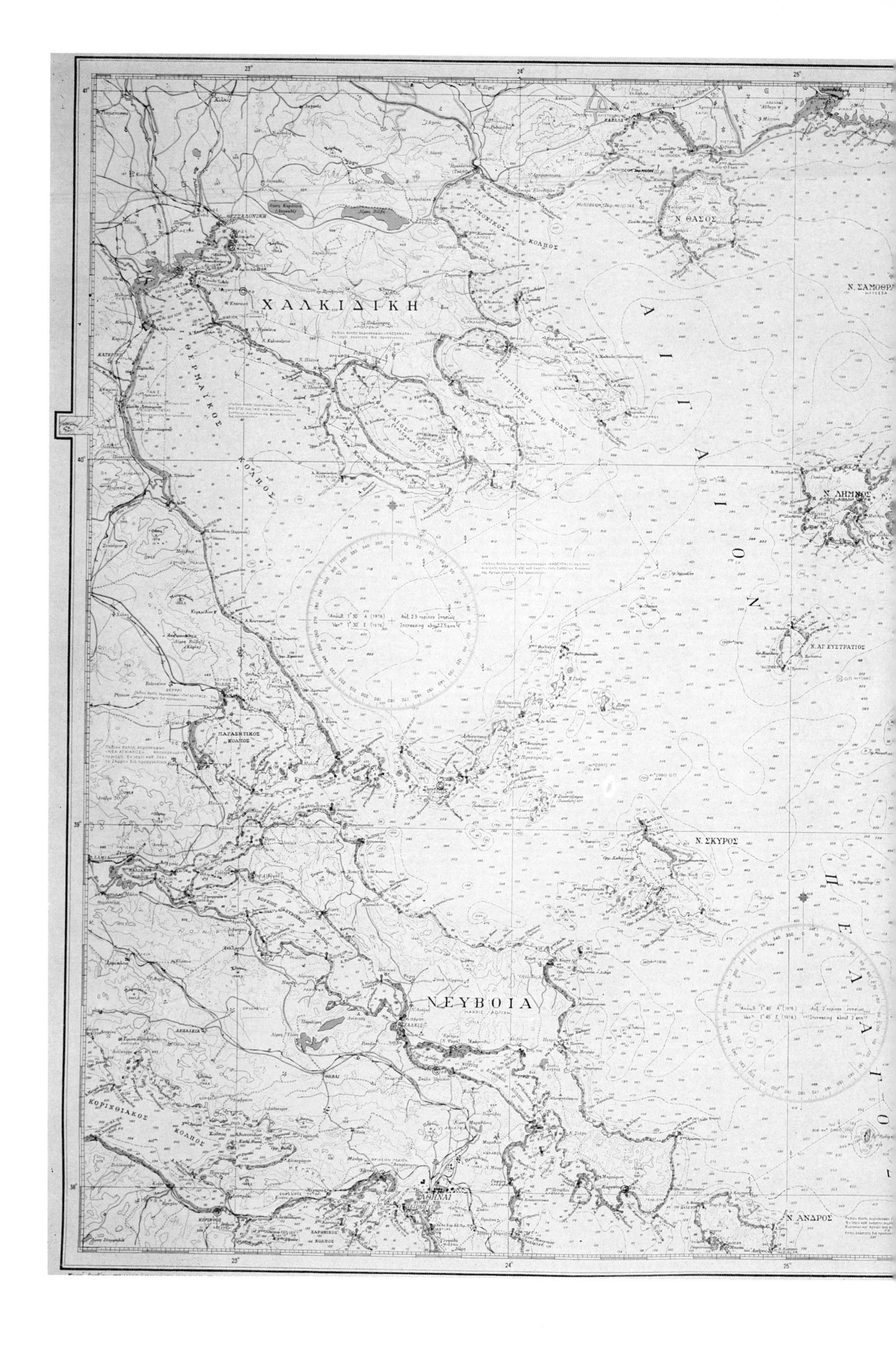
ΧΑΛΚΙΔΙΚΗ
ΘΕΡΜΑΪΚΟΣ ΚΟΛΠΟΣ
ΑΙΓΑΙΟΝ ΠΕΛΑΓΟΣ
Ν. ΘΑΣΟΣ
Ν. ΣΑΜΟΘΡΑ
Ν. ΛΗΜΝΟΣ
Ν. ΑΓ. ΕΥΣΤΡΑΤΙΟΣ
Ν. ΣΚΥΡΟΣ
Ν. ΕΥΒΟΙΑ
Ν. ΑΝΔΡΟΣ
ΠΑΓΑΣΗΤΙΚΟΣ ΚΟΛΠΟΣ
ΚΟΡΙΝΘΙΑΚΟΣ ΚΟΛΠΟΣ
ΣΑΡΩΝΙΚΟΣ ΚΟΛΠΟΣ
ΘΕΣΣΑΛΟΝΙΚΗ
ΑΘΗΝΑΙ
ΚΑΒΑΛΑ
ΚΟΡΙΝΘΟΣ
ΛΑΜΙΑ
ΧΑΛΚΙΣ
ΘΗΒΑΙ
ΛΕΒΑΔΕΙΑ
ΚΑΤΕΡΙΝΗ
23°
24°
25°
41°
40°
39°
38°
Increasing about 2.5 ann.
Increasing about 2' ann.

166. *Modern map of the northern Aegean, produced by the Hydrographical Service of the Greek Navy, on the basis of British Admiralty and US Navy charts.*

THE GREEK ARCHIPELAGO
A FAR-FLUNG CITY

"The city –locked within its walls– does not exist", concluded Ruggiero Romano at the close of a discussion on the city in Mediterranean history*. "Historians are well aware that the city is a place which makes its own space; that is, its own internal values give it the tendency to construct around itself a living space which may be extensive to a greater or lesser degree. One might think that this is the old and much-discussed city/country relationship. But no. We are dealing here with something much wider: with the fact that modern historiography (really modern historiography, that is) has entirely abandoned the older concept of the 'isolated city' (*isolierte Stadt*) of von Thünen, although of course the idea continues to be useful when talking of the economy. The past (and the present) of a city ought not to be seen as covering only its urban space, in the strictest sense of the word, and its immediate surroundings: the walls of the city cast a longer shadow than might at first be evident."

So much for the outward-facing, centralised city. But there are far-flung cities, too – cities which are aggregates or networks, and among them is the island complex of the Aegean. The text which follows attempts to examine these questions and become part of the appropriate historiographical viewpoint.

* 'The city in Mediterranean history' – the subject of one of the sessions of the International Study Conference organised by the "Istituto per i beni artistici, culturali e naturali della Regione Emilia - Romana", in Bologna, November 1983.

The Greek Archipelago, that unifying sea or plain-like expanse, has always been a focal point for the reception and transmission of cultures, throughout pre-history and recorded history, and has apportioned itself between isolation and a system of constant connections. Without a centre of its own, it has forged multiple links between the lands to its East and West; its fragmentary nature allowed its individualised organisational forms to survive throughout the long years of Turkish rule. Those forms – each a retreat into the self of the Archipelago – were typical of urban structuring and were for the most part formulated during the period of western rule. The community was founded on tax solidarity and organised in such a way as to tend to stabilise social mutuality, which in its turn permitted the perpetuation of internal balances imposed by two overriding factors: the disproportion between human and natural local resources, and a consequent dependence from the point of view of food supplies.

Not all coastal zones and not all nuclei of habitation are by nature the links in a perpetual chain of structure; the sea may provide opportunities for the continuity and unity of human space, but its cliffs are a frontier calling towards an isolation which exists but does not dominate.

Although the Archipelago is criss-crossed by mercantile and military fleets, it does not make its every island a waystation. Sometimes the crossing is made almost without a halt, as in the case of the journey of the Baron de Saint Blacard, who, in the winter of 1537, sailed from Negreponte to Constantinople calling only at Chios. The harbours on the islands are laid out according to the needs imposed by the safety of their little fleets; small bays protected by steep and fortified ground formations within which the town, too, nestles, it also being most frequently constructed as a defensive nucleus. Nonetheless, not every fortified point commands the sea, and the agglomerations of habitation with which the fortified points go to make up a whole do not constitute an equal number of points at which maritime movement could be received. They are part of the hinterland, as is the case in the Cyclades with the castle complexes of Kea, of Kimolos and of Emborio on Santorini. Along with settlements of this kind are others lying on the coast but built on the top of cliffs inaccessible from the sea, with which they communicate through other, more distant, anchorages. Two more types of fortified settlement can be found, in direct relation to the sea: this direct relation springs from their sites, which are either on heights crowning accessible inlets or bays or on low outcrops of ground in gulfs or inlets or along the shores of straits. These last two types of settlement can be found in the Cyclades on a number of islands, Syros, Sifnos, Ios, Serifos, Andros, Naxos, Mykonos, Paros and Antiparos.

Thus from the point of view of inhabited areas the way to the sea is both open and closed: this does not mean that these forms of inhabited area reflect an equal number of economic micro-systems, whether self-sufficient or transactional – the latter in the context of the connections between the islands or between the islands and the mainland. This is because the Greek Archipelago consists mainly of small islands, and depends on external input to fill in the gaps left by inadequate agricultural production. With the exception of some of the larger islands – Crete and Cyprus foremost among them – most of the others suffered from the disequilibrium between their sources of wealth and their demographic strength. This is even more evident in the case of an island like Crete, whose economy was above all agricultural. Yet even Crete, as early as the Venetian period, was dependent on external sources to meet its needs in wheat – Methone and Korone supplied Chania, Thessaloniki and Euboea supplied Herakleio, and, outside the area of Venetian conquest, the coast of Asia Minor and Alexandria provided extra supplies for the islands of the Duchy of the Aegean.

The response of the islanders – and especially of those living on the small islands – to the disproportion between natural sources of wealth and demographic strength consisted of occupational and productive specialisation: fishing, shipping and trade constituted a privileged area of activity which allowed this disproportion to be overcome while the local economies were transformed into money economies and a system of communications and interdependences was established. One should not believe that shipping was exclusively a response to a demand for sea transport facilities arising at the points where there was surplus production and at which products were directed into long-distance transactions: it was more a response to the demands of local economies and their manner of specialisation.

The fishing boats give proof of this in the islands which became specialised in sponge-fishing: Kalymnos, Syme, Chalke, and above all Kastellorizo. There can be no doubt that voyages which were not related to specialisation and local shortages of food had created flourishing commercial fleets – the examples of Hydra, Psara and Spetses during the blockade of Epirus have much to tell us, and the same is true of the fleets of other ports: Messolonghi, for instance, during the second half of the 18th century, and the little Aegean island fleets which secured constant communication with Venice. What is of prime importance, however, in the perspective of economic continuity in the Aegean has to do with connections of another kind: those between islands.

Neither the fact that the islands succeeded in maintaining maritime contact between the two halves of the Mediterranean which was long-term and which circumstances combined from time to time to make intensive, nor in addition, the fact that all routes from the Eastern to the Western Mediterranean had to pass through the islands, constitute the main reason for the economic unity which would allow us to say for certain that this watery world was in fact an urban complex. If the complex existed, then the main reason for its existence has to be sought elsewhere: in the constant to-ing and fro-ing of people, goods and ships from one island to another, in an economic osmosis, at least insofar as this is manifested through multiple connections which are simultaneously internally and externally-directed.

But before going on to present some examples related to these internal communications and interdependences, I would like to provide a reminder of a number of fairly obvious facts. The Greek Archipelago was always a part of wider state formations, in this case, of the Ottoman Empire; in addition, the rulers it experienced brought about its administrative fragmentation, but in all cases the islanders felt that they were part of a single administrative and state entity. The fact, however, that the islands were under the control of different rulers, and that they had contacts with both halves of the Mediterranean – with all the cultural offshoots which this contact implied – meant that the feeling of membership of an entity went hand-in-hand with the perpetuation of individualities. This situation was not without its interruptions, when political circumstances dislocated the interdependences, as happened with the Cretan war which broke off links between Patmos and Crete and Venice, and emptied Patmos of its non-money goods – "silver, gold and pearls, they took them down to the galleys in sacks". Sometimes, too, the islands's position within a state came into contradiction with obvious spatial facts: for the inhabitants of the Dodecanese, the 'journey inside' was the trip into the Adriatic, while that along the shores of Asia Minor was known as the 'journey outside'.

The Ottoman Empire had grouped most of the islands (the Cyclades, the Sporades, the Saronic Gulf islands and those of the Gulf of Argos, together with three of the Dodecanese) into one single administrative unit. Nonetheless, the community administrative system imposed Constantinople as the main point of political reference: it was there that the representatives of the island communities sought to resolve their collective affairs, each on behalf of his home island but also in conjunction with measures taken in respect of the other islands. More partial administrative units which were at the same time tax regions, reinforced relations between islands forced to bear the same burdens. Thus Naxos and Paros formed one province of the old Duchy of the Aegean, under the same bey, as did Andros with Syros and Melos with Santorini. "Andros and Syra are one" – and they were for the Turkish fief-holder of the two islands in the 18th century. Of course, this did not mean the formation of a city scattered across the waters, but it did strengthen mutuality. This mutuality can be seen more of less everywhere: in the islands' obligation to maintain vigilance over the seas and to keep in touch with fires by night and pillars of smoke by day; in the Kythnos community regulations for 1812, which forbade certain forms of behaviour as likely to shame the islanders in the eyes of others: "lest we become the laughing-stock of the surrounding islands"; in the jokes which one island told about the other, and, chiefly, in the distribution of roles, of which we shall have more to say later on.

If each island looked to its neighbour night and day, it was because they shared the same fate and trembled at the same fears, among which the most notorious were the pirates and corsairs, however benificent they may have been for some of the islands. There were other fears, too, of a daily nature, which had nothing to do with piracy or war but which nevertheless left their mark on the community of spirit, on the most intimate beliefs scarring the landscape of the soul – the vampires which wander freely almost everywhere impeding communication between the two worlds as it manifests itself in the worship of the memory of the dead, that game of submission and mutual guilt played between the human and the divine and confirmed by a multitude of churches and monasteries and represented by a numerous clergy and a well-organised monastic mechanism in the large foundations such as that of St. John the Divine on Patmos. Spiritual hegemonies – distinctive features of a broadly similar society ethnologically and religiously mixed here and there and constantly reinforced by internal and external migratory currents – varied in intensity and approached diversification from one place to another. Orthodox believers made up the essential portion of the population of the islands, but on Naxos, Tinos, Syros (where they were the majority) and elsewhere the Catholics formed aristocracies which despite mixed marriages were able to invoke their western origins and their submission to the church to set themselves apart from the rest of the population. At one time, indeeed, on Naxos, they became entrapped within a decaying atavism corresponding to the island's arthritic economy, which had turned in upon itself and relied on income from land rent, although it did not cease for this reason to provoke constant social tension.

Although the society of the islands was broadly speaking similar, social forms varied. The agricultural population was ever-present, but its demographic significance differed from island to island, and the same is true of the city/village dichotomy, which was marked in Rhodes, with a clear dividing line being imposed by the walled cities, whose gates were closed each evening against the coming and going of the villagers. We find a similar phenomenon in all the protected areas, but here the separation was due also to the economic features of the cities. We have proof of this in one of the chronicles of the late 16th century, which describes the typical famine/epidemic cycle: the classic mechanism analysed by Wilhem Abel. As happened everywhere, the starving villagers attack the walls of Herakleio; the city closes its gates to them and the nobility takes refuge in its fortified and well-supplied villages, leaving the "plebeians" to be decimated by the plague. As a result, handicrafts suffer from a shortage of working hands, and wages rise. These are urban phenomena, and they cannot be distinguished with the same clarity in the case of the smaller islands: on barren Serifos a population fall in the late 17th century did not mean a consequent restructuring of land ownership and a rise in family income. There are other similarities, too, relating to urban stratification: a class of nobility in the Western conquests and its remnants on some other islands during Ottoman rule; elsewhere, on the islands made rich by merchant shipping, the population was classified with exactness on the tax registers: "householders", priests, and labourers. Social stratification also revealed itself in more paltry symbolism: on poverty-stricken Skyros, which had no shipping to speak of, only the 'noble' families had the privilege of owning certain types of copper utensil, marks of wealth amidst the general impoverishment. But these social and economic similarities, the component parts of which are unequally distributed, are not sufficient by themselves to make a far-flung entity into an urban complex. They do, however, show that each human community on the islands sought to maintain its internal structure, the equilibrium, we might say, of its own totality, an essential pre-condition for individual totalities to become part of a general whole – and that general whole is the far-flung city.

Discharge of tax obligations is the primary condition for the maintenance of equilibrium in any society; as tax liability was collective, each island community had, in order to sustain its own existence, to operate a solidarity system which would allow it, through means-testing, to fix individual taxation. This reinforced social stratification and led to the sensitisation as 'citizens' of those who belonged to the upper strata – the merchants and the ship-owners and, here and there, nobility of Latinate origin and even local authorities, including the clergy, who were distinctive for their ownership of most of the islands' moderate agricultural wealth. For the collective body, as expressed through the codification of custom, the ideal equilibrium consisted of respect for the 'old' rules which stabilised the perpetual ownership of commodities within the family circle. In the succession of heirs, descent through the male line was usually the rule, though it did happen, where the right of primogeniture was enforced, and especially in Karpathos, that women were favoured. This osmosis at the level of custom, despite the sporadic occurrence of the right of primogeniture, constitutes one of the elements in the cultural unity of the islands; seen from the point of view of the mechanisms regulating the effecting of agricultural production, the unity of custom is a reflection of the disequilibrium between the islands' demographic strength and the natural (agricultural) sources of wealth. Indeed, this lack of land capable of cultivation led to an extreme degree of division into small-holdings, which was countered by the restructuring of family fortunes either by the right of primogeniture or through the exclusion of women from distribution of the paternal fortune (materna maternis, paterna paternis). These distinguishing features of the islands go to make up an integrated social and economic community, and this integrated community was confirmed within each island by individual institutions, community authorities and local codified customs. In order for all the above to exist the islands had to be open and to communicate.

As we have said, the islands of the Greek Archipelago counterbalanced their shortages in agricultural produce by creating production of other kinds, by providing services; they were, then, open and communicating societies. Their populations were formulated in relation to migratory movements, such as, for instance, Latinate and Albanian colonisation. There was, too, a reverse trend, from the island to the Asia Minor coast, exemplified by the settling of Naxiot winegrowers and barrelmakers in Smyrna in the mid-18th century, the establishment of people from Syros, Kythnos, Serifos, Sifnos and Amorgos in Constantinople and on the Asia Minor coast, and the movement to the same area of people from Chios, Lesbos, Samos and the Dodecanese. Migration is also apparent from one island to another, and names, among other evidence, can be used to prove this: of the 38 names indicating specific origin found on Kythnos, 21 are from Aegean islands; in 1673, 15% of the population of Patmos bore names of local origin, and so on. Whenever we have at our disposal dated records of a representative part of the population of the islands we can see the internal Aegean 'diaspora', with the contribution of Crete a feature, and the same is true of placenames. Inter-marriage was one of the causes of this movement – "we have many women of Tinos here, too," wrote the representatives of the Koinon of Syros in 1781 – due in part to the bonds forged between the Catholic communities. But let us return to maritime communications and the economic links which they brought about.

There were two types of communication; the first of which concerned communication by means of shipping which did not involve the inhabitants of the islands. Fleets or individual ships would stop at the harbours or inlets of the Archipelago to take on supplies or to shelter from bad weather, and here the spatial continuity, and especially the economic continuity, involved only those who travelled and not those who lived on the islands at which they called. The other form of communication involved participation on the part of the islanders themselves as either the direct agents of shipping or as its clients. The communication generated by this could be internal, external, or both together. The area of economic continuity is a correlation of this type of communication, and it is also in correlation with this area, economically *continuous for the islanders*, that we must define the far-flung city. The direct links between a port such as Chios and external centres by means of the arrival of individual ships or convoys did not sensitise the other islands, and the port of arrival despite the transactions taking place there, did not become a pole of attraction in the form of a caravanserai or a temporary city such as occurred in the case of fairs. This does not mean, however, that the presence of ships in a harbour securing extensive movement between the two halves of the Mediterranean did not provoke the interest of the island merchants: it simply means that the presence of ships did not set off a reaction equivalent to that of the caravanserai or the fair: important seasonal events, that is, localised in time and with sufficient power of attraction to orientate the movement of all the island's commodities towards the same pole.

The urban complex of the Archipelago was not only a corollary of transactions concluding in a market outside its own area; this market constituted a factor to the extent to which local production was subject to long-distance transport, further away than the coastline. It should not be forgotten that the islands did not indulge in long-range shipping: in about 1813, Kastellorizo may have sent 30 sponge-fishing vessels and some 450 seamen in search of sponges off the coast of Maghreb, but Serifos awaited the ships from Hydra to load its must at pre-determined prices. This last example is indicative of the way in which economic unity was achieved: the community authorities of the two islands defined the terms on which the one community absorbed the products of the other. Serifos must was to supply the market of Hydra, and each sale was to be made on the terms of the agreement drawn up by the community authorities of the two islands, which provided for sale elsewhere only after the requirements of the purchasing community had been met. Restrictions of this kind were innate in the functioning of the communities, and can be seen at various levels, perpetuating the right of 'preference' whether in regard to the disposal of land, or to the *annona* policy, or to the way in which the market operated, itself aimed at serving immediate consumer needs, which limited the range of the merchants.

All the evidence makes it plain that the economic unity of the islands was dictated by their interdependence in relation to foodstuffs, and did not concern external trade. Nor, with the exception of wheat, did the composition of the inter-island market reflect that of the external market. Let us examine some examples of this.

By the mid-17th century, Kimolos had lost the wealth which the pirates had brought. Its crops were divided between barley and cotton, and its consumer needs were met by importing wine from Melos. Its only exportable handicraft products, cotton socks, "supplied the neighbouring islands". Melos, in turn, was during the time of the pirates "the great bazaar of the Archipelago". Its booty, at bargain prices, made the fortune of the "middle class", which "sold it off at a profit". When the good years were past, the Meliots were content to export their handmills to Constantinople, Egypt, the Morea, Zakynthos, Cephallonia and Ancona. In Sifnos, too, they drank the wine of Melos. A fertile island itself, Sifnos produce all the cereals it needed and made cotton cloth. Thus it was able to absorb part of the cotton production of the surrounding islands and its straw hats were to be found throughout the Archipelago. It also exported honey, wax, onions and sesame seeds. There were other forms of movement beside commercial transactions: pilgrims, for instance, who "came to pray". In Andros, the locals worked in silk and built ships. The islanders controlled the means of transport and themselves exported their products to Chios, and in the villages they made baskets which were exported to all parts of the Archipelago. So there were handicrafts in the villages, too: most of the villages of Chios made textiles for local consumption and for export.

Santorini produced good wine which was exported to Chios, Smyrna, Constantinople and Crete, but lacked cereals, and so sent its boats to buy supplies from (for instance) Amorgos. Santorini also imported wood from Folegandros, which consumed its wine. Patmos had commercial communication with the coast of Asia Minor and the Gulf of Venice, but also with Egypt, Crete and the Aegean islands, of which Samos supplied it with timber for building, Santorini with sails, and Chalke and Kalymnos with sponges. An analytical sample drawn from collection of the 'commercium' (duties) in Patmos in 1783 illustrates the inflow from one island to another: of the islands which sent goods, Samos sent iron, cotton, onions, cheese, wine and wax; Kasos sent soap, jugs and pots; Mytilene sent oil; Hydra sent flax (and, of course, wheat); Chios sent pots; Syme sent soap, hides, sponges, cotton, canvas and salt; Crete sent oil and soap; Nisyros sent pots; Paros sent wine; Ikaria sent charcoal; Kalymnos sent sponges; Mykonos sent oil; Cephallonia sent flax, Kastellorizo sent rafters and planks. The list could be continued: in 1747 we find contributions from Santorini, Amorgos, Astypalaea, Skopelos, Leros and Tilos in addition to the above – a microcosm weaving a net of communications from one end to the other of the centreless sea-city of the Aegean.

The manufacture of textiles, sails, socks and gloves constituted an area of handicraft activity which favoured internal trade. In the second half of the 17th century, Chios imported 9,360 kilos of silk from Tinos and the Thessaloniki region, and from Samos as well, at a price of 8,000 scudos. The cloth made in Chios was not destined for the islands, where raw materials were sought, but for Constantinople and Smyrna. Movement was not always mutual, and not at all levels. There were inequalities and diversifications: the Chios merchants became the 'conquerors' of the Levant in the 19th century as traders and financiers, but what is important is that all the islands, with their inequalities of demography and economy, were forced to develop this form of communications amongst themselves. If there was a ranking of magnitudes, it was not due to one island dominating the other by compelling it to produce only agricultural commodities; it was a result of the fact that with primarily agricultural production the merchants were able to insert a part of the surplus, and, secondarily, a part of the handicrafts production into the big commercial circles. Some products were able to take part in this game: a case in point is that of the silk imported to Chios to cover the shortfall in its own production. But the real dependence of the islands is to be sought elsewhere, in their shortages of foodstuffs; from that point of view, imports of oil from Mytilene and Crete, of wine from Psara and Mykonos, and of wheat from Asia Minor provide a better illustration of the dependence of Chios on the islands as a whole and the dependence of these islands on the cash flowing in from Chios.

Interdependence led to a general complementariness of the island economy and to a complementariness of economic roles; it should not, however, escape us that both of these assume links with the mainland, which both provides and accepts. The Archipelago had no centre, and was thus not free of localised tension: Rhodes, for instance, with its multiple internal and external connections, which were, however, loose throughout the 18th century; Crete, with its lasting connection with Marseilles; even Kos, which sent the products of Karamania to Alexandria, or Hydra and its leading role at the time of the blockade of Epirus. The list could be a long one.

As we have already noted, some islands specialised in one main activity – the sponge-fishers of Kalymnos, Syme, Chalke and Kastellorizo are a typical instance of this. There were also other specialisations or distributions of roles: the ship-owners of Mykonos, acting on their own behalf, took building timber from Mount Athos to Alexandria, and on their way back carried coffee and rice, not only for the islands but for the mainland – the Morea – as well. The men of Mykonos, thought to be the Archipelago's best sailors, found work in the fleets. The men of Melos were reckoned the best pilots, those of Syme the best divers, much sought-after for the recovery of sunken ships, and the men of Paros were reputed to be the best settlers of disputes.

One could find endless examples of the direct and multiple links between the islands and the distribution of roles. One could insist equally well on the inequalities and diversifications which occurred in the sea-space and which made Psara, at the start of the 19th century, from an ordinary island into a company administering the economics of the other islands. One could also standardise the somewhat over-positive image which might arise from description of a mechanism as a whole rather than the systematic recording of the ways in which it was put into operation. Let us devote a little space to this positive image.

We are discussing here a maritime world with communications which were not always easy or uninterrupted, for the Aegean is not an easy sea at all times of the year, nor was the Aegean always an area throughout which peace reigned, nor are all the techniques equally able to control a ship at sea. On another plane, commercialisation too fell foul of that internal isolation which, as we said, exists without dominating: a classic example is that of 18th century Chios: "most of the mountain-dwellers will trade only by barter, and since they are forced to consume their own wine, because they cannot transport it, they would be penniless if they had not had the foresight to breed flocks". This testimony is indicative in two ways: on the one hand, it shows that trade was impeded by lack of communications in the hinterland of the island, and on the other it shows the introduction of even a limited degree of the use of money into human environments dominated by exchanges in kind rather than in cash.

To conclude, it will never be possible to prove with figures the significance of internal trade relations and the consequent ranking within an entity which remained rooted in an agricultural economy, which, on the larger islands – though not only there – constituted the heart of the economy as a whole. Our problem, however, lies elsewhere – the problem, that is, is whether "an expanse of sea, from which extrudes a host of islands, (with their towns, villages, and settlements, their ports, ship-lanes like roads and faint differences) may as a whole take on the form of one single city scattered throughout the area". Of all these elements, the one which creates cohesion is the network of internal communications: these exist, and through them the totality reaches equilibrium. This totality is a broad conglomeration with communication and interdependence, in which one-way connections are not the dominant ones. And is that not a description of a city?

Spyros I. Asdrahas

MAP INDEX

In this appendix the original title and the particulars of publication of each map are given. Where there have been repeated editions of a map, the date of the first edition is given.

1. "Portulano del Mar Egeo e Archipelago por Francisco Oliva", Messini 1615, Barcelona Maritime Museum (Photographic archive, National Bank of Greece).
1a. Venice, Korrer Museum (Photographic archive, National Bank of Greece).
2. British Museum (Photographic archive, National Bank of Greece).
3. Venice, Korrer Museum (Photographic archive, National Bank of Greece).
4. "I. Chios", from the *Liber Insularum Archipelagi* of Cr. Buondelmonti, manuscript of the 15th century.
5. "I. Rodos", *op. cit.*
6. "I. Andros", *op. cit.*
7. "I. Samos", *op. cit.*
8. "I. Amurgo", *op. cit.*
9. From the *Isolario* of Bartolomeo dalli Sonetti, Venice 1485.
10. [Sio], *op. cit.*
11. [Psara], *op. cit.*
12. [Sciati e Scopulo], *op. cit.*
13. [Samo], *op. cit.*
14. [Caloiero], *op. cit.*
15. [Lero], *op. cit.*
16. [Metelin], *op. cit.*
17. [Rodi], *op. cit.*
18. [Cipro], *op. cit.*
19. "Tabula Nova Candiae", edition of Ptolemy, Strasbourg 1522 and other subsequent editions.
20. [Siphano] from the *Isolario di Benedetto Bordone nel qual si ragiona di tutte l' isole del mondo... In Venetia per Francesco di Leno,* 1537.
21. [Patmo], *op. cit.*
22. [Greece], *op. cit.*

23. [Caloiero], *op. cit.*
24. [Cipro], *op. cit.*
25. [Nio - Cardiaci], *op. cit.*
26. [Nixia], *op. cit.*
27. [Sciro - Schiropola], *op. cit.*
28. [Candia], *op. cit.*
29. "Nova Graecia", from the *Geography* of Ptolemy, Basel edition, 1545.
30. "Scio Chio antiquam detta insula posta nella Archipelago", from *Isole famose, porti, fortezze e terre maritime,* Venice 1571-1575, Chios collection of Yannis Kanarios.
31. "Palmosa", from the same edition. War Museum collection.
32. "Tine", from the same edition. War Museum collection.
33. "Negroponte", from the same edition. War Museum collection.
34. "Arcipelago", from *L' isole più famose del mondo, descritte da Thomaso Porcacchi da Castiglione Arretino e intagliate da Girolamo Porro Padovano,* Venice 1572.
35. "Milo", *op. cit.*
36. "Cerigo", *op. cit.*
37. "Stalimene", *op. cit.*
38. "Rhodi", *op. cit.*
39. "Scarpanto", *op. cit.*
40. "Cipro", *op. cit.*
41. "Lesbos" from *Strabonis Rerum Geographicarum libri septemdecim. A Gulielmo Xylandro Angustano... Basileae, ex officina Henricpetrina* [1571].
42. "Ragionevol' forma et vera postura del' isola di Samo", from *Diporti notturni. Dialloghi familliari del Capo Franco Ferretti... con la dimonstratione figurale intagliata da Michel' Angelo Marrelli Anconitano, 1580.*
43. "Ragionevol' forma et vera postura del' isola di Cerigo", *op. cit.*
44. "Ragionevol' forma et vera postura del' isola di Scio", *op. cit.*
45. "Ragionevol' forma et vera postura del' isola di Stalimini", *op. cit.*
46. "Ragionevol' forma et vera postura del' isola di Necsia", *op. cit.*
47. "Ragionevol' forma et vera postura del' isola di Andria", *op. cit.*
48. "Ragionevol' forma et vera postura del' isola di Metellino", *op. cit.*
49. "Ragionevol' forma et vera postura del' isola di Tino", *op. cit.*
50. [Chios], from *La Cosmographie Universelle d' André Thevet, cosmographe du Roy... A Paris chez Guillaume Chaudière... 1575.* Chios collection of Yannis Kanarios.
51. [L' isle de Fermene], map drawn for the unpublished work of André Thevet, *Le grand insulaire et pilotage,* 1584.
52. [Namphio], *op. cit.*
53. [Les Dile jadis Delos / Delos ou Lesdille], *op. cit.*
54. [L' isle de Micole], *op. cit.*

55. [Sydra], *op. cit.*
56. [Specie], *op. cit.*
57. "Graeciae Universae Secundum Hodiernum situm Neoterica descriptio". The oldest printed map of 'Modern Greece' by J. Gastaldi. Printed for the first time at Venice in 1545. War Museum collection.
58. "Scarpanto", from *Viaggio da Venetia, a Costantinopoli, per mare e per terra... da Giuseppe Rosaccio... In Venetia.... 1598.*
59. "Palmosa", *op. cit.*
60. "Tine", *op. cit.*
61. "Negroponte", *op. cit.*
62. "Sciro", *op. cit.*
63. "Tenedo", *op. cit.*
64. "Zea Insula", *op. cit.*
65. "Nova totius Graeciae descriptio". Included in *Atlas sive Cosmographicae Meditationes...*, 1590-1641 and in other subsequent editions.
66. "Candia cum insulis aliquot circa Graeciam / Corfu - Zante - Milo - Nicsia - Santorini - Scarpanto", from which the previous map is taken.
67. "Cyprus Ins. - Stalimini I. - Chius Insul. - Mitilene Ins. - Negroponte In. - Cerigo Insul. - Rhodus Ins." Included in *Atlas sive Cosmographicae Meditationes...*, Amsterdam 1606 and in many subsequent editions.
68. "Cyprus Insula/Candia olim Creta", from *Theatrum Orbis Terrarum, 1570-1584.* Subsequent editions.
69. "Candia olim Creta", from *An Epitome of Ortelius his Theatre of World, where in the principal regions of the Earth are described in small mappes... At London...* [1603].
70. "Ἑλλάς - Graecia Sophiani / Ex conatibus geographicis Abrahami Ortelii Antwerpiensis". Included in the *Additamentum II, 1579,* and thence in the *Theatrum Orbis Terrarum (Parergon), 1579.*
71. "Archipelagi insularum aliquot descrip. / Candia insula - Metellino - Cerigo - Scarpanto - Nicsia - Santorini - Milo - Stalimene - Negroponte - Rodus - Scio". Included in the *Additamentum III, 1584,* and thence in the *Theatrum Orbis Terrarum, 1584.* Subsequent editions.
72. "Cyprus Insula nova descript. 1573 / Lemnos insula ex Petri Bellonij libro de Auibus, hoc in loco tanquam parergon adiecimus". Included in the *Additamentum I, 1573,* and thence in *Theatrum Orbis Terrarum, 1573* and subsequent editions.
73. "Insular aliquot Aegaei Maris Antiqua Descrip. / Ex conatibus geographicis Abrahami Ortelij Antwerpiani / Rhenia, Delus - Icaria - Euboea - Samos - Cia, Ceos - Rhodus - Chios / Cyprus Insula laeta choris, blandorum et mater amorum / Lesbos - Lemnos". Included in the *Additamentum III, 1584,* and thence in the *Theatrum Orbis Terrarum (Parergon), 1584.*
74. "Candia olim Creta", included in *Theatrum Orbis Terrarum sive Novus Atlas,* after 1640. Many subsequent editions.

75. "Cyprus Insula", included in *Theatrum Orbis Terrarum sive Novus Atlas, 1635.* Many subsequent editions.
76. "Hellas seu Graecia Universa. Autore I. Laurenbergio", from *A full and exact description of the Earth, or ancient Geography, both sacred and profane... by Georg. Hornius... Amsterdam... printed for John and Gillis Janssons... 1700.*
77. "Archipelagi Meridionalis seu Cycladum insularum accurata delineatio. Autore I. Laurenbergio". Included in *Atlas Novus,* 1638-1661 and in other editions.
78. "Insularum Archipelagi Septentrionalis seu Maris Aegei accurata delineatio. Autore I. Laurenbergio", *op. cit.*
79. "Arcipelago", from *L' Arcipelago con tutte le isole... In Venetia per Francesco Nicolini, 1658.*
80. "Il Regno di Candia", from *Il regno tutto di Candia delineato a parte a parte, et intagliato da Marco Boschini venetiano...,* Venice 1651.
81. "Isle et royaume de Candie tirée de divers mémoires / Par le Sr Sanson. A Paris chez l' auteur, avec privilège du Roy pour vingt ans", 1658.
82. "Carta maritima di tutto l' Arcipelago", from *Prima parte dello specchio del mare...1664.*
83. "Carta maritima che contiene come si posse vellegiare per l' isola Tenedo et la Natolia - Carta maritima dell' isola Lemnos... com'anche la carta maritima fra Metelino e il stretto di Constantinopoli - Carta maritima del Golfo overo stretto di Constantinopoli", *op. cit.*
84. "Plan de l' isle de Candie jadis Crète et des isles voisines / A Paris par le Chevalier de Beaulieu... / La Canée - Candie - Corfu - Zante - Milo - Nicsia - Santorini - Scarpanto", 1674.
85. "Candie ville métropolitaine de l' isle... / Isle de Candie par Pierre du Val géographe du Roy. A Paris chez l' auteur... avec privilège de S.M. 1677".
86. "Haaven-Kaart van Eenigo Voornaamste Haavens leggende in de Middelandsche zee en Archipelago...", from *De groote Nieuwe Vermerderde Zee Atlas ofte Water Werelt...* 1680-1734 and in subsequent editions.
87. "Pascaarte vande Archipelagusche Eylanden - Naakeurig opgestelt P. to S. Giorgio de Schiro in't Groot", *op. cit.*
88. "Insula Candia eiusque fortificatio edita per F. de Wit / Canea - Candia - Spina Longa - Retimo - Suda - Thine", from *Atlas sive descriptio terrarum orbis... 1680,* subsequent editions.
89. "Exactissima totius Archipelagi nec non Graeciae tabula in qua omnes subjacentes regiones et insulae distincte ostenduntur per Nicolaum Vissher. Amstel..." Included in *Atlas minor, 1682-1716* and other editions.
90. "Insula Candia olim Creta. N. Vissher exc. / Candia", from *Atlas minor, 1682-1716* and in other editions.

91. "Nio, Namphio, Sta Erini", from *Description de l' Univers contenant les différents systèmes du monde... Par Allain Manesson Mallet... A Paris,* 1683.
92. "Les isles de l' Archipel qui sont vers l' Asie", *op. cit.*
93. "Pelagnisi - Dromi", *op. cit.*
94. "D' Andro e Tine", *op. cit.*
95. "Accurata totius Archipelagi et Graeciae Universae tabula / Carte de la Grèce dressée sur un grand nombre de mémoires anciens et nouveaux, sur ceux de Mrs Wheler et Tournefort... Par G. de l' Isle de l' Académie R^le des Sciences et Ier Géographe du Roy. A Amsterdam chez Jean Covens et Corneille Mortier", from *Atlas nouveau, 1683-1761* of I. Covens and C. Mortier.
96. "Arcipelago Mar Egeo con le coste del Medesimo e l' isole che in esso si ritrovano descritto, con l' accrescinito di varie notizie da Giacomo Cantelli da Vignola...", Rome 1685. War Museum collection.
97. "Paskaarte vertoonende de Noorkuste van Negropont... / Paskaarte van der Zee Archipelago vertoonende hoemen door der Eylanden..." from *Zee Atlas, 1683.*
98. "Geoctrogeerde Haven Kaart van de Archipelagusche Ylande Gedruckt tot Amsterdam by Jacob Robijn", 1694.
99. "Paskaarte vande Archipelagusche Zee", from *Zee Atlas, 1683.*
100. "Archipelagus", from *Archipelagus turbatus oder der schönen Griechen Lands verwüstete und erödete Wasser-Felder. Augspurg,* edition of Jacob Enderling, 1686.
101. "Caloiero, Chirana, Lesindra", from *L' Egeo redivivo o' sia chorographia dell' Arcipelago... di Francesco Piacenza Napolitano... in Modena 1688.*
102. "Isole Gregarie, S. Elia, Scopulo, Schiatti", *op. cit.*
103. "Amorgo", *op. cit.*
104. "Micone", *op. cit.*
105. "Egeum mare", *op. cit.*
106. "Monte Santo e Tasso", *op. cit.*
107. "Cythnus, Ophiusa", *op. cit.*
108. "Nisarae, Calidnae Insulae", *op. cit.*
109. "S. Strati", *op. cit.*
110. "Agathonissi, Eleo, Fermaco, Arginussae Ins.", *op. cit.*
111. "Serphino", *op. cit.*
112. "Sirna", *op. cit.*
113. "Samos", *op. cit.*
114. "Scio", from *Description exacte des Isles de l' Archipel... Traduite du flamand d' O. Dapper. A Amsterdam 1703.* Chios collection of Yannis Kanarios.
115. "Insularum Archipelagi septentrionalis seu Maris Aegei accurata delineatio", from *Naakeurige, Beschryving der Eilanden in de Archipel,* Amsterdam 1688.

116. "Archipelagus meridionalis seu Cycladum insularum accurata delineatio", *op. cit.*
117. "Scio/I. Peeters excudit", from *Description des principales villes, havres et isles... 1690.* Chios collection of Yannis Kanarios.
118. "Cipre/Ciprus insula/I. Peeters excudit", *op. cit.*
119. "Tine/I. Peeters excudit", *op. cit.*
120. "Caloiero", from the *Isolario* of V.M. Coronelli, p. 280, 1696.
121. "Parallelo geographico dell' antico col moderno Arcipelago per istruzione dell' istoria dell' isole contenute in esso opera del P. Maestro Coronelli cosmografo della Serenissima Republica di Venezia...", from *Isolario,* Venice 1696.
122. "Parte meridionale del Archipelago dal P. Coronelli Cosmografo Publico", *op. cit.*
123. "Acamantis insula, hoggidi Cipro... dal P. Cosmografo Coronelli", *op. cit.*
124. "A new map of the islands of the Aegean Sea to-gether with the island of Crete and the adjoyning islands... F. J. Smith sculp.", from *A new set of maps... 1700-1738.*
125. "Insula Creta hodie Candia in sua IV territoria divisa cum adjacentibus Aegei Maris insulis ac praesertim nuperrimi ex abysso pelagi emergate nova Santorini insula... Ioh. Bapt. Homannus Norimbergae", from *Atlas novus terrarum... 1702-1773* and other subsequent editions.
126. "Nouvelle carte de l' Archipel fait par les Sieurs Michelot pilote royal et Bremond hydrographe du Roy, avec privilège 1715", included in *Carte des côtes de la Mer Méditerranée avec les îles et les ports, 1715-1726.*
127. "A new chart of the Archipelago corrected by J. Gaudy, included in *The English Pilot - Part III,* 1716-1803.
128. "Carte de l' Archipel / Presentée à Monseignr le Comte de Maurepas, par le Sr Grognard Pilote entretenu au département de Toulon. 1745 / Approbation - J' ai examiné par ordre de Mgr le Comte de Maurepas la carte de l' Archipel... et j'ai crû qu'elle pouvoit être de quelque utilité pour la Navigation... à Paris le 15 Septembre 1745. Signé Bellin, Ingénieur du Roy et Hydrographe de la Marine", included in *Le Neptune François ou recueil des cartes maritimes, 1753.*
129. "La Grèce tirée des mémoires de Monsieur l' Abbé Baudrand. A Paris chez le Sr Jaillot Géographe du Roy...", 1716.
130. "Ioura - Zea", from *Relation d' un voyage du Levant fait par ordre du Roy... Par M. Pitton de Tournefort... A Paris...,* 1717.
131. "Port de Micone", *op. cit.*
132. "L' Archipel avec toutes ses isles et les côtes des environs... mis au jour par Pierre Vander Aa, Marchand Libraire à Leide", from *La Galerie Agréable du monde... 1729.*
133. "Archipel septentrional ou Mer Egée avec toutes ses isles... par

Pierre Vander Aa...", *op. cit.* Chios collection of Yannis Kanarios.
134. "Les côtes de la Grèce et l' Archipel par le S^{r} d' Anville... 1756", from *Atlas Général... 1727-1780.*
135. "XII Feuille / avec privilège du Roy à Marseilles chez Joseph Roux Hydrographe du Roy sur le port à St Jean", from *Carte de la Méditerranée en 12 feuilles..., 1764.*
136. "XI Feuille / avec privilège du Roy à Marseilles chez Joseph Roux Hydrographe du Roy...", *op. cit.*
137. "Isle de Chateau Rouge", from *Recueil des principaux plans des Ports et Rades de la mer Méditerranée estraits de ma carte en Douze Feuilles... Par.. Joseph Roux Hydrographe du Roy. A Marseille 1764.*
138. "I. Ipsera", *op. cit.*
139. "Rade du Miconi / Grande isle Dellos", *op. cit.*
140. "Port St Ange au sud de l' isle de Simi", *op. cit.*
141. "I. Scio", *op. cit.*
142. "I. Milo", *op. cit.*
143. "Port Olivier / I. Metelin", *op. cit.*
144. "Isle Estampalie", *op. cit.*
145. "Greece, Archipelago and part of Anadoli by L.S. de la Rochette MDCCXC. London published for Willm Faden Geographer to the King. January 1st 1791", from *General Atlas, 1791,* published W. Faden.
146. "Carte de la Grèce et ses îles pour le voyage du jeune Anacharsis par M. Barbié du Bocage", from *Recueil des cartes géographiques, plans, vues et médailles de l' ancienne Grèce relatifs au voyage du jeune Anacharsis... chez Sanson et Compagnie, 1791.*
147, 148. *Map of Greece, in which are included its islands and a part of its numerous colonies in Europe and Asia Minor... now published for the first time by R. Velestinlis Thettalos... 1797.*
149. "Carte des îles de Lemnos, Imbros, Samothrace / Levée par M.M. Truguet... Gravé par P.F. Tardieu / Ecrit par Dien", from *Voyage pittoresque de la Grèce. Tome second, 1809.*
150. "Carte de la Grèce moderne", from *Voyage pittoresque de la Grèce, vol. I, 1782.*
151. "Carte générale de l' île de Paros / Levée par F. Kauffer en 1776 gravé par J. Perrier", from *Voyage pittoresque de la Grèce, vol. I, 1782.*
152. "Plan de l'île de Delos / Levé par le comte de Choiseul Gouffier en 1776 / Gravé par J. Perrier", from *Voyage pittoresque de la Grèce, vol. I, 1782.*
153. "Extended map of the Archipelago carefully drawn by Captain Nikolaos Kephalas of the island of Zakynthos, in which are recorded the true positions of the parts and the islands in relation to one another and are noted the various land masses and rocks observed by the same on his several voyages, for the use of his fellow Greeks". Paris 1818. / Humbly presented by me the publisher to the distinguished members of the newly-constituted Administration of the free united provinces and

the Ionian Islands".
154. "Plans des isles de Milo, de l' Argentière et de Polino", from *Atlas pour servir au voyage dans l' Empire Othoman, l' Egypte et la Perse, fait par ordre du gouvernement, pendant les six premières années de la République. Par G. A. Olivier. A Paris (An IX).*
155. "Golfe de la Sude en Candie", *op. cit.*
156. "Plan de l' île Théra ou Santorin", *op. cit.*
157. "Plan du port Parthéni au nord de l'isle de Léro", *op. cit.*
158. "Grèce, Archipel et partie de l'Asie Mineure", *op. cit.*
159. "Carte réduite de la partie septentrionale de l' Archipel rédigée d' après les travaux exécutés dans les années 1818 et 1819 par M. Gauttier... secondé par M. Benoist Ingénieur Hydrographe de la Marine... / Dépôt général de la Marine, 1827".
160. "Carte réduite de la partie méridionale de l' Archipel... 1827".
161. "Carte générale de la Morée et des Cyclades... Rédigée au Dépôt général de la Guerre... sous la direction de M. le lieutenant - général Pelet 1833", from *Expédition scientifique de Morée. Travaux de la Section des Sciences physiques... par M.M. Bory de Saint-Vincent, Peytier, Puillon-Boblaye... Atlas 1831-1835, Paris... Strasbourg 1835.*
162. "Carte de la Grèce et de l' Archipel. Dressée par Mr. Lapie colonnel...", 1838.
163. "Carte de la partie méridionale de la Grèce Moderne / Dressée principalement sur les Mémoires de M. Pouqueville membre de l' Institut et appuyé sur les observations Astronomiques de M. Gauttier / Par le Chr Lapie premier Géographe du Roi / 1827. Gravé par Flahaut".
164. "Andros Island and Doro Channel. Surveyed by Captain Thomas Graves, H.M.S. Beacon 1844".
165. "Grecian Archipelago (Ancient) by William Smith L.L.D., 1843.
166. "Aigaion Sea-Northern part. From Hellenic Surveys to 1967 with additions from B. Admiralty charts and U.S. Navy Sources to 1950".

GENERAL INDEX

This Index contains the names of cartographers and historical personages as well as geographical names connected with the Aegean area. The Index also contains a certain number of terms, mostly related to map-making. The italic numbers refer to maps, and the remainder to the text.

CONTENTS

"MAPS AND MAPMAKERS OF THE AEGEAN"
WAS PRINTED IN MAY, 1985, BY ASPIOTIS
ELKA S.A., ON BEHALF OF OLKOS EDITIONS,
5, IPATIA St., ATHENS, GREECE, TEL. 32.24.131.